TOEIC® L&R TEST
990点獲得
Part 1-4難問模試

MediaBeacon
メディアビーコン

無料音声
ダウンロード付

ベレ出版

はじめに

「TOEIC L&R TESTで高得点を取りたい!」
「最終的には990点を目指したい!」

本書は、そのように考えているあなたに必ず取り組んでいただきたい、TOEICリスニングパートの難問対策書です。

「リスニングはだいたい高めのスコアが取れているから大丈夫」
そう思っている方もいるかもしれません。

もちろん、リスニングパートよりもリーディングパートの方が難しいと言われることも多いです。しかし、それならなおさら、まずリスニングで安定して満点を取れる実力が必要になります。あなたの今のリスニング能力は、本当に十分でしょうか?

近年、TOEIC公開テストは難化傾向にあり、小手先のテクニックでは通用しなくなってきています。かつてリスニングパートで満点を継続して取れていた人が、ぽろぽろと問題を取りこぼしてしまうというケースも少なくありません。もし、あなたが「以前よりリスニングパートの正答率が下がっている」と感じているのなら、今のTOEICテストの傾向に合わせた、より質の高い英語学習をしなければならないのです。

私たちは常に最新のTOEICテストの傾向を把握するために、毎回公開テストを受験して研究や分析を重ねています。さらに、TOEICコーチングでは、高得点を狙う学習者の方への指導もしており、多くの学習者がつまずきやすいポイントも深く理解しています。

そんな私たちの知識と経験から、テスト本番に近い形で、かつ難易度の高い問題を作り上げ、ギュッと1冊に詰め込みました。本書を使って難問を解く練習をしていただければ、本番のテストで出題される難問に対応できる力がつきます。ぜひ本書で、あなたのリスニング力にさらなる磨きをかけてください。

目標スコアを達成し、あなたの人生がより豊かになることを心より願っています。

メディアビーコン

TOEIC® L&R TEST 990点獲得 Part 1-4難問模試
［目次］

本書の使い方

　本書では、Part 1〜4の5回分の模試を収録しています。それぞれの模試を解いて、難問に対応できる力をつけていきましょう。ただ、各模試を一度解くだけでは意味がありません。解いて復習することを何度も繰り返して初めて、その模試を自分のものにすることができます。

　下記に、各TESTを解く際の取り組み方、そして効果的な音読トレーニング法をまとめました。これらを参考にして、本書で得られる最大限の効果をぜひ体感してください。

各模試の基本的な取り組み方

① 問題を解く

　できるだけ1TESTを通しで解くようにしましょう。実際の試験では約45分間ずっと英語を聞くことになるので、本番でも通用する集中力を鍛えることが大切です。また、実際の試験となるべく同じ環境で模試を解くために、音声はイヤホンではなくスピーカーで聞くことが望ましいです。また、後の復習に生かせるよう、自信がない問題には問題番号に丸印を付けておきましょう。

② 答え合わせをする

　解答を確認し、丸付けをしましょう。繰り返し解いていく際に効果を確認できるよう、全体の正答率やどの問題を間違えたのかなどを記録しておくのがおすすめです。

③ 復習をする

　間違えた問題だけでなく、正答を選べている問題についても解説を読むようにしましょう。勘や推測で選んでたまたま合っていた可能性があるので、きちんと全て理解できていたのか確認することが満点を取るためのカギになります。特に難しいポイントは ⚠ **ここに注意！** でも解説しているので、そちらも参考にしてください。また、 語彙チェック を活用して、知らなかった単語や表現は覚えておくようにしましょう。曖昧に覚えていたものもそのままにせず、その場でしっかり定着させてください。

④ 音読トレーニングを行う

音読トレーニングは、8割以上内容を理解できている英文で行うのが効果的。必ずしっかりと復習をした後で行ってください。また、さまざまな音読トレーニング法がありますが、自分のレベルに合ったトレーニング法を活用することが重要です。次に紹介している音読トレーニング法の中で、自分に適したものを実践してみましょう。

おすすめの音読トレーニング法

Lv. 1：Read and Look up

まずは意味のまとまりごとに英文にスラッシュを入れます。その後、スラッシュごとに英文を見ながら音読して、直後に英文を見ないで（目線を上げて）音読します。慣れてきたら、1度に読む量を増やし、1文ずつできるように挑戦しましょう。

Lv. 2：オーバーラッピング

英文を目で追いながら、音声と一緒に声を出して音読します。スピードに追い付けるようになったら、意味を意識しながら音読しましょう。

Lv. 3：シャドーイング

英文を見ずに音声だけを聞いて、それに付いていくように音読します。意味を理解しながら、できるだけ感情を込めて読むのがコツです。速度に追い付けないようなら、オーバーラッピングに戻るようにしてください。

Lv. 4：瞬間英作文

1文ずつ日本語訳を読んで、英語で発話します。発話後すぐにスクリプトの英文を見て、抜けているところなどを確認します。何度も読んで英文を大体覚えている状態で行いましょう。

990点獲得のための
リスニングで満点をとる勉強法

　TOEIC L&R TESTのリスニングパートで満点を取るために必要なのはただ一つ、諦めずに努力を継続する力です。勉強しているのに点数が思ったように伸びなかったり、時には点数が下がってしまったりして、落ち込んでしまう経験は誰しもあるのではないでしょうか。ですが大事なのは、そこで折れることなく、苦手を分析したり勉強法を改善したりして、地道にコツコツ努力し続けることです。

　ここでは、リスニングで満点を獲得するために必要な勉強のポイントを5つ取り上げています。これらのポイントを意識して、ぜひ勉強を継続してみてください。きっと皆さんのリスニング満点獲得への手助けになるはずです。

1. 英語の音に慣れる

　自ら英語を聞く習慣をつけていかないと、英語の音を聞き取る感覚はすぐに忘れてしまいます。忙しくてなかなか時間が取れないときも、スキマ時間を有効に使って毎日英語を聞くようにしましょう。

　ここでポイントになるのが、すでに内容を理解できている状態の英語音声を繰り返し聞くようにすることです。リスニング力を高めるために、ひたすらいろいろな英語を聞く人もいますが、人によってはそれが効率の悪い勉強法になってしまうことがあります。まずは一度理解した英語音声を使って、聞いてすぐ理解できる状態までに仕上げていくことが大切です。

　また、TOEIC L&R TESTでは4カ国（アメリカ、イギリス、カナダ、オーストラリア）のナレーターが登場しますが、あなたが聞き取りにくいなと感じるナレーターはいませんか？もしいるのであれば、その人もしくはその国籍の人の英語を繰り返し聞いて、その発音やアクセントに耳を慣らしてしまうのが一番です。リスニングで満点を目指す方は、こういった自分の苦手も意識しながら英語を聞く習慣をつけていきましょう。

2. 語彙力を高める

リスニングパートはリーディングパートに比べると難しい語彙は少ないです。ですが、当然のことながらリスニングは「聞き取りのテスト」です。たとえ知っている英単語だったとしても、聞き取ることができなければ意味がありません。英単語を勉強するときには音声を活用して、英単語の意味だけでなく音もセットで覚えるようにしましょう。

それから、「単語帳を何周もしたからその中の英単語はカンペキに覚えている」と勝手に思い込んでしまっていませんか？ 意味を理解するのに少しでも時間がかかるのであれば、それはカンペキに覚えられているとは言えません。見た瞬間、聞き取った瞬間に意味がパッと分かる状態になるまで、英単語を体に染み込ませることを意識してください。

3. 英文法をしっかり理解する

「リスニングなのに英文法？」と思った方も、いらっしゃるかもしれません。ですが、英文法は英語の基礎。リスニングにおいてもかなり大事な要素になります。リスニング対策だからと言って、英文法の勉強を怠ってはいけません。

TOEIC L&R TESTは全体的に難化傾向にあり、リスニングパートでも複雑な文構造が登場しています。読んで理解することはできても、「聞いて理解する」となるとより難しくなります。自分の文法力を過信せずに、音で聞いてすぐに文構造を把握できるかということも再確認しましょう。

4. 予測する力をつける

リスニングで満点を獲得するためには、Part 3とPart 4の「設問文と選択肢から内容を予測する力」が大事なカギになります。そして、ここで必要になるのが、放送文を聞く前に設問文と選択肢を読む「先読み」です。実際にやっている人も多いと思いますが、近年のTOEIC L&R TESTを攻略していくためにはこの「先読み」のスキルが必須に

なってくると私たちは考えています。

　Part 3やPart 4では変わったシチュエーションが登場することが多くなっていますが、出題されうる全てのシチュエーションを対策するのは難しく、時間がかかります。ですが、設問と選択肢というヒントをうまく利用すれば、本文を聞く前に準備できることはかなりあります。事前に準備して予想しておくだけで理解力はぐんと上がるので、普段の勉強のときから「先読み」を意識して問題を解くようにしましょう。

5. 話し手の意図を読み取る力をつける

　状況描写の問題であるPart 1を除き、リスニングパートでは話し手の意図を読み取る力が求められます。特に近年のTOEIC L&R TESTでは、「発言の意図を読み取れないと答えられない問題」が非常に多くなっています。こういった問題は、言い換えれば「ちゃんと聞き取れて意味も理解していても、それだけでは答えられない問題」なので、高得点者でも苦手としている人が多いです。

　この種の問題は、代表的なもので言うとPart 3やPart 4のWhat does the man mean when he says, "〜"?といった問題ですが、Part 2でも話し手の意図を読み取らなければならない問題が多く出てきます。例えば、聞かれていることに対して直接的には答えていない応答でも、「話し手の意図を読み取ると会話が成り立つもの」が正解になることもあります。

　ただ、勘違いしてはいけないのが、それらは無理やり分かりにくくした不自然な英語ではなく、現実にありうる英語のやりとりだということです。よりリアルな状況を思い浮かべて、話し手が何を思ってその発言をしているのかを想像する癖をつけていきましょう。

■ 付属のダウンロード音声について

　本書の音声は、スマートフォンやタブレット、またはパソコンで聞くことができます。音声は全て無料でお聞きいただけます。

スマートフォン・タブレットの場合

AI英語教材アプリabceed（株式会社Globee提供）

①アプリストアで「abceed」をダウンロード。
②アプリを立ち上げ、本書の名前を検索して音声を使用。

https://www.abceed.com

パソコンの場合

「ベレ出版」ホームページ

①「ベレ出版」ホームページ内、『TOEIC L&R TEST990点獲得 Part 1-4難問模試』の
　詳細ページにある「音声ダウンロード」ボタンをクリック。
　(https://www.beret.co.jp/books/detail/835)
②8ケタのコードを入力して「ダウンロード」ボタンをクリック。

　ダウンロードコード　（ pWAkfAuA ）

③ダウンロードされた圧縮ファイルを解凍して、お使いの音声再生ソフトに取り
　込んで音声を使用。

＊ダウンロードされた音声はMP3形式となります。
＊zipファイルの解凍方法、iPod等のMP3携帯プレイヤーへのファイル転送方法、パソコン、
　ソフトなどの操作方法については、メーカー等にお問い合わせいただくか、取扱説明書を
　ご参照ください。小社での対応はできかねますこと、ご理解ください。
☞音声の権利・利用については、小社ホームページ内［よくある質問］にてご確認ください。

TEST 1

解答&解説

正解一覧

Part 1				Part 2				Part 3			
問題番号	正解	1	2	問題番号	正解	1	2	問題番号	正解	1	2
1	B	☐	☐	7	B	☐	☐	32	A	☐	☐
2	C	☐	☐	8	A	☐	☐	33	B	☐	☐
3	A	☐	☐	9	C	☐	☐	34	C	☐	☐
4	C	☐	☐	10	B	☐	☐	35	C	☐	☐
5	A	☐	☐	11	B	☐	☐	36	A	☐	☐
6	D	☐	☐	12	C	☐	☐	37	D	☐	☐
				13	A	☐	☐	38	A	☐	☐
				14	C	☐	☐	39	A	☐	☐
				15	C	☐	☐	40	D	☐	☐
				16	A	☐	☐	41	B	☐	☐
				17	B	☐	☐	42	D	☐	☐
				18	C	☐	☐	43	D	☐	☐
				19	A	☐	☐	44	C	☐	☐
				20	B	☐	☐	45	B	☐	☐
				21	A	☐	☐	46	C	☐	☐
				22	B	☐	☐	47	D	☐	☐
				23	A	☐	☐	48	C	☐	☐
				24	C	☐	☐	49	A	☐	☐
				25	C	☐	☐	50	A	☐	☐
				26	A	☐	☐	51	B	☐	☐
				27	B	☐	☐	52	C	☐	☐
				28	A	☐	☐	53	D	☐	☐
				29	C	☐	☐	54	A	☐	☐
				30	B	☐	☐	55	D	☐	☐
				31	A	☐	☐	56	B	☐	☐

Part 4

問題番号	正解	1 2
57	D	☐☐
58	D	☐☐
59	C	☐☐
60	B	☐☐
61	C	☐☐
62	A	☐☐
63	D	☐☐
64	B	☐☐
65	A	☐☐
66	B	☐☐
67	D	☐☐
68	C	☐☐
69	B	☐☐
70	B	☐☐

問題番号	正解	1 2
71	D	☐☐
72	B	☐☐
73	D	☐☐
74	A	☐☐
75	B	☐☐
76	A	☐☐
77	C	☐☐
78	B	☐☐
79	C	☐☐
80	C	☐☐
81	A	☐☐
82	D	☐☐
83	B	☐☐
84	B	☐☐
85	D	☐☐
86	A	☐☐
87	C	☐☐
88	B	☐☐
89	A	☐☐
90	C	☐☐
91	C	☐☐
92	D	☐☐
93	B	☐☐
94	D	☐☐
95	C	☐☐

問題番号	正解	1 2
96	D	☐☐
97	B	☐☐
98	C	☐☐
99	A	☐☐
100	C	☐☐

Part 1

1 　　　　　　　　　　　　　□□□　正解 **B**　　▶TRACK_002

(A) He's putting on a helmet for safety.

(B) He's hammering a wall.

(C) He's replacing some bricks.

(D) He's breaking a ceiling with a tool.

(A) 彼は安全のためにヘルメットを被っているところである。

(B) 彼は壁をハンマーでたたいている。

(C) 彼はれんがを取り替えている。

(D) 彼は天井を工具で壊している。

ハンマーを手に持った男性の動作について述べている(B)が正解。hammerには「ハンマー、金づち」という名詞の意味の他に、「～をハンマーでたたく」という動詞の意味もある。

語彙チェック　□put on ～　～を身に着ける　□brick　れんが　□ceiling　天井

2 　　　　　　　　　　　　　□□□　正解 **C**　　▶TRACK_003

(A) One of the women is standing at a podium.

(B) One of the women is sampling an item.

(C) Some lighting has been fixed on the ceiling.

(D) Some merchandise has been lined up on the floor.

(A) 女性の1人は演壇に立っている。

(B) 女性の1人は商品を試している。

(C) 照明が天井に固定されている。

(D) 商品が床に並べられている。

天井の照明について説明している(C)が正解。fixには「～を修理する」といった意味もあるが、ここでは「～を固定する、～を取り付ける」という意味で使われていることに注意。

語彙チェック　□podium　演壇　□sample　～を実際に試す　□fix　～を取り付ける　□merchandise　商品　□line up ～　～を並べる

🙀 **ここに注意！**

(A)のpodium「演壇」はそこまで出題頻度が高いわけではないので、知らなかった人もいるかもしれない。知らない単語が聞こえてきても不安にならずに、他の選択肢をしっかり聞き取ることで確実な答えを導き出そう！

3 | □□□ 正解 **A** | ▶TRACK_004

(A) He is extending his arm into a cabinet.
(B) He is rolling up his sleeves.
(C) A water faucet has been turned on.
(D) A cup has been left beneath a shelf.

(A) 彼は腕を戸棚の中へ伸ばしている。
(B) 彼は袖をまくり上げているところである。
(C) 水道の蛇口の栓が開けられている。
(D) 棚の下にコップが残されている。

現在進行中の男性の動作について説明している(A)が正解。extendは多義語で、「～を伸ばす」の他に、「～を表す」や「～を延長する」といった意味もある。

語彙チェック □cabinet 戸棚 □roll up ～ ～を巻き上げる □sleeve 袖 □faucet 蛇口

---

4 | □□□ 正解 **C** | ▶TRACK_005

(A) Some potted plants are being placed on the ground.
(B) Some houses are under construction.
(C) Some bicycles are propped up against a wall.
(D) Some window panes are being cleaned.

(A) いくつかの鉢植えが地面に置かれているところである。
(B) 何軒かの家が建設中である。
(C) 何台かの自転車が壁に立て掛けられている。
(D) いくつかの窓ガラスが掃除されているところである。

写真の左側に注目すると、壁に立て掛けられた自転車が何台か写っている。よって、(C)が正解。be propped up against ～は、Part 1に頻出の表現。

語彙チェック □potted plant 鉢植え □be propped up against ～ ～に立て掛けられている □window pane 窓ガラス

> 🐾 **ここに注意!**
> (A)は地面に置かれた鉢植えが写っているので正解に思えるが、「今まさに～されているところである」という状況を表す現在進行形の受動態が使われているため誤り。動詞の時制に注意しよう!

(A) The woman is resting her hand on a counter.
(B) The woman is taking off her glasses.
(C) One of the men is handing over a briefcase.
(D) One of the men is entering a waiting area.

(A) 女性は手をカウンターの上に置いている。
(B) 女性は眼鏡を外しているところである。
(C) 男性の1人は書類かばんを手渡している。
(D) 男性の1人は待合室に入っているところである。

女性は片手をカウンターの上に置いているので、(A) が正解。動詞のrestには「休む、休憩する」の他に、「～を置く」という意味もある。

語彙チェック □rest ～を置く □hand over ～ ～を手渡す □briefcase 書類かばん

> 🐾 ここに注意！
> 正答の(A)で使われている表現に注目。rest自体は簡単な単語ではあるが、今回のように、一般的にはあまり知られていない意味で使われる場合があるので要注意！

(A) A worker is examining a pair of shoes.
(B) A worker is hanging some items on the wall.
(C) Some shelves are being stocked with tools.
(D) Some garments have been spread out on a desk.

(A) 作業員は1足の靴を調べている。
(B) 作業員はいくつかの品物を壁に掛けている。
(C) 棚に道具が入れられているところである。
(D) 衣服が机に広げられている。

衣服が机の上に広げられているという状態を説明している (D) が正解。衣服を表す単語のclothingやclothesは不可算名詞だが、garmentは可算名詞であり、1着の服を指す語。

語彙チェック □examine ～を調べる □hang ～を掛ける □stock *A* with *B* AにBを入れる □garment 衣服 □spread out ～ ～を広げる

Part 2

7 M 🇺🇸　W 🇬🇧　□□□　正解 **B**　▶ TRACK_009

Weren't these shirts scheduled to be picked up yesterday?

(A) They want us to clean the cabinet.

(B) I'll call the customer to check.

(C) It has been placed in the lobby.

これらのシャツは昨日引き取られる予定ではなかったのですか。

(A) 彼らは私たちに戸棚を掃除してほしいそうです。

(B) お客さまに電話して確認します。

(C) それはロビーに置かれています。

否定疑問文でシャツの引き取り予定について尋ねている。昨日引き取りの予定だったことを受けて、「お客さまに電話して確認する」と申し出ている (B) が正解。

語彙チェック　□ be scheduled to *do*　〜する予定である　□ pick up 〜　〜を受け取る

---

8 M 🇦🇺　W 🇬🇧　□□□　正解 **A**　▶ TRACK_010

Why's Ms. Jones absent from today's meeting?

(A) I thought you knew that.

(B) In Conference Room B.

(C) Oh, the agenda is clear.

なぜJonesさんは今日の会議を欠席するのですか。

(A) あなたはそのことを知っていると思っていました。

(B) 会議室Bでです。

(C) ああ、議題が明確ですね。

Jonesさんが今日の会議を欠席している理由を尋ねているのに対し、「あなたはそのことを知っていると思っていた」と驚きを示している (A) が正解。

語彙チェック　□ absent from 〜　〜に欠席の　□ agenda　議題

---

9 W 🇨🇦　M 🇺🇸　□□□　正解 **C**　▶ TRACK_011

What's the company going to hire more staff for?

(A) It's about twenty people in total.

(B) The clothing industry.

(C) Our new plant will begin operating.

会社は何のためにより多くの従業員を雇う予定なのですか。

(A) 合計で約20人です。

(B) 衣料品産業です。

(C) 新しい工場が稼働し始める予定なのです。

会社がより多くの従業員を雇う予定であることについて、その目的を尋ねている。新しい工場の稼働に伴い、新たに人手が必要であることを示唆している (C) が正解。

語彙チェック　□ in total　合計で　□ industry　産業　□ plant　工場　□ operate　操業する

> 🐾 ここに注意！
> What 〜 for? は目的を問う表現で、Whyと同じような役割を持つ。最後までしっかり聞かなければ、何が問われているかを判断することができないのが難しいポイント！

TEST 1

TEST 2

TEST 3

TEST 4

TEST 5

Would you like this gift wrapped or unwrapped?

(A) Yes, my colleagues gave it to me.

(B) I'll decorate it myself later.

(C) Ted will leave the company soon.

このギフトは包みますか、それとも包みませんか。

(A) そうです、私の同僚からもらいました。

(B) 後で自分で飾り付けます。

(C) Ted はもうすぐ退職します。

ギフトを包むのと包まないのとどちらがいいかを選択疑問文で尋ねているのに対し、「後で自分で飾り付ける」と伝えている (B) が正解。間接的にギフトは包まないようお願いしている。

語彙チェック　□wrapped　包装した　□unwrapped　包装していない　□decorate　〜を飾る

There's a long line at the cafeteria.

(A) Of course, I'd like to.

(B) I have already reserved our seats.

(C) We have to arrange items in line.

カフェテリアに長い行列があります。

(A) もちろんです、ぜひしたいです。

(B) 私たちの席はすでに予約しましたよ。

(C) 商品を一列に並べる必要があります。

問いかけ文は平叙文で、カフェテリアに長い行列があることを相手に伝えている。これに対し、「席はすでに予約した」と相手を安心させている (B) が正解。

語彙チェック　□reserve　〜を予約する　□arrange　〜を並べる　□in line　一列に

Ian is going on a business trip next week, isn't he?

(A) Yes, he was reimbursed the expenses.

(B) Because it'll be a long trip.

(C) I was appointed to replace him.

Ian は来週出張に行く予定ですよね？

(A) そうです、彼は経費を払い戻されました。

(B) 長旅になる予定だからです。

(C) 私が彼に代わるよう指名されました。

付加疑問文で Ian さんの来週の出張予定について尋ねている。「私が彼に代わるよう指名された」と答えることで、Ian さんは来週出張に行く予定がなくなったことを間接的に伝えている (C) が正解。

語彙チェック　□business trip　出張　□reimburse *A B*　A に B を返済する　□expenses　経費
□appoint　〜を指名する　□replace　〜に取って代わる

> **⚠️ ここに注意！**
> この問いかけ文は冒頭にいきなり人名がきているので、混乱した人も多いかもしれない。人名は自分の知らない英単語だと思ってしまう可能性もあるので、文全体を聞いて人名だと推測する力も必要になる！

13　W 🇬🇧　M 🇦🇺　□□□　正解 **A**　▶TRACK_015

Which company should we ask about catering services?

(A) Our top priority now is searching for a venue.

(B) We need at least 10 more attendees.

(C) I prefer the outside table.

どちらの会社にケータリングサービスについて尋ねるべきでしょうか。

(A) 今私たちの最優先事項は会場を探すことです。

(B) 少なくともあと10人の参加者が必要です。

(C) 私は外の席の方がいいです。

Which company 〜?で「どちらの会社にケータリングサービスについて尋ねるべきか」意見を求めているのに対し、直接的に質問に答えることはせず、現在の最優先事項として行うべきことを説明している (A) が正解。

語彙チェック　□priority　優先事項　□venue　会場　□at least　少なくとも
　　　　　　□attendee　参加者

14　M 🇺🇸　W 🇬🇧　□□□　正解 **C**　▶TRACK_016

Isn't that personal organizer on the podium yours?

(A) Now I have to contact them.

(B) That was an interesting talk.

(C) Thanks for telling me.

演壇の上にあるあのシステム手帳は、あなたのものではないのですか。

(A) 今や彼らに連絡を取る必要があります。

(B) それは興味深い話でした。

(C) 伝えていただきありがとうございます。

演壇にあるシステム手帳について、否定疑問文で「あなたのものではないのか」と確認している。これに対し、教えてくれたことへの感謝を述べている (C) が正解。間接的にそのシステム手帳が自分のものであることを伝えている。

語彙チェック　□personal organizer　システム手帳　□podium　演壇

> 🐾 **ここに注意！**
> この問いかけ文の主語は、that personal organizer on the podiumの部分。このように主語が長い文は、瞬時に文構造を取るのが難しくなるので注意！

15　W 🇨🇦　M 🇺🇸　□□□　正解 **C**　▶TRACK_017

Could you take a look at this copy machine, or should I ask someone else?

(A) Yes, it shows how to reload the paper.

(B) Mr. Adkins has been there before.

(C) Is there anything wrong?

このコピー機を見ていただけますか、それとも他の誰かに頼むべきでしょうか。

(A) はい、それは紙を入れ直す方法を示しています。

(B) Adkinsさんは以前そこに行ったことがあります。

(C) 何か問題があるのですか。

「コピー機を見てもらえるか、それとも他の誰かに頼むべきか」ということを尋ねている。これに直接答えるのではなく、「何か問題があるのか」と聞き返している (C) が正解。

語彙チェック　□take a look at 〜　〜を見る　□reload　〜を入れ直す

16　M 🇦🇺　W 🇬🇧　□□□　正解 A　⏵TRACK_018

When's our contact information on the Web site going to be updated?

(A) It seems to be new now.

(B) In the IT department.

(C) Online reviews are valuable for us.

いつウェブサイトにある当社の連絡先は更新される予定なのですか。

(A) もう新しくなっているようです。

(B) IT部門でです。

(C) オンラインレビューは私たちにとって貴重です。

ウェブサイト上の連絡先情報について、いつ更新予定なのかを尋ねている。これに対し、「もう新しい連絡先になっているようだ」とサイトの現状を伝えている(A)が正解。

17　M 🇺🇸　W 🇨🇦　□□□　正解 B　⏵TRACK_019

I've heard Amanda will be retiring next month.

(A) There were few visitors this month.

(B) I'm sure we'll miss her.

(C) That's a great promotion.

Amandaが来月退職する予定だと聞きました。

(A) 今月はほとんど訪問者はいませんでした。

(B) 私たちはきっと彼女がいなくなることを寂しく思います。

(C) あれは素晴らしいプロモーションです。

平叙文で「Amandaが来月退職する予定だと聞いた」ということを伝えている。これを受け、「私たちはきっと彼女がいなくなることを寂しく思う」と、Amandaさんの退職について気持ちを述べている(B)が正解。

語彙チェック　□retire　退職する　□promotion　プロモーション

18　W 🇬🇧　M 🇦🇺　□□□　正解 C　⏵TRACK_020

What do you think of having experts analyze the customer survey?

(A) We can conduct the survey online.

(B) Some parts of that product were defective.

(C) It costs a lot, right?

専門家に顧客調査を分析してもらうことについてどう思いますか。

(A) オンラインで調査を行うことができます。

(B) その製品の一部の部品に欠陥がありました。

(C) 多額の費用がかかりますよね？

What do you think of 〜? で「専門家に顧客調査を分析してもらうこと」に対する意見を尋ねている。これに対し、費用面の懸念点を伝えている(C)が正解。主語である代名詞のitは、having experts analyze the customer surveyを指している。

語彙チェック　□expert　専門家　□analyze　〜を分析する　□defective　欠陥のある

> 🈲 ここに注意！
> 問いかけ文のhaving experts analyze the customer surveyは、使役動詞haveを使った構文。have A doで「Aに〜してもらう」という意味になる。知識として知っている構文だとしても、音声だけで聞くと瞬時に意味が取れないことがあるので要注意！

19 M 🇦🇺 W 🇨🇦 □□□ 正解 **A** ⓟTRACK_021

Where can I get the expense report form?

(A) I'll e-mail you the link.
(B) You need your supervisor's signature on them.
(C) Thanks, it took me a lot of time.

どこで経費報告書の用紙を手に入れることができますか。

(A) あなたにEメールでリンクを送りますね。
(B) それらにはあなたの上司の署名が必要です。
(C) ありがとうございます、とても時間がかかりました。

経費報告書の用紙を手に入れることができる場所について尋ねているのに対し、直接的に場所を教えるのではなく、「Eメールでリンクを送る」と申し出ている(A)が正解。

語彙チェック □supervisor　上司

20 W 🇬🇧 M 🇺🇸 □□□ 正解 **B** ⓟTRACK_022

We've got the file cabinet you requested.
(A) Could you show me the file?
(B) Oh, but I wanted the silver one.
(C) That document is located in my drawer.

あなたが頼んだ書類整理棚がきました。
(A) そのファイルを見せていただけますか。
(B) ああ、しかし私はシルバーのものが欲しかったのです。
(C) あの書類は私の引き出しにあります。

注文していた書類整理棚が届いたという知らせを受け、それに対するリアクションをしつつ、「シルバーのものが欲しかった」と自分の希望の色と違っていたことを伝えている(B)が正解。

語彙チェック □cabinet　整理棚　□be located in ～　～にある　□drawer　引き出し

> **⚠️ここに注意！**
> 問いかけ文のWe'veはWe haveが短縮された形。このように、会話では主語に続くhaveが短縮されることも多い。弱く発音されて聞き取りづらくなるので注意しよう！

21 M 🇦🇺 W 🇬🇧 □□□ 正解 **A** ⓟTRACK_023

How's the preparation for next month's exhibition?

(A) There're not so many things left to do.
(B) We've had a number of visitors.
(C) I found a customer showing interest.

来月の展示会の準備はどうですか。

(A) 残りやるべきことはそれほど多くないです。
(B) 大勢の来客がありました。
(C) 興味を示している顧客を見つけました。

来月の展示会の準備の状態を尋ねているのに対し、「残りやるべきことはそれほど多くない」と進捗を報告している(A)が正解。

語彙チェック □exhibition　展示会　□a number of ～　多数の～　□interest　興味

22 M 🇦🇺 W 🇨🇦 　□□□　正解 B　⏵TRACK_024

What made you interested in this job?

(A) The repair work took a month.

(B) I studied marketing in university.

(C) To the New York branch.

なぜこの仕事に興味を持ったのですか。

(A) 修理作業は1カ月かかりました。

(B) 私は大学でマーケティングを勉強したのです。

(C) New York支店へです。

問いかけ文は、直訳すると「何があなたにこの仕事に興味を持たせたのですか」という意味。すなわち、興味を持った理由を尋ねていると分かる。大学でマーケティングを勉強したことがきっかけだったと述べている(B)が正解。

語彙チェック　□branch　支店

23 W 🇨🇦 M 🇺🇸 　□□□　正解 A　⏵TRACK_025

Have we gotten all the products for the trade show?

(A) We're ready to go.

(B) He's arranged the tables.

(C) There's a crowd of people.

見本市のための製品は全てそろいましたか。

(A) 行く準備はできています。

(B) 彼はテーブルを並べました。

(C) 人だかりがあります。

現在完了の疑問文で「見本市のための製品は全てそろったのか」と尋ねている。これに対し、「行く準備はできている」と答えることで、製品は全てそろっていることを示唆している(A)が正解。

語彙チェック　□trade show　見本市　□be ready to *do*　～する準備ができている
□arrange　～を並べる　□crowd　群衆

24 M 🇺🇸 W 🇬🇧 　□□□　正解 C　⏵TRACK_026

Who's in charge of the accounting department?

(A) Ms. Acker did it yesterday.

(B) We've already confirmed the payment.

(C) I am the accounting manager.

経理部を管理しているのは誰ですか。

(A) Ackerさんが昨日それをしました。

(B) 私たちは支払いをすでに確認しました。

(C) 私が経理部長です。

Who ～?で経理部を管理している人物について尋ねているのに対し、自分自身が経理部長であると名乗り出ている(C)が正解。

語彙チェック　□in charge of ～　～を担当して、～を管理して　□confirm　～を確認する
□payment　支払い

25　W 🇬🇧　M 🇦🇺　□□□　正解 C　▶TRACK_027

Shouldn't we put away this projector now?

(A) Actually, it's a new project.

(B) They've put it in the back of the room.

(C) Another meeting will begin in fifteen minutes.

今このプロジェクターを片付けておくべきではないのですか。

(A) 実は、それは新しい企画なのです。

(B) 彼らはそれを部屋の奥に置きました。

(C) 別の会議が15分後に始まる予定なのです。

否定疑問文で「今このプロジェクターを片付けておくべきではないのか」と尋ねているのに対し、すぐに別の会議が始まる予定であることを伝えることで、間接的にプロジェクターはそのままでよいと示唆している (C) が正解。

語彙チェック　□put away ～　～を片付ける　□projector　プロジェクター

26　W 🇬🇧　M 🇦🇺　□□□　正解 A　▶TRACK_028

When will Andy's Café reopen after the renovation?

(A) They are in business now.

(B) I'll be on vacation next week.

(C) You can get some discounts.

改装後、Andy'sカフェはいつ再開するのですか。

(A) 現在営業中ですよ。

(B) 私は来週休暇に入る予定です。

(C) いくらか割引がもらえますよ。

Andy'sカフェの営業再開時期を尋ねている。これに対し、「現在営業中だ」と答え、カフェはすでに営業を開始していることを伝えている (A) が正解。

語彙チェック　□reopen　再開する　□renovation　改装　□be in business　営業している
□discount　割引

> 🐾ここに注意！
> 質問をしている人物は「カフェはまだ改装中だ」と思っているが、実際はもう営業を再開しているという状況。このように、話し手が前提として持っている情報が間違っている、というパターンに注意しよう！

27　M 🇺🇸　W 🇨🇦　□□□　正解 B　▶TRACK_029

Does it rain often in this area?

(A) No, it is a historic district.

(B) I always carry an umbrella.

(C) On Fourth Avenue.

この地域ではよく雨が降りますか。

(A) いいえ、それは歴史地区です。

(B) 私はいつも傘を持ち歩きます。

(C) 第4大通りです。

「この地域ではよく雨が降るのか」と尋ねているのに対し、「いつも傘を持ち歩く」と答えることで、間接的によく雨が降るということを示唆している (B) が正解。

語彙チェック　□historic　歴史上重要な　□district　地区　□avenue　大通り

28　W 🇬🇧　M 🇦🇺　□□□　正解 A　▶TRACK_030

Why don't we add some more items to the questionnaire?

(A) We don't want it to take longer to answer.

(B) Because they don't have any in stock.

(C) Mr. Smith has arranged them on the shelf.

アンケート用紙にもっと項目を増やしてはどうですか。

(A) 回答するのに長く時間を取らせたくないのです。

(B) 彼らは在庫に何もないからです。

(C) Smith さんがそれらを棚に並べました。

提案の表現 Why don't we 〜? で、アンケート用紙にもっと項目を増やすことを提案している。「回答するのに長く時間を取らせたくない」とアンケート用紙に項目を増やしたくない理由を述べている (A) が正解。

語彙チェック　□questionnaire　アンケート用紙　□have 〜 in stock　〜の在庫がある

29　M 🇺🇸　W 🇨🇦　□□□　正解 C　▶TRACK_031

Who will join the advertising department?

(A) Ms. Stoney is in charge of its design.

(B) I don't know about the advertising strategy.

(C) It will be announced by our manager.

誰が宣伝部に入る予定なのですか。

(A) Stoney さんはデザインを担当しています。

(B) 私は広告戦略のことは分かりません。

(C) 私たちの部長によって発表される予定です。

Who 〜? で宣伝部に入る予定の人物を尋ねているのに対し、人名を答えるのではなく、「私たちの部長によって発表される予定だ」と説明している (C) が正解。

語彙チェック　□in charge of 〜　〜を担当して　□strategy　戦略

30　W 🇨🇦　M 🇦🇺　□□□　正解 B　▶TRACK_032

The launch of our new mobile phone was a resounding success, right?

(A) Yes, you can borrow my phone.

(B) It definitely was.

(C) You should carry a mobile battery.

私たちの新しい携帯電話の発売は大成功でしたよね？

(A) はい、私の電話を借りてもいいですよ。

(B) 本当にそうでしたね。

(C) あなたは携帯充電器を持ち歩くべきですよ。

付加疑問文で、新しい携帯電話の発売が大成功だったかどうかを尋ねている。これに対し、「本当にそうでしたね」と同意している (B) が正解。主語の it は問いかけ文の The launch of our new mobile phone を指している。

語彙チェック　□launch　発売　□resounding　決定的な、圧倒的な　□battery　充電器

> 🙈 ここに注意！
> (B) では was の後ろに、a resounding success が省略されていると考えられる。繰り返しを避けるために、このように文の要素が一部省略されることもあるので注意しよう！

The auditors will begin the inspection of our department today.

(A) Should we prepare anything for that?

(B) He's out of the city tomorrow.

(C) Yes, there's one in stock.

監査官は今日、私たちの部署の監査を始める予定です。

(A) そのために何か用意するべきですか。

(B) 彼は明日街を離れます。

(C) はい、在庫に1つあります。

平叙文で、監査官が部署の監査を今日始める予定であることを伝えている。これに対し、「監査のために何か用意するべきか」と、準備について聞き返している (A) が正解。

語彙チェック ☐auditor 監査官 ☐inspection 監査

Part 3

M 🇦🇺 **W** 🇨🇦　　　　　　　　　　会話 ▶TRACK_035　　問題 ▶TRACK_036

Questions 32 through 34 refer to the following conversation.

M: Hi. My name's Trevor Young. I'm from TRJ Productions. I have an appointment to see Ms. Harper.

W: Good morning Mr. Young. Umm. I see your appointment is at one twenty. You're a little early.

M: Yes, sorry. Is that a problem?

W: No, not at all. But, I'm afraid Ms. Harper is still speaking with one of her clients. You're welcome to wait here, though.

M: Thank you. I'll just work on some things on my computer until she's ready.

W: Thank you for understanding. Can I get you something to drink while you're waiting? We have coffee, tea, or bottled water.

問題32-34は次の会話に関するものです。

男性：こんにちは。Trevor Young と申します。TRJ Productions 社から参りました。Harper さんにお会いする約束があります。

女性：おはようございます、Young さん。えーと。あなたの約束は1時20分かと思います。少し早いですね。

男性：はい、すみません。それは問題でしょうか。

女性：いいえ、全くそんなことはございません。ただ、申し訳ないのですが、Harper さんはまだお客さまの1人とお話し中です。こちらで自由にお待ちいただいて構いませんが。

男性：ありがとうございます。彼女の準備ができるまで、パソコンで少し作業します。

女性：ご理解いただきありがとうございます。お待ちの間、何かお飲み物をお持ちしましょうか。コーヒー、紅茶、ミネラルウォーターがございます。

32　　　　　　　　　　□□□　正解 A

Where does the conversation most likely take place?	会話はどこで行われていると考えられますか。
(A) At a reception desk	(A) 受付
(B) At a bus stop	(B) バス停
(C) At a movie theater	(C) 映画館
(D) At a parking garage	(D) 駐車場ビル

男性は冒頭で名前と所属を述べた後、I have an appointment to see Ms. Harper. と、Harper さんとの約束があることを女性に伝えている。それに対して女性は、I see your appointment is at one twenty. と言っており、男性と Harper さんとの約束の時間を確認しているため、女性は受付のスタッフであると考えられる。よって、正解は (A)。

33

□□□ 正解 **B**

What does the woman say about Ms. Harper?

(A) She will be late.

(B) She is meeting one of her clients.

(C) She has changed the meeting location.

(D) She is on a business trip.

女性はHarperさんについて何と言っていますか。

(A) 彼女は遅刻してくる。

(B) 彼女は顧客の1人と面会している。

(C) 彼女はミーティングの場所を変更した。

(D) 彼女は出張中である。

Harperさんとの約束の時間よりも早く到着した男性に対して、女性は Ms. Harper is still speaking with one of her clients と伝えている。よって、(B)が正解。

34

□□□ 正解 **C**

What does the woman offer the man?

(A) A brochure

(B) A pen

(C) A beverage

(D) An invitation

女性は男性に何を勧めていますか。

(A) パンフレット

(B) ペン

(C) 飲み物

(D) 招待状

Harperさんの準備ができるまで待っていると発言している男性に対し、女性は Can I get you something to drink while you're waiting? と申し出て、提供できる飲み物の種類を伝えている。よって、(C)が正解。

W 🇬🇧　M 🇦🇺

会話 ▶TRACK_037　問題 ▶TRACK_038

Questions 35 through 37 refer to the following conversation.

W: The next stop on our tour of the City of London is the famous clock tower. Does anyone have any questions?

M: Excuse me. Is there a trash can on the bus? I have some food wrappers I'd like to get rid of.

W: Yes, we have one here in the front. We'll be stopping in a few minutes, so you can throw them out as you get off the bus.

M: Thank you. Um, can I ask, how long will we be spending at the clock tower? I'd like to buy some souvenirs.

問題35-37は次の会話に関するものです。

女性：私どものロンドン市内観光ツアーの次の降車地は、有名な時計台です。ご質問がある方はいらっしゃいますか。
男性：すみません。このバスにごみ箱はありますか。処分したい食品の包み紙があるのですが。
女性：はい、こちら前列にございます。あと数分で停車いたしますので、バスを降りる際にお捨ていただけます。
男性：ありがとうございます。ええと、時計台にどのくらい滞在するのか聞いてもいいですか。お土産を買いたいのですが。

語彙チェック　□trash can　ごみ箱　□wrapper　包み紙　□get rid of ～　～を処分する
□throw ～ out　～を処分する　□souvenir　土産

35　　　□□□　正解 C

Who most likely is the woman?　　女性は誰だと考えられますか。

(A) An engineer　　　　　　　(A) 技術者
(B) A politician　　　　　　　(B) 政治家
(C) A tour guide　　　　　　　(C) ツアーガイド
(D) A park ranger　　　　　　(D) 公園整備士

女性は冒頭で、The next stop on our tour of the City of London is the famous clock tower. と案内している。その後、男性はごみの処分についての質問や、時計台の滞在時間などについての質問を女性に尋ねていることから、女性の職業はツアーガイドだと判断できる。よって、正解は(C)。

28

36

What does the man ask about?

(A) Throwing out some garbage
(B) Inviting some colleagues
(C) Changing a schedule
(D) Planning an event

男性は何について尋ねていますか。

(A) ごみを処分すること
(B) 同僚を何人か招待すること
(C) スケジュールを変更すること
(D) イベントを計画すること

質問がある人はいるかという女性の呼びかけに対し、男性は Is there a trash can on the bus? とごみ箱の有無を尋ねた後、I have some food wrappers I'd like to get rid of. 「処分したい食品の包み紙がある」と理由を説明している。よって、正解は(A)。

語彙チェック □garbage ごみ

37

What does the man say he would like to do?

(A) Eat a meal
(B) Take a break
(C) Take some photographs
(D) Do some shopping

男性は何をしたいと言っていますか。

(A) 食事をとる
(B) 休憩する
(C) 写真を撮る
(D) 買い物をする

男性は最後に I'd like to buy some souvenirs. と述べている。「お土産を買う」を「買い物をする」と言い換えた(D)が正解。

Questions 38 through 40 refer to the following conversation.

W: Good afternoon Mr. Ling. Please come through here. <u>I'll explain the work we've carried out on your car.</u> It needed a lot more attention than we expected, I'm afraid.

M: I see. <u>Will I be able to take it home this afternoon?</u>

W: Oh, yes. <u>It's ready for you now.</u> I just wanted to show you the parts we replaced and explain why we needed to change them.

M: <u>It might be beyond me.</u>

W: That's OK. <u>I won't use any technical terms.</u>

問題38-40は次の会話に関するものです。

女性：こんにちは、Lingさん。どうぞこちらへ。お客さまのお車に行った作業についてご説明いたします。申し訳ないのですが、予想以上にかなり多くの手入れが必要でした。

男性：分かりました。今日の午後、家に持って帰れますか。

女性：ああ、できますよ。現在準備ができております。取り替えた部品をお見せして、なぜそれらを変える必要があったのかご説明だけさせていただきたいのですが。

男性：私には分からないかもしれません。

女性：大丈夫です。専門用語は用いません。

語彙チェック □carry out 〜　〜を実行する　□attention　手当て、手入れ
　　　　　　　　□beyond　（〜の範囲）を超えて　□technical term　専門用語

38　　　　　　　　　□□□　正解 **A**

Who most likely is the woman?	女性は誰だと考えられますか。
(A) A mechanic	(A) 整備士
(B) A doctor	(B) 医者
(C) A construction worker	(C) 建設作業員
(D) A film producer	(D)映画プロデューサー

女性の冒頭のI'll explain the work we've carried out on your car.という発言から、女性は男性の車に何か処置をしたことが分かる。また、It needed a lot more attention than we expectedのattentionは「手当て、手入れ」という意味で、車は予想以上に手入れが必要だったと言っている。これらから、女性は男性の車の修理をしたと判断できる。よって、正解は(A)。

> ⚠ **ここに注意！**
> この問題は、最初の女性の発言にあるcarを聞き取れれば正解できるが、それ以降に正答を絞ることができるキーワードがほとんど出てこない。1語1語をしっかり聞き取れないと正解できない難問だ！

39 □□□ 正解 **A**

What does the man ask about?

(A) When some work will be completed
(B) Who will be invited to an event
(C) What will be served at a dinner
(D) Where some guests will be seated

男性は何について尋ねていますか。

(A) いつ作業が完了するのか
(B) 誰がイベントに招待されるのか
(C) 何が夕食で提供されるのか
(D) どこにゲストが着席するのか

男性のWill I be able to take it home this afternoon? という質問は「車の手入れは今日の午後には終わるのか」という意味を含み、それに対し女性はIt's ready for you now. と答えている。車の手入れの完了時期について話していることが分かるので、(A)が正解。

語彙チェック □seat　〜を着席させる

40 □□□ 正解 **D**

What does the man mean when he says, "It might be beyond me"?

(A) He may not be able to attend a meeting.
(B) He is not qualified to carry out a task.
(C) He does not have enough time.
(D) He may not understand the woman's explanation.

男性は "It might be beyond me" という発言で、何を意味していますか。

(A) 彼は会議に出席できないかもしれない。
(B) 彼は仕事を遂行する資格を持っていない。
(C) 彼には十分な時間がない。
(D) 彼は女性の説明を理解できないかもしれない。

「交換部品を見せて説明したい」という女性の申し出に、男性はIt might be beyond me. と答えている。beyondは「(〜の範囲) を超えて」という意味で、beyond meで「私の理解の範囲を超える」となる。男性のその発言に対し、女性も「専門用語は使わない」と言っている。これらのことから、男性は「女性の説明が難しくて理解できないかもしれない」と考えていると判断できる。よって、正解は(D)。

語彙チェック □be qualified to *do*　〜をする資格を持っている

Questions 41 through 43 refer to the following conversation.

W: Hi Jack. What brings you to Bronson Bus Lines today?

M: Hi Helen. I'm meeting Hide Tanaka for lunch. We're going to try out that new restaurant on Douglass Street. Why don't you join us?

W: That sounds great. I'd really love to, but I'm busy working on a report. I have to get it done by three o'clock. Let me know next time you make plans, though.

M: Sure thing. We usually get together on Tuesdays, so come along whenever you feel like it.

問題41-43は次の会話に関するものです。

女性：こんにちはJack。今日はどのような件でBronson Bus Linesにいらっしゃいましたか。

男性：こんにちはHelen。ランチにHide Tanakaと会う予定なのです。Douglass通りのあの新しいレストランに試しに行ってみるつもりです。あなたも一緒に行きませんか。

女性：いいですね。ぜひ行きたいのですが、報告書に取り組むのに忙しくて。3時までに仕上げなくてはいけないのです。でも、次回計画を立てたときには教えてください。

男性：もちろんです。たいてい火曜日に集まるので、気が向いたらいつでも来てください。

語彙チェック □try out 〜　〜を試してみる　□make a plan　計画を立てる
□Sure thing.　もちろん。　□get together　集まる　□come along　一緒に来る

41   □□□ 正解 B

What does the woman ask the man about?	女性は男性に何について尋ねていますか。
(A) The duration of an event	(A) イベントの期間
(B) The purpose of his visit	(B) 彼の訪問の目的
(C) The opening hours of a business	(C) 企業の営業時間
(D) The deadline of an assignment	(D) 課題の締め切り

冒頭のWhat brings you to Bronson Bus Lines today? という女性の発言は、「何があなたをBronson Bus Linesに連れて来るのか」、つまり「なぜあなたはBronson Bus Linesに来たのか」という意味である。よって、正解は(B)。

語彙チェック □duration　期間　□assignment　課題

42

☐☐☐ 　正解 **D**

What is the woman invited to do?	女性は何をするように勧められていますか。
(A) Become a club member	(A) クラブ会員になる
(B) Sample a product	(B) 製品を試す
(C) Attend a conference	(C) 会議に出席する
(D) Have something to eat	(D) 何か食べ物を食べる

男性はランチをしにDouglass通りの新しいレストランへ行くことを話し、Why don't you join us? と女性を誘っている。「ランチをしにレストランへ行く」ことを言い換えている (D) が正解。

語彙チェック ☐sample 〜を実際に試す

43

☐☐☐ 　正解 **D**

What does the woman say she will do today?	女性は今日何をすると言っていますか。
(A) Review a product	(A) 製品の見直しをする
(B) Meet a client	(B) 顧客に会う
(C) Leave work early	(C) 仕事を早退する
(D) Complete a report	(D) 報告書を完成させる

女性は男性からレストランに行かないかと誘われた後、I'd really love to, but I'm busy working on a report. I have to get it done by three o'clock. と述べている。get 〜 done は「〜を終わらせる」という意味で、itは a report を表していることから、「報告書を3時までに終わらせないといけない」となる。よって、正解は (D)。

Questions 44 through 46 refer to the following conversation with three speakers.

M1: Next month we're holding the annual employee banquet. I need someone to lead the organizing committee. Do any of you have time?

W: I'd be happy to do it. I was working on the Freeman Advertising project, but since that's been canceled, I have plenty of time to organize the banquet.

M1: OK. Well, please meet with Pete Rose. He organized last year's event. He can give you all the files you need.

M2: I know his number, so I can e-mail it to you later.

W: Thanks, Lucas. I'll call Pete right after I receive it. I want to get started as soon as possible.

問題44-46は3人の話し手による次の会話に関するものです。

男性１：来月、毎年恒例の社員の宴会を開催します。企画委員会をまとめる人が必要です。誰か時間がある人はいますか。

女性　：喜んでやります。Freeman広告プロジェクトに取り組んでいたのですが、それはキャンセルになったので、宴会を企画する時間はたっぷりあります。

男性１：そうですか。では、Pete Roseに会ってください。彼は去年のイベントを企画しました。彼はあなたが必要とするファイルを全てくれますよ。

男性２：彼の電話番号を知っているので、後でEメールで送りますよ。

女性　：ありがとうございます、Lucas。それを受け取ったらすぐに、Peteに電話をかけます。できるだけ早く始めたいと思います。

語彙チェック　☐banquet　宴会　☐lead　〜を率いる、〜を指導する　☐committee　委員会　☐plenty of 〜　たくさんの〜、十分な〜

44　　　　　　　☐☐☐　正解 **C**

What does the woman offer to do?

(A) Introduce a client

(B) Teach a course

(C) Arrange a function

(D) Check some reviews

女性は何をすることを申し出ていますか。

(A) 顧客を紹介する

(B) 講習を教える

(C) 宴会を準備する

(D) レビューを確認する

1人目の男性は Next month we're holding the annual employee banquet. と発言した後、企画委員会をまとめる人が必要だと述べている。これに対し、女性は I'd be happy to do it. と答えた後、I have plenty of time to organize the banquet とも言っている。これらから、女性は宴会を企画すると申し出ていることが分かる。よって、(C)が正解。

語彙チェック　☐arrange　〜を手配する、〜を準備する　☐function　宴会、大会合

45 　　　　正解 B

Why is the woman asked to meet Mr. Rose?

(A) To express gratitude
(B) To get some documents
(C) To return some equipment
(D) To provide some feedback

なぜ女性はRoseさんに会うよう求められていますか。

(A) 感謝を表すため
(B) 書類をもらうため
(C) 備品を返却するため
(D) フィードバッグを与えるため

1人目の男性は、女性にplease meet with Pete Roseと指示した後、その理由をHe organized last year's event. He can give you all the files you need.と説明している。よって、正解は(B)。本文のfilesをdocuments「書類」と言い換えている。

46 　　　　正解 C

What will the woman most likely do?

(A) Send an e-mail
(B) Place an advertisement
(C) Make a phone call
(D) Complete a report

女性は何をすると考えられますか。

(A) Eメールを送る
(B) 広告を出す
(C) 電話をかける
(D) 報告書を完成させる

女性は1人目の男性からPete Roseに会うよう指示されている。その後、2人目の男性からその人の電話番号をEメールで共有すると伝えられたのに対し、女性はI'll call Pete right after I receive it.と述べている。よって、(C)が正解。

Questions 47 through 49 refer to the following conversation.

M: Thank you for coming in and meeting me, Ms. Paulson. I'd like to talk to you about the process and requirements before we can host an exhibition of your work. <u>There's a lot to it.</u>

W: <u>All the planning and paperwork can't be an easy job.</u>

M: Thanks for understanding. <u>Did you receive the guidelines that I sent you last night? I sent the e-mail at about seven</u> ₚ.ₘ.

W: Yes, I read them carefully. <u>Actually, I have a couple of questions. Can I ask you now?</u>

問題47-49は次の会話に関するものです。

男性：会いに来ていただきありがとうございます、Paulsonさん。あなたの作品の展示会を開催する前に、その手順と必要条件についてお話しさせていただきたいと思っています。<u>それには多くのことがございまして。</u>

女性：<u>全ての企画立案と文書業務は簡単な仕事ではないでしょう。</u>

男性：ご理解いただきありがとうございます。<u>昨夜お送りしたガイドラインはお受け取りになりましたか。午後7時ごろEメールをお送りしたのですが。</u>

女性：はい、よく読みました。<u>実はいくつか質問があります。今伺ってもよろしいですか。</u>

語彙チェック　□process　手順　□requirement　必要条件　□exhibition　展示会　□paperwork　書類事務

47　　　□□□　正解 **D**

Why does the man say, "<u>There's a lot to it</u>"?

(A) They should distribute an instruction manual.

(B) A shipment will be very heavy.

(C) There are several routes to choose from.

(D) Some preparations will be complicated.

男性はなぜ"<u>There's a lot to it</u>"と言っていますか。

(A) 彼らは取扱説明書を配布すべきだ。

(B) 積み荷がとても重くなる。

(C) 選ぶ経路がいくつかある。

(D) ある準備が複雑である。

冒頭の男性の発言から、展示会を開催する手順や条件があることが分かる。また、男性が下線部の発言をした後、女性は All the planning and paperwork can't be an easy job. と述べている。つまり、展示会を開催するまでに企画や書類作業が必要で、それらが簡単ではないことが考えられる。よって、正解は (D)。

語彙チェック　□distribute　〜を配布する　□shipment　積み荷

⚠ **ここに注意！**
今回の問題47-49のように、3問のうち1問目が「発言の意図を問う問題」になっているパターンは危険。「発言の意図を問う問題」を解くのに時間をかけ過ぎて、残りの2問を無駄にしてしまわないように注意しよう！

48　　　　　　　　□□□　正解 **C**

What does the man say he has done?	男性は何をしたと言っていますか。
(A) Written a manual	(A) 説明書を書いた
(B) Interviewed a candidate	(B) 候補者を面接した
(C) Sent an e-mail	(C) Eメールを送った
(D) Read a book	(D) 本を読んだ

　展示会の準備について説明を始める際、男性は Did you receive the guidelines that I sent you last night? と言ってから、I sent the e-mail at about seven P.M. と述べている。よって、正解は (C)。

語彙チェック　□candidate　候補者

49　　　　　　　　□□□　正解 **A**

What does the woman say she would like to do?	女性は何をしたいと言っていますか。
(A) Ask some questions	(A) 質問をする
(B) Order some food	(B) 食べ物を注文する
(C) Look at a menu	(C) メニューを見る
(D) Speak with an expert	(D) 専門家と話す

　男性から受け取ったガイドラインをよく読んだと言う女性は、Actually, I have a couple of questions. Can I ask you now? と尋ねている。よって、正解は (A)。

Questions 50 through 52 refer to the following conversation.

W: I've been looking at the designs for the new restaurant. I think they look great. The views from the dining room will be amazing.

M: I agree. <u>I'm worried about the employee bathrooms, though. The location looks very inconvenient.</u> They're too far from the kitchen. I'd like to have a talk with the architect.

W: Well, everything has to be finalized by Tuesday afternoon. <u>We're submitting the plans to the council on Wednesday.</u> I will contact the architect today.

M: Thanks. <u>I'll ask the staff members if they see anything else that they want to change.</u>

問題50-52は次の会話に関するものです。

女性：新しいレストランの設計図を見ています。素晴らしいと思います。ダイニングルームからの眺めは見事でしょうね。

男性：同感です。しかし、従業員用のトイレが心配です。場所がとても不便そうです。キッチンから遠過ぎるのです。建築家と話をしたいと思っています。

女性：ええと、火曜日の午後までに全て仕上げなくてはいけません。水曜日に評議会に計画を提出する予定なので。今日、建築家に連絡しますね。

男性：ありがとうございます。他に何か変更したいところがあるか、スタッフたちに聞いてみます。

語彙チェック　□inconvenient　不便な　□finalize　〜を終了させる、〜を仕上げる
　　　　　　　　　□council　評議会

50　　　　　　　□□□　正解 A

What does the man say is inconvenient?　　男性は何が不便だと言っていますか。

(A) The bathrooms　　　　(A) トイレ

(B) The dining room　　　(B) ダイニングルーム

(C) The entryway　　　　(C) 通路

(D) The parking lot　　　(D) 駐車場

男性は I'm worried about the employee bathrooms, though. と従業員用のトイレについて言及し、The location looks very inconvenient. と述べている。つまり、「従業員用のトイレの場所が不便そうだ」ということなので、正解は (A)。

> 🈁 **ここに注意！**
> この設問を先読みした場合 inconvenient がキーワードになるが、会話文で inconvenient が出てきたときにはすでに、根拠となる I'm worried about the employee bathrooms, though. という部分は読まれた後である。キーワードにとらわれ過ぎずに、会話の流れを理解することが大切！

51 正解 B

When does the woman say they will submit the plans?
(A) On Tuesday
(B) On Wednesday
(C) On Thursday
(D) On Friday

女性は彼らはいつ計画を提出すると言っていますか。
(A) 火曜日
(B) 水曜日
(C) 木曜日
(D) 金曜日

男性が「建築家と話をしたい」と言っているのに対し、女性は「火曜日の午後までに全て仕上げなければいけない」と述べている。その後、We're submitting the plans to the council on Wednesday. と説明しているので、正解は (B)。

52 正解 C

What does the man say he will do?
(A) Call an architect
(B) Visit the council building
(C) Speak with employees
(D) Sit by the window

男性は何をすると言っていますか。
(A) 建築家に電話する
(B) 議会の建物を訪れる
(C) 従業員と話す
(D) 窓辺に座る

「建築家に連絡をする」と言う女性に対し、男性は I'll ask the staff members if they see anything else that they want to change. と述べ、設計図について他に変更したい部分があるかスタッフに聞いてみることを伝えている。よって、(C) が正解。

ここに注意！
誤答の選択肢の (A) をうっかり選んでしまった人も多いかもしれない。たしかに I will contact the architect today. という発言はあるが、発言しているのは男性ではなく女性。誰の発言なのかも意識して聞こう！

Questions 53 through 55 refer to the following conversation.

M: It's a public holiday tomorrow, so we need to get everything ready for Thursday's product demonstration today.

W: Right. I forgot about that. I still have to pick up the product samples from the factory. Can I use the van this afternoon?

M: I don't think anyone's reserved it. I'd check the reservation system first, though. I'll ask some of the other staff to help set up the chairs and tables in the hall downstairs.

W: Thanks for that. I've prepared a floor plan. I'll get that to you today.

問題53-55は次の会話に関するものです。

男性：明日は祝日なので、木曜日の製品デモンストレーションのために、今日全部準備を済ませておかなければいけませんよ。

女性：そうですね。そのことを忘れていました。まだ工場から製品サンプルを取ってこないといけないのです。今日の午後、ワゴン車を使ってもいいですか。

男性：誰も予約していないと思いますよ。まず予約システムを確認してみますけど。下の階のホールに椅子とテーブルを並べるのを手伝ってくれるように、他のスタッフに頼んでおきますね。

女性：ありがとうございます。間取り図は準備できています。今日あなたに渡しますね。

語彙チェック □public holiday　祝日　□demonstration　実演、デモンストレーション　□van　ワゴン車　□set up 〜　〜を配置する　□floor plan　間取り図

53　　　　　　　　□□□　正解 D

What does the man say will happen tomorrow?

(A) A conference room will be used.
(B) Invitations will be sent out.
(C) Some products will be delivered.
(D) The staff will have a day off.

男性は明日何が起こると言っていますか。

(A) 会議室が使用される。
(B) 招待状が発送される。
(C) 商品がいくつか配達される。
(D) スタッフが休暇を取る。

男性は It's a public holiday tomorrow と述べた後、「今日中に全ての準備を終える必要がある」と伝えている。これらから、明日は祝日のためスタッフは休みだと考えられる。よって、正解は (D)。

語彙チェック □send out 〜　〜を発送する　□day off　休日

54 □□□ 正解 A

What does the woman say she has to do?

(A) Obtain some product samples
(B) Prepare a presentation
(C) Review a production schedule
(D) Do some vehicle maintenance

女性は何をしなければならないと言っていますか。

(A) 製品サンプルを入手する
(B) プレゼンテーションの準備をする
(C) 製造スケジュールを再検討する
(D) 乗り物のメンテナンスをする

製品デモンストレーションの準備について話をする中で、女性は I still have to pick up the product samples from the factory. と述べている。pick up 〜は「〜を受け取る」という意味で、これを obtain「〜を入手する」に言い換えた (A) が正解。

55 □□□ 正解 D

What does the woman say she has prepared?

(A) A meeting schedule
(B) A shipping label
(C) A product catalog
(D) A room layout

女性は何を準備したと言っていますか。

(A) 会議のスケジュール
(B) 配送ラベル
(C) 製品カタログ
(D) 部屋の配置図

男性が「椅子とテーブルを並べるのを手伝うように他のスタッフにお願いする」と申し出たのに対し、女性は I've prepared a floor plan. と答えている。この a floor plan を言い換えている (D) が正解。

Questions 56 through 58 refer to the following conversation.

M: Greenslopes Greens. Queensland's premier golf course. How may I help you?

W: I'm interested in holding a corporate golf tournament, and I'm looking for a venue. We have forty people on our staff, all of whom will be playing in the tournament. I'm wondering if you could host something like that. Naturally, we would need access to golf carts and so on. A lot of the participants will need to rent equipment as well.

M: Depending on the date you have in mind, I'm sure we could accommodate you. Will you be requiring refreshments and lunch in the clubhouse restaurant? We have a variety of menu plans for large groups. I could send you a copy of our brochure as an e-mail attachment if you'd like.

問題56-58は次の会話に関するものです。

男性：Queenslandの最高級のゴルフ場、Greenslopes Greensです。どのようなご用件でしょうか。

女性：会社のゴルフトーナメントを開催したいと思っておりまして、会場を探しています。40人のスタッフがいて、全員がトーナメントに参加する予定です。そちらでそのようなものを主催していただけないかと思いまして。当然ですが、ゴルフカートなどの利用が必要になるでしょう。参加者の多くは備品もレンタルする必要があります。

男性：お考えいただいている日にちによりますが、受け入れできると思います。クラブハウスのレストランでの軽食や昼食は必要ですか。人数の多い団体用にさまざまなメニュープランをご用意しております。もしよろしければ、パンフレットのコピーをEメールに添付してお送りいたします。

語彙チェック　□premier　最高級の　□naturally　当然　□access to ～　～の利用
　　　　　　　　　□have ～ in mind　～を計画している、～を考慮している
　　　　　　　　　□accommodate　～を収容できる　□refreshment　軽食
　　　　　　　　　□a variety of ～　さまざまな～　□brochure　パンフレット

> 🐾 **ここに注意！**
> この問題のように、1人の1回の発言が長いものも出題される。Part 3は複数人の会話のやりとりだが、こういった、会話の往復が少ない問題でペースが崩されないように気を付けよう！

56　　　　　　　　　□□□　正解 B

Where does the man work?	男性はどこで働いていますか。
(A) At a catering company	(A) ケータリング会社
(B) At a golf course	(B) ゴルフ場
(C) At a travel agency	(C) 旅行代理店
(D) At a sports store	(D) スポーツ用品店

男性は冒頭で、Greenslopes Greens. Queensland's premier golf course. と言っている。その後、「どのようなご用件でしょうか」と用件を伺っていることからも、男性はこのゴルフ場の職員であることが分かる。よって、正解は (B)。

57

□□□ 正解 **D**

How many people will participate in the event?

(A) 10

(B) 20

(C) 30

(D) 40

何人がイベントに参加しますか。

(A) 10

(B) 20

(C) 30

(D) 40

女性は会社のゴルフトーナメントの開催を考えていると説明した後、We have forty people on our staff, all of whom will be playing in the tournament. と伝えている。設問のthe eventはこのゴルフトーナメントを指し、社員40人全員がそのイベントに参加すると述べられているので、正解は(D)。

58

□□□ 正解 **D**

What does the man ask about?

(A) The woman's contact details

(B) An event location

(C) The size of a budget

(D) Dining requirements

男性は何について尋ねていますか。

(A) 女性の連絡先

(B) イベントの場所

(C) 予算の規模

(D) 食事の条件

男性は女性に対し、Will you be requiring refreshments and lunch in the clubhouse restaurant? と軽食や昼食が必要かどうかを尋ねている。よって、正解は(D)。

Questions 59 through 61 refer to the following conversation with three speakers.

M: Helen, have you seen my phone? I can't find it anywhere.

W1: You must have left it on the table in the conference room. I saw you put it there. By the way, did you notice that the projector was flickering? I think we need to replace it.

M: I was thinking the same thing. I'll send an e-mail to Mr. Hawkins in administration.

W1: If they're going to replace it, can you suggest getting one with wireless capabilities? I don't want to connect wires every time I use the projector.

W2: That's a great idea. My computer uses an older video cable, so it's always a hassle.

問題59-61は3人の話し手による次の会話に関するものです。

男性　　：Helen、私の電話を見ませんでしたか。どこにも見当たらなくて。

女性１：会議室のテーブルの上に置き忘れたに違いありませんよ。あなたがそこにそれを置くのを見ました。ところで、プロジェクターがちらついているのに気付きましたか。取り替える必要があると思います。

男性　　：私も同じことを考えていました。管理部のHawkinsさんにEメールを送りますね。

女性１：もし取り替えるのであれば、ワイヤレス機能が付いているものを手に入れるよう提案していただけませんか。毎回プロジェクターを使うたびに配線をつなげたくないのです。

女性２：素晴らしいアイデアですね。私のパソコンは古いビデオケーブルを使っているので、いつも面倒なのです。

語彙チェック　□flicker　明滅する、ちらつく　□administration　管理部
　　　　　　　　　□wireless　ワイヤレス　□capability　能力、機能　□hassle　面倒なこと、問題

> 🐾 **ここに注意！**
> この会話文では、3人目の話し手が最後に突然登場する。先読みをする際に61.の設問にあるwomenなどから、女性が2人登場することも意識して心の準備をしておくこともポイント！

59 | □□□ 正解 C

Why does the man speak to Helen?

(A) He wants to see a guest list.

(B) He needs a client's contact details.

(C) He is looking for a mobile phone.

(D) He would like her to work additional hours.

男性はなぜHelenに話しかけていますか。

(A) 彼は来客名簿を見たいと思っている。

(B) 彼は顧客の連絡先が必要である。

(C) 彼は携帯電話を探している。

(D) 彼は彼女に残業をしてもらいたいと思っている。

冒頭で男性は女性にHelenと呼びかけ、have you seen my phone? と尋ねている。その後、I can't find it anywhere.と言っていることから、男性は自分の携帯電話を探していると考えられる。よって、(C)が正解。

60 | □□□ 正解 B

What does Helen say about the projector?

(A) It was recently installed.

(B) It was malfunctioning.

(C) It is a well-known brand.

(D) It has been removed.

プロジェクターについて、Helenは何と言っていますか。

(A) それは最近設置された。

(B) それは正常に作動していなかった。

(C) それはよく知られたブランドである。

(D) それは撤去された。

男性からHelenと呼びかけられた女性は、プロジェクターについて男性にdid you notice that the projector was flickering? と尋ねている。その後、I think we need to replace it.とも言っているので、プロジェクターは正常に作動していないと考えられる。よって、(B)が正解。

語彙チェック □malfunction 正常に作動しない

61 | □□□ 正解 C

What do the women agree about?

(A) Hiring temporary staff members

(B) Refurbishing a building

(C) Using a wireless connection

(D) Rescheduling a meeting

女性たちは何について同意していますか。

(A) 臨時社員を雇うこと

(B) 建物を改装すること

(C) ワイヤレス接続を使うこと

(D) 会議のスケジュールを変更すること

調子が悪いプロジェクターの交換について話し合う中で、Helenと呼ばれる1人目の女性がcan you suggest getting one with wireless capabilities? と提案したのに対し、2人目の女性はThat's a great idea.と答えている。よって、正解は(C)。

語彙チェック □refurbish ～を改装する

Questions 62 through 64 refer to the following conversation and map.

W: Where shall we hold this year's banquet? Everyone was pleased with Furnivall's Kitchen last year.

M: I know, but we've grown a lot this year. I don't think there'd be enough room. I'm thinking of that new conference center on Tina Street.

W: Good idea. They're still offering discounts for new clients. This would be a good opportunity to take advantage of that.

M: Can you call them and figure out how much it'll cost? I know they have their own catering service.

問題62-64は次の会話と地図に関するものです。

女性：今年の宴会はどこで開催しましょうか。昨年は皆さん Furnivall's Kitchen に満足していましたね。

男性：そうですね、でも今年は人数がかなり増えました。十分なスペースがないと思います。私は Tina 通りにできた新しいカンファレンスセンターを考えています。

女性：いい考えですね。そこはまだ新規顧客向けの割引をやっていますよ。それを利用するいい機会になるでしょう。

男性：そこに電話して、いくらかかるか計算してくれませんか。そこには独自のケータリングサービスがあります。

語彙チェック   □banquet　宴会　□take advantage of 〜　〜を利用する
□figure out 〜　〜を計算する　□catering　ケータリング、仕出し

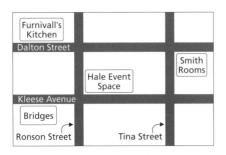 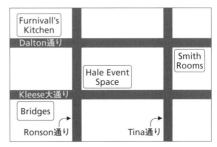

62 ☐☐☐ 正解 **A**

What are the speakers planning?

(A) A dinner

(B) A clearance sale

(C) An information session

(D) A reunion

話し手たちは何を計画していますか。

(A) 夕食会

(B) 在庫処分セール

(C) 説明会

(D) 同窓会

冒頭で、女性が男性に Where shall we hold this year's banquet? と尋ねている。その後も、その宴会の会場候補について話しているので、(A) が正解。

63 ☐☐☐ 正解 **D**

Look at the graphic. Which venue will the speakers most likely choose?

(A) Furnivall's Kitchen

(B) Bridges

(C) Hale Event Space

(D) Smith Rooms

図を見てください。話し手たちはどの会場を選ぶと考えられますか。

(A) Furnivall's Kitchen

(B) Bridges

(C) Hale Event Space

(D) Smith Rooms

男性が I'm thinking of that new conference center on Tina Street. と述べ、女性も Good idea. と賛成している。地図を見ると、Tina 通りにある会場は (D) Smith Rooms だと分かる。(A) Furnivall's Kitchen については、男性が「今年は人数が増えたので、十分なスペースがないと思う」と述べているため、不正解。

64 ☐☐☐ 正解 **B**

What is the woman instructed to do?

(A) Check their product inventory

(B) Get a price estimate

(C) Update a Web site

(D) Schedule a holiday

女性は何をするよう指示されていますか。

(A) 彼らの製品の在庫を確認する

(B) 見積もりをもらう

(C) ウェブサイトを更新する

(D) 休暇の予定を組む

男性は女性に対して、Can you call them and figure out how much it'll cost? と尋ねている。カンファレンスセンターに電話をして金額を出すということは、見積もりをもらうということなので、(B) が正解。

語彙チェック ☐inventory 在庫

M 🎌 　**W** 🇬🇧　　　　　　　　　　会話 ▶TRACK_057　問題 ▶TRACK_058

Questions 65 through 67 refer to the following conversation and graph.

M: The quarterly sales results are in. Look how much sales in Hartford and Durant have improved. The new marketing strategy is really paying off.

W: True. It's clear where we need to focus our efforts next. Let's invite their sales team down to the head office for a little motivation.

M: We'd better check with the president, first. We might have to schedule the visit for a date when he's in town.

W: I agree, but Mr. Hargraves will be busy until the end of the month negotiating to buy a sawmill in Redfern. We'd probably have to wait until July.

問題65-67は次の会話とグラフに関するものです。

男性：四半期の売上成績が出ました。HartfordとDurantの売り上げがどれくらい伸びたかをご覧ください。新しいマーケティング戦略が非常に功を奏しています。

女性：そうですね。次にどこに力を入れる必要があるのかが明確です。モチベーションを少し上げるために、そこの販売チームを本部に招待しましょう。

男性：まず社長に確認した方がいいですよ。彼が町にいるときに訪問日を設定しなくてはならないかもしれません。

女性：そうですね、でもHargravesさんは今月末までRedfernの製材所を買収する交渉で忙しいでしょう。おそらく7月まで待たなければなりませんね。

語彙チェック　□quarterly　四半期の　□pay off　効果を生む、報われる　□head office　本部
　　　　　　　　　□president　社長　□negotiate to *do*　交渉して～することを取り決める
　　　　　　　　　□sawmill　製材所

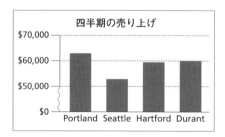

🐾ここに注意！

この会話文では、男性はかなり速いスピードで話し、女性はゆっくりのスピードで話している。このように、ナレーターの話すスピードに差があると、ペースを崩されやすいので注意しよう！

65 □□□ 正解 **A**

What is mentioned about two of the branches?	2つの支店について何が述べられていますか。
(A) They are using a new marketing strategy.	(A) 彼らは新しいマーケティング戦略を使っている。
(B) They will hire new staff members this month.	(B) 彼らは今月新しい社員を雇用する予定だ。
(C) They will have their offices renovated.	(C) 彼らはオフィスを改装してもらう予定だ。
(D) They have hired an analyst.	(D) 彼らは分析者を雇った。

男性は売上成績のグラフを見せながら、Hartford と Durant の2つの支店の成績が向上したことを取り上げ、The new marketing strategy is really paying off. と言っている。よって、正解は (A)。

66 □□□ 正解 **B**

Look at the graphic. Which sales team will be invited to the head office?	図を見てください。どの販売チームが本部に招かれますか。
(A) Portland	(A) Portland
(B) Seattle	(B) Seattle
(C) Hartford	(C) Hartford
(D) Durant	(D) Durant

男性から売上成績について話を聞いた女性は、It's clear where we need to focus our efforts next. と述べた後、Let's invite their sales team down to the head office for a little motivation. と提案している。つまり、売上成績が振るわない支店の販売チームが、モチベーションを上げるために、本部に呼ばれると考えられる。グラフから、Seattle の売上成績が最も低いことが分かるので、正解は (B)。

67 □□□ 正解 **D**

Who most likely is Mr. Hargraves?	Hargraves さんは誰だと考えられますか。
(A) A sales representative	(A) 販売責任者
(B) An accountant	(B) 会計士
(C) A new recruit	(C) 新入社員
(D) A company president	(D) 企業の社長

女性が販売チームを本部に呼ぶことを提案すると、男性は We'd better check with the president, first. と述べ、社長が町にいるときに訪問日を設定することを勧めている。これを受けて、女性は I agree, but Mr. Hargraves will be busy until the end of the month と答え、「おそらく7月まで待たなければならない」と伝えている。よって、Hargraves さんは社長であると考えられるので、(D) が正解。

Questions 68 through 70 refer to the following conversation and list.

W: Here's a list of the television programs we're considering for the advertisements for our new electric motorcycles. Advertising in these time slots costs about the same.

M: I expect that the new model will be popular with middle-aged people. We should choose a program they watch. People in their 20s and 30s probably won't have enough money to purchase them.

W: Good point. I spoke with the production company this morning. Apparently, they've finished editing the commercial. Shall we head over there this afternoon to take a look?

M: Sounds good. I'm free from two o'clock.

問題68-70は次の会話と一覧表に関するものです。

女性：新しい電動バイクの広告を出すのを検討しているテレビ番組の一覧表です。これらの時間帯で広告を出すのはほぼ同額の費用がかかります。

男性：新モデルは中年層に人気が出ると私は予想しています。彼らが視聴する番組を選ぶべきです。20代から30代はおそらく購入するのに十分なお金を持っていないでしょう。

女性：いいポイントですね。今朝制作会社と話をしました。どうやらコマーシャルの編集が終わっているようです。今日の午後、見に行きましょうか。

男性：それはいいですね。私は2時以降は時間があります。

語彙チェック　□electric motorcycle　電動バイク　□time slot　時間帯
　　　　　　　　　□middle-aged　中年の　□apparently　見たところは～らしい
　　　　　　　　　□commercial　（テレビ・ラジオなどの）コマーシャル

Program	Average Viewer Age
Brighton Bake Off	68
Home Reno Challenge	45
This Week Today	30
Fun and Games Show	22

番組	視聴者の平均年齢
Brighton Bake Off	68
Home Reno Challenge	45
This Week Today	30
Fun and Games Show	22

68 □□□ 正解 C

What product do the speakers want to sell?

(A) Mobile phones
(B) Desserts
(C) Motorcycles
(D) Fashion items

話し手たちはどのような製品を販売したいと思っていますか。

(A) 携帯電話
(B) デザート
(C) バイク
(D) ファッション雑貨

女性は一覧表について、Here's a list of the television programs we're considering for the advertisements for our new electric motorcycles. と説明している。「新しい電動バイクの広告を検討している」と言っていることから、(C) が正解。

69 □□□ 正解 B

Look at the graphic. Which program are the speakers most likely to choose?

(A) Brighton Bake Off
(B) Home Reno Challenge
(C) This Week Today
(D) Fun and Games Show

図を見てください。話し手たちはどの番組を選ぶと考えられますか。

(A) Brighton Bake Off
(B) Home Reno Challenge
(C) This Week Today
(D) Fun and Games Show

新商品の電動バイクについて、男性は I expect that the new model will be popular with middle-aged people. と述べ、さらに We should choose a program they watch. と言っているので、中年層が見るテレビ番組を選ぶ。図を見ると、Home Reno Challenge は視聴者の平均年齢が45歳なので、(B) が正解。

70 □□□ 正解 B

What does the woman suggest?

(A) Asking for a discount
(B) Viewing an advertisement
(C) Conducting a survey
(D) Visiting a broadcaster

女性は何を提案していますか。

(A) 割引を要求すること
(B) 広告を見ること
(C) 調査を行うこと
(D) 放送局を訪問すること

女性は「制作会社はコマーシャルの編集が終わったようだ」と述べ、男性に Shall we head over there this afternoon to take a look? と提案している。制作会社のところに行き、コマーシャルを見てみることを提案していると分かるので、(B) が正解。

Part 4

M 🇦🇺　　　　　　　　　　　　トーク ▶TRACK_062　　問題 ▶TRACK_063

Questions 71 through 73 refer to the following telephone message.

Hi there. It's Ronald Furze from Furze Plumbing. I'm at the property at 45 Wilcox Street. I've been asked to fix the leaking water pipes under the driveway, but I can't get in. The front gate is locked and no one is answering the doorbell. I have another job to get to in Carrara this afternoon, so I can't afford to spend a long time waiting here. I'm going to stay here for another 20 minutes. Please call me back if you get in touch with the tenants or if you can bring me a key. Otherwise, I'll have to come back later in the week.

問題71-73は次の電話のメッセージに関するものです。

こんにちは。Furze配管工事社のRonald Furzeです。今Wilcox通り45番地の物件にいます。私道下の水道管の水漏れ修理を依頼されているのですが、中に入れません。正面ゲートは鍵がかかっていて、誰もドアベルに答えないのです。今日の午後、Carraraで着手する別の仕事があるので、ここで長いこと待つ余裕はありません。あと20分はここにいるつもりです。入居者に連絡を取っていただくか、もしくは鍵を持ってきていただける場合は、折り返しお電話ください。そうでなければ、週の後半にまたお伺いします。

語彙チェック　　□plumbing　配管工事　□property　物件、土地、建物　□leak　漏れる
　　　　　　　　　□driveway　私道、車道　□get to 〜　〜に着手する
　　　　　　　　　□afford to do　（金銭的、時間的に）〜する余裕がある
　　　　　　　　　□get in touch with 〜　〜と連絡を取る　□tenant　住人、居住者
　　　　　　　　　□otherwise　そうでなければ

71　　　　　　　　□□□　正解 D

Who is the speaker?　　　　　　　話し手は誰ですか。
(A) A real estate agent　　　　　　(A) 不動産業者
(B) A security guard　　　　　　　(B) 警備員
(C) A taxi driver　　　　　　　　　(C) タクシー運転手
(D) A plumber　　　　　　　　　　(D) 配管工

話し手は冒頭でIt's Ronald Furze from Furze Plumbing.と自分の名前と所属を言い、I've been asked to fix the leaking water pipes under the drivewayと今回の訪問の目的を説明している。plumbing「水道工事、配管工事」やfix the leaking water pipes「水道管の水漏れを修理する」という言葉から、話し手の職業は配管工だと考えられる。よって、正解は(D)。

72 ☐☐☐ 正解 B

What does the speaker say about the property at 45 Wilcox Street?	話し手はWilcox通り45番地の物件について、何と言っていますか。
(A) The gate is hard to find.	(A) ゲートが見つけにくい。
(B) He cannot gain access.	(B) 彼は中に入れない。
(C) The power is disconnected.	(C) 電気が通っていない。
(D) Some guests have arrived.	(D) 客が到着した。

話し手はWilcox通り45番地の物件にいて、水道管の修理を依頼されていると説明した後、but I can't get inと伝えている。その後も、The front gate is locked and no one is answering the doorbell. と物件に入れない理由を説明している。よって、正解は(B)。

語彙チェック ☐gain access （建物などに）入る、侵入する

73 ☐☐☐ 正解 D

Why does the speaker mention Carrara?	話し手はなぜCarraraについて述べていますか。
(A) His company is based there.	(A) 彼の会社はそこを拠点にしている。
(B) It is outside his territory.	(B) そこは彼の担当地区ではない。
(C) There is a traffic jam in the area.	(C) その地域で交通渋滞が起きている。
(D) He has to go there for his next job.	(D) 彼は次の仕事のためにそこへ行かなければならない。

話し手はI have another job to get to in Carrara this afternoonと述べており、「ここで長く待つ余裕はない」と伝えているので、正解は(D)。

W 🇬🇧
トーク ▶TRACK_064　問題 ▶TRACK_065
Questions 74 through 76 refer to the following talk.

Thank you for coming to this information session for Perry Energy Solutions' new products. Our new solar panels are perfect for residential applications. They can be assembled into complex shapes to make the most of your roof space, ensuring you get maximum exposure to sunlight year-round. Our panels come with a fifteen-year replacement warranty. This means that if any of your panels drop below eighty percent efficiency within fifteen years of your purchase, we'll replace them free of charge. Typically, in just five years, installing the panels pays for itself in energy savings. You can't go wrong.

問題74-76は次の話に関するものです。

Perry Energy Solutionsの新商品説明会にお越しいただき、ありがとうございます。当社の新しい太陽光パネルは住宅用に最適です。お客さまの屋上スペースを最大限利用するために複雑な形状に組み立てることができ、年間を通して最大限の日光の照射を得ることを保証しております。当社のパネルは15年間の交換保証が付いております。ご購入から15年以内に、お客さまのパネルの発電効率が80パーセントを下回った場合には、無料で交換いただけるということです。通常、たったの5年間で、エネルギー節約の点からパネル設置代金の元を取ることができます。パネルはこちらをお選びになれば間違いありません。

語彙チェック	□information session　説明会　□solar panel　太陽光パネル、ソーラーパネル
	□assemble *A* into *B*　Aを組み立ててBにする
	□make the most of 〜　〜を最大限に利用する　□ensure　〜を保証する
	□exposure　さらすこと、照射　□sunlight　日光　□free of charge　無料で
	□pay for itself　採算が取れる、元が取れる
	□energy saving　電力の節約、省エネルギー

74　　　□□□　正解 A

What is the purpose of the talk?

(A) To promote a product
(B) To explain an installation procedure
(C) To attract new investors
(D) To thank an employee

この話の目的は何ですか。

(A) 製品の販売を促進すること
(B) 取り付け手続きを説明すること
(C) 新しい投資者を引き付けること
(D) ある従業員に感謝すること

冒頭のThank you for coming to this information session for Perry Energy Solutions' new products.という発言で、新商品説明会での場面だと分かる。その後もOur new solar panels are 〜と新商品の説明が続く。新商品説明会の目的は販売促進だと考えられるので、正解は(A)。

語彙チェック	□promote　〜を促進する、〜を宣伝する　□installation　取り付け

75

正解 B

Why are the solar panels perfect for residential use?

(A) They are lightweight.

(B) They are highly customizable.

(C) They can be purchased in small lots.

(D) They are easy to install.

太陽光パネルはなぜ住宅用に最適なのですか。

(A) 軽量だから。

(B) 高度にカスタマイズ可能だから。

(C) 小口で購入できるから。

(D) 取り付けが簡単だから。

話し手は Our new solar panels are perfect for residential applications. と述べた後、その理由を、They can be assembled into complex shapes to make the most of your roof space と説明している。よって、これを言い換えている (B) が正解。

語彙チェック □highly 高度に □customizable カスタマイズ可能な □small lot 小口、少量

76

正解 A

What does the speaker mean when she says, "You can't go wrong"?

(A) The product is a safe investment.

(B) The instructions are easy to follow.

(C) The store is conveniently located.

(D) The company provides free shipping.

話し手は "You can't go wrong" という発言で、何を意味していますか。

(A) その製品は安全な投資である。

(B) 説明が分かりやすい。

(C) 店舗が便利な場所にある。

(D) 会社は無料配送を行っている。

話し手は太陽光パネルについて、「15年間の保証付き」であり、かつ「保証期間中は無料で交換可能」と述べている。その後、in just five years, installing the panels pays for itself in energy savings と、パネル設置代金も5年で元が取れることを説明している。これらから「この商品は購入しても将来的に問題ない、安心だ」ということを話し手は伝えたいと考えられるので、正解は (A)。

語彙チェック □investment 投資

> 🄰 ここに注意！
> 「発言の意図を問う問題」は前後の会話の流れから正解を選ぶことが多いが、ここでは問われている発言が話の最後の発言になっている。問われる発言の後に根拠があると思いこまず、会話の全体の流れを意識しよう！

Questions 77 through 79 refer to the following telephone message.

Hello Ms. Jackson. This is Rod Bellman from Cartman Publishing house. I'm calling to let you know that we've been approached by a Japanese publisher that would like to distribute a Japanese language version of your book in Japan. We think it'd be a wonderful opportunity for you to reach a large new audience. I'd like to invite you to our office in New York next week to discuss the topic. Please call me back today and let me know when you'll be available.

問題77-79は次の電話のメッセージに関するものです。

こんにちは、Jacksonさん。Cartman出版社のRod Bellmanです。あなたの本の日本語版を日本で流通させたいという日本の出版社から話があったことをお知らせするために、お電話を差し上げております。多くの新しい読者に読んでもらうために、あなたにとって素晴らしい機会になるだろうと思います。このことについて話し合うために、来週New Yorkにある私どものオフィスに招待させていただきたく存じます。本日中に折り返しお電話していただき、ご都合をお知らせください。

語彙チェック □publishing house 出版社 □approach ～に話を持ちかける
□reach （影響などが）～に広がる、～に及ぶ □audience 読者

77   □□□ 正解 C

Who most likely is the listener?   聞き手は誰だと考えられますか。
(A) An actor   (A) 俳優
(B) A scientist   (B) 科学者
(C) An author   (C) 作家
(D) A musician   (D) 音楽家

まず、話し手は冒頭でCartman出版社の者だと名乗っている。また、電話の用件を説明する中で、a Japanese language version of your bookと発言している。話し手は出版社の人で、「あなたの本の日本語版」と言っていることから、聞き手はある本の作者だと考えられる。よって、正解は(C)。

78 　　　□□□　正解 **B**

What is the purpose of the call?	電話の目的は何ですか。
(A) To announce a decision	(A) 決定事項を知らせること
(B) To describe an offer	(B) オファーについて説明すること
(C) To explain a condition	(C) 状況について説明すること
(D) To congratulate a colleague	(D) 同僚を祝福すること

話し手は、I'm calling to let you know that we've been approached by a Japanese publisher that would like to distribute a Japanese language version of your book in Japan. と電話した理由を説明している。「日本の出版社があなたの本の日本語版を出版したいと話を持ちかけてきている」ということは、「仕事の依頼があった」と判断できる。よって、正解は (B)。

> 🐾 **ここに注意！**
>
> 1つ前の設問77.は、中盤で登場する your book という部分を聞き取らないと正解を絞ることができないが、このキーワードは次の78.の正答根拠が述べられている中に含まれている。77.の根拠を探すのに集中し過ぎると、78.の根拠を聞き逃してしまう！

79 　　　□□□　正解 **C**

When is the listener invited to the speaker's office?	聞き手はいつ話し手のオフィスに招かれますか。
(A) Today	(A) 今日
(B) Tomorrow	(B) 明日
(C) Next week	(C) 来週
(D) Next month	(D) 来月

話し手は、日本の出版社からの依頼について話し合うため、I'd like to invite you to our office in New York next week と伝えている。よって、正解は (C)。

トーク ⏵TRACK_068　問題 ⏵TRACK_069

Questions 80 through 82 refer to the following excerpt from a meeting.

The last item on the agenda for today's meeting is the Russell Bridge Project. We've had crews working on it for almost eight months. According to the schedule, we have to complete construction by the end of this month, or we lose our early completion bonus. That's £20,000, so I'd really like to make sure we finish on time. If any of you can spare people from the projects you're managing, please send them to help on Russell Bridge.

問題80-82は次の会議の抜粋に関するものです。

本日の会議の議題の最後の項目は、Russell橋プロジェクトです。私たちはおよそ8カ月間、作業チームにこれに取り組んでもらっています。スケジュールによると、私たちは今月末までに工事を終了させなくてはなりません。できない場合は、早期完成のボーナスがもらえません。それは20,000ポンドですから、確実に予定通りに終わらせたいと思います。現在管理しているプロジェクトから人を出せる場合は、Russell橋の応援に送ってください。

語彙チェック □agenda 議題　□on time 時間通りに　□spare 〜を貸す、〜を割く

80　□□□　正解 C

Where does the speaker most likely work?　話し手はどこで働いていると考えられますか。

(A) At an educational institution　(A) 教育機関

(B) At a printing firm　(B) 印刷会社

(C) At a construction company　(C) 建設会社

(D) At a cruise provider　(D) クルーズ船プロバイダー

話し手は会議の最後の議題が the Russell Bridge Project であると述べて、We've had crews working on it for almost eight months. と説明している。その後、「今月末までに工事を終了させなくてはならない」とも話している。これらから、話し手の会社は橋の建設を進めていると考えられる。よって、正解は (C)。

81

□□□ 正解 **A**

What will happen at the end of this month?

(A) A deadline will pass.

(B) A payment will be made.

(C) A new rule will be created.

(D) An employee will retire.

今月末に何が起こりますか。

(A) 期限が切れる。

(B) 支払いがされる。

(C) 新しい規則が作られる。

(D) 従業員が退職する。

話し手はスケジュールについて、we have to complete construction by the end of this month, or we lose our early completion bonus と説明している。つまり、今月末で早期完成のボーナスの期限が切れてしまうということなので、正解は (A)。

82

□□□ 正解 **D**

What does the speaker say listeners should do?

(A) Spend money on upgrading a bridge

(B) Send a document to the speaker

(C) Reduce spending on a project

(D) Dispatch workers to a certain project

話し手は聞き手が何をすべきだと言っていますか。

(A) 橋の改良に資金を費やす

(B) 話し手に書類を送る

(C) プロジェクトにおける支出を減らす

(D) あるプロジェクトに作業員を送る

話し手は工事の期限について説明すると、If any of you can spare people from the projects you're managing, please send them to help on Russell Bridge. と聞き手にお願いしている。可能であれば Russell 橋プロジェクトに人員を割くように言っているので、(D) が正解。

語彙チェック □dispatch ～を派遣する、～を送る

Questions 83 through 85 refer to the following excerpt from a speech.

Thank you for inviting me here to give the keynote speech at the annual Dental Convention. It certainly came out of the blue as far as I was concerned. Just two years back, I was here as an attendee for the first time, and I was excited to meet the famous dentists that I'd read about when I was in university. Thanks to my connection with Dr. Carter, who invited me to collaborate on her research project, I've been attached to a famous new medical procedure. And today, I have the honor of speaking about it to all of you gathered here. I've brought along some footage of the procedure, which I would like you all to take a look at first.

問題83-85は次のスピーチの抜粋に関するものです。

今年度の Dental Convention で基調講演を行うためにお招きいただき、ありがとうございます。私としては、まさに青天のへきれきでした。ちょうど2年前、私は初めてこちらに出席者として参加しまして、大学時代に読んで知った有名な歯科医の方々にお会いし、興奮しておりました。研究プロジェクトを共同でやろうと私を誘ってくださった Carter 先生とのつながりのおかげで、私はある有名な新しい医療に携わっています。そして本日、光栄なことに、ここにお集まりいただいた皆さまにそれについてお話しさせていただきます。その治療の映像をお持ちしましたので、最初にそちらを皆さまにご覧いただきたいと思います。

語彙チェック　□keynote speech　基調講演
　　　　　　　　□come out of the blue　突然やってくる、青天のへきれきである
　　　　　　　　□as far as I was concerned　私の考えとしては、私としては
　　　　　　　　□collaborate on 〜　〜を共同してやる　□be attached to 〜　〜に所属している
　　　　　　　　□medical procedure　医療、治療法　□honor　光栄、名誉
　　　　　　　　□footage　フィルム映像、ビデオ

83　　　　　　　　　　　　　　□□□　正解 B

What does the speaker say about the event?

(A) He helped organize it.
(B) He did not expect to be invited.
(C) He likes the new venue.
(D) He will leave before the end.

話し手はイベントについて何と言っていますか。

(A) 彼はそれの企画を手伝った。
(B) 彼は招待されると思っていなかった。
(C) 彼は新しい会場が気に入っている。
(D) 彼は閉会前に退席する。

話し手は Thank you for inviting me here 〜と、基調講演のため会議に招待されたことに感謝を示した後、It certainly came out of the blue と言っている。come out of the blue は「不意にやってくる、青天のへきれきである」という意味なので、話し手は講演するために会議に招待されるとは考えてもいなかったことが分かる。よって、(B)が正解。

84

☐☐☐ 正解 **B**

When did the speaker first attend the event?	話し手が初めてイベントに出席したのはいつですか。
(A) One year ago	(A) 1年前
(B) Two years ago	(B) 2年前
(C) Three years ago	(C) 3年前
(D) Four years ago	(D) 4年前

話し手はこの会議について、Just two years back, I was here as an attendee for the first timeと述べている。この発言から、話し手が初めて会議に参加したのは2年前だと分かる。よって、正解は(B)。

> 🐾 **ここに注意!**
> Just two years backと分かりやすく発言してはいるが、そのキーワードは1つ前の設問83.の正答根拠のすぐ後に述べられているので聞き逃してしまいやすい。さらに「初めてイベントに出席した」という内容もその後に出てくるので、気付いたときにはもう根拠が述べられているということが起こりうる!

85

☐☐☐ 正解 **D**

What will the listeners most likely do next?	聞き手は次に何をすると考えられますか。
(A) Open an envelope	(A) 封筒を開ける
(B) Take a seat	(B) 着席する
(C) Ask questions	(C) 質問をする
(D) Watch a video	(D) ビデオを見る

話し手は、これからするスピーチの内容について触れた後に、I've brought along some footage of the procedure, which I would like you all to take a look at first.と伝えている。footageは「フィルム映像、ビデオ」という意味で、話し手は聞き手に、治療の映像をまず見てもらいたいと言っている。よって、これを言い換えた(D)が正解。

Questions 86 through 88 refer to the following telephone message.

This is Kate Dunphy from Reynolds Real Estate. I spoke with you earlier today about commercial properties in Algester. We didn't have anything suitable at the time, but one's just come up. I think it'll be perfect for your needs, but you should visit it first. If you have time this afternoon, I'd love to take you there and show you around. The rent is very reasonable, and the owner doesn't mind if you make alterations to the building. Please call me back on this number if you're interested.

問題86-88は次の電話のメッセージに関するものです。

こちらはReynolds不動産のKate Dunphyです。Algesterの商業用物件について、先ほどお話しさせていただきました。そのときはふさわしいものがございませんでしたが、ただ今1件出てまいりました。あなたの条件にぴったりだと思いますが、まずそちらをお訪ねいただいた方がよろしいかと思います。今日の午後お時間がございましたら、ぜひこちらへお連れしてご案内させていただきたいと思っております。賃料は大変お手頃で、所有者はあなたが建物を改築しても構わないとおっしゃっています。もし興味がございましたら、こちらの番号におかけ直しください。

> **語彙チェック**　□real estate　不動産　□commercial property　商業用不動産
> □come up　現れる、出る　□show ~ around　~を案内する
> □make alterations to ~　~を改造する、~に変更を加える

86　　　　□□□　正解 **A**

What does the speaker mean when she says, "you should visit it first"?

(A) She needs the listener to confirm the location's suitability.

(B) There is no time to consider other choices.

(C) The listener must lead a group in the future.

(D) There is a discount for first-time visitors.

話し手は "you should visit it first" という発言で、何を意味していますか。

(A) 彼女は聞き手にその場所が適当かどうか確認してもらう必要がある。

(B) 他の選択肢を検討する時間がない。

(C) 聞き手は将来グループを率いていかなければならない。

(D) 新規訪問者向けの割引がある。

> 冒頭から話し手は不動産業者だと分かる。Algesterのcommercial properties「商業用物件」について1件見つかったという状況で、I think it'll be perfect for your needsと述べた後、but you should visit it firstと伝えている。話し手はすでに聞き手が求める条件を知っているが、まずそこを見てもらいたいと言っていることから、「条件に本当に合っているか確認してもらいたい」という意図がくみ取れる。よって、正解は(A)。

> **語彙チェック**　□confirm　~を確認する　□suitability　適合性

87

□□□ 正解 **C**

What benefit does the speaker mention?	話し手はどんな利点について述べていますか。
(A) Modern design	(A) 現代的なデザイン
(B) High visibility	(B) 高い視認性
(C) Low cost	(C) 費用の安さ
(D) Popular area	(D) 人気の地域

話し手は、今回紹介する物件について The rent is very reasonable と説明している。賃料がとても手頃だということは、費用があまりかからないということなので、正解は (C)。

語彙チェック □visibility　視界、可視性

88

□□□ 正解 **B**

What is the listener asked to do?	聞き手は何をするよう求められていますか。
(A) Stock a product	(A) 製品を仕入れる
(B) Return a call	(B) 電話をかけ直す
(C) Get a qualification	(C) 資格を取得する
(D) Provide a reference	(D) 参考資料を提供する

話し手は物件について説明した後、最後に Please call me back on this number if you're interested. と伝えている。すなわち、話し手が聞き手にしてもらいたいことは折り返しの電話をすることなので、(B) が正解。

語彙チェック □stock　〜を仕入れる

W 🇬🇧

トーク ▶TRACK_074　問題 ▶TRACK_075

Questions 89 through 91 refer to the following advertisement.

White Car Wash is Washington's largest chain of car washes — <u>now with 12 super convenient locations around the state</u>. <u>This week we're celebrating the opening of our newest location in Greenwind.</u> Come in this Saturday or Sunday and get a complete car wash for just five dollars. This includes a regular wash, windshield cleaning, and a wax coating. We're at 221 Hale Street in Greenwind — right next to the Greenwind Shopping Mall. <u>Mention hearing this advertisement and get a free members card</u> that entitles you to lots of great savings.

問題89-91は次の広告に関するものです。

White Car WashはWashington最大の洗車チェーン店です―現在、Washington州中にとても便利な12店舗を展開しております。今週は、Greenwindの新店舗開店をお祝いします。今週土曜日か日曜日にご来店いただくと、たった5ドルで完全な洗車ができます。通常の洗浄、フロントガラスの洗浄、そしてワックスがけも込みのお値段です。場所はGreenwindのHale通り221番地―Greenwindショッピングモールのすぐ隣です。この広告を聞いたとお申し出いただくと、たくさん節約することができるメンバーズカードを無料で差し上げます。

語彙チェック　□car wash　洗車　□windshield　フロントガラス　□wax coating　ワックスがけ
□entitle *A* to *B*　Aに Bを得る権利を与える

89　□□□　正解 **A**

What does the speaker mention about White Car Wash locations?	話し手は White Car Washの店舗について、何と述べていますか。
(A) They are easy to get to.	(A) 行きやすい。
(B) They all have the same equipment.	(B) 全ての店舗に同じ設備がある。
(C) They are looking for new staff members.	(C) 新しいスタッフを募集している。
(D) They have luxurious waiting rooms.	(D) 豪華な待合室がある。

White Car Washの店舗について、話し手は冒頭で now with 12 super convenient locations around the state と述べている。super convenient locations「とても便利な店舗」ということは「店舗は行きやすい場所にある」ということなので、(A)が正解。

語彙チェック　□waiting room　待合室

90　正解 C

What is the company celebrating this week?

会社は今週何を祝う予定ですか。

(A) An anniversary

(A) 記念日

(B) The completion of a merger

(B) 合併の完了

(C) A grand opening

(C) グランドオープン

(D) The launch of a new service

(D) 新サービスの開始

話し手は This week と始めて、we're celebrating the opening of our newest location in Greenwind と説明している。よって、(C) が正解。

語彙チェック　□grand opening　グランドオープン、開店

91　正解 C

How can listeners get a members card?

聞き手はどのようにしてメンバーズカードを入手できますか。

(A) By filling out an online application form

(A) オンライン申込フォームに入力することによって

(B) By purchasing one from a vending machine

(B) 自動販売機で購入することによって

(C) By telling staff that they heard the commercial

(C) 広告放送を聞いたと店員に伝えることによって

(D) By introducing a customer to the business

(D) 会社に顧客を紹介することによって

話し手はメンバーズカードについて、Mention hearing this advertisement and get a free members card と案内している。この広告放送を聞いたことを伝えればメンバーズカードを無料で入手できると分かるので、(C) が正解。

Questions 92 through 94 refer to the following telephone message.

Hi Kate. It's Peter Dunn. <u>I know I was supposed to discuss the plans for the new shed with you today</u>, <u>but a water pump here broke</u>. <u>I'll have to spend the morning at the farm fixing it. Can we meet tomorrow instead? I have to go to the bank in the morning</u>, so sometime between twelve and two would be perfect. <u>I'll be bringing one of my neighbors with me.</u> He's looking at getting a similar shed, so I'd like to introduce him to you.

問題92-94は次の電話のメッセージに関するものです。

こんにちはKate。Peter Dunnです。今日あなたと新しい物置の計画を話し合うことになっていたかと思いますが、ここの水揚げポンプが故障しました。午前中を使って、農場でそれを修理しなければなりません。代わりに明日お会いできますか。午前中に銀行に行かなくてはならないので、12時から2時の間のどこかだと助かります。近所の人を1人連れていく予定です。彼はよく似た物置を購入することを検討しているので、ぜひ彼をあなたに紹介したいと思います。

語彙チェック   □ be supposed to *do*   〜することになっている   □ shed   物置、小屋
       □ look at 〜   〜を検討する

92   ☐☐☐   正解 **D**

Why does the speaker say, "<u>but a water pump here broke</u>"?

(A) To suggest a change of location
(B) To ask the listener for some assistance
(C) To encourage a quick response
(D) To explain why he can't make an appointment

話し手はなぜ "but a water pump here broke" と言っていますか。

(A) 場所の変更を提案するため
(B) 聞き手に支援を求めるため
(C) 迅速な対応を促すため
(D) なぜ約束に行けないのかを説明するため

話し手は but a water pump here broke という発言をする前に、I know I was supposed to discuss the plans for the new shed with you today と言っているため、聞き手と話し手が今日話し合う約束をしていたことが分かる。さらに話し手は、水揚げポンプが故障したことについて、I'll have to spend the morning at the farm fixing it. と言い、Can we meet tomorrow instead? と聞き手にお願いしている。つまり、今日は水揚げポンプを修理するため約束に行けないので、明日に予定を変更してもらえないかということである。これらのことから、正解は (D)。

93　　　　□□□　正解 **B**

What does the speaker say he will do tomorrow morning?	話し手は明日の午前に何をすると言っていますか。
(A) Meet with Kate	(A) Kate に会う
(B) Visit the bank	(B) 銀行に行く
(C) Work on the farm	(C) 農場で仕事をする
(D) Complete some paperwork	(D) 書類作業を終える

話し手は Can we meet tomorrow instead? と明日会うことができるかを尋ねた後、I have to go to the bank in the morning と言い、「だから12時から2時の間がいい」と説明している。この流れから I have to go to the bank in the morning の in the morning は「明日の午前中」のことだと分かる。よって、正解は (B)。

> 🔥 **ここに注意！**
> 話し手は I'll have to spend the morning at the farm fixing it. とも言っているが、この the morning とは「今日の午前」のこと。話の流れを追えていないと、間違って (C) を選んでしまう可能性があるので注意が必要な問題！

94　　　　□□□　正解 **D**

Who does the speaker say he will bring to the meeting?	話し手は誰を打ち合わせに連れていくと言っていますか。
(A) A colleague	(A) 同僚
(B) An accountant	(B) 会計士
(C) A relative	(C) 親戚
(D) A neighbor	(D) 近所の人

話し手は聞き手に「代わりに明日会えるか」と尋ね、都合の良い時間帯を伝えた後、I'll be bringing one of my neighbors with me. と言っている。よって、正解は (D)。

Questions 95 through 97 refer to the following announcement and table.

Good morning, everyone. This is the final day of the annual county fair. The weather forecast is for clear skies so we expect a record turnout. The gates will open at eleven A.M., but we need every ticket booth to be staffed during the busiest time. That should be around two P.M. Most of the food stalls will be busy all day long, but they typically get busiest at around six o'clock. Make sure you're ready for extra orders. There will be a meeting for security staff in my office in five minutes. Please make your way there now if you are part of the security team.

問題95-97は次のお知らせと表に関するものです。

皆さん、おはようございます。今日は毎年恒例の農産物品評会の最終日です。天気予報は快晴なので、記録的な来場者数を予想しています。入り口は午前11時に開きますが、最も忙しい時間の間は全てのチケット売り場にスタッフが入らなければいけません。それは午後2時ごろのはずです。屋台のほとんどは1日中忙しいですが、例年6時ごろに最も忙しくなります。追加注文の準備を確実にするようにしてください。5分後に私のオフィスで警備スタッフの打ち合わせがあります。警備チームの方はそこへ行ってください。

語彙チェック □country fair 農産物品評会 □clear sky 晴天 □turnout 来場者数
□staff ～にスタッフを配置する □food stall 屋台
□typically 例によって、決まって □security staff 警備スタッフ
□make *one's* way 進む、行く

Annual County Fair Schedule			
Friday	Saturday	Sunday	Monday
Set up	Day One	Day Two	Cleanup

年次農産物品評会のスケジュール			
金曜日	土曜日	日曜日	月曜日
準備	1日目	2日目	片付け

95 　　　　　　　　 正解 C

Look at the graphic. When does the announcement take place?

(A) On Friday

(B) On Saturday

(C) On Sunday

(D) On Monday

図を見てください。このお知らせはいつ行われていますか。

(A) 金曜日

(B) 土曜日

(C) 日曜日

(D) 月曜日

冒頭で話し手は This is the final day of the annual county fair. と述べているので、今日がイベントの最終日だと分かる。Annual County Fair Schedule と題された表を見ると、Monday は Cleanup「片付け」となっているので、Sunday の Day Two「2日目」がイベントの最終日だと判断できる。よって、正解は (C)。

⚠️ ここに注意！

この図表問題では、図表の中の要素が放送文の中で一切読まれていないのが難問ポイント。図表に書かれているキーワードだけに集中しないように注意しよう！

96 　　　　　　　　 正解 D

Why does the speaker mention 2:00 P.M.?

(A) The parking lot may be full.

(B) The main event will take place.

(C) An announcement will be made.

(D) Ticket booths should be fully staffed.

話し手はなぜ午後2時について述べているのですか。

(A) 駐車場が満車になるかもしれない。

(B) メインイベントが行われる。

(C) お知らせが発表される。

(D) チケット売り場はスタッフが十分に配置されなければならない。

話し手は we need every ticket booth to be staffed during the busiest time と述べた後、That should be around two P.M. と付け加えている。That が指すのは the busiest time であり、午後2時ごろは最も忙しい時間であると分かる。そして、その時間は各チケット売り場にスタッフを配置しなければならないということなので、正解は (D)。

97 　　　　　　　　 正解 B

What will the speaker most likely do next?

(A) Inspect some venues

(B) Hold a meeting

(C) Explain a procedure

(D) Introduce a guest

話し手は次に何をすると考えられますか。

(A) 会場を視察する

(B) 打ち合わせを開く

(C) 手順を説明する

(D) ゲストを紹介する

話し手は最後に There will be a meeting for security staff in my office in five minutes. と言っている。「5分後に私のオフィスで警備スタッフの打ち合わせがある」と言っているので、この後話し手自身が打ち合わせを開くと予想される。よって、正解は (B)。

Questions 98 through 100 refer to the following talk and map.

This concludes the guided portion of our visit to Hampton Gardens. I hope you all learned a lot about the history of this important local landmark. You have about thirty minutes of free time before we get back on the bus. The bus will be waiting at the special bus parking area at the end of Fergal Lane. There are bathrooms on Sharkey Path and a small gift shop on Valley Walk. Please make sure you're on the bus by three twenty. We'll leave immediately for the hotel. We hope to arrive there by four o'clock.

問題98-100は次の話と地図に関するものです。

これで私たちのHampton Gardens 見学の案内部分は終了です。皆さまにこの重要な地元の史跡の歴史について、多くのことを知っていただけたのなら幸いです。バスに戻る前に、約30分の自由時間がございます。バスはFergal Laneの端にある特別バス駐車場でお待ちしております。Sharkey Pathにお手洗いが、Valley Walkに小さな土産屋がございます。必ず3時20分までにバスにお戻りください。すぐにホテルに向けて出発いたします。4時までにそこへ到着したいと思っております。

語彙チェック □portion 部分、一部 □landmark 史跡 □immediately 直ちに

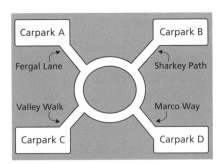
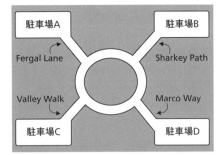

98 □□□ 正解 C

What is mentioned about Hampton Gardens?

(A) It has won an award.
(B) It charges an admission fee.
(C) It has historical significance.
(D) It is publicly owned.

Hampton Gardensについて何が述べられていますか。

(A) そこは賞をもらったことがある。
(B) そこは入場料がかかる。
(C) そこは歴史的意義がある。
(D) そこは公営である。

話し手はHampton Gardensの案内の終了を告げると、I hope you all learned a lot about the history of this important local landmark. と述べている。このthis important local landmarkはHampton Gardensのことを指していることから、Hampton Gardensは歴史がある重要な場所だと考えられるので、正解は(C)。

語彙チェック □significance 重要性、意義

99 □□□ 正解 A

Look at the graphic. Where will the listeners get on the bus?

(A) At Carpark A
(B) At Carpark B
(C) At Carpark C
(D) At Carpark D

図を見てください。聞き手はどこでバスに乗車しますか。

(A) 駐車場A
(B) 駐車場B
(C) 駐車場C
(D) 駐車場D

話し手は、バスについて The bus will be waiting at the special bus parking area at the end of Fergal Lane. と説明している。バスが待っているのはFergal Laneの端の駐車場ということなので、地図から、正解は(A)。

 ここに注意！
(A)の選択肢につながるFergal Lane、(B)の選択肢につながるSharkey Path、(C)の選択肢につながるValley Walkが放送文中に登場している。このように、複数の選択肢につながるキーワードが登場する問題もあるので、混乱してしまわないように注意が必要！

100 □□□ 正解 C

What time will the bus depart?

(A) At 2:20 P.M.
(B) At 3:00 P.M.
(C) At 3:20 P.M.
(D) At 4:00 P.M.

バスは何時に出発しますか。

(A) 午後2時20分
(B) 午後3時
(C) 午後3時20分
(D) 午後4時

話し手は聞き手たちに Please make sure you're on the bus by three twenty. と指示し、We'll leave immediately for the hotel. と説明している。このことから3時20分がバスの出発時間だと考えられる。よって、正解は(C)。

TEST 2

解答＆解説

Part 1

問題番号	正解	1 2
1	D	☐☐
2	B	☐☐
3	D	☐☐
4	A	☐☐
5	C	☐☐
6	A	☐☐

Part 2

問題番号	正解	1 2
7	C	☐☐
8	C	☐☐
9	A	☐☐
10	B	☐☐
11	A	☐☐
12	B	☐☐
13	B	☐☐
14	C	☐☐
15	A	☐☐
16	C	☐☐
17	C	☐☐
18	A	☐☐
19	A	☐☐
20	B	☐☐
21	C	☐☐
22	A	☐☐
23	C	☐☐
24	A	☐☐
25	B	☐☐
26	A	☐☐
27	B	☐☐
28	A	☐☐
29	C	☐☐
30	C	☐☐
31	A	☐☐

Part 3

問題番号	正解	1 2
32	A	☐☐
33	B	☐☐
34	C	☐☐
35	C	☐☐
36	B	☐☐
37	C	☐☐
38	C	☐☐
39	A	☐☐
40	D	☐☐
41	A	☐☐
42	A	☐☐
43	D	☐☐
44	B	☐☐
45	C	☐☐
46	D	☐☐
47	D	☐☐
48	C	☐☐
49	A	☐☐
50	A	☐☐
51	B	☐☐
52	D	☐☐
53	D	☐☐
54	A	☐☐
55	D	☐☐
56	B	☐☐

Part 4

問題番号	正解	1 2
57	D	☐☐
58	D	☐☐
59	C	☐☐
60	B	☐☐
61	C	☐☐
62	A	☐☐
63	B	☐☐
64	B	☐☐
65	A	☐☐
66	B	☐☐
67	D	☐☐
68	D	☐☐
69	C	☐☐
70	B	☐☐

問題番号	正解	1 2
71	A	☐☐
72	A	☐☐
73	B	☐☐
74	D	☐☐
75	B	☐☐
76	D	☐☐
77	C	☐☐
78	A	☐☐
79	D	☐☐
80	B	☐☐
81	C	☐☐
82	D	☐☐
83	A	☐☐
84	C	☐☐
85	C	☐☐
86	A	☐☐
87	D	☐☐
88	D	☐☐
89	C	☐☐
90	B	☐☐
91	D	☐☐
92	A	☐☐
93	C	☐☐
94	B	☐☐
95	D	☐☐

問題番号	正解	1 2
96	B	☐☐
97	C	☐☐
98	A	☐☐
99	D	☐☐
100	B	☐☐

Part 1

(A) Some vehicles are parked in a garage.
(B) Some plants are growing from the ground.
(C) Some chairs have been stacked on a table.
(D) Some sunshades extend over furniture.
(A) 数台の車が車庫に駐車されている。
(B) 植物が地面から生えている。
(C) 椅子がテーブルの上に積み重ねられている。
(D) 日よけが家具の上方に広がっている。

写真の右側に注目。日よけがテーブルや椅子などの家具の上に広がっているので、これを説明している(D)が正解。

語彙チェック □stack ～を積み重ねる □sunshade 日よけ □extend 伸びる、広がる

2 □□□ 正解 B ▶TRACK_084

(A) One of the women is reaching for a suitcase.
(B) One of the women is putting a phone to her ear.
(C) The man is taking off his jacket.
(D) The man is handing a tool over a counter.
(A) 女性の1人はスーツケースに手を伸ばしている。
(B) 女性の1人は電話を耳に当てている。
(C) 男性はジャケットを脱いでいるところである。
(D) 男性はカウンターの上で道具を手渡している。

カウンターの奥に座っている女性が電話機を耳に当てているので、これを説明している(B)が正解。

語彙チェック □reach for ～ ～に手を伸ばす

> 🔔 **ここに注意！**
> 正答の(B)の文は少し長く、最後にはto her earと短い単語が続いている。短い音が続くとかなり聞き取りにくくなるので、より高いリスニング力が必要！

3 🇨🇦   □□□ 正解 D ▶TRACK_085

(A) They are serving some customers.
(B) They are bending over some notes.
(C) Windows are being wiped with a cloth.
(D) A table is being sanitized.

(A) 彼らはお客さんに応対しているところである。
(B) 彼らはメモの上にかがみ込んでいる。
(C) 窓が布で拭かれているところである。
(D) テーブルが消毒されているところである。

テーブルがスタッフによって消毒されているので、(D)が正解。正答(D)は物を主語にした現在進行形の受動態の文で、間接的に人物の動作を問われているとも言える。

語彙チェック □bend　かがむ　□wipe　〜を拭く　□cloth　布　□sanitize　〜を消毒する

4 🇬🇧   □□□ 正解 A ▶TRACK_086

(A) A wheelbarrow is loaded with blocks.
(B) Some houses are being built by the water.
(C) The man is mowing the lawn.
(D) The man is kneeling down on the ground.

(A) 手押し車にブロックが載せられている。
(B) 何軒かの家が水辺に建てられているところである。
(C) 男性は芝生を刈っている。
(D) 男性は地面に膝を付いている。

ブロックが手押し車に載せられている状態を説明している(A)が正解。load *A* with *B*で「AにBを載せる」という意味。

語彙チェック □wheelbarrow　手押し車　□mow　〜を刈る　□kneel down　膝を付く

🙅 **ここに注意！**

動詞 load は Part 1 で頻出の単語だが、ここで使われている load *A* with *B*「AにBを載せる」の他に、load *A* into[onto] *B*「AをBに載せる」という表現もある。「載せる物」と「載せる先の物」を置く位置が変わるので注意しよう！

(A) Some drawers have been left open.
(B) Some shelves are being assembled.
(C) The man is grabbing an item with one hand.
(D) The man is standing with his arms folded.

(A) いくつかの引き出しが開いたままにされている。
(B) いくつかの棚が組み立てられているところである。
(C) 男性は片手で物をつかんでいる。
(D) 男性は腕を組んで立っている。

写真の手前の男性は、棚に置かれている箱を片手でつかんでいる。よって、この動作を説明した(C)が正解。with one hand で「片手で」という意味になる。

語彙チェック □drawer 引き出し □assemble 〜を組み立てる □grab 〜をつかむ

(A) She's drawing on an easel.
(B) She's opening a curtain to get more light in.
(C) She's organizing a pen case on a table.
(D) She's holding a can of paint.

(A) 彼女はイーゼルの上で絵を描いている。
(B) 彼女はより光を取り込むためにカーテンを開けているところである。
(C) 彼女はテーブルの上の筆箱を整理しているところである。
(D) 彼女は絵の具の缶を手に持っている。

イーゼルの上で絵を描いている女性について説明している(A)が正解。イーゼルは絵を描くときに使用する道具で、キャンバスを載せる台のことである。

語彙チェック □easel イーゼル

> 🐾 **ここに注意！**
> 正答の(A)にある単語easelが何かを知っていて、かつそれを聞き取ることができるかがポイント！ (B)のような長い選択肢に引っ張られないように注意しよう。

7 M 🇦🇺 W 🇬🇧 □□□ 正解 C ▶TRACK_090

Where can I find the instructions for this paper cutting machine?
(A) Black and white, please.
(B) Has today's paper been delivered?
(C) I saw Oliver reading it.

この紙裁断機の説明書はどこで見つけられますか。
(A) 白黒でお願いします。
(B) 今日の新聞は届きましたか。
(C) Oliver がそれを読んでいるのを見ました。

紙裁断機の説明書の場所を尋ねているのに対し、「Oliver がそれを読んでいるのを見た」と答えることで、Oliver が説明書を持っているのではないかということを間接的に伝えている (C) が正解。see A doing で「A が〜しているところを見る」の意味になる。

語彙チェック □instructions 説明書 □cutting machine 裁断機

8 W 🇨🇦 M 🇦🇺 □□□ 正解 C ▶TRACK_091

When's the maintenance report due?
(A) Repair work on the kitchen.
(B) I have already been there today.
(C) Noon, next Monday.

メンテナンス報告書の提出期限はいつですか。
(A) キッチンでの修理作業です。
(B) 今日すでにそこに行きました。
(C) 来週の月曜日の正午です。

メンテナンス報告書の提出期限を尋ねているのに対し、締め切りの具体的な日時を答えている (C) が正解。

語彙チェック □maintenance メンテナンス □due 提出期限がきた

9 M 🇺🇸 W 🇬🇧 □□□ 正解 A ▶TRACK_092

What role is Ms. Gaster playing in the advertising department?
(A) She is the section head.
(B) We have some rules to follow.
(C) Here's the design for our poster.

Gaster さんは、宣伝部でどんな役割を担っていますか。
(A) 彼女は部長です。
(B) 守るべきルールがいくつかあります。
(C) これが私たちのポスターのデザインです。

What role で Gaster さんの宣伝部での役割を尋ねているので、Gaster さんの役職を答えている (A) が正解。

> 🏯 ここに注意！
> 疑問詞 what で始まる疑問文の場合は、このように直後に名詞が続くパターンもあるので注意が必要。今回の what role のように、あまり聞き慣れない音には惑わされないように気を付けよう！

What do you think of the proposed security policy?
(A) I can do it by the end of the day.
(B) I couldn't attend the meeting yesterday.
(C) Are you sure you locked the door?

提案されたセキュリティーポリシーについてどう思いますか。
(A) 今日中にできます。
(B) 昨日は会議に参加できませんでした。
(C) 確かにドアに鍵をかけましたか。

What do you think of 〜? を使って、提案されたセキュリティーポリシーに関する意見を尋ねている。これに対し、「昨日は会議に参加できなかった」と伝えることで、暗にまだそのポリシーについて確認できていないことを示している (B) が正解。

語彙チェック □proposed　提案された　□attend　〜に参加する　□lock　〜に鍵をかける

Won't you be leaving earlier than usual today?
(A) My dentist appointment was postponed.
(B) Yes, I want to leave it here at the office.
(C) Thanks, but it's too expensive.

今日はいつもより早く帰る予定ではないのですか。
(A) 歯医者の予約が延期になったのです。
(B) はい、それをオフィスに置いておきたいです。
(C) ありがとうございます、でも高過ぎます。

否定疑問文で「今日はいつもより早く帰る予定ではないのか」と尋ねているのに対し、予定の変更により早く帰る必要性がなくなったことを示唆している (A) が正解。

語彙チェック □dentist　歯医者　□appointment　予約　□postpone　〜を延期する

🐾 **ここに注意!**

will be doing は「〜することになっている」という未来の予定を表す。この問いかけ文のように、否定疑問文の形になると意味を取りにくくなるので注意!

78

12　W 🇬🇧　M 🇦🇺　□□□　正解 B　▶TRACK_095

The product sample we ordered arrived this morning.

(A) OK, I'll do that later in the afternoon.

(B) It was scheduled to be here by yesterday.

(C) Can you revise the order form?

私たちが注文した商品サンプルが今朝届きました。

(A) 分かりました、後で午後にやっておきます。

(B) それは昨日までにここに届く予定でした。

(C) 注文用紙を修正できますか。

平叙文で「注文した商品サンプルが今朝届いた」と報告しているのに対し、予定より配達が遅れていたことを示唆している(B)が正解。主語である代名詞のItは、問いかけ文のThe product sampleを指している。

語彙チェック　□sample　サンプル　□be scheduled to *do*　〜する予定である
□revise　〜を修正する　□form　用紙

13　M 🇺🇸　W 🇨🇦　□□□　正解 B　▶TRACK_096

Have you seen the inspector entering the building?

(A) Not yet, I will work on it next week.

(B) I suppose the inspection is tomorrow.

(C) Please enter your passcode here.

視察の方が建物に入っていくのを見ましたか。

(A) まだです、来週それに取り組みます。

(B) 視察は明日だと思います。

(C) ここにパスコードを入力してください。

現在完了の疑問文で「視察の方が建物に入っていくのを見たか」と尋ねている。これに対し、視察は今日ではなく明日であることを伝えている(B)が正解。質問をしている人は、視察のスケジュールを勘違いしていると考えられる。

語彙チェック　□inspector　視察官　□work on 〜　〜に取り組む　□inspection　視察

14　W 🇬🇧　M 🇦🇺　□□□　正解 C　▶TRACK_097

You did a great job on your presentation at the marketing event.

(A) There was an open position.

(B) He's applying for a job in marketing.

(C) Oh, I didn't think you attended it.

販促イベントでのあなたのプレゼンテーションは素晴らしい出来でした。

(A) 空いている職がありました。

(B) 彼はマーケティングの仕事に応募する予定です。

(C) ああ、あなたが参加していたとは思いませんでした。

プレゼンテーションの感想を伝えている平叙文での問いかけに対し、「あなたが参加していたとは思わなかった」と、それが予想外の出来事であったということを伝えている(C)が正解。代名詞のitは、問いかけ文のthe marketing eventを指している。

Should we reserve our seats in advance, or buy same-day tickets?

事前に席を予約するべきでしょうか、それとも当日券を買うべきでしょうか。

(A) Well, that movie is attracting a lot of attention.

(A) そうですね、その映画はとても注目されています。

(B) No, I don't think we can afford it.

(B) いいえ、その余裕はないと思います。

(C) They visited our company on the same day.

(C) 彼らは同じ日に私たちの会社を訪れました。

選択疑問文で、事前に席を予約するべきか、当日券を買うべきかを尋ねている。これに対し、映画の注目度の高さから、事前に席を予約した方がいいことを示唆している(A)が正解。

語彙チェック □in advance 事前に □attract ～を引く □attention 注目

> 🐾ここに注意！
> 選択疑問文に対し、明確にどちらとは答えていないが、間接的に一方の選択肢を選んでいる応答。「事前に予約をするべき」と考える理由を説明している！

Who's assigned to give an estimate for the project in June?

誰が6月の企画の見積もりを出すことを割り当てられましたか。

(A) Mr. Hurley signed the letter.

(A) Hurleyさんが手紙に署名しました。

(B) There's an error on our system.

(B) 私たちのシステムにエラーがあります。

(C) That hasn't been decided yet.

(C) それはまだ決まっていません。

企画の見積もりを出すよう割り当てられた人は誰なのかを尋ねているのに対し、人名を答えるのではなく「まだ決まっていない」と現在の状況を伝えている(C)が正解。

語彙チェック □assign ～を割り当てる □estimate 見積もり □sign ～に署名する

Which aisle should I arrange these groceries in?

これらの食料品はどの通路に並べればいいですか。

(A) Oh, that's a good idea.

(A) ああ、それは良い考えですね。

(B) I'd like a window seat, please.

(B) 窓側の席でお願いします。

(C) They should be kept in the stockroom.

(C) それらは倉庫に保管されるべきです。

Which aisle ～ ? でどの通路に食料品を並べればいいかを尋ねている。これに対し、食料品の保管場所について、通路ではなく倉庫に保管すべきだと伝えている(C)が正解。

語彙チェック □aisle 通路 □grocery 食料雑貨 □stockroom 倉庫

18　W 🇨🇦　M 🇦🇺　　□□□　正解 A　▶TRACK_101

Isn't it possible for us to downsize the budget?

(A) There's room for consideration.

(B) No, I cannot arrive in time.

(C) Please send me a smaller shirt.

予算を削減することは可能ではないのですか。

(A) 検討する余地はあります。

(B) いいえ、私は間に合うように到着することができません。

(C) より小さいシャツを送ってください。

否定疑問文で、予算の削減が可能かどうかを尋ねているのに対し、可能かどうかを明言するのではなく、「検討する余地はある」と婉曲的に答えている (A) が正解。

語彙チェック　□downsize　〜を削減する　□room　余地　□in time　間に合って

🐾 ここに注意！
正答の (A) にある room は「部屋」ではなく、「余地」という意味で使われている。文脈に応じて適切な意味を思い浮かべられるようにしておこう！

19　M 🇺🇸　W 🇨🇦　　□□□　正解 A　▶TRACK_102

Why's the admission fee to the museum discounted today?

(A) Is it cheaper than the last time we came?

(B) At the entrance, I think.

(C) We have to buy the tickets in July.

なぜ今日は、博物館の入場料が割引されているのですか。

(A) 前回私たちが来たときよりも安いですか。

(B) 入り口でだと思います。

(C) 7月にチケットを買う必要があります。

問いかけ文では、博物館の入場料が割引されている理由を尋ねている。これに対し、「前回私たちが来たときよりも安いのか」と聞き返している (A) が正解。

20　M 🇦🇺　M 🇺🇸　　□□□　正解 B　▶TRACK_103

How can we alleviate the traffic congestion in this area?

(A) Let's have our car repaired as soon as possible.

(B) We need to conduct some more research.

(C) Visit our Web site to choose fabric samples.

どうしたら、この地域の交通渋滞を緩和できるでしょうか。

(A) できるだけ早く私たちの車を修理してもらいましょう。

(B) もっと調査を行う必要があります。

(C) 生地サンプルを選ぶには、私たちのウェブサイトをご覧ください。

地域の交通渋滞を緩和する方法について意見を求めているのに対し、その方法を見つけるためにはもっと調査を行う必要があるということを伝えている (B) が正解。

語彙チェック　□alleviate　〜を緩和する　□congestion　渋滞　□fabric　生地

I'm looking for the athletic shoes featured in this magazine.

(A) Sorry, it is out of paper right now.

(B) They will run in a marathon.

(C) Thank you for your interest.

この雑誌に特集されている運動靴を探しています。

(A) 申し訳ないですが、ただ今用紙が切れています。

(B) 彼らはマラソンで走ります。

(C) ご興味を持っていただきありがとうございます。

問いかけ文は平叙文で「雑誌に特集されている運動靴を探している」と伝えている。運動靴に興味を持ってくれたことに対する感謝の言葉を述べている(C)が正解。

語彙チェック □athletic 運動用の □feature ～を特集する

Would you mind dropping by my office to talk with me?

(A) I have a meeting until seven.

(B) Sure, your clothing is ready for pickup.

(C) Can we use these boxes instead?

話をするために私のオフィスに寄っていただけませんか。

(A) 7時まで会議があります。

(B) もちろんです、あなたの服は受け取り可能です。

(C) 代わりにこれらの箱を使えませんか。

Would you mind *doing* ～? という表現を使い、「オフィスに寄っていただけませんか」と相手に依頼している。これに対し、すでに予定が入っているので依頼に応じるのは難しい、もしくは7時以降であれば可能であるということを示唆している(A)が正解。

語彙チェック □drop by ～ ～に立ち寄る □clothing 衣類 □pickup 受け取ること

Did Sam book our train tickets to Munich?

(A) You can also enjoy a live performance.

(B) No, it was published recently.

(C) Yes, he prepared everything for us.

Munichまでの私たちの電車の切符はSamが予約したのですか。

(A) ライブパフォーマンスも楽しめます。

(B) いいえ、それは最近出版されました。

(C) そうです、彼が私たちのために全部準備してくれました。

問いかけ文は「電車の切符はSamが予約したのか」という内容。Yesと答え、Samが全て準備してくれたことを伝えている(C)が正解。

> **🐵ここに注意!**
> Yes / No疑問文に対する基本の応答となるYesとNoが、(B)と(C)の両方に登場している。冒頭のYesやNoの部分だけで判断せず、内容が問いかけと一致しているか最後まで注意して聞くようにしよう!

24 W 🇬🇧 M 🇦🇺 ☐☐☐ 正解 A ▶TRACK_107

Could you review this revised application form, please?

(A) Let me know what's been changed.

(B) They are on their way to the station.

(C) Some customers don't have a smartphone.

この修正した申込書を見直していただけますか。

(A) 何が変更されたか教えてください。

(B) 彼らは駅に向かっている途中です。

(C) スマートフォンを持っていない顧客もいます。

Could you ～?という表現を使い、修正した申込書の見直しを依頼している。これに対し、変更点を教えてほしいと伝えることで、間接的に依頼を承諾していると考えられる(A)が正解。

語彙チェック ☐review ～を見直す ☐revise ～を修正する ☐application 申し込み ☐form 用紙

25 W 🇨🇦 M 🇺🇸 ☐☐☐ 正解 B ▶TRACK_108

Will the new employee report to this office or the Sydney office?

(A) Yes, we need to move.

(B) He lives near here.

(C) The financial report.

その新入社員はこのオフィスに出勤しますか、それともSydneyのオフィスに出勤しますか。

(A) はい、私たちは移転する必要があります。

(B) 彼はこの近くに住んでいます。

(C) 財務報告書です。

選択疑問文で、ある新入社員がこのオフィスとSydneyのオフィスのどちらに出勤する予定かを尋ねている。「彼はこの近くに住んでいる」と伝えることで、間接的にこのオフィスに出勤してもらうことを伝えている(B)が正解。

語彙チェック ☐report to ～ ～に出頭する、～に出向く ☐financial 財務の

26 M 🇺🇸 W 🇬🇧 ☐☐☐ 正解 A ▶TRACK_109

Why are some of the customers unsatisfied with our service?

(A) It's obvious from the survey results.

(B) In the sales department.

(C) We are offering free shipping.

なぜ一部のお客さまは、私たちのサービスにご満足いただけないのでしょうか。

(A) それは調査の結果から明らかです。

(B) 営業部です。

(C) 無料発送を提供しています。

一部のお客さんがサービスに満足していない理由を尋ねているのに対し、直接的に質問に答えることはせず、調査結果を見れば分かることだと伝えている(A)が正解。

語彙チェック ☐unsatisfied 満足していない ☐obvious 明らかな ☐shipping 発送

How many people are expected to come to the exposition?

(A) You can reserve online.

(B) I guess more than last year.

(C) It'll be three-days long.

展覧会にはどのくらいの人数が来ると想定されていますか。

(A) オンラインで予約できますよ。

(B) 去年より多いと思います。

(C) 3日間あります。

How many 〜?で、想定される展覧会の来場者数を尋ねている。これに対し、「去年より多いと思う」と自身の予想を述べている (B) が正解。

語彙チェック □expect A to do　Aが〜するだろうと思う　□exposition　展覧会
□reserve　〜を予約する

> 🐾**ここに注意！**
> 数を尋ねるHow many 〜?という質問に対して、数字を使わずに答えることも多い。数字を含む(C)のような選択肢に惑わされないように！

What kind of devices are available in your meeting space?

(A) Here's the list of our equipment.

(B) A staff member in the IT department.

(C) The rental fee is on our Web site.

会議スペースでは、どのような種類の装置が利用できますか。

(A) これが備品のリストです。

(B) IT部門のスタッフです。

(C) レンタル料金は私たちのウェブサイトに載っています。

What kind of 〜?で、会議スペースで利用できる装置の種類を尋ねている。この質問に直接答えるのではなく、備品のリストを確認するように促している (A) が正解。

語彙チェック □device　装置　□equipment　備品　□fee　料金

Shouldn't we arrange the transportation first?

(A) I used to work there.

(B) About the company policy.

(C) Thanks for reminding me.

まず初めに交通手段を手配するべきではないですか。

(A) 私はそこで以前働いていました。

(B) 会社の方針についてです。

(C) 思い出させてくれてありがとうございます。

否定疑問文で「最初に交通手段を手配すべきではないか」と尋ねているのに対し、「思い出させてくれてありがとうございます」と相手に感謝を示している (C) が正解。

語彙チェック □arrange　〜を手配する

30 M 🇦🇺 M 🇺🇸 ☐☐☐ 正解 C ▶TRACK_113

This new construction project will cost too much, won't it?

(A) Sure, that looks great.

(B) Thanks, this is my favorite.

(C) I'm sure it's worth the price.

この新しい建設計画は費用がかかり過ぎますよね。

(A) もちろんです、よさそうですね。

(B) ありがとうございます、これは私のお気に入りです。

(C) 価格に見合う価値はあると思います。

付加疑問文で「新しい建設計画は費用がかかり過ぎる」という意見に同意を求めているのに対し、「価格に見合う価値はあると思う」と自身の意見を述べている (C) が正解。

語彙チェック ☐construction　建設　☐worth　～に値する

31 W 🇨🇦 M 🇺🇸 ☐☐☐ 正解 A ▶TRACK_114

When is the elevator near platform 2 going to be available?

(A) The inspection will be finished by noon.

(B) The next train arrives in two minutes.

(C) The north gate of the station.

プラットフォーム 2 近くのエレベーターは、いつ利用できるようになりますか。

(A) 点検は正午までには終わる予定です。

(B) 次の電車は2分後に到着します。

(C) 駅の北口ゲートです。

「プラットフォーム2近くのエレベーターがいつ利用できるようになるのか」を尋ねているのに対し、点検が終わる予定時刻を答えている (A) が正解。

語彙チェック ☐elevator　エレベーター　☐platform　プラットフォーム　☐inspection　点検

Part 3

Questions 32 through 34 refer to the following conversation.

M: Gina. Has Mr. Daniels arrived yet? He has a one o'clock appointment.

W: He hasn't arrived yet. It's only twelve fifty. Your clock might be running a little fast again.

M: Oh, it must be. I thought it was one o'clock. Anyway, show Mr. Daniels directly to my office when he gets here.

W: Will do. Would you like me to bring in something to drink, or is it just a short meeting?

M: That won't be necessary, but can you see about getting me a new clock?

問題32-34は次の会話に関するものです。

男性：Gina、Danielsさんはもう到着しましたか。彼は1時に約束があるのですが。

女性：彼はまだ到着していません。まだ12時50分ですよ。あなたの時計はまた少し早く進んでいるのかもしれませんね。

男性：ああ、そうに違いないですね。1時だと思っていました。とにかく、Danielsさんがこちらに到着したら、直接私のオフィスに案内してください。

女性：そうします。何か飲み物をお持ちしましょうか。それともちょっとした打ち合わせですか。

男性：飲み物はいりませんが、新しい時計を持ってきてもらえませんか。

語彙チェック ☐ show ～を案内する ☐ see about *doing* ～するよう取り計らう

---

32   ☐☐☐   正解 A

What does the man say he is waiting for?   男性は何を待っていると言っていますか。

(A) A visitor   (A) 訪問客

(B) A delivery   (B) 配達

(C) A taxi   (C) タクシー

(D) A broadcast   (D) 放送

男性は冒頭で「Danielsさんは到着したか」と尋ね、He has a one o'clock appointment. と述べている。このことから、男性はこれから面会の約束があるDanielsさんを待っていることが分かる。その後も男性は女性に、Danielsさんを直接オフィスに案内するように言ったり、女性も飲み物が必要か尋ねていたりすることから、Danielsさんは訪問客だと考えられる。よって、正解は(A)。

33 □□□ 正解 B

What does the woman say about the clock?

(A) It was recently installed.
(B) It may be showing the wrong time.
(C) It is the same model as hers.
(D) It needs new batteries.

女性は時計について何と言っていますか。

(A) それは最近取り付けられた。
(B) それは誤った時刻を示しているかもしれない。
(C) それは彼女のものと同じモデルだ。
(D) それは新しい電池が必要だ。

男性が、1時に約束がある Daniels さんはもう到着しているかどうか尋ねると、女性は「まだ12時50分だ」と返答し、Your clock might be running a little fast again. と指摘している。running a little fast を showing the wrong time と言い換えている (B) が正解。

34 □□□ 正解 C

What does the woman offer to do?
(A) Call a client
(B) Purchase an item
(C) Supply some beverages
(D) Schedule a meeting

女性は何をすることを申し出ていますか。
(A) 顧客に電話する
(B) 商品を買う
(C) 飲み物を提供する
(D) 打ち合わせの予定を立てる

男性から Daniels さんを直接オフィスに案内するよう言われた女性は、Would you like me to bring in something to drink と尋ねている。よって、(C) が正解。

語彙チェック □beverage （水以外の）飲み物

Questions 35 through 37 refer to the following conversation.

M: Hi. We're from Now and Again Used Goods. We're here to pick up some furniture.
W: I see. I haven't heard anything about that. Who did you speak to?
M: Umm. It was a Ms. Cranston, I believe. She asked us to come and get a large table and some chairs. I think she also mentioned a small sofa. She called me this morning.
W: I see. She works in Building B. You should take your truck over there. Just follow the driveway down. You'll see it on the right. I'll give her a call and let her know you're coming.

問題35-37は次の会話に関するものです。

男性：こんにちは。Now and Again 中古品店です。家具の回収に伺いました。
女性：そうですか。私はそれについて何も聞いておりません。あなたは誰と話をしましたか。
男性：ええと。Cranston さんという方だったと思います。彼女から大きなテーブルと椅子の回収を依頼されました。小さなソファのことも言っていたと思います。今朝彼女からお電話いただきました。
女性：そうですか。彼女は Building B に勤務しております。そちらへトラックを回すといいでしょう。私道をずっと行ってください。建物は右側に見えてきますよ。彼女に電話をして、あなたたちが向かっていると知らせておきますね。

語彙チェック　□used goods　中古品　□pick up 〜　〜を集める、〜を受け取る
　　　　　　　　□mention　〜を話に出す　□driveway　私道

35　　　　　　　　　　　□□□　正解 C

Where does the man most likely work?　　　男性はどこで働いていると考えられますか。
(A) At a construction company　　　　　　(A) 建設会社
(B) At the city council　　　　　　　　　(B) 市議会
(C) At a second-hand store　　　　　　　(C) 中古品店
(D) At a fitness center　　　　　　　　　(D) フィットネスセンター

男性は We're from Now and Again Used Goods. と所属を述べた後、We're here to pick up some furniture. と訪問の理由を説明している。その後も、テーブルや椅子などの回収を依頼されたと述べている。これらのことから、男性は中古品店の従業員で家具の回収に来たと分かるので、正解は (C)。

36 □□□ 正解 B

What does the man say about
Ms. Cranston?

(A) He has worked with her before.
(B) He spoke with her today.
(C) She was nominated for an award.
(D) She is taking a day off from work.

男性はCranstonさんについて何と言っていますか。

(A) 彼は以前彼女と一緒に働いたことがある。
(B) 彼は今日彼女と話をした。
(C) 彼女は賞にノミネートされた。
(D) 彼女は仕事を1日休んでいる。

家具の回収依頼について、女性にWho did you speak to?と尋ねられると、男性はIt was
a Ms. Cranston, I believe.と返答し、She called me this morning.と最後に付け加えてい
る。男性はCranstonさんと今朝電話で話をしたことが分かるので、正解は(B)。

37 □□□ 正解 C

What does the woman say she will do?

(A) Rent a vehicle
(B) Provide a map
(C) Call a colleague
(D) Confirm a schedule

女性は何をすると言っていますか。

(A) 乗り物をレンタルする
(B) 地図を提供する
(C) 同僚に電話する
(D) スケジュールを確認する

女性は男性にCranstonさんがBuilding Bに勤務していることを伝え、そこへの行き方を
説明した後、最後にI'll give her a call and let her know you're coming.と言っている。
give her a callのherはCranstonさんのことである。また、女性とCranstonさんは同じ
会社で働いている同僚だと考えられる。これらのことから、正解は(C)。

語彙チェック □colleague　同僚

Questions 38 through 40 refer to the following conversation.

W: Did you see our advertisement in the newspaper? <u>It was much bigger than I requested.</u>

M: I didn't see it. <u>I hope they don't charge us more than we agreed to pay.</u> <u>We have a tight marketing budget.</u>

W: I don't think they will. We were just lucky. Sometimes they increase the size when there aren't enough advertisements to fill the page.

M: I see. In that case, it'll be interesting to see whether or not this affects sales. <u>Can you ask someone to analyze our sales this week and determine the effect it has?</u>

問題38-40は次の会話に関するものです。

女性：新聞に載っている私たちの広告を見ましたか。私が依頼したものよりずっと大きかったです。

男性：見ていません。私たちが支払うと同意した金額より多く請求してこないといいのですが。マーケティング予算には余裕がありません。

女性：それはしないと思いますよ。ただラッキーだっただけです。彼らは紙面を埋めるだけの十分な広告がないときには、サイズを大きくすることがあるんですよ。

男性：そうですか。その場合、これが売り上げに影響するかどうか見てみたら面白いでしょうね。今週の売り上げを分析して効果を究明するよう、誰かに頼んでもらえませんか。

語彙チェック □charge　〜に請求する　□budget　予算　□in that case　その場合　□whether or not 〜　〜かどうか　□affect　〜に影響を及ぼす　□determine　〜を究明する　□effect　効果

38   □□□   正解 C

What does the woman say about the advertisement?

女性は広告について何と言っていますか。

(A) It will appear tomorrow.

(B) It was published accidentally.

(C) It was larger than expected.

(D) It has been very successful.

(A) それは明日掲載される。

(B) それは誤って発行された。

(C) それは予想以上に大きかった。

(D) それはとても成功している。

女性は男性に新聞の広告を見たか尋ねた後、It was much bigger than I requested. と述べている。よって、これを言い換えている(C)が正解。than expected は「予想以上に、思っていたより」という意味。

39 　　　 正解 A

What is the man concerned about?

(A) The expense
(B) The timing
(C) An error
(D) A delay

男性は何について心配していますか。

(A) 費用
(B) 時期
(C) 誤り
(D) 遅延

広告のサイズが依頼したものよりも大きかったと聞いて、男性は I hope they don't charge us more than we agreed to pay. と述べ、We have a tight marketing budget. とも言っている。これらのことから、男性は支払い料金について心配していると分かるので、正解は (A)。

40 　　　 正解 D

What is the woman instructed to do?

(A) Purchase a newspaper
(B) Cancel an advertisement
(C) Conduct a customer survey
(D) Allocate some work

女性は何をするよう指示されていますか。

(A) 新聞を買う
(B) 広告を取り消す
(C) 顧客調査を行う
(D) 仕事を割り振る

男性は広告が売り上げに影響するかどうかを見るために、女性に Can you ask someone to analyze our sales this week and determine the effect it has? と依頼している。「今週の売り上げを分析して効果を究明するよう、誰かに頼む」ことを「仕事を割り振る」と言い換えた (D) が正解。

語彙チェック □allocate 〜を配分する、〜を割り振る

Questions 41 through 43 refer to the following conversation.

W: Hi. My name's Jo Clapper. I rented a carpet cleaner from you this morning. I'm having trouble turning it on. I can't find the switch anywhere. Are you familiar with the machine?

M: Yes. I'm sorry, I should have included the operating instructions. You'll find the switch on the cable. Once you switch it on there, you should be able to control it with the handle.

W: On the cable? That's a new one. I wouldn't have thought to look there. Thanks for that. I'll give you a call if I need any more assistance.

問題41-43は次の会話に関するものです。

女性：こんにちは。Jo Clapperと申します。今朝そちらでカーペットクリーナーをレンタルしました。それの電源を入れるのに困っています。どこにもスイッチが見当たらないのです。この機械に詳しいですか。

男性：はい。申し訳ございません、取扱説明書を入れるべきでした。スイッチはケーブルの上に付いております。一度そこのスイッチを入れていただくと、ハンドルを持って操作できるはずです。

女性：ケーブルの上ですか。それは新しいですね。そこを見るなんて思い付きもしませんでした。ありがとうございます。何か他に助けが必要だったら、また電話します。

語彙チェック　□ have trouble *doing*　〜するのに困る、〜するのに苦労する
　　　　　　　　□ be familiar with 〜　〜をよく知っている、〜に詳しい
　　　　　　　　□ operating instructions　取扱説明書

41　　　　　　　　　□□□　正解 A

Where does the man most likely work?　　　男性はどこで働いていると考えられますか。

(A) At an equipment rental company　　　(A) 機器のレンタル会社
(B) At a carpet cleaning business　　　(B) カーペットのクリーニング業者
(C) At a clothing manufacturer　　　(C) 衣料品メーカー
(D) At a furniture store　　　(D) 家具店

女性は I rented a carpet cleaner from you this morning. と言っているので、男性の店からカーペットクリーナーをレンタルしたことが分かる。また、その後、男性は女性にそのカーペットクリーナーの使い方を説明している。これらのことから、男性が働いているところは、カーペットクリーナーのような機器をレンタルしている会社だと考えられる。よって、正解は(A)。

> 🐧 **ここに注意！**
> 会話の中でcarpet cleanerという語句が登場しているので、(B)が非常に紛らわしい選択肢になっている。会話の内容から、話し手たちの立場や関係性をしっかりと読み取って正解を選ぶ必要がある！

42 □□□ 正解 A

What does the man say he forgot to do? | 男性は何をし忘れたと言っていますか。

(A) Provide some directions | (A) 指示書を提供する
(B) Take a reservation | (B) 予約を受ける
(C) Return some goods | (C) 商品を返却する
(D) Charge the woman | (D) 女性に請求する

「カーペットクリーナーの電源を入れるのに困っている」という女性の問い合わせを受け、男性はI'm sorry, I should have included the operating instructions. と謝罪している。つまり、男性は取扱説明書を女性に渡していなかったということが分かるので、正解は(A)。(A)では男性の発言のthe operating instructionsをsome directionsに言い換えている。

43 □□□ 正解 D

Why does the woman say, "That's a new one"? | 女性はなぜ "That's a new one" と言っていますか。

(A) To introduce a colleague | (A) 同僚を紹介するため
(B) To assign some work | (B) 仕事を割り当てるため
(C) To recommend an item | (C) 商品を勧めるため
(D) To express surprise | (D) 驚きを表現するため

男性からスイッチがケーブルの上にあると説明された後、女性はThat's a new one. と言い、I wouldn't have thought to look there. と付け加えている。「ケーブルの上を確認しようとは思わなかった」ということは、彼女にとってスイッチがケーブルの上に付いていたということは意外だったと考えられる。よって、正解は(D)。

W 🇨🇦　M 🇺🇸　　　　　　　　　　　　　会話 ▶TRACK_124　問題 ▶TRACK_125

Questions 44 through 46 refer to the following conversation.

W: George, can you give me a hand with my presentation later? I need some help formatting some of the slides.

M: Sure. I'll look at it after we finish installing the new accounting software. Where will I find you?

W: I'll be in Conference Room 5. I'm working there to get away from distractions.

M: OK. Give me about twenty minutes. I should be there by four thirty.

W: Great. I'm going to get some coffee. Would you like me to make you one, too?

M: No thanks. I won't have time to drink it.

問題44-46は次の会話に関するものです。

女性：George、後で私のプレゼンテーションを手伝ってもらえませんか。何枚かスライドの書式を整えるのに手助けが必要なのです。

男性：いいですよ。新しい会計ソフトウェアのインストールが終わったら見ます。どこにいますか。

女性：会議室5にいます。気が散らないように、そこで作業しています。

男性：分かりました。約20分ください。4時30分までにはそこに行けるはずです。

女性：よかったです。私はコーヒーを淹れてきます。あなたにも一杯淹れましょうか。

男性：いいえ、結構です。飲んでいる時間がありませんから。

語彙チェック　□give A a hand with B　AのBを手伝う　□format　〜の書式を整える
　　　　　　　　　□get away from 〜　〜から離れる、〜を避ける　□distraction　気を散らすもの

44　　　　　　　　　□□□　正解 B

What does the man ask about?　　　　　男性は何について尋ねていますか。

(A) The length of a presentation　　　　(A) プレゼンテーションの長さ

(B) A meeting location　　　　　　　　(B) 打ち合わせの場所

(C) A presentation topic　　　　　　　(C) プレゼンテーションのトピック

(D) An accounting seminar　　　　　　(D) 会計セミナー

男性は、プレゼンテーション用のスライドの書式設定を手伝ってほしいという女性の依頼を承諾した後、Where will I find you? と尋ねている。「どこであなたを見つけられるか」、すなわち「どこにいるか」ということを質問しているので、正解は(B)。

45

□□□ 正解 **C**

When will the man be available?	男性はいつ応対できますか。
(A) In 5 minutes	(A) 5分後
(B) In 10 minutes	(B) 10分後
(C) In 20 minutes	(C) 20分後
(D) In 30 minutes	(D) 30分後

女性がどこにいるかを確認した後、男性はGive me about twenty minutes. I should be there by four thirty. と言っている。20分後には女性のところに行けるということなので、正解は(C)。

46

□□□ 正解 **D**

Where will the woman most likely go next?	女性は次にどこへ行くと考えられますか。
(A) To a bathroom	(A) トイレ
(B) To a restaurant	(B) レストラン
(C) To a garage	(C) 車庫
(D) To a kitchen	(D) キッチン

女性は最後に、I'm going to get some coffee. Would you like me to make you one, too? と言っているので、オフィス内のどこでコーヒーを淹れるのかを考える。よって、正解は(D)。

Questions 47 through 49 refer to the following conversation.

M: Hi. I'm ready to check out. Can I pay with this?

W: Yes, sir. We take all major cards.

M: Great. Oh, and thanks for changing my room last night.

W: No problem at all. Was there something wrong with the room we assigned you at first?

M: No no, it was fine. I was just hoping to stay in a room with a view of the bridge. I forgot to mention that when I made my booking.

W: I'm glad we were able to make the switch. We're usually fully booked. There must have been a last-minute cancellation.

問題47-49は次の会話に関するものです。

男性：こんにちは。チェックアウトの準備ができています。これで支払いできますか。

女性：はい、お客さま。主要なカードは全て取り扱っております。

男性：そうですか。ああ、それから昨夜は部屋を変更してくださりありがとうございました。

女性：全く問題ございません。初めにご案内したお部屋は何か不備がございましたか。

男性：いえいえ、大丈夫でしたよ。ただ、橋が見られる部屋に泊まりたいと思ったのです。予約をするときに伝えるのを忘れてしまいました。

女性：変更することができてよかったです。通常は満室なのです。直前にキャンセルが出たのだと思います。

語彙チェック　　□assign *A B*　AにBを割り当てる　　□make a booking　予約する
□switch　変更　□fully　完全に　□book　〜を予約する
□last-minute　直前の、間際の

47　　　　　　　　□□□□　正解 D

What does the man ask about?

(A) Vehicle parking

(B) Luggage storage

(C) A key return system

(D) A payment method

男性は何について尋ねていますか。

(A) 乗り物の駐車

(B) 荷物保管所

(C) 鍵の返却システム

(D) 支払い方法

男性は冒頭でCan I pay with this?と尋ねている。それに対し、女性がWe take all major cards.と答えていることから、男性は支払い方法について質問していることが分かるので、正解は(D)。

48

☐☐☐ 正解 **C**

Why did the man ask for a change of room?

(A) His room was too noisy.

(B) He wanted to stay near a colleague.

(C) He was unsatisfied with the scenery.

(D) His room was smaller than he expected.

男性はなぜ部屋の変更を要求したのですか。

(A) 彼の部屋はうるさ過ぎた。

(B) 彼は同僚の近くに泊まりたかった。

(C) 彼は景色に満足していなかった。

(D) 彼の部屋は予想していたよりも小さかった。

男性が部屋の変更について女性にお礼を言うと、女性は最初に案内した部屋に何か問題があったのか尋ねている。これに対し男性は、I was just hoping to stay in a room with a view of the bridge. と説明している。「橋が見える部屋に泊まりたかった」ということから、男性は景色について満足していなかったと考えられる。よって、正解は (C)。

49

☐☐☐ 正解 **A**

What does the woman say about the hotel?

(A) It is unusual to have a vacancy.

(B) It only accepts online bookings.

(C) It has locations in most cities.

(D) It is popular among vacationers.

女性はホテルについて何と言っていますか。

(A) 空室があるのは珍しい。

(B) オンライン予約しか受け付けていない。

(C) たいていの都市に店舗がある。

(D) 行楽客の間で人気がある。

男性の客室変更について、女性は「変更することができてよかった」と伝え、We're usually fully booked. と説明している。これを言い換えた (A) が正解。

語彙チェック ☐vacancy　空き、空室　☐vacationer　行楽客

Questions 50 through 52 refer to the following conversation with three speakers.

W1: Hi, we're looking for the paint section. Paint, brushes, ladders — that kind of thing.

M:　That's aisle eight. It's on the other end of the store, I'm afraid. Except for ladders, um... They're in aisle two — the next one over.

W1: Thanks. Jane, why don't you ask him about your voucher, too?

W2: I have this discount voucher. I got it the last time I was here. Can I use this today?

M:　It's expired, I'm afraid.

W2: That makes sense. I got it about four months ago.

M:　We're having a year-end sale, right now. Most of the stock is on sale, so you'll still get a great deal.

問題50-52は3人の話し手による次の会話に関するものです。

女性１：こんにちは、ペンキ売り場を探しています。ペンキ、ブラシ、はしご―そういった類のものです。

男性　：そちらは8番通路です。申し訳ございませんが、店の反対側の端でございます。はしごは別で、ええと… 2番通路にございます―この次の通路です。

女性１：ありがとうございます。Jane、あなたの割引券についても彼に聞いてはどうですか。

女性２：この割引券を持っているのですが。前回ここに来たときにもらいました。これは今日使えますか。

男性　：申し訳ございませんが、期限が切れております。

女性２：そうですよね。4カ月ぐらい前にもらったので。

男性　：ちょうど今は、年末セールを行っております。在庫のほとんどがセール中ですので、まだお買い得品をお求めいただけますよ。

語彙チェック	□paint　ペンキ、絵の具　□brush　ブラシ　□ladder　はしご　□aisle　通路
	□discount voucher　割引券　□on sale　特価で　□great deal　お買い得品

50　　　　　□□□　正解 A

Where does the conversation most likely take place?

会話はどこで行われていると考えられますか。

(A) At a hardware store

(B) At an educational institution

(C) At a radio station

(D) At a supermarket

(A) ホームセンター

(B) 教育施設

(C) ラジオ局

(D) スーパーマーケット

1人目の女性は冒頭でHi, we're looking for the paint section. Paint, brushes, ladders — that kind of thing. と発言している。すなわち、「ペンキ、ブラシ、はしご」といったものを売っている場所での会話だと判断できるので、正解は(A)。

51 ☐☐☐ 正解 B

What does Jane ask about?	Janeは何について尋ねていますか。
(A) A rental service	(A) レンタルサービス
(B) A discount coupon	(B) 割引クーポン
(C) Advertising rates	(C) 広告料金
(D) Home delivery	(D) 宅配便

2人目の女性Janeは I have this discount voucher. と言った後、Can I use this today? と質問している。持っている割引券が使えるかどうかを尋ねているので、(B)が正解。

52 ☐☐☐ 正解 D

When did Jane last come to the business?	Janeは最後にいつ来店しましたか。
(A) 1 month ago	(A) 1カ月前
(B) 2 months ago	(B) 2カ月前
(C) 3 months ago	(C) 3カ月前
(D) 4 months ago	(D) 4カ月前

2人目の女性Janeは持っている割引券について I got it the last time I was here. と説明している。その後、男性に割引券が期限切れだと言われると、I got it about four months ago. と述べている。これらから、Janeが最後に来店したのは4カ月前だと分かる。よって正解は(D)。

> 🐾 ここに注意！
>
> 根拠となる four months ago というキーワードはそのまま出てくるが、設問は「最後にいつ来店したか」なので、少し前の発言のI got it the last time I was here.も聞き取らなくてはならない。このように根拠となる文が離れているパターンに注意しよう！

M 🇦🇺　W 🇨🇦　　　　　　　　　　　　会話 ▶TRACK_130　　問題 ▶TRACK_131

Questions 53 through 55 refer to the following conversation.

M: Hi Wendy. What did you think of that movie last night?

W: It wasn't the best. Jennifer liked it, though. Perhaps you should ask her.

M: I need to talk to her about our marathon team, too. She's organizing it this year.
　 Do you know where she is?

W: I saw her in the break room about ten minutes ago. Are you going to take part in
　 the marathon, too?

M: I'd like to if there's still room on the team. I've been training since March.

問題53-55は次の会話に関するものです。

男性：こんにちはWendy。昨晩のあの映画をどう思いましたか。

女性：あまり良くありませんでした。Jenniferは気に入ったようですが。よろしければ彼女に聞いてみる
　　　といいですよ。

男性：私たちのマラソンチームについても、彼女に話をする必要があります。彼女は今年それをまとめ
　　　ているのです。彼女がどこにいるか知っていますか。

女性：10分くらい前に休憩室で彼女を見ましたよ。あなたもマラソンに参加する予定なのですか。

男性：まだチームに空きがあれば、参加したいと思っています。3月からトレーニングをしているのです。

語彙チェック □perhaps　できましたら、よろしければ　□organize　〜を計画する
　　　　　　　　 □break room　休憩室　□take part in 〜　〜に参加する

53　　　　　　　　　　　　　　　　□□□　正解 D

What does the woman mean when she
says, "It wasn't the best"?

(A) She preferred another movie.

(B) She wanted to go to another cinema.

(C) She disagreed with a review.

(D) She disliked the movie.

女性は "It wasn't the best" という発言で、何を意味
していますか。

(A) 彼女は他の映画の方が好きだった。

(B) 彼女は他の映画館に行きたかった。

(C) 彼女はレビューに同意できなかった。

(D) 彼女はその映画が好きではなかった。

　昨日の映画の感想を聞かれた女性は It wasn't the best. と答えた後、Jennifer liked it,
though. Perhaps you should ask her. と述べている。「でもJenniferはそれ（映画）を気
に入っていたので、彼女に聞いてみるといい」と言っているということは、自分自身は
映画が気に入らなかったと考えられるので、正解は (D)。

54　　　正解 A

What does the man say about Jennifer?

(A) She is in charge of a team.
(B) She has already gone home.
(C) She has a new qualification.
(D) She regularly goes to the movies.

男性はJenniferについて何と言っていますか。

(A) 彼女はチームの責任者である。
(B) 彼女はすでに帰宅した。
(C) 彼女は新しい資格を持っている。
(D) 彼女は定期的に映画を見に行く。

映画の感想について、Jenniferに尋ねるよう女性に言われると、男性は I need to talk to her about our marathon team, too. She's organizing it this year. と述べている。it は our marathon team を指しているので、Jenniferはマラソンチームをまとめていると分かる。よって、(A) が正解。

55　　　正解 D

What does the man say he has been doing?

(A) Watching a movie
(B) Speaking with a client
(C) Fixing some machinery
(D) Preparing for a sporting event

男性は何をしていると言っていますか。

(A) 映画を見ている
(B) 顧客と話している
(C) 機械を修理している
(D) スポーツイベントに備えている

マラソンに参加するのかと質問されると、男性はチームに空きがあれば参加したいと答え、I've been training since March. と述べている。よって、(D) が正解。(D) では「マラソン」を sporting event と言い換えている。

語彙チェック　□machinery　機械

Questions 56 through 58 refer to the following conversation with three speakers.

W: Rod, Marco. I'm glad I found the two of you. I just had a call from the gallery. They'd like us to make some changes to the arrangements for the fundraiser.

M1: I hope they're not big changes. We've settled on the details. I've already placed an order with the caterer.

M2: I thought we agreed on everything last week. It'll cause a lot of trouble if they make changes at the last minute.

W: A major contributor has suddenly decided to attend, and they want to do something special to show their appreciation.

M1: What are the details of the changes?

W: You can get all the information you need from the e-mail I sent this morning. Fortunately, it won't affect any of the arrangements you've already made. They just need to extend the welcome speech and make some amendments to the seating plan.

問題56-58は3人の話し手による次の会話に関するものです。

女性　：Rod、Marco。あなたたち2人を見つけられてよかったです。ちょうどギャラリーから電話をもらいました。私たちに資金集めの行事の計画に変更をしてもらいたいとのことです。

男性1：大きな変更でないといいのですが。詳細についてはもう決定していますし、私はすでにケータリング業者に注文をしてしまいましたよ。

男性2：先週全て同意したと思っていました。間際で変更すると、多くのトラブルを引き起こすことになりますよ。

女性　：主要な寄付者が突然出席することに決まって、彼らは感謝を示すために何か特別なことをしたいと思っているのです。

男性1：変更の詳細は何ですか。

女性　：私が今朝送ったEメールから必要な情報は全て得られますよ。幸いにも、あなたがすでに手配したものには影響はありません。彼らはただウェルカムスピーチの延長と座席プランの修正が必要なだけです。

語彙チェック　□arrangement　計画、予定　□fundraiser　資金集めの行事
　　　　　　　　□settle on ～　～を決める　□place an order with ～　～に注文する
　　　　　　　　□at the last minute　直前に、間際になって　□contributor　寄付者
　　　　　　　　□extend　～を延長する　□amendment　修正

56　□□□　正解 B

What are the speakers discussing?　話し手たちは何について話し合っていますか。

(A) A photography exhibition　(A) 写真展

(B) A charity event　(B) チャリティーイベント

(C) A musical performance　(C) ミュージカル公演

(D) An award ceremony　(D) 授賞式

冒頭で女性は「ちょうどギャラリーから電話をもらったところだ」と述べ、They'd like us to make some changes to the arrangements for the fundraiser. と発言している。よって、fundraiser「資金集めの行事」を言い換えた (B) が正解。

57　　　　　正解 D

What do the men say about the plans?

(A) They will be expensive.

(B) They have been distributed.

(C) They include entertainment.

(D) They have been finalized.

男性たちは計画について何と言っていますか。

(A) 費用が高い。

(B) 割り当てられている。

(C) 余興が含まれている。

(D) 最終決定されている。

計画を変更してほしいとギャラリーから要望があったことを女性が伝えると、1人目の男性は We've settled on the details. と述べ、2人目の男性も I thought we agreed on everything last week. と付け加えている。つまり、イベントの詳細はすでに決まっていたと考えられるので、正解は(D)。

語彙チェック　□distribute　〜を割り当てる

58　　　　　正解 D

What does the woman say she has done?

(A) Approved a purchase

(B) Reserved some equipment

(C) Met with a guest

(D) Provided some information

女性は何をしたと言っていますか。

(A) 購入を承認した

(B) 機器を予約した

(C) ゲストに会った

(D) 情報を提供した

男性が変更の詳細を尋ねると、女性は You can get all the information you need from the e-mail I sent this morning. と答えている。この発言から、女性は今朝必要な情報を全てEメールで送ったということが分かるので、正解は(D)。

M 🇦🇺　W 🇬🇧　　　　　　　　　　　　会話 ▶TRACK_134　問題 ▶TRACK_135

Questions 59 through 61 refer to the following conversation.

M: Hi Trudy. It's me, Harry. I'm looking for someone who can drive the bus. Greg Teller has just called in sick, and I have to take a group of visitors around the facility.

W: I don't think anyone else has a license to drive it. I could call Mr. Tanaka. He retired last year, but he might be willing to come in and work for one day.

M: Can you try him, then? I need him to be here by two P.M.

W: Sure. He lives in Redcliff, so he should be able to get here in time.

問題59-61は次の会話に関するものです。

男性：こんにちはTrudy。Harryです。バスを運転できる人を探しています。Greg Tellerが具合が悪くて休むと電話してきたところなのですが、私は施設に団体客を案内しないといけないのです。

女性：他にバスの運転免許を持っている人は誰もいないと思います。Tanakaさんに電話しましょうか。彼は去年退職しましたが、喜んで1日働きに来てくれるかもしれません。

男性：それでは彼にお願いしてみてもらえますか。彼に午後2時までにここに来てもらう必要があります。

女性：いいですよ。彼はRedcliffに住んでいますから、間に合うようにここに到着できるはずです。

語彙チェック　□call in sick　病欠の電話をする　□license　免許　□retire　退職する
　　　　　　　□be willing to do　進んで〜する、喜んで〜する　□in time　間に合って

59　☐☐☐　正解 C

Why did the man call the woman?

(A) He would like her to take over a project.

(B) He will arrive at work late today.

(C) He needs someone with a certain skill.

(D) He forgot to take a map of the area.

男性はなぜ女性に電話したのですか。

(A) 彼は彼女にプロジェクトを引き継いでもらいたい。

(B) 彼は今日仕事に遅れて到着する。

(C) 彼はある技術を持っている人を必要としている。

(D) 彼はその地域の地図を持ってくるのを忘れた。

男性は冒頭でI'm looking for someone who can drive the bus.と伝えている。「バスを運転できる人」をsomeone with a certain skillと言い換えた(C)が正解。

語彙チェック　□take over 〜　〜を引き継ぐ、〜を引き受ける

60 □□□ 正解 B

What does the woman mention about Mr. Tanaka?	女性はTanakaさんについて何と述べていますか。
(A) He is on a business trip this afternoon.	(A) 彼は今日の午後出張中である。
(B) He is no longer employed at the company.	(B) 彼はもう会社に雇われていない。
(C) He has experience in hospitality.	(C) 彼はサービス業での経験がある。
(D) He is a factory employee.	(D) 彼は工場の従業員である。

「バスを運転できる人を探している」という男性の発言に対し、女性はTanakaさんに電話することを提案した後、Tanakaさんについて He retired last year と説明している。「Tanakaさんは去年退職した」ということを言い換えている(B)が正解。

語彙チェック □no longer 〜 もはや〜でない

61 □□□ 正解 C

What will the woman most likely do next?	女性は次に何をすると考えられますか。
(A) Pick up a colleague	(A) 同僚を迎えに行く
(B) Search for a bus service	(B) バスの便を探す
(C) Call Mr. Tanaka	(C) Tanakaさんに電話する
(D) Cancel a visit	(D) 訪問をキャンセルする

女性の「Tanakaさんに電話しましょうか」という申し出に対して男性はCan you try him, then?と女性に依頼しており、女性はSure.と承諾している。この流れから、女性はこの後Tanakaさんに電話すると考えられるので、正解は(C)。

語彙チェック □service （バスなどの）便

Questions 62 through 64 refer to the following conversation and catalog.

W: We need to get a new filing cabinet to hold more patient files.
M: There's only about fifty centimeters of space left along that wall. Get the biggest one you can, but make sure it fits.
W: I'll see what I can find online. By the way, how about canceling some of the magazine subscriptions for the waiting room? Most of the patients seem to use their mobile phones these days.
M: Good idea. I'll talk to the doctor about offering them free Wi-Fi instead.

問題62-64は次の会話とカタログに関するものです。

女性：より多くの患者ファイルを収納できる新しい書類整理棚を購入する必要があります。
男性：その壁に沿って50cm くらいのスペースしか残っていませんよ。できるだけ大きいものを買ってください。でもぴったり合うようにしてくださいね。
女性：オンラインで何があるか見てみます。ところで、待合室用の雑誌の定期購読をいくつかキャンセルするのはいかがですか。最近、ほとんどの患者さまは自分の携帯電話を使っているようです。
男性：いいアイデアですね。代わりに無料の Wi-Fi を提供することについて、医師に相談してみます。

語彙チェック　□subscription　定期購読　□waiting room　待合室
　　　　　　　　□seem to *do*　～するように思える

Truman
Three-draw
Filing Cabinet

Height: 110cm
Depth: 42cm

Four width options
Slim: 35cm
Regular: 45cm
Wide: 55cm
Ultra-Wide: 65cm

Truman
引き出し3つの
書類整理棚

高さ: 110cm
奥行き: 42cm

4種類の幅の選択肢
スリム: 35cm
レギュラー: 45cm
ワイド: 55cm
ウルトラワイド: 65cm

⚠ ここに注意！
この会話では、最初は書類整理棚について話しているが、女性が By the way, と言ってからは、雑誌の定期購読について話し始めている。このように途中で急に話題が変わると、ペースを乱されやすいので要注意！

62 □□□ 正解 A

Where do the speakers most likely work?　話し手たちはどこで働いていると考えられますか。

(A) At a clinic
(B) At an appliance store
(C) At an office supply store
(D) At a publishing house

(A) 診療所
(B) 家電量販店
(C) 事務用品店
(D) 出版社

冒頭の女性の発言のpatient files、2回目の女性の発言のthe waiting room、最後の男性の発言のI'll talk to the doctorなどから、話し手たちは医療関係の職場に勤めていると考えられる。よって、正解は(A)。

63 □□□ 正解 B

Look at the graphic. Which filing cabinet will the woman probably order?　図を見てください。女性はおそらくどの書類整理棚を注文しますか。

(A) Slim
(B) Regular
(C) Wide
(D) Ultra-Wide

(A) スリム
(B) レギュラー
(C) ワイド
(D) ウルトラワイド

女性が「書類整理棚を購入する必要がある」と発言すると、男性はThere's only about fifty centimeters of space left along that wall.と述べ、Get the biggest one you can, but make sure it fits.と付け加えている。つまり男性は幅が50cm以下で最大のものを選ぶように言っている。カタログから(B)が正解だと分かる。

> 🐾 ここに注意！
>
> この問題は、Get the biggest oneだけを聞くと一番大きいサイズの(D)を選んでしまうのでなかなかの難問。リスニング満点を目指すなら、1つ1つの要素を聞き逃さないように集中力を鍛えよう！

64 □□□ 正解 B

What does the woman suggest?　女性は何を提案していますか。

(A) Scanning some documents
(B) Ending some subscriptions
(C) Purchasing some magazines
(D) Refurbishing an office

(A) 書類をスキャンすること
(B) 定期購読を終了すること
(C) 雑誌を購入すること
(D) オフィスを改装すること

女性は中盤でBy the wayと話題を変え、how about canceling some of the magazine subscriptions for the waiting room?と提案している。よって、(B)が正解。

語彙チェック　□refurbish　〜を改装する

M 🇦🇺 W 🇬🇧　　　　　　　　　　会話 ▶TRACK_138　問題 ▶TRACK_139

Questions 65 through 67 refer to the following conversation and map.

M: I just got a call from someone at Hayman National Park. Apparently, a tree has fallen over the path and they can't get to Stinson Campground. We'd better send one of the rangers over to take care of it.

W: I'll do it myself. I'm tired of doing paperwork. Which one of the trucks has the tools in it?

M: That'd be Truck 4, but it's got a flat tire. Let me help you move the tools into one of the other trucks.

W: Thanks, Tim. You'd better fix that tire as soon as possible. We need to be able to drive all the trucks in case there's an emergency.

M: I'll do it today. I can't do it in the morning, though. I have to plant some trees on South Ridge before it gets too hot.

問題65-67は次の会話と地図に関するものです。

男性：Hayman国立公園にいる人からちょうど電話がありました。どうやら木が通り道に倒れて、Stinsonキャンプ場に行けないようです。それを処理するために森林警備隊員を1人派遣した方がよさそうです。

女性：私がやりますよ。書類仕事にうんざりしています。どのトラックに道具が入っていますか。

男性：トラック4だと思いますが、タイヤがパンクしています。他のトラックに道具を移動させるのをお手伝いさせてください。

女性：ありがとうございます、Tim。できるだけ早くそのタイヤを修理した方がいいですよ。緊急事態に備えて、全てのトラックを運転できるようにしておく必要があります。

男性：今日修理します。午前中はできませんが。暑くなり過ぎる前にSouth Ridgeに木を植えなくてはならないのです。

語彙チェック　□apparently　どうやら〜らしい　□path　通路、小道　□ranger　森林警備隊員
□take care of 〜　〜を処理する　□paperwork　書類仕事
□get a flat tire　タイヤがパンクする
□in case 〜　〜だといけないから、〜の場合に備えて

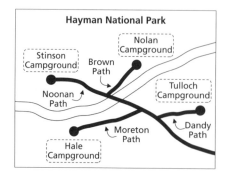
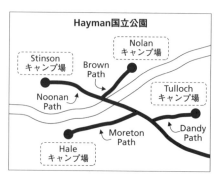

65

☐☐☐　正解 **A**

Look at the graphic. Which path are the speakers discussing?	図を見てください。話し手たちはどの通り道について話し合っていますか。
(A) Noonan Path	(A) Noonan Path
(B) Brown Path	(B) Brown Path
(C) Moreton Path	(C) Moreton Path
(D) Dandy Path	(D) Dandy Path

冒頭で男性が Apparently, a tree has fallen over the path and they can't get to Stinson Campground. と説明している。「木が通り道に倒れて Stinson キャンプ場に行けない」ということなので、Stinson キャンプ場に続く通り道について話していると分かる。地図から、正解は (A)。

66

☐☐☐　正解 **B**

What does the man say about Truck 4?	男性はトラック4について何と言っていますか。
(A) It is in the main garage.	(A) それはメインガレージにある。
(B) It needs some repairs.	(B) それは修理が必要である。
(C) It is out of fuel.	(C) それは燃料切れである。
(D) It has been taken by a colleague.	(D) それは同僚が乗って行った。

女性がどのトラックに道具が入っているのか尋ねたのに対し、男性は That'd be Truck 4, but it's got a flat tire. と答えている。さらに、その後女性が You'd better fix that tire as soon as possible. と言っていることから、トラック4はタイヤがパンクがしていて、修理が必要だと分かる。よって、正解は (B)。

67

☐☐☐　正解 **D**

What does the man say he will do this morning?	男性は今日の午前中に何をすると言っていますか。
(A) Check a fence	(A) フェンスの点検をする
(B) Guide some visitors	(B) 観光客を案内する
(C) Purchase some tires	(C) タイヤを購入する
(D) Plant some trees	(D) 木を植える

女性がタイヤのパンクを直すよう指示したのに対し、男性は I can't do it in the morning と返事をし、その理由を I have to plant some trees on South Ridge before it gets too hot. と説明している。つまり、男性は午前中は South Ridge に木を植える予定だと分かるので、正解は (D)。

Questions 68 through 70 refer to the following conversation and list.

W: Hi. I'm interested in joining this historical tour of Boston. What time does it leave?

M: That one leaves at nine thirty in the morning. It finishes at twelve thirty. The Breakfast Tour leaves at eight A.M. The others start at ten A.M.

W: Nine thirty is a bit early for me. I'll take this one, then.

M: Sure. That'll be 133 dollars. There's an additional fee if you need us to pick you up from your hotel.

W: That won't be necessary. I'm staying right across the road.

問題68-70は次の会話と一覧表に関するものです。

女性：こんにちは。このボストン歴史ツアーへの参加に興味があるのですが。何時に出発しますか。

男性：そちらは午前9時30分に出発します。終了は12時30分です。朝食ツアーは午前8時に出発します。他のものは午前10時出発です。

女性：9時30分は少し早いですね。そうしたら、こちらのものにします。

男性：かしこまりました。133ドルです。ホテルへのお迎えが必要であれば、追加料金がかかります。

女性：その必要はありません。道路のすぐ向かい側に宿泊しているので。

語彙チェック   □historical   歴史の   □additional fee   追加料金

Morning Tour Options		
8:00	Breakfast Tour	$155.00 per person
9:30	Historical Tour	$145.00 per person
10:00	Pop Culture Tour	$133.00 per person
10:00	Landmark Tour	$130.00 per person

朝ツアーの選択肢		
8:00	朝食ツアー	1人あたり155.00ドル
9:30	歴史ツアー	1人あたり145.00ドル
10:00	ポップカルチャーツアー	1人あたり133.00ドル
10:00	名所ツアー	1人あたり130.00ドル

68 ☐☐☐ 正解 D

What does the woman ask about?

(A) A menu option
(B) A pickup location
(C) A tour duration
(D) A departure time

女性は何について尋ねていますか。

(A) メニューの選択肢
(B) 送迎の場所
(C) ツアーの長さ
(D) 出発時刻

女性は冒頭でボストン歴史ツアーに興味があると述べた後、それについて What time does it leave? と尋ねている。それに対し、男性も「午前9時30分に出発する」と出発時刻を答えているので、正解は (D)。

69 ☐☐☐ 正解 C

Look at the graphic. Which tour will the woman take?

(A) Breakfast Tour
(B) Historical Tour
(C) Pop Culture Tour
(D) Landmark Tour

図を見てください。女性はどのツアーを選びますか。

(A) 朝食ツアー
(B) 歴史ツアー
(C) ポップカルチャーツアー
(D) 名所ツアー

男性からボストン歴史ツアーの時間の詳細を聞いた後、女性は Nine thirty is a bit early for me. と言い、I'll take this one, then. と他のツアーを選択している。それに対し、男性はThat'll be 133 dollars. と料金を答えている。表から、出発時刻が9時30分より遅く、料金が133ドルのツアーを選ぶ。正解は (C)。

🐾 ここに注意！

表には、選択肢にあるツアー名に加え、時間と金額という2つの要素が書かれている。図表に含まれる要素が多い場合は特に、音声を聞く前に何が書かれているのかをよく見て整理しておこう！

70 ☐☐☐ 正解 B

What does the woman mention about her accommodations?

(A) It provides a shuttle service.
(B) She is staying nearby.
(C) She will change hotels.
(D) It will not store her luggage.

女性は宿泊施設について何と述べていますか。

(A) そこは送迎サービスを提供している。
(B) 彼女は近くに宿泊している。
(C) 彼女はホテルを変更する予定である。
(D) そこは彼女の荷物が置けない。

男性がホテルへの送迎サービスについて説明すると、女性はそれは必要ないと答え、その理由を I'm staying right across the road. と説明している。よって、正解は (B)。

語彙チェック ☐ shuttle 定期往復便 ☐ store ～を入れる余地がある

Part 4

W 🇬🇧

トーク ▶TRACK_143　問題 ▶TRACK_144

Questions 71 through 73 refer to the following announcement.

Good morning, everyone. <u>We have a big day planned</u>. <u>We're moving all the furniture and equipment in this office and our storage closet in Building B into the new office in Building D.</u> You can leave all of the heavy items to the professionals we've hired from Hills Moving Company. <u>Staff members should just collect their personal belongings in boxes and carry them over.</u> We won't be able to get much work done until the movers arrange your desks and chairs in the new office, <u>so feel free to take a long lunch today.</u> Just try to be back by three so that you can put your things back in your desks by the end of the workday.

問題71-73は次のお知らせに関するものです。

おはようございます、皆さん。今日は大変な一日を予定しています。このオフィスとBuilding Bの倉庫にある全ての家具と備品をBuilding Dの新しいオフィスに移動させます。重い物は全て、私たちがHills引っ越し会社から雇ったプロにおまかせします。スタッフは箱に私物を集めて運ぶだけです。引っ越し業者が新しいオフィスに机と椅子を配置するまで、私たちは作業があまりできないと思いますので、今日は遠慮なく長いランチタイムをとってください。就業時間の終わりまでには自分のデスクに荷物を戻せるように、3時までには戻るようにしてください。

語彙チェック　□storage closet　倉庫　□personal belongings　私物
□feel free to *do*　遠慮なく〜する　□workday　1日の勤務時間

71 □□□ 正解 **A**

What does the speaker mean when she says, "We have a big day planned"?

(A) A lot of changes will be made.
(B) Employees will be very busy.
(C) A popular event will be held.
(D) A product will be launched.

話し手は "We have a big day planned" という発言で、何を意味していますか。

(A) 多くの変化がもたらされる。
(B) 従業員はとても忙しくなる。
(C) 人気のイベントが開催される。
(D) 製品が発売される。

話し手はWe have a big day planned.と言った後、We're moving 〜と、家具と備品を全て別の建物の新しいオフィスに移動させることについて説明している。引っ越し業者が入るとも言っていることから大掛かりなものだと予想される。よって、**(A)** が正解。

72

□□□ 正解 **A**

What are employees asked to do?	従業員は何をするよう求められていますか。
(A) Package some items	(A) 荷物をまとめる
(B) Call a moving company	(B) 引っ越し業者に電話する
(C) Fill out a form	(C) 用紙を記入する
(D) Purchase some furniture	(D) 家具を購入する

重い物は引っ越し業者に運んでもらうと説明する一方で、話し手は従業員がやるべきことについて、Staff members should just collect their personal belongings in boxes and carry them over. と伝えている。よって、**(A)** が正解。

語彙チェック □package 〜をまとめる、〜の荷造りをする

73

□□□ 正解 **B**

What does the speaker say about lunch?	話し手はランチについて何と言っていますか。
(A) It will be provided by the company.	(A) 会社から支給される。
(B) Employees can take extra time.	(B) 従業員は時間を延長してもよい。
(C) Food and beverages will be sold at booths.	(C) 食べ物と飲み物が売店で売られる。
(D) A receipt is needed for reimbursements.	(D) 払い戻しのために領収書が必要である。

話し手は、机や椅子が新しいオフィスに配置されるまでは私たちができる作業はあまりないと述べ、so feel free to take a long lunch today と伝えている。従業員はランチタイムを長めにとることができるということなので、これを言い換えている **(B)** が正解。

語彙チェック □booth 屋台の店、売店 □reimbursement 払い戻し

Questions 74 through 76 refer to the following talk.

I'd like to welcome you all to Sydney. I'll be your tour guide this morning. You're all staying at the Promenade Hotel in downtown Sydney until May 17. On the way to the hotel, we'll be making just one stop. That'll be for lunch at a popular local restaurant called Matador. In order to save a little time, I'd like to confirm your meal choices before we get there. In a few moments, I'll come by and ask each of you to let me know your preference. We have steak, chicken, and Atlantic salmon for you to choose from.

問題74-76は次の話に関するものです。

皆さまSydneyへようこそ。私が本日の午前中のツアーガイドでございます。お客さまは全員5月17日までSydneyの繁華街にあるPromenadeホテルに滞在します。ホテルへ向かう途中、1か所だけ立ち寄る予定です。Matadorという名前の人気のローカルレストランでのランチのためになります。少し時間を節約するために、そこへ到着する前にお客さまのお食事の選択を確認させていただきたいと思います。少ししたら、お客さまそれぞれにご希望を伺いに参ります。ステーキ、チキン、アトランティックサーモンの中からお選びいただけます。

語彙チェック　□downtown　繁華街の、都心の　□on the way to ～　～へ向かう途中で
　　　　　　　　□come by　立ち寄る　□preference　好み、選択

74　　　　　　　　　□□□　正解 **D**

Who is the speaker?
(A) A training officer
(B) A waiter
(C) A bus driver
(D) A tour guide

話し手は誰ですか。
(A) 指導員
(B) ウエーター
(C) バス運転手
(D) ツアーガイド

　話し手はI'd like to welcome you all to Sydney.と呼びかけた後、I'll be your tour guide this morning.と自己紹介している。よって、正解は(D)。

75

□□□ 正解 **B**

What will happen on May 17?

(A) The listeners will attend a performance.

(B) The listeners will check out of a hotel.

(C) The listeners will be assigned positions.

(D) The listeners will receive a discount.

5月17日に何が起こりますか。

(A) 聞き手は公演を観に行く。

(B) 聞き手はホテルをチェックアウトする。

(C) 聞き手は職責を与えられる。

(D) 聞き手は割引を受ける。

話し手は自己紹介をした後、You're all staying at the Promenade Hotel in downtown Sydney until May 17. と述べている。5月17日までPromenadeホテルに宿泊するということは、5月17日にはホテルをチェックアウトすると判断できる。よって、正解は (B)。

🐾 ここに注意！

この問題では、キーワードとなる May 17 が聞こえたときにはすでに、5月17日に起こった内容が述べられた後である。日付のキーワードは言い換えられることも少ないため分かりやすいが、キーワードばかり待ち過ぎてしまわないように注意しよう！

76

□□□ 正解 **D**

What does the speaker say he will do next?

(A) Deliver some drinks

(B) Explain a procedure

(C) Hand out a guidebook

(D) Take a meal order

話し手は次に何をすると言っていますか。

(A) 飲み物を届ける

(B) 手順を説明する

(C) ガイドブックを配る

(D) 食事の注文をとる

話し手は I'd like to confirm your meal choices と言った後、In a few moments, I'll come by and ask each of you to let me know your preference. と伝えている。話し手は聞き手のもとに食事を何にするか聞きに来るということなので、(D) が正解。

Questions 77 through 79 refer to the following telephone message.

Hi, Ms. Yasukura. It's Claire Cho from Sander's Beats. <u>We've received your guitar back from the workshop.</u> I'm sorry it took a little longer than we anticipated. <u>Some of the parts had to be ordered from the UK,</u> which took a couple of weeks. You can come in any day this week to pick it up. Um... any day except Tuesday. That's our day off. <u>If you can't come in, we have a delivery service for just 30 dollars to anywhere within the state.</u> Oh... by the way, your carry strap is almost worn out. <u>We've replaced it with a new one for free.</u> We've kept the old one in case it has some sentimental value.

問題77-79は次の電話のメッセージに関するものです。

こんにちは、Yasukuraさん。Sander's BeatsのClaire Choです。作業場からお客さまのギターを受け取りりました。予想より少々お時間がかかってしまい申し訳ございません。イギリスからいくつか部品を取り寄せる必要がありまして、それに2〜3週間かかってしまいました。今週いつでもお受け取りにいらしてください。いや…火曜日以外ですね。その日は休業日です。もしお越しいただけない場合は、州内ならどこでも、ちょうど30ドルで配達サービスがございます。ああ…ところで、お客さまのキャリーストラップはほとんど擦り切れています。無料で新しいものにお取り換えしました。思い入れがあるものかもしれませんので、古いものは保管してあります。

語彙チェック　□workshop　作業場　□anticipate　〜を予期する　□come in　入る、入ってくる
□day off　休日　□carry strap　キャリーストラップ
□wear out 〜　〜を擦り減らす　□replace *A* with *B*　A を B と取り換える
□in case 〜　〜するといけないから、万一〜するのに備えて
□sentimental value　愛着のあるもの、思い入れがあるもの

77　　正解 C

Where does the speaker most likely work?　話し手はどこで働いていると考えられますか。

(A) At a concert venue　　　　　　　(A) コンサート会場

(B) At a garage　　　　　　　　　　(B) 自動車修理工場

(C) At a music store　　　　　　　　(C) 楽器屋

(D) At a construction firm　　　　　(D) 建設会社

話し手は自分の名前と店名を述べた後、We've received your guitar back from the workshop.と言っている。聞き手のギターを作業場から受け取り返却するという流れや、キャリーストラップを交換しておいたという発言などから、話し手は楽器屋で働いていると考えられる。よって、正解は(C)。

78 | 正解 A

Why did the work take longer than expected?

(A) Some parts were shipped internationally.

(B) Some employees were on holiday.

(C) There was some inclement weather.

(D) The work was complicated.

作業はなぜ予想よりも時間がかかりましたか。

(A) いくつかの部品が国際輸送された。

(B) 何人かの従業員が休暇中だった。

(C) 天候不良だった。

(D) 作業が複雑だった。

話し手は予想より時間がかかったことに対して謝罪を述べた後、その理由を Some of the parts had to be ordered from the UK と説明している。部品を外国から取り寄せるのに時間がかかったということなので、(A) が正解。

語彙チェック □ship 〜を輸送する □inclement 荒天の

79 | 正解 D

What can the speaker provide for an additional fee?

(A) An accessory

(B) Some clothing

(C) After-hours service

(D) Home delivery

話し手は追加料金で何を提供できますか。

(A) アクセサリー

(B) 衣料品

(C) 時間外サービス

(D) 宅配便

話し手は聞き手にギターを受け取りに来るように言っているが、一方で If you can't come in, we have a delivery service for just 30 dollars to anywhere within the state. とも述べている。すなわち、30ドルの宅配サービスがあるということなので、正解は (D)。

語彙チェック □after-hours 営業時間後の

> 🐾 ここに注意!
> 後半で carry strap の取り換えについて説明しているが、それは無料で提供しているものなので (A) An accessory は正解にはならない。

トーク ▶TRACK_149　問題 ▶TRACK_150

Questions 80 through 82 refer to the following excerpt from a meeting.

Thanks for coming at such short notice. The reason I've asked you all here is that I've made a decision regarding the timing of the product launch. I'm moving it up because I've learned that a competitor is getting ready to release their new model. Jerry, I'd like you to handle marketing. Please talk to Ms. Donaldson in accounting about your budget. Kim and Rhod, I'm putting you in charge of the presentation on the special features of the new photocopier and the product demonstration. Please try to show why ours is the best on the market in terms of function and value for money.

問題80-82は次の会議の抜粋に関するものです。

このような突然の呼び出しにお越しいただきありがとうございます。皆さんにお集まりいただいた理由は、私が製品発売の時期に関して決定を下したからです。競合企業が新しいモデルの発売準備をしていると知ったので、私たちの製品の発売時期を繰り上げる予定です。Jerry、あなたにマーケティングを指揮してもらいたいと思います。会計部のDonaldsonさんにあなたの予算について話をしてください。Kimと Rhod、あなたたちには新しいコピー機の特徴についてのプレゼンテーションと製品デモンストレーションを担当してもらいたいと思います。機能と金銭的価値の点から、私たちの製品がなぜ市場の中で最も優れているのかを示すようにしてください。

語彙チェック　□short notice　突然の呼び出し　□regarding　〜に関して　□launch　発売
□move 〜 up　〜を繰り上げる　□handle　〜を指揮する
□put *A* in charge of *B*　AにBを任せる　□photocopier　コピー機
□in terms of 〜　〜に関して、〜の点から

80　　　正解 B

What does the speaker say about the meeting?	話し手は会議について何と言っていますか。
(A) It will end soon.	(A) それはすぐに終わる。
(B) It was called suddenly.	(B) それは突然開かれた。
(C) Some people did not attend.	(C) 何人か出席しなかった。
(D) The location was changed.	(D) 場所が変更された。

話し手は冒頭でThanks for coming at such short notice. と感謝を表している。short noticeは「突然の呼び出し」という意味で、冒頭のこの発言から、会議が突然開かれたということが分かる。よって、正解は (B)。

語彙チェック　□call　（会議）を招集する

> 🙅 **ここに注意！**
> 正答根拠がトークの一言目に登場するパターン。油断して聞き逃さないように、音声が流れ始まる前に集中モードをしっかり作っておこう！

81

□□□ 正解 **C**

What does the speaker say about a product launch?

(A) It will be handled by a new employee.
(B) It has had a budget cut.
(C) It has been rescheduled.
(D) It will be attended by a journalist.

話し手は製品の発売について何と言っていますか。

(A) それは新入社員が指揮する。
(B) それは予算がカットされた。
(C) それは予定が変更された。
(D) それにジャーナリストが出席する。

話し手はI've made a decision regarding the timing of the product launchと述べ、I'm moving it upと付け加えている。itは直前のthe timing of the product launchを指し、「製品の発売時期を繰り上げる」ということである。つまり、製品発売の予定が変更されたと分かるので、正解は(C)。

82

□□□ 正解 **D**

What kind of products does the company produce?

(A) Motor vehicles
(B) Sporting goods
(C) Software titles
(D) Office equipment

会社はどのような種類の製品を製造していますか。

(A) 自動車
(B) スポーツ用品
(C) ソフトウェア
(D) オフィス機器

話し手はスタッフへの指示の中で、I'm putting you in charge of the presentation on the special features of the new photocopier and the product demonstrationと発言している。photocopier「コピー機」はoffice equipment「オフィス機器」と言い換えることができるので、(D)が正解。

M

Questions 83 through 85 refer to the following telephone message.

Hello, Mr. Papas. It's Colin Day at Redmond Dental Clinic. Unfortunately, Dr. Redmond will be unable to keep his appointment with you this morning. He's attending a conference in Toronto, and his return flight was canceled due to the weather. I can offer you an appointment at ten A.M. on Wednesday instead. By the way, a lot of patients are using text messages to communicate with the dental clinic recently. It makes things a lot easier. If it suits you, too, please let us know your mobile phone number when you call me back.

問題83-85は次の電話のメッセージに関するものです。

こんにちは、Papasさん。Redmond歯科クリニックのColin Dayです。あいにくRedmond医師は今朝のあなたの診察予約に来られません。彼はTorontoでの会議に出席していましたが、帰りのフライトが天候のせいでキャンセルになりました。代わりに水曜日の午前10時の予約をお取りできます。ところで、最近は多くの患者さまがテキストメッセージでクリニックと連絡のやりとりをされています。それによって物事がはるかに簡単になります。もしあなたにとっても好都合であれば、お電話をかけ直していただくときに、携帯電話の番号を教えてください。

語彙チェック　□dental　歯の、歯科の　□unfortunately　不運にも、あいにく
　　　　　　　□patient　患者　□suit　〜に好都合である

83　□□□　正解 A

Who is the listener?
(A) A dental patient
(B) A cleaner
(C) A salesperson
(D) A business consultant

聞き手は誰ですか。
(A) 歯科患者
(B) 清掃業者
(C) 販売員
(D) 事業コンサルタント

冒頭のIt's Colin Day at Redmond Dental Clinic.という発言より、歯科クリニックからの電話だと分かる。その後の「あなたの今朝の予約に医師が来られない」という説明や、患者とクリニックの連絡方法についての説明などから、聞き手はこの歯科クリニックに予約した患者だと考えられる。よって、正解は(A)。

84 □□□ 正解 C

Why does the speaker mention Toronto?

(A) He will open a new branch there.

(B) He will meet the listener there.

(C) His employer is currently there.

(D) His flight will stop there.

話し手はなぜTorontoについて述べているのですか。

(A) 彼はそこに新しい支店を開く。

(B) 彼はそこで聞き手と会う。

(C) 彼の雇用主が現在そこにいる。

(D) 彼のフライトはそこに止まる。

話し手は、Redmond 医師が診察予約に来られない理由を He's attending a conference in Toronto, and his return flight was canceled due to the weather. と説明している。つまり、話し手の雇用主である Redmond 医師はフライトがキャンセルされて、Toronto から出発できないということなので、(C) が正解。

85 □□□ 正解 C

What does the speaker suggest?

(A) Meeting at the airport

(B) Registering for a conference

(C) Providing some contact details

(D) Obtaining a qualification

話し手は何を提案していますか。

(A) 空港で会うこと

(B) 会議に登録すること

(C) 連絡先を提供すること

(D) 資格を取得すること

話し手は、患者の多くがテキストメッセージでクリニックと連絡を取り合っていると説明し、If it suits you, too, please let us know your mobile phone number と伝えている。よって、(C) が正解。「携帯電話の番号」が contact details「連絡先」と言い換えられている。

Questions 86 through 88 refer to the following advertisement.

If you're on your feet all day working hard, you need a pair of Halliday brand shoes. They're not the kind of thing you wear to a fancy dinner. They're made from rugged materials and have a utilitarian design. Halliday shoes are water and dirt-resistant, while remaining light, cool, and comfortable. They're guaranteed to last for at least 24 months of heavy use, so it's worth paying a bit more. They're only available from our Web site, so search for Halliday brand shoes on your favorite search engine.

問題86-88は次の広告に関するものです。

もしあなたが1日中立ったままの状態で一生懸命に働いているのなら、あなたにはHallidayブランドの靴が必要です。それらは豪華なディナーに履いていくようなものではありません。丈夫な素材から作られていて、実用的なデザインをしています。Hallidayの靴は軽さ、通気性、そして快適さを残したまま、防水性と防汚性があります。少なくとも24カ月間多用しても耐えられることが保証されていますので、もう少しお高くても、お支払いいただく価値があります。こちらはウェブサイトからのみご購入いただけますので、お好きな検索エンジンでHallidayブランドの靴を検索してください。

語彙チェック □on *one's* feet　立っている状態で　□fancy　装飾的な、高級な
　　　　　　　□rugged　丈夫な、しっかりした　□utilitarian　実用的な
　　　　　　　□water and dirt-resistant　防水性と防汚性のある　□last　（物が）長持ちする
　　　　　　　□at least　少なくとも　□worth *doing*　〜する価値がある

86　　　　　□□□　正解 **A**

Why does the speaker say, "They're not the kind of thing you wear to a fancy dinner"?

(A) To avoid a misunderstanding
(B) To explain a dress requirement
(C) To recommend a different option
(D) To stress the reasonable price

話し手はなぜ"They're not the kind of thing you wear to a fancy dinner"と言っていますか。

(A) 誤解を防ぐため
(B) 服装の条件を説明するため
(C) 別の選択肢をお勧めするため
(D) 手頃な価格を強調するため

話し手はHallidayブランドの靴について、「丈夫な素材から作られている」、「実用的なデザインをしている」と説明している。つまり、素材やデザインに関して「豪華なディナー用ではない」と強調したい話し手の意図がくみ取れる。よって、正解は(A)。

語彙チェック □stress　〜を強調する

87 □□□ 正解 D

How long is the product warranty?	製品保証はどのくらいの期間ですか。
(A) One month	(A) 1カ月
(B) Six months	(B) 6カ月
(C) One year	(C) 1年
(D) Two years	(D) 2年

話し手は靴の性能について They're guaranteed to last for at least 24 months of heavy use と述べている。よって、24 months「24カ月」を Two years「2年」と言い換えている (D) が正解。

88 □□□ 正解 D

How can people buy the product?	人々は製品をどうやって買うことができますか。
(A) By ordering from a catalog	(A) カタログから注文することによって
(B) By going to a specialty store	(B) 専門店に行くことによって
(C) By attending a special event	(C) 特別なイベントに参加することによって
(D) By visiting an online store	(D) オンラインストアを訪れることによって

話し手は製品について、They're only available from our Web site と言っているので、製品を購入するためにはウェブサイトへアクセスしなくてはいけないと分かる。よって、(D) が正解。

語彙チェック □specialty 専門

Questions 89 through 91 refer to the following broadcast.

Good evening, listeners. I'm Chaz Gooding, and you're listening to *Chats with Chaz* on Radio 6KP. Today, we have a special guest all the way from the USA. It's well-known novelist Clayton Porteous. He's just released the fourth novel in his series of adventure books for children. He's signing books at Watts Bookseller stores all over Australia, starting here in Melbourne on December 3. Now, Clayton, you started your career as a chemical engineer at a major chemical company. In that field, you made a name for yourself by developing several very effective bonds and lubricants. What made you take up writing?

問題89-91は次の放送に関するものです。

リスナーの皆さん、こんばんは。Chaz Goodingです。ラジオ6KPのChats with Chazをお聞きいただいております。今日ははるばるアメリカからスペシャルゲストをお迎えしています。有名な小説家のClayton Porteousです。彼は子ども向けアドベンチャーシリーズの4作目の小説を発表したばかりです。彼はオーストラリア中のWatts Booksellerの店舗で書籍のサイン会を開催する予定で、12月3日にここMelbourneでスタートします。それではClayton、あなたは大手化学薬品会社で化学エンジニアとしてキャリアをスタートしました。あなたはその分野で、とても効果的な接着剤と潤滑油をいくつか開発したことで有名になりました。何がきっかけで、執筆を始めたのですか。

語彙チェック　□all the way　はるばる　□well-known　よく知られた、有名な
□adventure　冒険、アドベンチャー　□chemical engineer　化学エンジニア
□make a name for *oneself*　名を上げる、有名になる　□bond　接着剤
□lubricant　潤滑油　□take up ～　～を始める、～に取りかかる

> ⚠ **ここに注意！**
> この問題で登場しているlubricantは「潤滑油」という意味の難単語。リスニングでは専門用語のような難しめの単語が時々登場するが、そこまで多くは出てこないので、知らない単語が出ても深追いし過ぎずに話の全体の流れをつかむことに集中しよう！

89 　　　　　　　　　□□□　正解 C

Who is the speaker?　　　　　　　話し手は誰ですか。
(A) A musician　　　　　　　　　　(A) 音楽家
(B) A scientist　　　　　　　　　　(B) 科学者
(C) A radio personality　　　　　　(C) ラジオパーソナリティー
(D) A talent agent　　　　　　　　(D) タレントエージェント

話し手は冒頭でGood evening, listeners.と聞き手にあいさつをし、I'm Chaz Goodingと自分の名前を述べた後、you're listening to *Chats with Chaz* on Radio 6KPと言っている。その後も「今日はゲストをお迎えしています」と話を続けていることから、話し手はラジオパーソナリティーだと考えられる。よって、正解は(C)。

90 — 正解 B

What is the purpose of Mr. Porteous' trip?
(A) To help develop new chemicals
(B) To promote a fiction publication
(C) To speak at a conference
(D) To attend a ceremony

Porteousさんの旅の目的は何ですか。
(A) 新しい化学薬品の開発を支援すること
(B) 小説出版物の販売を促進すること
(C) 会議で演説をすること
(D) 式典に参列すること

話し手はPorteousさんについて、「有名な小説家」で「4作目の小説を発表したばかり」と紹介し、He's signing books at Watts Bookseller stores all over Australiaと述べている。サイン会は販売促進の1つであると考えられるので、正解は(B)。

語彙チェック □chemicals 化学薬品 □fiction 小説、フィクション

91 — 正解 D

What does the speaker ask Mr. Porteous about?
(A) An employment contract
(B) A work schedule
(C) A film adaptation
(D) A career change

話し手はPorteousさんに、何について尋ねていますか。
(A) 雇用契約
(B) 仕事の予定
(C) 映画化
(D) キャリアチェンジ

話し手はPorteousさんを紹介した後、Now, Claytonと呼びかけ、インタビューを始めている。you started your career as a chemical engineer at a major chemical companyと述べた後、最後にWhat made you take up writing?と尋ねている。これらのことから、Porteousさんはもともと化学エンジニアで、そこから小説家に転向したことが分かる。話し手はPorteousさんに小説の執筆を始めたきっかけを尋ねているので、(D)が正解。

Questions 92 through 94 refer to the following excerpt from a speech.

We all know why we're here this evening. We're celebrating Gina Forbes' winning the National Architecture Award. We're all really proud of her and extremely thankful for the prestige she's brought to the firm. We've been receiving inquiries from all around the state. Some of them have been for huge projects such as the new Thurston City Hall. It's very unfortunate that Ms. Forbes couldn't be here with us this evening. She had some urgent family business to take care of at the last minute. She has, however, given me a letter, which she asked me to read to all of you.

問題92-94は次のスピーチの抜粋に関するものです。

なぜ今夜お集まりいただいたかは皆さんお分かりですね。Gina Forbesの全国建築賞の受賞祝いです。私たちは皆彼女を心から誇りに思いますし、事務所の評判を高めてくれたことに非常に感謝しております。州中からお問い合わせを頂いています。その中には新しいThurston市役所のような巨大プロジェクトもいくつかあります。Forbesさんに今夜こちらにお越しいただけなかったことは非常に残念です。土壇場になって、対応しなくてはならない緊急の家庭の事情があったとのことです。しかしながら、彼女からお手紙を頂きまして、皆さまに読んでほしいとのお願いがありました。

語彙チェック	□be proud of 〜　〜を誇りに思う　□extremely　極めて、とても
	□prestige　名声　□inquiry　問い合わせ、質問　□urgent　緊急の
	□at the last minute　直前に、土壇場になって

92 ☐☐☐ 正解 A

What is the purpose of the gathering?

(A) To praise an employee
(B) To celebrate a retirement
(C) To show appreciation to a client
(D) To launch a new service

集まりの目的は何ですか。

(A) 従業員を褒めたたえること
(B) 定年退職を祝うこと
(C) 顧客に感謝を表すこと
(D) 新しいサービスを始めること

話し手は冒頭で「なぜ今夜お集まりいただいたかは皆さんお分かりですね」と投げかけ、We're celebrating Gina Forbes' winning the National Architecture Award. と集まりの目的を説明している。その後、Forbesさんのことを誇りに思っていることや、彼女が事務所の評判を高めてくれたことに感謝していることなどを伝えているので、Forbesさんは話し手の会社の従業員であると考えられる。従業員のForbesさんの受賞を祝うということなので、正解は(A)。

語彙チェック	□praise　〜を褒める、〜を賞賛する

93

正解 C

What does the speaker imply when he says, "We've been receiving inquiries from all around the state"?

(A) Ms. Forbes has been asked to speak at other firms.

(B) The firm had been put up for sale by its owners.

(C) Ms. Forbes has made the firm more attractive to clients.

(D) The new products have been getting positive reviews.

話し手は "We've been receiving inquiries from all around the state" という発言で、何を示唆していますか。

(A) Forbesさんは別の事務所での講演を依頼された。

(B) 事務所は所有者によって売りに出されていた。

(C) Forbesさんは事務所を顧客にとってより魅力的なものにした。

(D) 新製品は肯定的な評価を受けている。

この発言の直前に、話し手は We're all really proud of her and extremely thankful for the prestige she's brought to the firm. と述べている。Forbesさんの受賞によって事務所の評判が上がったということは、Forbesさんのおかげで顧客がより事務所に注目するようになったと考えられる。よって、正解は(C)。

語彙チェック □put up 〜 for sale （家など）を売り出す

94

正解 B

What will the speaker most likely do next?

(A) Distribute a document

(B) Convey a message

(C) Introduce a guest

(D) Explain a schedule

話し手は次に何をすると考えられますか。

(A) 書類を配布する

(B) メッセージを伝える

(C) ゲストを紹介する

(D) スケジュールについて説明する

話し手は「今夜Forbesさんはここに来られなかった」ことを伝えた後、She has, however, given me a letter, which she asked me to read to all of you. と述べている。この後、話し手はForbesさんから預かった手紙を代わりに読むと予想される。よって、正解は(B)。

語彙チェック □convey 〜を伝える

ここに注意！
正答の (B) Convey a message という表現は、あまりなじみのない人も多いかもしれない。convey には「〜を運ぶ」という意味の他に、「〜を伝える」という意味があることも覚えておこう。(B)は、Pass on a message、Deliver a message とも言い換えられる！

M 🇺🇸

Questions 95 through 97 refer to the following telephone message and catalog.

Hi Ms. Waters. It's Randy. I looked for you in your office, but you seem to have stepped out. Anyway, <u>I've finished installing the dishwasher in the kitchen</u>. I'd like to test it with a load of plates. <u>Can you get one of the kitchen hands to come in and load it up with some dirty dishes for me?</u> Once we've confirmed that everything is working, <u>I'll need your signature on the job completion form</u> that I handed you earlier. Oh, and you mentioned that you were thinking of buying a new refrigeration unit as well. I asked one of our salespeople to e-mail you a copy of the catalog. <u>I suggest getting the second largest one.</u> I know you wanted something even bigger, but there's just not enough space for it.

問題95-97は次の電話のメッセージとカタログに関するものです。

こんにちはWatersさん。Randyです。オフィスであなたを探しましたが、外出中のようですね。それはそうとして、キッチンの食器洗浄機の取り付けが終了しました。たくさんのお皿を使って試運転したいと思っております。調理助手の1人に何枚か汚れたお皿を入れに来させてもらえませんか。全て作動していることが確認できたら、以前にお渡しした作業終了フォームにあなたの署名を頂かなくてはいけません。ああ、新しい冷蔵装置の購入も検討されているとおっしゃっていましたね。私たちの販売員の1人に、カタログを1部Eメールであなたに送るようにお願いしました。私は2番目に大きいものをお勧めします。もっと大きいものをご希望だったと思いますが、それにはちょっと十分なスペースがありません。

語彙チェック ☐step out　外出する　☐dishwasher　食器洗浄機　☐a load of 〜　たくさんの〜　☐kitchen hand　調理助手　☐signature　署名　☐refrigeration unit　冷蔵装置

Small	1m x 1m	$2,000
Standard	1m x 2m	$2,500
Roomy	2m x 2m	$3,500
Extra Roomy	2m x 3m	$4,000

小型タイプ	1m x 1m	2,000ドル
標準タイプ	1m x 2m	2,500ドル
広々タイプ	2m x 2m	3,500ドル
超広々タイプ	2m x 3m	4,000ドル

95 ☐☐☐ 正解 D

Where does the listener most likely work?
(A) At an appliance store
(B) At a supermarket
(C) At a construction firm
(D) At a restaurant

聞き手はどこで働いていると考えられますか。
(A) 家電量販店
(B) スーパーマーケット
(C) 建設業者
(D) レストラン

話し手は冒頭で I've finished installing the dishwasher in the kitchen と伝えている。その後、「試運転のために、調理助手にお皿を入れに来させてくれないか」と尋ねている。キッチンやお皿、調理助手といった言葉から、聞き手はレストランで働いていると考えられるので、正解は(D)。

96 ☐☐☐ 正解 B

What does the speaker ask the listener to do?
(A) Call a supplier
(B) Sign a form
(C) Read a contract
(D) Write a review

話し手は聞き手に何をするよう求めていますか。
(A) 供給業者に電話する
(B) フォームに署名する
(C) 契約書を読む
(D) レビューを書く

話し手は、食器洗浄機の試運転について述べた後、I'll need your signature on the job completion form と言っている。よって、正解は(B)。

語彙チェック ☐sign ～に署名する

97 ☐☐☐ 正解 C

Look at the graphic. Which model does the speaker recommend?
(A) Small
(B) Standard
(C) Roomy
(D) Extra Roomy

図を見てください。話し手はどのモデルを勧めていますか。
(A) 小型タイプ
(B) 標準タイプ
(C) 広々タイプ
(D) 超広々タイプ

冷蔵装置が欲しいという聞き手の要望に対し、話し手は「販売員にカタログを1部Eメールで送るよう依頼した」と述べ、I suggest getting the second largest one. と提案している。表から、2番目に大きいものは (C) Roomy だと分かる。

語彙チェック ☐roomy 広々した、ゆったりした

W 🍁

Questions 98 through 100 refer to the following excerpt from a meeting and map.

One more point before we conclude the meeting. <u>Since Tuesday, members of the accounting department have been complaining about the noise from the construction site across the road.</u> Unfortunately, <u>the accounting department is closest to the noisy worksite</u>, and none of the vacant offices in the building are large enough for the whole department. There's just not much we can do about it. <u>One solution that's been suggested is allowing accounting staff to work from home until the noisiest work is over.</u> Does anyone have any objections?

問題98-100は次の会議の抜粋と地図に関するものです。

会議を終える前にもう1点だけございます。火曜日以降、経理部のメンバーから、道路の向かい側の建設現場の騒音について苦情が出ています。あいにく、経理部は騒がしい作業現場に1番近く、また、この建物の空きオフィスはどれもその部署全体を移動するには十分な大きさではありません。これについて私たちにできることはあまりありません。提案された1つの解決策は、最も騒音がひどい作業が終わるまで、経理部の社員が自宅で仕事をするのを許可することです。反対意見がある人はいますか。

語彙チェック　□conclude　～を終える、～を締めくくる　□accounting department　経理部
□complain about ～　～について苦情を言う　□construction site　建設現場
□worksite　作業現場　□vacant　空いている　□objection　反対、異議

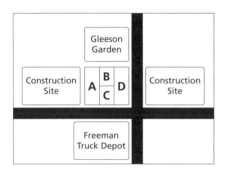 

98 正解 A

When did the construction work probably start? | 建設工事はおそらくいつ始まりましたか。
(A) On Tuesday | (A) 火曜日
(B) On Wednesday | (B) 水曜日
(C) On Thursday | (C) 木曜日
(D) On Friday | (D) 金曜日

話し手は冒頭で、Since Tuesday, members of the accounting department have been complaining about the noise from the construction site across the road. と述べている。「火曜日以降、建設現場の騒音について苦情が出ている」ということなので、工事はおそらく火曜日に始まったと考えられる。よって、正解は(A)。

99 正解 D

Look at the graphic. In which office is the accounting department? | 図を見てください。経理部はどのオフィスにありますか。
(A) In Office A | (A) オフィス A
(B) In Office B | (B) オフィス B
(C) In Office C | (C) オフィス C
(D) In Office D | (D) オフィス D

話し手は建設現場について the construction site across the road と述べ、the accounting department is closest to the noisy worksite と説明している。道路の向かい側に建設現場があり、そこに最も近い場所が経理部のオフィスだと分かるので、地図から正解は(D)。

100 正解 B

What suggestion does the speaker mention? | 話し手はどんな提案について述べていますか。
(A) Allowing flexible work hours | (A) 柔軟な勤務時間を許可すること
(B) Having some employees work remotely | (B) 従業員にリモート勤務させること
(C) Moving some employees to a different office | (C) 何人かの従業員を別のオフィスに移動させること
(D) Postponing the construction work | (D) 建設工事を延期すること

話し手は「問題解決のためにできることはあまり多くない」と言いつつも、One solution that's been suggested is allowing accounting staff to work from home until the noisiest work is over. と解決策について言及している。よって、work from home を work remotely と言い換えている(B)が正解。

TEST 3

解答&解説

Part 1

問題番号	正解	1 2
1	B	☐☐
2	C	☐☐
3	D	☐☐
4	A	☐☐
5	B	☐☐
6	A	☐☐

Part 2

問題番号	正解	1 2
7	C	☐☐
8	B	☐☐
9	C	☐☐
10	C	☐☐
11	A	☐☐
12	A	☐☐
13	A	☐☐
14	C	☐☐
15	B	☐☐
16	B	☐☐
17	A	☐☐
18	C	☐☐
19	C	☐☐
20	B	☐☐
21	B	☐☐
22	C	☐☐
23	B	☐☐
24	C	☐☐
25	A	☐☐
26	A	☐☐
27	C	☐☐
28	B	☐☐
29	B	☐☐
30	A	☐☐
31	C	☐☐

Part 3

問題番号	正解	1 2
32	A	☐☐
33	B	☐☐
34	C	☐☐
35	C	☐☐
36	C	☐☐
37	D	☐☐
38	B	☐☐
39	D	☐☐
40	D	☐☐
41	C	☐☐
42	B	☐☐
43	A	☐☐
44	A	☐☐
45	A	☐☐
46	D	☐☐
47	D	☐☐
48	C	☐☐
49	A	☐☐
50	A	☐☐
51	B	☐☐
52	C	☐☐
53	D	☐☐
54	D	☐☐
55	A	☐☐
56	B	☐☐

Part 4

問題番号	正解	1 2
57	D	☐☐
58	D	☐☐
59	C	☐☐
60	B	☐☐
61	C	☐☐
62	A	☐☐
63	C	☐☐
64	D	☐☐
65	C	☐☐
66	A	☐☐
67	D	☐☐
68	B	☐☐
69	C	☐☐
70	B	☐☐

問題番号	正解	1 2
71	D	☐☐
72	B	☐☐
73	D	☐☐
74	C	☐☐
75	A	☐☐
76	D	☐☐
77	D	☐☐
78	B	☐☐
79	D	☐☐
80	B	☐☐
81	C	☐☐
82	D	☐☐
83	A	☐☐
84	C	☐☐
85	C	☐☐
86	C	☐☐
87	B	☐☐
88	D	☐☐
89	A	☐☐
90	C	☐☐
91	B	☐☐
92	A	☐☐
93	B	☐☐
94	A	☐☐
95	C	☐☐

問題番号	正解	1 2
96	A	☐☐
97	C	☐☐
98	B	☐☐
99	D	☐☐
100	B	☐☐

Part 1

1 🇺🇸 □□□ 正解 B ▶TRACK_164

(A) He's searching through a cabinet.
(B) He's standing on metal equipment.
(C) He's assembling a shelf to store tools.
(D) He's putting an organizer on his lap.

(A) 彼は収納棚を念入りに調べている。
(B) 彼は金属の備品の上に立っている。
(C) 彼は工具を保管しておくために棚を組み立てている。
(D) 彼は膝の上にシステム手帳を置いている。

はしごに上って立っている男性の状態について述べている(B)が正解。写真に写っているはしごをmetal equipment「金属の備品」と言い表している。

語彙チェック □search through ~ ~を念入りに調べる □assemble ~を組み立てる
□store ~を保管する □organizer システム手帳 □lap 膝

> 🐾**ここに注意！**
> この写真にははしごが写っているが、Part 1に頻出の単語ladder「はしご」を使わずに
> metal equipmentと言い換えている。リスニング満点を目指すなら、王道の単語や表現
> ばかりに頼らないこともポイント！

2 🇬🇧 □□□ 正解 C ▶TRACK_165

(A) Cyclists are gathering around the river.
(B) Boats are docking at a pier.
(C) A tower is reflected in the water.
(D) Vehicles are stuck in traffic.

(A) 自転車に乗った人が川の周辺に集まっている。
(B) ボートが桟橋に着いている。
(C) タワーが水面に反射している。
(D) 乗り物が渋滞に巻き込まれている。

水面に反射されたタワーの様子を説明している(C)が正解。物がたくさん写っている情報量の多い写真も、1つ1つ選択肢と写真を照らし合わせて解答することがポイント。

語彙チェック □cyclist 自転車に乗る人 □dock （船が）波止場に着く □pier 桟橋
□reflect ~を反射する

正解 D ▶TRACK_166

(A) One of the women is packing her backpack.
(B) Some people are waiting for a bus.
(C) The window is covered with a curtain.
(D) A chair outside has been occupied.

(A) 女性の1人はリュックサックに荷物を詰めているところである。
(B) 何人かの人々はバスを待っているところである。
(C) 窓がカーテンで覆われている。
(D) 外にある椅子は使用中である。

外に椅子が置かれており、その椅子には人が座っているのが分かる。よって、この椅子の状態について説明している(D)が正確。

語彙チェック □occupy 〜を使用する、〜を占有する

⚠️ここに注意！

正答の(D)は、「座っている」という人物の動作を直接説明するのではなく、「椅子」というモノに焦点を当てた文になっていることがポイント。人が写っていても、人の動作や状態ばかりに視点を置かないように注意！

---

4 🇨🇦 正解 A ▶TRACK_167

(A) A notebook is held close to his chest.
(B) A cable is coiled around a headset.
(C) He is turning on a computer on a desk.
(D) He is drinking from a cup at a workspace.

(A) ノートが胸の近くで抱えられている。
(B) ケーブルがヘッドホンに巻き付けられている。
(C) 彼は机の上のコンピューターの電源を点けているところである。
(D) 彼は作業場でコップから飲み物を飲んでいる。

男性が胸にノートを抱えている状態を表した(A)が正解。「〜を持っている」という意味のholdが、受動態の形で使われている。

語彙チェック □coil A around B AをBに巻き付ける □headset ヘッドホン

(A) The man is putting on a coat.
(B) The man is grasping a bag.
(C) Some groceries are removed from a car.
(D) Posters are being attached to a wall.

(A) 男性はコートを着ているところである。
(B) 男性は袋をつかんでいる。
(C) 食料品が車から取り除かれている。
(D) ポスターが壁に貼り付けられているところである。

男性は袋をつかんでいるところであり、この動作を説明している(B)が正解。プラスチック製の袋に加えて、布製や紙製のものも bag という語で表すことができる。

語彙チェック　□grasp　〜をつかむ　□grocery　食料雑貨　□attach　〜を貼り付ける

> (🐾) ここに注意！
> 誤答の(C)は、最後のcarがcartであれば正解になりうる。Part 1で全問正解するためには、細かい部分の聞き取りでミスをしないように1語1語集中してよく聞こう！

(A) The woman is stirring the mixture in a bowl.
(B) The man is using a cutting machine.
(C) Some utensils have been arranged in a drawer.
(D) Some vegetables have been placed in a sink.

(A) 女性は混ぜ合わせたものをボウルの中でかき混ぜている。
(B) 男性は裁断機を使っている。
(C) 調理器具が引き出しの中に並べられている。
(D) 野菜がシンクの中に置かれている。

ボウルの中で何かをかき混ぜている女性の動作について説明した(A)が正解。bowl「ボウル」などのキッチン用品の単語と合わせて、(C)にある utensil「調理器具」という単語も押さえておこう。

語彙チェック　□stir　〜をかき混ぜる　□cutting machine　裁断機　□utensil　調理器具
　　　　　　　□arrange　〜をきちんと並べる

7 W 🇬🇧 M 🇺🇸   □□□ 正解 C   ▶TRACK_171

Which branch will you work at starting next month?

(A) I want something with a salad.

(B) Due to the shortage in the workforce.

(C) How did you know about my transfer?

来月以降どの支店で働き始めるのですか。

(A) サラダ付きのものが欲しいです。

(B) 労働力の不足が原因です。

(C) どうやって私の異動を知ったのですか。

Which branch ～? で、「来月以降どの支店で働き始めるのか」を尋ねている。これに対し、質問に答えるのではなく、どうして来月以降別の支店で働き始めることを知っているのか疑問に思い、尋ねている (C) が正解。

語彙チェック　□branch　支店　□due to ～　～のために、～が原因で　□shortage　不足　□workforce　労働力　□transfer　異動

8 W 🇨🇦 M 🇺🇸   □□□ 正解 B   ▶TRACK_172

I wonder if I should ask you to bring your camera to the event.

(A) Push here to turn it on.

(B) Either is fine with me.

(C) It is discounted here.

イベントにカメラを持ってくるようあなたに頼んだ方がいいかと思っているのですが。

(A) オンにするにはここを押してください。

(B) 私はどちらでも大丈夫ですよ。

(C) それはここで割引されています。

相手にカメラを持ってくるよう頼もうかどうかと考えていることを I wonder if ～ で伝えているのに対し、「どちらでも、どちらも」という意味の代名詞 either を使って自身の考えを述べている (B) が正解。

語彙チェック　□turn ～ on　～をオンにする　□either　どちらでも、どちらも

9 M 🇦🇺 W 🇬🇧   □□□ 正解 C   ▶TRACK_173

When's Norman Pharmacy going to open for business?

(A) They added some additional menu items.

(B) Next to the post office.

(C) There is a sign in front of their door.

Norman 薬局はいつ開店する予定ですか。

(A) 彼らはいくつか追加のメニューの品を増やしました。

(B) 郵便局の隣です。

(C) ドアの前に看板がありますよ。

薬局の開店予定について尋ねているのに対し、具体的な日時を答えるのではなく、「ドアの前に看板がある」と伝えることで、その情報をどこで得ることができるのかを示唆している (C) が正解。

語彙チェック　□pharmacy　薬局　□additional　追加の

I'd like you to take some time to review this marketing plan.

(A) Sure, she has a lot of knowledge.

(B) We should update our account information.

(C) When should I finish it?

このマーケティング案を見直すお時間を取っていただきたいのですが。

(A) もちろんです、彼女は知識が豊富です。

(B) 私たちの口座情報を更新するべきです。

(C) いつ終わらせればいいですか。

問いかけ文は I'd like you to 〜で相手に対する自分の要求を伝えている平叙文。「マーケティング案を見直す時間を取ってほしい」という要望に対し、when を使って作業の期限を聞き返している (C) が正解。

語彙チェック　☐review　〜を見直す　☐knowledge　知識　☐account　口座

How did your company hear about our catering service?

(A) I saw your poster on the train.

(B) We are considering the cheapest course.

(C) It has been about three years.

御社はどのようにして弊社のケータリングサービスについて耳にしたのですか。

(A) 電車で広告を見ました。

(B) 最安値のコースを検討しています。

(C) 約3年になります。

「どのようにして自社のケータリングサービスについて耳にしたのか」、その方法を尋ねている。これに対し、「電車で広告を見た」とサービスを知ったきっかけを答えている (A) が正解。

One of our photocopiers doesn't seem to be working properly either.

(A) The repair person hasn't come yet.

(B) It was very kind of him to help us.

(C) I'll show you the property tomorrow morning.

私たちのコピー機の1つも、きちんと作動していないみたいです。

(A) 修理の人はまだ来ていないのです。

(B) 私たちを助けてくれるなんて彼はとても優しいですね。

(C) 明日の朝に物件を見せます。

問いかけ文ではコピー機の不調を伝えている。これに対し、「修理の人がまだ来ていない」と現状を伝えることで、これから修理が行われることを説明している (A) が正解。

語彙チェック　☐photocopier　コピー機　☐properly　きちんと、適切に　☐property　物件

> 🐾 ここに注意！
> この問いかけ文は平叙文。疑問文ではなく平叙文のときは、応答の仕方が予想しにくいので難しい。何かを尋ねているわけではなくても、その発言をしている意図や背景を想像するようにしよう！

13　W 🇬🇧　M 🇺🇸　□□□　正解 A　▶TRACK_177

Weren't you going to try Amy's Café after work today?
(A) I didn't know it was that far away.
(B) Yes, she is out of town today.
(C) No, it wasn't my original dish.

今日の仕事後に Amy's Café に行ってみる予定ではなかったのですか。
(A) あんなに遠いとは知らなかったのです。
(B) はい、彼女は今日街を離れています。
(C) いいえ、それは私のオリジナル料理ではありません。

否定疑問文で、仕事の後のカフェに行く予定について尋ねている。これに対し、「あんなに遠いとは知らなかった」と答えることで、カフェに行く予定を取り止めたことを示唆している (A) が正解。

語彙チェック □that それほど、そんなに　□far away 遠く離れて

14　M 🇦🇺　W 🇨🇦　□□□　正解 C　▶TRACK_178

Will the safety inspection be conducted for the main building or the other one?
(A) Tomorrow afternoon.
(B) They are certified inspectors.
(C) It was announced by e-mail.

安全点検はメインビルで行われますか、それとももう1つのビルで行われますか。
(A) 明日の午後です。
(B) 彼らは資格を持った調査の方々です。
(C) Eメールで知らされていましたよ。

選択疑問文で、安全点検は2つのビルのうちどちらで行われる予定かを尋ねている。これに対し、どちらのビルで行われるのかを明言するのではなく、間接的にその情報を得られる方法を伝えている (C) が正解。

語彙チェック □inspection 点検　□conduct ～を行う　□certified 資格のある　□inspector 調査官

⚠ ここに注意！
このように長い問いかけ文も、ときどき登場する。1文が長いと文構造が取りにくかったり、内容を忘れてしまったりしがちなので注意したい！

15　W 🇬🇧　M 🇦🇺　□□□　正解 B　▶TRACK_179

How often do you come to this art museum?
(A) Twice as large as yours.
(B) This is my first time.
(C) From their Web site.

どのくらいの頻度でこの美術館に来るのですか。
(A) あなたのより2倍大きいです。
(B) 今回が初めてです。
(C) ウェブサイトからです。

How often ～? で美術館を訪問する頻度について尋ねているのに対し、「今回が初めて」と今までは一度も来たことがないことを伝えている (B) が正解。

What do you think of the tentative plan for our factory tour?
(A) Yes, I think so.
(B) Let's discuss it tomorrow.
(C) Many joined that tour.

私たちの工場見学の仮計画についてどう思いますか。
(A) はい、そう思います。
(B) それについて明日話し合いましょう。
(C) そのツアーには多くの人が参加しました。

What do you think of ～?で工場見学の仮計画についての意見を尋ねているのに対し、「明日話し合おう」と提案している(B)が正解。

語彙チェック　□tentative　仮の　□tour　見学、ツアー

Doesn't our cafeteria need renovation?
(A) It was only built 10 years ago.
(B) No, it is the previous one.
(C) Are you familiar with that dish?

私たちの食堂は改装が必要ではないのですか。
(A) ほんの10年前に建てられたばかりですよ。
(B) いいえ、それは以前のものです。
(C) その料理をよく知っていますか。

問いかけ文は、「食堂を改装する必要があるのではないか」という意見を伝える否定疑問文。ほんの10年前に建てられたばかりである、すなわち食堂はまだ建てられてから日が浅いと伝えることで、間接的に改装の必要はないと答えている(A)が正解。

語彙チェック　□cafeteria　食堂　□renovation　改装　□previous　以前の

🐾ここに注意！
正答の(A)は間接的な応答。「10年前に建てられた」という事実をどのような意図やニュアンスで伝えているのかを理解するために、副詞onlyが重要なポイントとなっている！

The presentation slides were completed yesterday, weren't they?
(A) Of course, it would be bigger for you.
(B) That should be Sam's wallet.
(C) I just need to correct some data.

プレゼンテーションのスライドは昨日完成しましたよね？
(A) もちろん、あなたにはもっと大きいでしょう。
(B) それはSamの財布のはずです。
(C) いくつかのデータを訂正する必要があるだけです。

問いかけ文は「プレゼンテーションのスライドが昨日完成しているか」を確認する付加疑問文。これに対し、訂正作業が少し残っていると答えることで、間接的にスライドはまだ完成していないことを伝えている(C)が正解。

語彙チェック　□complete　～を完成させる　□wallet　財布　□correct　～を訂正する

19 M 🇺🇸 W 🇨🇦 　　　□□□　正解 C　▶TRACK_183

Why's the train to Shibuya behind schedule?

(A) In the north of the station.

(B) Our office is under construction.

(C) Please check the schedule for weekends.

なぜ渋谷行きの電車は遅れているのですか。

(A) 駅の北側です。

(B) 私たちのオフィスは工事中です。

(C) 週末の時刻表を確認してください。

問いかけ文では、電車が遅れている理由を尋ねている。これに対し、週末の時刻表を確認するように促している (C) が正解。すなわち、週末は普段と電車のダイヤが異なるため、渋谷行きの電車は遅れているわけではないということを伝えていると考えられる。

語彙チェック　□behind schedule　定刻に遅れて　□construction　建築工事

20 W 🇨🇦 M 🇦🇺 　　　□□□　正解 B　▶TRACK_184

Who used this projector last?

(A) The same software.

(B) Was it left on?

(C) The manager approved this purchase order.

最後に誰がこのプロジェクターを使いましたか。

(A) 同じソフトウェアです。

(B) 作動したままだったのですか。

(C) 部長がこの注文書を承認しました。

最後にプロジェクターを使った人を尋ねているのに対し、特定の人物を答えるのではなく、プロジェクターがついたままだったのかと聞き返している (B) が正解。

語彙チェック　□projector　プロジェクター　□approve　〜を承認する
　　　　　　　□purchase order　注文書

> ⚠️ **ここに注意！**
> 正答の (B) は、相手が聞いていることに対して答えるのではなく、どうして最後にプロジェクターを使ったのが誰か知りたいのか、相手の質問の意図を尋ねる応答になっている。

21 M 🇺🇸 W 🇬🇧 　　　□□□　正解 B　▶TRACK_185

An error message appeared on my computer.

(A) The sales data is accurate.

(B) That happened to me, too.

(C) I'm sure you'd like that letter set.

私のコンピューターにエラーメッセージが出てきました。

(A) 売上データは正確です。

(B) 私のところにも起こりました。

(C) あなたはあのレターセットをきっと気に入ると思います。

問いかけ文ではコンピューターに発生した問題を報告しているのに対し、自身にも同様のことが起こったと反応している (B) が正解。代名詞の That は、「コンピューターにエラーメッセージが出てきた」という問いかけ文の内容全体を指している。

Are these sculpture workshops intended for beginners?

(A) Anyone can access the internet for free here.

(B) Please send me your work shift schedule.

(C) Most of the participants are experienced.

これらの彫刻教室は初心者向けですか。

(A) ここでは、誰でも無料でネットにアクセスできます。

(B) あなたの仕事のシフト表を私に送ってください。

(C) 参加者のほとんどが経験者です。

彫刻教室が初心者向けかどうか尋ねているのに対し、参加者のほとんどが経験者であることを伝えることで、初心者向けではないことを示唆している (C) が正解。

語彙チェック　□sculpture　彫刻　□be intended for 〜　〜に向けられている

> ⚠ **ここに注意！**
> 問いかけ文の beginner「初心者」という単語と、正答の experienced「経験を積んだ」という単語が対比関係になっていることを押さえておこう！

You studied business administration in college, didn't you?

(A) I prefer to work in a small company.

(B) It should help me do a good job here.

(C) How about going to some job fairs?

大学で企業経営を勉強したのですよね？

(A) 私は小さい会社で働く方がいいです。

(B) それをここで活かすことができるはずです。

(C) 就職説明会に行くのはいかがですか。

付加疑問文で、相手が大学で企業経営を勉強したということを確認している。これに対し、学んだことを仕事で活かすことができると思うと答えている (B) が正解。

語彙チェック　□administration　管理、経営　□job fair　就職説明会

> ⚠ **ここに注意！**
> 問いかけ文に business administration「企業経営」という難易度の高い語彙が含まれている。ビジネス関連の単語はぜひ押さえておこう！

24　M 🇺🇸　W 🇨🇦　☐☐☐　正解 C　▶TRACK_188

Could you please take notes for me at the management seminar?

(A) Yes, I will change the date.

(B) There's an opening for a manager.

(C) Do you have client meetings?

経営セミナーで私のためにメモを取っていただけませんか。

(A) はい、日付を変更しておきます。

(B) マネージャー職に空きがあります。

(C) 顧客との会議があるのですか。

依頼の表現Could you please 〜？で経営セミナーでメモを取ることを依頼しているのに対し、質問に直接答えるのではなく、「顧客との会議があるのか」と経営セミナーに出られない理由を尋ねている(C)が正解。

語彙チェック ☐take notes　メモを取る　☐opening　（職などの）空き

25　M 🇦🇺　M 🇺🇸　☐☐☐　正解 A　▶TRACK_189

Where are the new desks going to be placed?

(A) That purchase wasn't approved.

(B) Let's meet in the lobby.

(C) Mr. Dudley sent it by express delivery.

新しい机はどこに置かれる予定ですか。

(A) あの購入は認められませんでした。

(B) ロビーでお会いしましょう。

(C) Dudleyさんが速達で送ってくれました。

新しい机を置く予定の場所を尋ねているのに対し、「あの購入は認められなかった」と答えている(A)が正解。机を購入する予定だったが、それが承認されなかったため購入しないことになった、という状況。

語彙チェック ☐purchase　購入　☐approve　〜を承認する　☐express delivery　速達便

26　W 🇬🇧　M 🇦🇺　☐☐☐　正解 A　▶TRACK_190

What made it possible to catch up on the deadline?

(A) We hired more assistants.

(B) They will visit us in September.

(C) You must submit it in person.

どうやって締め切りの遅れを取り戻したのですか。

(A) より多くのアシスタントを雇いました。

(B) 彼らは9月に訪ねてくる予定です。

(C) それは直接提出しなければいけません。

「どうやって締め切りの遅れを取り戻したのか」を尋ねているのに対し、アシスタントの数を増やしたと、実行した解決策を述べている(A)が正解。

語彙チェック ☐catch up on 〜　〜の遅れを取り戻す　☐deadline　締め切り
☐in person　自分で、本人が

🐾 **ここに注意！**
問いかけ文は、直訳すると「何が締め切りの遅れを取り戻すことを可能にしたのか」という意味。What made 〜？で、方法を尋ねている！

Should we offer loyal customers discount coupons or new product samples?

(A) Its reasonable price is the main reason.

(B) Oh, I forgot to bring my coupon.

(C) We can also offer them free delivery.

常連客には割引クーポン券を提供するべきですか、それとも新しい試供品を提供するべきですか。

(A) その手頃な価格が主な理由です。

(B) ああ、クーポン券を持ってくるのを忘れました。

(C) 無料配送を提供することもできますね。

選択疑問文で「割引クーポン券と新しい試供品のどちらを常連客に提供するべきか」を尋ねている。「無料配送を提供することもできる」と答えることで、提示されている2つとはまた別の方法を提案している (C) が正解。

語彙チェック ☐loyal 義理堅い、忠実な ☐reasonable （値段が）あまり高くない

Was there anything left in the meeting room?

(A) The sales in the last quarter.

(B) Ms. Miles found someone's pen case.

(C) No, it's on the first floor.

会議室に何か忘れ物はありましたか。

(A) 第4四半期の売り上げです。

(B) Milesさんが誰かの筆箱を見つけました。

(C) いいえ、1階にあります。

問いかけ文では、「会議室に何か忘れ物があったか」と尋ねている。これに対し、「Milesさんが誰かの筆箱を見つけた」と答えることで、忘れ物があったという事実を伝えている (B) が正解。

語彙チェック ☐quarter 四半期

Why don't we hire a financial consultant?

(A) Because of the weather.

(B) I have an acquaintance to recommend.

(C) The personnel department manager.

財務コンサルタントを雇いませんか。

(A) 天候のせいです。

(B) お薦めしたい知人がいます。

(C) 人事部の部長です。

Why don't we ～? で財務コンサルタントを雇うことを提案しているのに対し、紹介したい人物がいることを伝えることで、間接的にコンサルタントを雇うことに賛成している (B) が正解。

語彙チェック ☐financial 財務の ☐consultant 顧問、コンサルタント
☐acquaintance 知り合い、知人

30 M 🇦🇺 W 🇨🇦 　☐☐☐　正解 **A**　▶TRACK_194

When will you be finished reading the booklet?

(A) I can give you a copy if you want.

(B) The room was booked online.

(C) Their work was completed yesterday.

その小冊子をいつ読み終わりますか。

(A) よろしければ1部お渡ししますよ。

(B) その部屋はオンラインで予約されました。

(C) 彼らの仕事は昨日完了しました。

「小冊子をいつ読み終わるか」と尋ねているのに対し、具体的な「時」を答えるのではなく、「よろしければ1部お渡しします」と申し出ている(A)が正解。相手の質問からうかがえる要望に対して、代案を提示していると考えられる。

語彙チェック ☐booklet 小冊子 ☐copy 部、冊 ☐book ～を予約する

31 W 🇬🇧 M 🇦🇺 　☐☐☐　正解 **C**　▶TRACK_195

Haven't we used this restaurant as an event venue before?

(A) It's too small for my office.

(B) There're not so many people here.

(C) That was a welcome party for Bella.

このレストランをイベント会場として以前使いませんでしたか。

(A) 私のオフィスには小さ過ぎます。

(B) ここにはそれほど多くの人はいません。

(C) それはBellaのための歓迎パーティーでした。

否定疑問文で、以前このレストランをイベント会場として使用したことがあるのではないかと尋ねている。これに対し、「それはBellaのための歓迎パーティーだった」と答えることで、以前も同じ会場を使用したことがあることを示唆している(C)が正解。

語彙チェック ☐venue 会場

> 🐾ここに注意！
>
> この問いかけ文はかなり速く読まれているので、聞き取れなかった人も多いのではないだろうか。このように突然速い問いかけ文が出題されることもあるので、音声が流れる前にしっかりと身構えておこう！

W 🇬🇧 M 🇦🇺   会話 ▶TRACK_197   問題 ▶TRACK_198

Questions 32 through 34 refer to the following conversation.

W: Hello, Jeff. Ms. Carter is retiring at the end of this month. We're getting some flowers for her farewell party. We're all putting in some money. Would you like to contribute?

M: I'd be happy to. When are we having the party?

W: It'll be on March 24. We'll go to a local restaurant after work. The company is covering the costs. We've chosen one of their banquet plans so the food should be suitable for everyone.

M: Sounds great. Oh, how much should I give for the flowers?

問題32-34は次の会話に関するものです。

女性：こんにちは、Jeff。Carterさんが今月末に退職するのです。彼女の送別会のために花を買う予定で、みんなでお金を出し合っています。あなたも協力しませんか。

男性：喜んで。いつ送別会をする予定ですか。

女性：3月24日です。仕事の後、地元のレストランに行く予定です。会社が費用を負担してくれます。宴会プランの中の1つを選んだので、食べ物は全員に合うはずです。

男性：いいですね。ああ、私は花代にいくら出せばいいですか。

語彙チェック　□farewell party　送別会　□put in ～　（分担金など）を払う
　　　　　　　　　□contribute　貢献する、寄付する　□banquet　宴会
　　　　　　　　　□suitable for ～　～にふさわしい、～に適切な

---

32   □□□ 正解 A

What does the woman say about Ms. Carter?	女性はCarterさんについて何と言っていますか。
(A) She will leave the company.	(A) 彼女は会社を辞める。
(B) She has broken a sales record.	(B) 彼女は売上記録を更新した。
(C) She did some volunteer work.	(C) 彼女はボランティア活動をした。
(D) She has been promoted.	(D) 彼女は昇進した。

女性は冒頭でCarterさんについて、Ms. Carter is retiring at the end of this month. と述べている。よって、(A)が正解。

語彙チェック　□break a record　記録を破る、更新する　□promote　～を昇進させる

33　　　□□□　正解 B

What does the man agree to do?	男性は何をすることに同意していますか。
(A) Change a date	(A) 日付を変更する
(B) Contribute some money	(B) お金を支払う
(C) Order some flowers	(C) 花を注文する
(D) Make a speech	(D) スピーチをする

女性は「Carter さんに花を贈るために、みんなでお金を出し合っている」と説明し、Would you like to contribute? と男性に尋ねている。これに対し、男性は I'd be happy to. 「喜んで」と答えている。すなわち、男性は「花代としてお金を出すこと」に同意していると判断できるので、正解は (B)。

> 🐾 ここに注意！
>
> (C) の選択肢は、会話の内容にかなり絡んでいるので正解に思ってしまいやすい。「花を買う」こと自体は決まっている程で話しているので、男性がここで同意している内容としては (C) は間違い！

34　　　□□□　正解 C

What does the woman say about the party?	女性はパーティーについて何と言っていますか。
(A) It has been postponed.	(A) それは延期された。
(B) An employee will perform a song.	(B) ある従業員が歌を披露する。
(C) The company will pay the bill.	(C) 会社が代金を支払う。
(D) It will be held at a hotel.	(D) それはホテルで開催される。

女性は送別会の詳細を説明する中で、The company is covering the costs. と述べている。よって、(C) が正解。

語彙チェック　□ perform （歌）を歌う

Questions 35 through 37 refer to the following conversation.

M: Hi. My name's Greg Trembley. I'm a reporter for the Hamburg Times. I understand that the Orley Gallery will host an exhibition by Tina Yates this week.

W: That's correct. The exhibition will take place over three days starting on Friday evening. Are you interested in purchasing tickets?

M: Not exactly. I'd like to interview Ms. Yates for an article we're writing about her. I was hoping that you could arrange a meeting.

W: You should speak to her publicist about that. I could certainly give you the phone number of her publicist, but I can't speak with Ms. Yates on your behalf.

問題35-37は次の会話に関するものです。

男性：こんにちは。Greg Trembleyと申します。Hamburg Timesの記者です。今週、OrleyギャラリーがTina Yatesの展示会を開催すると伺っています。

女性：その通りです。展示会は金曜日の夜から3日間開催されます。チケットを購入されますか。

男性：そういうわけではありません。私たちが彼女について執筆している記事のために、Yatesさんにインタビューしたいと思っています。こちらで面会を手配していただけないかと思いまして。

女性：それについては彼女の広報係に話をしてください。彼女の広報係の電話番号をお渡しすることはできますが、あなたの代わりにYatesさんにお話しすることはできかねます。

語彙チェック　□take place　開催される　□interview　〜にインタビューする
　　　　　　　　□publicist　広報係　□on *one's* behalf　〜に代わって、〜の代理として

35　　　　　　□□□　正解 C

What is the purpose of the phone call? 電話の目的は何ですか。

(A) To inquire about some furnishings (A) 備品について尋ねること

(B) To suggest a venue (B) 会場を提案すること

(C) To schedule an interview (C) インタビューの予定を立てること

(D) To introduce an artist (D) アーティストを紹介すること

男性は冒頭で、自分は記者だと名乗り、その後I'd like to interview Ms. Yatesと伝えI was hoping that you could arrange a meeting.と依頼している。つまり、男性が電話をかけた理由は、インタビューをするためにYatesさんと面会できるよう手配してもらうためだと判断できる。よって、(C)が正解。

語彙チェック　□inquire about 〜　〜について尋ねる　□furnishings　（家・部屋の）備品
　　　　　　　　□venue　会場

36 □□□ 正解 C

How long is the exhibition?

(A) Two weeks

(B) One week

(C) Three days

(D) One day

展示会はどのくらいの期間ですか。

(A) 2週間

(B) 1週間

(C) 3日間

(D) 1日間

男性に展示会について尋ねられると、女性は The exhibition will take place over three days starting on Friday evening. と答えている。この発言から、展示会は3日間にわたり開催されると分かるので、(C) が正解。

37 □□□ 正解 D

What does the woman offer to do?

(A) Send some free tickets

(B) Sell some artwork

(C) Take a photograph

(D) Provide contact details

女性は何をすることを申し出ていますか。

(A) 無料チケットを送る

(B) 芸術作品を売る

(C) 写真を撮る

(D) 連絡先を提供する

男性が「Yates さんとの面会の手配をしてほしい」と依頼すると、女性は「彼女の広報係に話をしてください」と伝え、I could certainly give you the phone number of her publicist と言っている。電話番号を渡すことを「連絡先を提供する」と言い換えた (D) が正解。

語彙チェック □artwork 芸術作品

M 🇺🇸　W 🇬🇧　　　　　　　　　会話 ▶TRACK_201　問題 ▶TRACK_202

Questions 38 through 40 refer to the following conversation.

M: Hi, Wendy. I have a bit of a problem I'm afraid. Some of the flowers got damaged in the back of the delivery van. I need you to remake a couple of arrangements.

W: I see. Can you give me the order numbers so I know what kind of flower arrangements I should prepare?

M: I'll send you a text message with the details. We need to get them delivered by three o'clock this afternoon.

W: That might be a bit difficult. I'll phone the customer and see if they can give us a little more time.

問題38-40は次の会話に関するものです。

男性：こんにちは、Wendy。申し訳ないのですが、少し問題がありまして。配達トラックの後ろに載せてある花がいくつか駄目になってしまいました。あなたに2,3個アレンジメントを作り直してもらう必要があります。

女性：分かりました。どの種類のフラワーアレンジメントを用意すればいいか分かるように、注文番号をもらえますか。

男性：詳細をテキストメッセージで送りますね。今日の午後3時までにそれらを配達された状態にしないといけません。

女性：それは少し難しいかもしれません。お客さまに電話をして、もう少し時間を頂けないか確認してみます。

語彙チェック　□van　トラック　□need *A* to *do*　Aに～してもらう必要がある
　　　　　　　□remake　～を作り直す　□get *A B*　AをBの状態にする
　　　　　　　□phone　～に電話をかける

38　　　　　　　□□□　正解 B

Who most likely is the woman?
(A) An event planner
(B) A florist
(C) A mechanic
(D) A hotel manager

女性は誰だと考えられますか。
(A) イベントプランナー
(B) 花屋
(C) 機械工
(D) ホテル経営者

男性は「花がいくつか駄目になってしまった」と言い、I need you to remake a couple of arrangements. と女性に依頼している。それに対し、女性は Can you give me the order numbers so I know what kind of flower arrangements I should prepare? と尋ねている。これらから、女性はフラワーアレンジメントを作り直すと考えられるので、女性の職業は花屋だと判断できる。よって、正解は (B)。

39

□□□ 正解 **D**

What does the man say has happened?

(A) Some parcels were mislabeled.

(B) A delivery arrived late.

(C) A meeting has been rescheduled.

(D) Some goods have been damaged.

男性は何が起こったと言っていますか。

(A) 小包のラベルが間違って貼られていた。

(B) 配達の到着が遅れた。

(C) 会議の予定が変更された。

(D) いくつかの商品が破損した。

男性は冒頭でI have a bit of a problem と話し始め、Some of the flowers got damaged in the back of the delivery van. と述べている。商品である花がいくつか駄目になってしまったことを伝えているので、(D)が正解。

語彙チェック □parcel 小包 □mislabel ～にラベルを貼り違える
□reschedule ～の予定を変更する

> **⚠ ここに注意！**
>
> この問題の正答根拠は、1つ前の38.の正答根拠となる部分と入り混じって登場している。このように根拠の箇所が重なっていたりすることがあるので、聞き取るべき情報を先読みの際に整理しておこう！

40

□□□ 正解 **D**

What does the woman say she will do?

(A) Offer a discount

(B) Load a vehicle

(C) Speak with a colleague

(D) Call a customer

女性は何をするつもりだと言っていますか。

(A) 割引する

(B) 車に荷物を積む

(C) 同僚と話をする

(D) お客さんに電話をする

「午後3時までに花を配達しなければいけない」と言う男性に対し、女性は「それは少し難しいかもしれない」と答え、I'll phone the customer and see if they can give us a little more time. と言っている。よって、正解は(D)。

語彙チェック □load ～に荷を積む

M 🇺🇸   W1 🇬🇧   W2 🇨🇦   会話 ▶TRACK_203   問題 ▶TRACK_204

Questions 41 through 43 refer to the following conversation with three speakers.

M: We need to find a time when you're both free this week.
W1: What for?
M: We need to interview the applicants for the receptionist position and choose someone by Friday.
W2: But, Jack, that's so soon!
W1: Yeah, it's really short notice.
M: I'm sure we can manage. I'll invite the candidates to come in on Wednesday. How's your schedule for Wednesday?
W2: Um... let me see. I have a meeting with the landscaping company. It'll take most of the morning.
M: Can you reschedule that for Friday? I don't think that work is urgent.
W1: I'm free on Wednesday.

問題41-43は3人の話し手による次の会話に関するものです。

男性　：今週あなたたちが両方とも手の空いている時間を見つけなければいけません。
女性1：何のためにですか？
男性　：受付係の仕事の応募者の面接をして、金曜日までに誰か選ばなければいけないのです。
女性2：でも、Jack、それは早過ぎますよ！
女性1：ええ、とても急な話ですね。
男性　：私たちなら何とかできますよ。志願者には水曜日に来るようにお願いするつもりです。あなたたちの水曜日の予定はどうですか。
女性2：ええと…そうですね。私は造園会社との打ち合わせがあります。午前中ほとんどかかります。
男性　：それを金曜日に予定変更してくれませんか。その仕事は緊急ではないと思います。
女性1：私は水曜日は時間がありますよ。

語彙チェック　□receptionist　受付係　□short notice　急な話
　　　　　　　　□manage　どうにか成し遂げる　□landscaping　造園
　　　　　　　　□reschedule　～の予定を変更する　□urgent　緊急の

41　　　　　　　　　　　□□□　正解 C

What does the man say they should do?　　男性は彼らが何をすべきだと言っていますか。
(A) Provide feedback on a presentation　　(A) プレゼンテーションのフィードバックをする
(B) Discuss a sales report　　　　　　　　(B) 販売報告書について話し合う
(C) Choose a candidate　　　　　　　　　(C) 候補者を選ぶ
(D) Revise a travel schedule　　　　　　　(D) 旅行の予定を修正する

「今週あなたたちが手が空いている時間を見つけなければいけない」と言う男性に、1人目の女性が What for? とその目的を尋ねている。それに対し、男性は We need to interview the applicants for the receptionist position and choose someone by Friday. と説明している。よって、正解は (C)。

語彙チェック　□feedback　フィードバック　□revise　～を修正する

42　　　　正解 B

Why are the women concerned?　　女性たちはなぜ心配していますか。

(A) There are too few candidates.　　(A) 志願者が少な過ぎる。

(B) They do not have enough time.　　(B) 彼らには十分な時間がない。

(C) There are not any rooms available.　　(C) 利用できる部屋がない。

(D) They have already spent their budget.　　(D) 彼らは予算をすでに使ってしまった。

「受付係の仕事の応募者の面接をして、金曜日までに誰か選ばなければいけない」と言う男性に対し、女性たちは But, Jack, that's so soon! や Yeah, it's really short notice. と反応している。これらの発言から、女性たちは時間がないことを心配していることが分かるので、正解は (B)。

43　　　　正解 A

What does the man mean when he says, "I'm sure we can manage"?　　男性は "I'm sure we can manage" という発言で、何を意味していますか。

(A) He thinks they can find a solution.　　(A) 彼は解決策を見つけられると思っている。

(B) He does not want to hire a new manager.　　(B) 彼は新しいマネージャーを雇いたくない。

(C) He will start a new business.　　(C) 彼は新しい事業を始める。

(D) He does not need assistance.　　(D) 彼は支援を必要としていない。

下線部の発言は、女性たちの「それは急過ぎる」という反応を受けたものである。この発言後、How's your schedule for Wednesday? と女性たちのスケジュールを確認したり、Can you reschedule that for Friday? とスケジュールの変更を依頼したりしていることから、男性が何とかこの問題を解決しようとしている様子がうかがえる。つまり、男性は解決策を見つけられると考えており、下線部の発言をしていると言える。よって、正解は (A)。

> 🐾 ここに注意！
> こういった「発言の意図を問う問題」は、多くの人が苦手意識を持っている問題。ここでは特に、42.の正答根拠のすぐ後の発言が取り上げられているため、聞き逃してしまいやすくなっている！

Questions 44 through 46 refer to the following conversation.

W: This is Margaret Timms from Structure magazine. I'm calling to speak with the head architect on the Manhattan Regency project.

M: Good morning Ms. Timms. That would be Kate Crenshaw. She led the team that designed that building. I'm afraid I can't put you through to her at the moment. She's out of the office this morning.

W: Would you mind asking her to call me back when she has time? She's been nominated for an award, and I need to speak with her about whether or not she'll attend the ceremony.

問題44-46は次の会話に関するものです。

女性：こちらはStructure誌のMargaret Timmsです。Manhattan Regencyプロジェクトの代表建築家とお話ししたくお電話を差し上げております。

男性：おはようございます、Timmsさん。それはKate Crenshawだと思われます。彼女がその建物を設計したチームをまとめていました。申し訳ございませんが、ただ今彼女におつなぎすることができません。彼女は午前中、外出しております。

女性：時間があるときに電話をかけ直すよう、彼女にお願いしていただけませんか。彼女は賞にノミネートされていて、式典に出席するかどうかについて彼女と話をしなければいけないのです。

語彙チェック □put A through to B　BにAの電話をつなぐ　□at the moment　ちょうど今
□nominate A for B　AをBに推薦する

44　　　　　　　　　　□□□　正解 **A**

What type of business does the man work for?

(A) An architecture firm
(B) A financial institution
(C) A clothing manufacturer
(D) A travel agency

男性はどのような企業で働いていますか。

(A) 建築事務所
(B) 金融機関
(C) 衣料メーカー
(D) 旅行代理店

女性は冒頭で、「Manhattan Regencyプロジェクトの代表建築家と話がしたいため電話をかけている」と述べている。それに対し男性はThat would be Kate Crenshaw.と答え、She led the team that designed that building.と説明している。これらから、男性は建築関係の会社で働いていると考えられる。よって、正解は(A)。

45

□□□　正解 **A**

What does the man say about Ms. Crenshaw?	男性はCrenshawさんについて何と言っていますか。
(A) She is unavailable.	(A) 彼女は手が空いていない。
(B) She has a new phone number.	(B) 彼女は新しい電話番号を持っている。
(C) She will give a speech.	(C) 彼女はスピーチをする予定である。
(D) She is dependable.	(D) 彼女は頼りになる。

女性が話をしたいと言っている人物について、男性は「それは Kate Crenshaw だと思われる」と答えているが、その後 I'm afraid I can't put you through to her at the moment. と伝え、その理由を She's out of the office this morning. と説明している。すなわち、Crenshaw さんは外出中で手が空いておらず、話ができないということなので、正解は (A)。

語彙チェック □unavailable　手が空いていない　□dependable　頼りになる、信頼できる

46

□□□　正解 **D**

What does the woman want to discuss?	女性は何について話し合いたいと思っていますか。
(A) The design of an award	(A) 賞のデザイン
(B) A magazine subscription	(B) 雑誌の購読
(C) The cost of a construction project	(C) 建設プロジェクトの費用
(D) An invitation to an event	(D) イベントへの招待

女性は男性に「Crenshaw さんに電話をかけ直すようお願いしてもらえないか」と言っており、その理由を She's been nominated for an award, and I need to speak with her about whether or not she'll attend the ceremony. と説明している。つまり女性は、式典への招待を受けるかどうかについて Crenshaw さんと話し合いたいと思っていることが分かるので、正解は (D)。

語彙チェック □subscription　購読

M 🇺🇸　W 🇬🇧 会話 ▶TRACK_207　問題 ▶TRACK_208

Questions 47 through 49 refer to the following conversation.

M: We have a large group coming to the restaurant today. The reservation is for twenty five people, so I expect we'll be extremely busy. <u>At about eleven thirty, we'll also have a visit from a town inspector.</u> I'll be showing her around for about twenty minutes.

W: <u>That might be a problem. Unfortunately, Tim Cleminson just called in sick.</u> I was hoping you could help out in the kitchen today.

M: I see. <u>I'll give the town a call and ask if they can reschedule the inspection.</u> I'm not sure if they can do that, though. Is there anyone who could come in on short notice?

W: I'll check with the evening staff.

問題47-49は次の会話に関するものです。

男性：今日は大きな団体がレストランにいらっしゃいます。予約は25名ですので、極めて忙しくなると思います。11時30分ごろには、町の視察官の訪問もあります。私が約20分間彼女を案内して回る予定です。

女性：それは問題かもしれません。あいにく、Tim Cleminson からちょうど病欠すると連絡がありました。今日はあなたに調理場を手伝ってもらいたかったのですが。

男性：そうですか。町に電話をして、視察の予定を変更してもらえないか聞いてみます。彼らがそれをできるかは分かりませんが。急なお願いでも来てくれそうな人はいませんか。

女性：夜シフトのスタッフに確認してみます。

語彙チェック　□extremely　極めて　□inspector　視察官
□show ~ around　~を案内して回る　□call in sick　病欠の電話をする
□help out　手伝う　□reschedule　~の予定を変更する　□inspection　視察
□on short notice　急な通知で

47　　　□□□　正解 D

What does the man say will happen today?

(A) Some food will be delivered.
(B) An athletic event will be held.
(C) He will make a presentation.
(D) An inspection will take place.

男性は今日何が起こると言っていますか。

(A) 食べ物が配達される。
(B) スポーツイベントが開催される。
(C) 彼はプレゼンテーションをする。
(D) 視察が行われる。

今日の予定について、男性は冒頭で25名の団体客が来ると説明した後、At about eleven thirty, we'll also have a visit from a town inspector. と続けている。よって、今日は外部から視察が入る予定であると分かるので、正解は(D)。

語彙チェック　□athletic　運動の　□take place　行われる

156

48 ☐☐☐ 正解 C

What problem does the woman mention?	女性はどんな問題について述べていますか。
(A) There is a shortage of ingredients.	(A) 材料が不足している。
(B) Some reservations were canceled.	(B) 予約がキャンセルされた。
(C) An employee is absent.	(C) ある従業員が欠勤する。
(D) Some equipment is malfunctioning.	(D) 機器が故障している。

「視察官を案内して回る予定だ」と言う男性に対し、女性はThat might be a problem. と発言し、Unfortunately, Tim Cleminson just called in sick. と説明している。病欠の電話を入れてきたということは、Tim Cleminsonはレストランの従業員であることが分かるので、正解は(C)。

語彙チェック ☐shortage 不足　☐ingredient 材料　☐absent 欠勤の
☐malfunction 正常に作動しない

49 ☐☐☐ 正解 A

What does the man say he will do?	男性は何をすると言っていますか。
(A) Call a town office	(A) 町役場に電話する
(B) Attend a banquet	(B) 宴会に出席する
(C) Speak with an athlete	(C) アスリートと話す
(D) Take part in a tour	(D) ツアーに参加する

欠勤のスタッフが出たので、女性は男性に調理場を手伝ってほしいと思っていたことを伝えている。それに対し、男性はI'll give the town a call and ask if they can reschedule the inspection. と申し出ている。このgive the town a callを言い換えている(A)が正解。

語彙チェック ☐banquet 宴会　☐athlete 運動選手、アスリート
☐take part in 〜　〜に参加する

Questions 50 through 52 refer to the following conversation.

W: The envelopes that I'm handing out now have everything you need for this new employee orientation session. Please check the list I've written on the whiteboard to make sure you have everything.

M: Excuse me. It looks like mine is missing a copy of the employee handbook.

W: Oh, I'm sorry. I'll have someone bring you one in a minute. I'm going to talk about the company policies this afternoon, so we don't need it now.

M: I see. Thanks. Oh... I'm missing the schedule, too.

問題50-52は次の会話に関するものです。

女性：私が今お配りしている封筒の中に、今回の新入社員説明会で必要な物が全て入っています。全てそろっているか、ホワイトボードに書いたリストを確認してください。

男性：すみません。私のものには従業員ハンドブックの冊子が入っていないようです。

女性：ああ、失礼いたしました。誰かにすぐに持ってくるようお願いしますね。今日の午後は企業方針についてお話しする予定ですので、今はそれは必要ありません。

男性：そうですか。ありがとうございます。ああ…予定表も入っていません。

語彙チェック　□envelope　封筒　□hand out 〜　〜を配る
　　　　　　　　□orientation session　説明会、オリエンテーション

50　　　　　　　　　　　□□□　正解 A

What kind of event are the speakers attending?

(A) An employee orientation
(B) A shareholders' meeting
(C) A product launch
(D) A business conference

話し手たちはどのようなイベントに出席していますか。

(A) 従業員説明会
(B) 株主総会
(C) 製品発売
(D) 営業会議

冒頭の女性の The envelopes that I'm handing out now have everything you need for this new employee orientation session. という発言から、話し手たちは新入社員説明会に参加していると判断できる。よって、(A)が正解。

語彙チェック　□shareholder　株主　□launch　売り出し

51 □□□ 正解 B

Why does the man address the woman?
(A) He plans to leave early.
(B) He has not been given a document.
(C) He does not have anywhere to sit.
(D) He would like to ask a question.

男性はなぜ女性に話しかけていますか。
(A) 彼は途中退席する予定である。
(B) 彼は書類をもらっていない。
(C) 彼は座るところがない。
(D) 彼は質問をしたいと思っている。

封筒の中身が全てそろっているか確認するよう女性が伝えると、男性は Excuse me. と女性に話しかけ、It looks like mine is missing a copy of the employee handbook. と申し出ている。この発言から男性は従業員ハンドブックをもらっていないということが分かるので、正解は (B)。

語彙チェック □address 〜に話しかける

> 🖐 **ここに注意！**
> この設問文で使われている address は「〜に話しかける」という意味。リスニングの設問文はシンプルなものが多いが、こういった少し珍しい表現のものも出てくるので、先読みの際にしっかりと意味を理解して準備しておこう！

52 □□□ 正解 C

What will the woman talk about this afternoon?
(A) Timeline of an event
(B) New features of an item
(C) Some company policies
(D) Some membership benefits

女性は今日の午後、何について話しますか。
(A) イベントのスケジュール
(B) 商品の新しい特徴
(C) 企業方針
(D) 会員特典

「従業員ハンドブックの冊子が入っていない」と申し出た男性に対し、女性は I'm going to talk about the company policies this afternoon, so we don't need it now. と説明している。よって、女性は午後に企業方針について話をすると分かるので、(C) が正解。

語彙チェック □timeline スケジュール、予定

W 🇬🇧　M 🇺🇸　　　　　　　　　　会話 ▶TRACK_211　問題 ▶TRACK_212

Questions 53 through 55 refer to the following conversation.

W: Hi. I'm looking for a sofa that I noticed in the catalog. I can't see it among the items on display here.

M: A lot of the furniture has sold out, unfortunately. I have a copy of the catalog here. Which sofa were you interested in?

W: This one, with the high back. Do you have any in stock?

M: We do. They are still in the box, though. Would you like us to assemble one for you?

W: It's fine as it is. I only have a small van. I don't think there would be enough room if it were fully assembled.

M: I see. I'll have one of the stockroom people load it for you.

問題53-55は次の会話に関するものです。

女性：こんにちは。カタログで見つけたソファを探しています。こちらで展示されている商品の中には見当たりません。

男性：あいにく多くの家具が売り切れております。カタログが1部こちらにございます。どのソファをお求めでしたか。

女性：これです、高い背もたれが付いているものです。在庫はありますか。

男性：ございますよ。でもまだ箱に入ったままです。組み立てましょうか。

女性：そのままでいいですよ。小型トラックしかないのです。完全に組み立てられていると、十分なスペースがないと思います。

男性：分かりました。倉庫係の1人に、それを積んでもらうようにいたしますね。

語彙チェック　□on display　展示されて　□back　背もたれ　□assemble　〜を組み立てる　□van　ワゴン車、トラック　□fully　完全に　□stockroom　倉庫　□load　〜を積む

53　　　□□□　正解 D

Why does the woman speak to the man?　女性はなぜ男性に話しかけていますか。

(A) She wants to see a catalog.　(A) 彼女はカタログが見たいと思っている。

(B) She would like to exchange an item.　(B) 彼女は商品を交換したいと思っている。

(C) She needs an instruction manual.　(C) 彼女は取扱説明書が必要である。

(D) She cannot find a product.　(D) 彼女は商品を見つけられない。

女性は I'm looking for a sofa that I noticed in the catalog. と男性に話しかけ、その後 I can't see it among the items on display here. と伝えている。ここから、女性は「探しているソファがあるが、それを見つけられない」と言っていることが分かる。よって、正解は (D)。

語彙チェック　□instruction manual　取扱説明書

160

54 ☐☐☐ 正解 D

Why does the woman say, "<u>I only have a small van</u>"?	女性はなぜ "<u>I only have a small van</u>" と言っていますか。
(A) To request an alternative	(A) 代案を要求するため
(B) To make a suggestion	(B) 提案するため
(C) To explain an expense	(C) 費用について説明するため
(D) To turn down an offer	(D) 申し出を断るため

「ソファは箱の中に入ったままだから、それを組み立てましょうか」という男性の申し出に対し、女性は「そのままでいい」と答え、理由を I only have a small van. と説明している。さらに女性は、続けて I don't think there would be enough room if it were fully assembled. と説明を加えている。これらから、この発言で女性は、「ソファを組み立てましょうか」という男性の申し出を断っていると判断できる。よって、正解は (D)。

語彙チェック □turn down 〜　〜を断る

55 ☐☐☐ 正解 A

Who will the man ask for assistance?	男性は誰に助けを求めますか。
(A) A warehouse worker	(A) 倉庫係
(B) A sales assistant	(B) 販売員
(C) A mechanic	(C) 修理工
(D) A store manager	(D) 店長

女性がソファを組み立てずにそのまま持って帰ることを伝えると、男性は I'll have one of the stockroom people load it for you. と伝えている。「荷積みを倉庫係の1人にお願いする」ということだが、この one of the stockroom people を言い換えている (A) が正解。

語彙チェック □warehouse　倉庫

Questions 56 through 58 refer to the following conversation with three speakers.

M1: We're from Dalton Logistics. We have an appointment to speak with Ms. Wu. She's relocating her office to another building.

M2: We're here to provide a price estimate for the move.

W: I'm Rebecca Wu. I wasn't expecting you just yet. Would you mind waiting a couple of minutes while I prepare? I'll have someone bring you something to drink. Would you like tea or coffee?

M1: That's not necessary.

M2: We stopped for a coffee on the way here. Please take your time.

W: OK. Well, please have a seat in our conference room over here. I'll be back in a moment.

問題56-58は3人の話し手による次の会話に関するものです。

男性１：Dalton Logistics 社から参りました。Wu さんとお話をする約束をしております。彼女はオフィスを他の建物に移転させる予定です。

男性２：引っ越しの見積書をお渡しに伺いました。

女性　：私が Rebecca Wu です。まだあなた方がいらっしゃるとは、とても予想していませんでした。準備する間、2、3分お待ちいただけますか。誰かに飲み物を持ってきてもらいますね。紅茶かコーヒーはいかがですか。

男性１：その必要はありませんよ。

男性２：ここへ来る途中にコーヒーを飲んできたのです。ゆっくりで構いませんよ。

女性　：そうですか。では、こちらの会議室でかけてお待ちください。すぐに戻ります。

語彙チェック　□relocate　〜を移転させる　□price estimate　見積書
　　　　　　　　□just yet　今のところはまだ　□stop for 〜　〜を求めて立ち寄る
　　　　　　　　□on the way　途中で　□take *one's* time　ゆっくりやる
　　　　　　　　□have a seat　着席する　□in a moment　すぐに

56　　　　　　　　　　　□□□　正解 B

Where do the men most likely work?　　男性たちはどこで働いていると考えられますか。

(A) At a catering company　　　　　　　(A) ケータリング会社

(B) At a moving company　　　　　　　(B) 引っ越し業者

(C) At a construction firm　　　　　　　(C) 建設会社

(D) At an accounting firm　　　　　　　(D) 会計事務所

冒頭で1人目の男性が、「Wu さんと話をする約束がある」と述べ、Wu さんについて She's relocating her office to another building. と言っている。その後、2人目の男性が We're here to provide a price estimate for the move. と、今回の訪問の目的を説明している。Wu さんのオフィス移転の件について、引っ越しの見積書を持ってきたということから、男性たちは引っ越し業者で働いていると考えられる。よって、正解は (B)。

57

☐☐☐ 正解 D

What does the woman offer the men?

(A) An invitation
(B) A contract
(C) A ride
(D) A beverage

女性は男性たちに何を申し出ていますか。

(A) 招待状
(B) 契約
(C) 送迎
(D) 飲み物

女性は男性たちの訪問に対し、「準備する間、2、3分お待ちいただけますか」と伝えた後、I'll have someone bring you something to drink. と申し出て、Would you like tea or coffee? と男性たちに尋ねている。よって、(D) が正解。

58

☐☐☐ 正解 D

Where does the woman direct the men?

(A) To a loading bay
(B) To a dining room
(C) To a waiting room
(D) To a meeting room

女性は男性たちをどこへ案内していますか。

(A) 搬入口
(B) ダイニングルーム
(C) 待合室
(D) 会議室

女性は男性たちに「準備する間、2、3分お待ちいただけますか」とお願いし、その後、Well, please have a seat in our conference room over here. と会議室に案内している。よって、(D) が正解。

Questions 59 through 61 refer to the following conversation.

M: Hi. I'd like to bring a group of tourists to see the caves on Tuesday next week. Do you have any guides that could give us a tour?

W: We don't have any on staff, but we can put you in touch with some professional tour guides who regularly lead groups through the caves.

M: That'd be great. If possible, we'd like someone who can speak German. Of course, English is fine if there aren't any German speakers.

W: I don't know anything about their language abilities. If you give me your phone number, I'll have one of them call you back. You can negotiate with them directly.

問題59-61は次の会話に関するものです。

男性：こんにちは。来週の火曜日に、洞窟を見に団体観光客を連れていきたいと思っています。ツアーをしてくれるガイドはいませんか。

女性：そのようなスタッフはおりませんが、定期的に団体を洞窟へ案内しているプロのツアーガイドにあなたを紹介することはできますよ。

男性：それはありがたいです。もしできたら、ドイツ語を話せる人をお願いしたいと思います。もちろん、ドイツ語を話す人がいなければ、英語でも構いません。

女性：彼らの言語能力については分かりかねます。あなたの電話番号を頂ければ、彼らの1人に電話をかけ直してもらいます。直接彼らと交渉していただけますよ。

語彙チェック　□cave　洞窟　□put *A* in touch with *B*　AにBと接触させる
　　　　　　　　　□negotiate with ～　～と交渉する

59　　　　　　　□□□　正解 **C**

What does the man ask about?　　　男性は何について尋ねていますか。

(A) Admission fees　　　　　　　　(A) 入場料金

(B) Dress recommendations　　　　(B) お勧めの服装

(C) Guided tours　　　　　　　　　(C) ガイド付きのツアー

(D) Accommodation availability　　(D) 宿泊施設の空室状況

男性は「団体観光客を洞窟へ連れていきたいと思っている」と伝え、Do you have any guides that could give us a tour?「ツアーをしてくれるガイドはいないか」と尋ねている。つまり、男性はガイド付きのツアーを考えており、そのためのガイドがいないかを女性に尋ねていると分かる。よって、正解は (C)。

60　　　　　　　　　　　正解 B

What does the woman offer to do?

(A) Reserve a room
(B) Provide an introduction
(C) Check a timetable
(D) Recommend a restaurant

女性は何をすることを申し出ていますか。

(A) 部屋の予約をする
(B) 紹介をする
(C) 予定表を確認する
(D) レストランを勧める

「ツアーをしてくれるガイドはいないか」という質問に対し、女性は「そのようなスタッフはいない」と答えているが、we can put you in touch with some professional tour guidesと申し出ている。よって、正解は(B)。

語彙チェック　□timetable　時刻表、予定表

61　　　　　　　　　　　正解 C

What does the woman say she is unsure of?

(A) Operating hours
(B) A maintenance schedule
(C) Language skills
(D) Weather conditions

女性は何について確信がないと言っていますか。

(A) 営業時間
(B) メンテナンスの予定
(C) 語学力
(D) 天候

紹介してもらうプロのツアーガイドについて、男性はIf possible, we'd like someone who can speak German. と希望を伝えている。これに対し、女性はI don't know anything about their language abilities. と答えている。このlanguage abilitiesを言い換えている(C)が正解。

語彙チェック　□be unsure of 〜　〜に確信がない

W 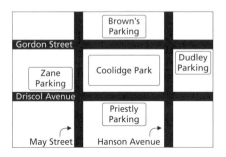 M 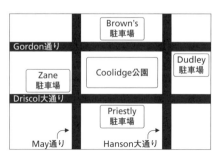　　　　　　　　　　会話 ▶TRACK_217　　問題 ▶TRACK_218

Questions 62 through 64 refer to the following conversation and map.

W: I've been looking forward to the convention all month. I hope some of the people we met last year show up.

M: I saw Jim Robeson a few minutes ago. Let's invite him to have lunch with us later.

W: Good idea. Oh, my phone's almost out of power. I think I left my phone charger in the van. Where did you end up parking it?

M: I don't remember the name of the parking lot. It was on the corner of Gordon Street and Hanson Avenue. I'll go with you.

W: We'd better go now. I don't want to miss anything.

問題62-64は次の会話と地図に関するものです。

女性：1カ月ずっと総会を楽しみにしていました。昨年会った人たちが来るといいですね。

男性：数分前にJim Robesonに会いましたよ。後で彼をランチに誘いましょう。

女性：いい考えですね。ああ、私の電話は充電が切れかかっています。電話の充電器をワゴン車に置いてきてしまったと思います。結局どこに駐車しましたか。

男性：駐車場の名前は覚えていません。Gordon通りとHanson大通りの角でした。一緒に行きますよ。

女性：今すぐ行った方がいいですね。私は何も聞き逃したくないので。

語彙チェック 　□look forward to 〜　〜を楽しみにする　□convention　総会
　　　　　　　　　□show up　現れる、来る　□out of power　充電が切れて
　　　　　　　　　□phone charger　電話の充電器　□van　ワゴン車、トラック
　　　　　　　　　□end up *doing*　結局［最後には］〜する　□parking lot　駐車場

62 □□□ 正解 A

Who most likely are the speakers?	話し手たちは誰だと考えられますか。
(A) Conference attendees	(A) 会議の出席者
(B) Restaurant patrons	(B) レストランの常連客
(C) Film critics	(C) 映画評論家
(D) Financial experts	(D) 金融専門家

冒頭で I've been looking forward to the convention all month. と述べていることから、女性は総会に参加すると判断できる。また、その後の I hope some of the people we met last year show up. という発言から、男性も昨年総会に参加し、今回も同行していると推測できる。これらから、2人は総会の出席者だと考えられる。よって、(A) が正解。

63 □□□ 正解 C

What does the woman say she has done?	女性は何をしたと言っていますか。
(A) Purchased some tickets	(A) チケットを購入した
(B) Invited a colleague to an event	(B) 同僚をイベントに誘った
(C) Left one of her belongings behind	(C) 彼女の持ち物の1つを置き忘れてきた
(D) Sent some product samples	(D) 商品サンプルを送った

女性は「電話の充電が切れかかっている」と言った後、I think I left my phone charger in the van. と述べている。よって、これを言い換えている (C) が正解。

語彙チェック □leave ～ behind ～を置き忘れる

64 □□□ 正解 D

Look at the graphic. Where will the speakers probably go next?	図を見てください。話し手たちは次にどこへ行くと考えられますか。
(A) To Zane Parking	(A) Zane 駐車場
(B) To Brown's Parking	(B) Brown's 駐車場
(C) To Priestly Parking	(C) Priestly 駐車場
(D) To Dudley Parking	(D) Dudley 駐車場

女性は電話の充電器を取りに行くために、男性に車を駐車した場所を尋ねている。男性は「駐車場の名前は覚えていない」と言いながらも、駐車場の場所を It was on the corner of Gordon Street and Hanson Avenue. と説明している。地図を見ると、Gordon 通りと Hanson 大通りの角にある駐車場は Dudley 駐車場。その後、男性は I'll go with you. と言っているので、話し手たちはこの後 Dudley 駐車場に向かうと分かる。よって、正解は (D)。

Questions 65 through 67 refer to the following conversation and report.

W: Hi Frank. I'm glad you're here to start work. I've been really busy at reception all night.

M: It's rare for people to be checking in that late. Were there any problems?

W: Well... Here's the nightly incident report. Just a couple of things. I had to move this guest because there was too much noise coming from one of the neighboring rooms. And, I offered this customer a discount when they complained about the size of the room. And, one of the air-conditioners was broken, but we were able to fix the problem from here, so that wasn't a big problem.

M: I see. I'll say sorry for the problems when I check them out. See you tomorrow, Tina.

問題65-67は次の会話と報告書に関するものです。

女性：こんにちは Frank。あなたが仕事を始めに来てくれてうれしいです。私は一晩中ずっと受付で本当に忙しかったのです。

男性：こんなに遅い時間に人々がチェックインしているのは珍しいですね。何か問題はありましたか。

女性：ええと…　これが夜の事故報告書です。2、3個だけですね。近隣の客室の1つからの騒音がひどかったので、こちらのお客さまを移動させなくてはいけませんでした。それから、こちらのお客さまから客室のサイズについて苦情があったので、料金を割引しました。そして、エアコンの1つが壊れたのですが、ここから問題を解決することができたので、これは大きな問題ではありませんでした。

男性：分かりました。お客さまをチェックアウトさせるときに、問題についてお詫びを言っておきます。また明日、Tina。

語彙チェック　□reception　受付　□rare　珍しい　□nightly　夜の　□incident　事故、出来事
　　　　　　　　□neighboring　近隣の　□complain about 〜　〜について苦情を言う

Room / Incident	
Hoover (457)	Noise
Bobson (1041)	Broken air conditioner
Kelly (987)	Luggage sent to the wrong room
Oda (546)	Room too small

部屋 / 事故	
Hoover (457)	騒音
Bobson (1041)	エアコンの故障
Kelly (987)	手荷物が違う部屋へ送られた
Oda (546)	部屋が狭過ぎる

65 　　　　正解 C

What does the woman say about the man?
(A) He has been hired to repair a device.
(B) He works in the evenings.
(C) He is at the beginning of his shift.
(D) He reported a problem to reception.

女性は男性について何と言っていますか。
(A) 彼は機器を修理するために雇われた。
(B) 彼は夜間勤務をしている。
(C) 彼は彼のシフトを開始する。
(D) 彼は受付に問題を報告した。

冒頭で女性は男性に対し、I'm glad you're here to start work. と声をかけている。この発言から男性は仕事を始めるところだと分かる。その後も、女性から事故報告書の引き継ぎを受けたり、See you tomorrow と女性にあいさつしたりしていることから、男性は女性と交代でシフトに入ると考えられる。よって、(C) が正解。

66 　　　　正解 A

Look at the graphic. Which guest was moved to another room?
(A) Hoover
(B) Bobson
(C) Kelly
(D) Oda

図を見てください。どの宿泊客が他の客室に移動させられましたか。
(A) Hoover
(B) Bobson
(C) Kelly
(D) Oda

女性は事故報告書の説明の中で、I had to move this guest because there was too much noise coming from one of the neighboring rooms. と述べている。ここから、客室移動の原因は騒音だと分かる。図を見ると、Noise「騒音」の報告があったのは Hoover さんの部屋と記載されているので、この宿泊客を移動させたと判断できる。よって、正解は (A)。

67 　　　　正解 D

What does the man say he will do?
(A) Order a device
(B) Cancel a reservation
(C) Request some repairs
(D) Apologize to a guest

男性は何をすると言っていますか。
(A) 機器を注文する
(B) 予約をキャンセルする
(C) 修理を頼む
(D) 宿泊客に謝罪する

女性の事故報告を聞くと、男性は I'll say sorry for the problems when I check them out. と述べている。よって、(D) が正解。

語彙チェック □apologize to 〜　〜に謝罪する

Questions 68 through 70 refer to the following conversation and floor plan.

W: Hello, I'd like to discuss renting a meeting room for a day. I need somewhere private to speak with some local business contacts.

M: Sure. As you can see from this floor plan, we have various meeting rooms on the first floor. They all have chairs, tables, a whiteboard, and Internet access. It just comes down to what size you require. When are you planning on using it?

W: Is this one available tomorrow morning? The small one directly across from the reception desk.

M: That one's taken, I'm afraid. But the one beside it isn't taken yet. It's the same size.

W: That'll be fine. How much is it?

M: That'll cost you 350 dollars for the full day. It's 10 dollars cheaper if you charge it to your room.

問題68-70は次の会話と間取り図に関するものです。

女性：こんにちは、会議室を1日レンタルすることについて伺いたいのですが。地元の事業者と話すために、人目につかない場所が必要なのです。

男性：かしこまりました。こちらの間取り図からお分かりいただけるように、1階にさまざまな会議室がございます。そちらには全て椅子、テーブル、ホワイトボード、そしてインターネット接続がございます。あとは、お客さまがどちらのサイズをご希望かということ次第です。いつお使いになるご予定ですか。

女性：こちらは明日の午前中に利用できますか。受付デスクの真向かいの小さなところです。

男性：申し訳ございませんが、そちらは予約済みです。しかし、そちらの隣のお部屋はまだ残っていますよ。サイズは同じです。

女性：そちらで結構です。おいくらですか。

男性：1日利用で350ドルです。お客さまのお部屋代に付けますと、10ドルお安くなります。

語彙チェック　□come down to ～　～次第である
　　　　　　　　□plan on *doing*　～するつもりである
　　　　　　　　□directly across from ～　～の真向かいの　□reception　受付
　　　　　　　　□beside　～の隣に　□charge ～ to *one's* room　～の料金を部屋付けにする

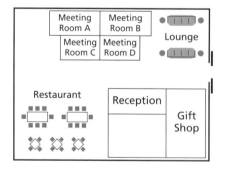

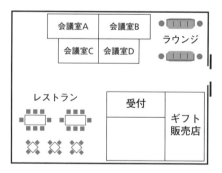

68

What does the woman say she will do?

(A) Interview some candidates
(B) Have confidential meetings
(C) Make a presentation
(D) Arrange an event

女性は何をすると言っていますか。

(A) 候補者の面接をする
(B) 内密の会議をする
(C) プレゼンテーションをする
(D) イベントの準備をする

女性は冒頭で「会議室を1日レンタルすることについて伺いたい」と述べ、その理由を I need somewhere private to speak with some local business contacts. と説明している。この発言から、女性は地元の事業者と人に知られないように打ち合わせをすると分かる。よって、正解は (B)。

語彙チェック □confidential 秘密の、内密の

69

Look at the graphic. Which room will the woman probably rent?

(A) Meeting Room A
(B) Meeting Room B
(C) Meeting Room C
(D) Meeting Room D

図を見てください。女性はおそらくどの部屋をレンタルしますか。

(A) 会議室A
(B) 会議室B
(C) 会議室C
(D) 会議室D

女性は会議室の希望を The small one directly across from the reception desk. と述べている。それに対し男性は、その会議室が予約済みであることを伝えた後、But the one beside it isn't taken yet. It's the same size. と代案を提示している。これを女性は That'll be fine. と承諾しているため、女性がレンタルする会議室は「受付デスクの真向かいの小さな会議室の隣に位置する同じサイズの部屋」だと判断できる。よって、正解は (C)。

> **⚠️ ここに注意！**
> このように、1つのものを希望した後にそれが変更される場合があるので、すぐに判断せずに最後までよく聞くことが大事！

70

What is mentioned about the meeting rooms?

(A) They have projectors installed in them.
(B) Hotel guests can get a discount.
(C) They are available 24-hours a day.
(D) Furniture must be rented separately.

会議室について何が述べられていますか。

(A) それらにはプロジェクターが設置されている。
(B) ホテルの宿泊客は割引が受けられる。
(C) それらは24時間利用可能である。
(D) 家具はレンタル料が別途かかる。

最後に女性が会議室のレンタル料を尋ねると、男性は1日利用で350ドルだと答えた後、It's 10 dollars cheaper if you charge it to your room. と説明している。この発言から、このホテルの宿泊客はレンタル料の割引を受けられると考えられる。よって、正解は (B)。

Part 4

トーク ▶TRACK_224　　問題 ▶TRACK_225

Questions 71 through 73 refer to the following broadcast.

Welcome to AM Drive on Radio 8TK — Chicago's number one morning radio show. I'm your host, Col Van and I'll be with you for the next three hours. Our first guest this morning is Binita Singh. She's been in the news a lot recently following her amazing world-record run at the track and field championships in Boston last week. She's using the attention she's getting to promote an environmental protection group called the Coastal Care Association. Ms. Singh has been an active member of the group for four years, and she was recently appointed as its leader and chief spokesperson. It's an unpaid position, which takes a lot of her free time.

問題71-73は次の放送に関するものです。

Radio 8TKのAM Drive—Chicagoでナンバーワンのモーニングラジオショーへようこそ。ホストである私、Col Vanが、これから3時間皆さんとご一緒いたします。今朝の最初のゲストはBinita Singhです。先週のボストンでの陸上大会において世界記録を達成した素晴らしい走りで、彼女は最近たくさんニュースになっています。彼女は、現在集めている注目を利用し、Coastal Care協会と呼ばれる環境保護団体の周知活動を行っています。Singhさんは4年間この団体のメンバーとして活発に活動し、最近ではそのリーダー、そして広報局長に任命されました。これは無報酬の仕事ですが、多くの彼女の時間を費やしています。

語彙チェック　□track and field　陸上　□promote　～を宣伝する、～を促進する
□environmental protection group　環境保護団体　□association　協会
□appoint *A* as *B*　AをBに任命する　□chief　長、局長
□spokesperson　広報担当者　□unpaid　無報酬の

71　　　　　正解 D

What is mentioned about AM Drive?
(A) It has multiple presenters.
(B) It does not have any advertisements.
(C) It features a competition.
(D) It lasts three hours.

AM Driveについて何が述べられていますか。
(A) それには多数の司会者がいる。
(B) それは広告が全くない。
(C) それは競技会を特集している。
(D) それは3時間続く。

話し手は冒頭でAM Driveというラジオ番組名と、自分が番組ホストであるということを紹介した後、I'll be with you for the next three hoursと述べている。「これから3時間皆さんとご一緒いたします」ということは、番組の長さが3時間だと考えられる。よって、正解は(D)。

語彙チェック　□multiple　多数の　□presenter　（テレビ、ラジオなどの）司会者
□feature　～を特集する

72

□□□ 正解 **B**

Who is Ms. Singh?

(A) An entertainer

(B) An athlete

(C) A politician

(D) A scientist

Singhさんとは誰ですか。

(A) 芸能人

(B) アスリート

(C) 政治家

(D) 科学者

話し手はゲストとしてBinita Singhさんを紹介し、彼女がニュースになっている理由を her amazing world-record run at the track and field championshipsと述べている。この ことから、Singhさんは陸上競技の選手だと判断できる。よって、正解は(B)。

73

□□□ 正解 **D**

What will Ms. Singh most likely speak about?

(A) Her recent discovery

(B) Her upcoming holiday

(C) Her retirement plans

(D) Her volunteer activity

Singhさんは何について話すと考えられますか。

(A) 彼女の最近の発見

(B) 彼女の次の休暇

(C) 彼女の引退計画

(D) 彼女のボランティア活動

話し手は、Singhさんについて、She's using the attention she's getting to promote an environmental protection group called the Coastal Care Association.と説明している。 その後、彼女が最近その団体のリーダーと広報局長に任命されたことや、It's an unpaid position 「これは無報酬の仕事だ」との説明もある。よって、Singhさんはボランティア として行っている環境保護団体の活動について話すと考えられるので、(D)が正解。

語彙チェック □upcoming 来たるべき

Questions 74 through 76 refer to the following excerpt from a meeting.

The next item on the agenda is the upcoming Bay to City Fun Run. <u>We're funding the event</u> in exchange for the rights to display our company logo along the course, on the tents, and on all of the official merchandise. We'll also be supporting participants by handing out drinks as they pass the various checkpoints. I'm having a special uniform created for us by a local garment factory. <u>Please take a look at the samples. I think they look quite nice. Right after the meeting, I'd like everyone to visit the manufacturer's Web site and choose their appropriate size. Staff members can use this code to place their orders.</u> The manufacturer will send them to our office by Thursday next week.

問題74-76は次の会議の抜粋に関するものです。

議題の次の項目は、まもなく開催されるBay to City Fun Runです。コース沿道やテント、そして全ての公式グッズに当社のロゴを付ける権利と引き換えに、私たちはイベントに資金提供をする予定です。参加者がさまざまなチェックポイントを通過するときにドリンクを手渡すことで、彼らの支援もします。こちらは地元の衣料品工場に、私たちのために作っていただいたスペシャルユニフォームです。サンプルをご覧ください。かなりすてきに見えると思います。会議の直後に、皆さんにメーカーのウェブサイトにアクセスしていただいて、ふさわしいサイズを選んでもらいたいと思います。スタッフメンバーは、注文するのにこのコードを使うことができます。来週木曜日までに、メーカーからオフィスにそれらを送ってもらいます。

語彙チェック   □upcoming 来たるべき   □fund ～に資金を提供する
□in exchange for ～ ～と交換に   □hand out ～ ～を配る
□pass ～のそばを通り過ぎる   □garment 衣料品
□appropriate 適切な、ふさわしい   □place an order 注文する

---

74   正解 C

What is the company going to do soon?   会社はまもなく何をする予定ですか。
(A) Open a new store   (A) 新しい店を開店する
(B) Relocate to another city   (B) 他の街へ移転する
(C) Sponsor an event   (C) イベントのスポンサーになる
(D) Release a product   (D) 製品を発売する

話し手は冒頭で、次の会議の議題がBay to City Fun Runであると伝えている。その後、We're funding the eventと述べており、その代わりに沿道やテント、イベントの公式グッズに自社のロゴを付けるということから、話し手の会社はイベントのスポンサーになると判断できる。よって、正解は(C)。

語彙チェック   □relocate 移転する   □sponsor ～のスポンサーになる、～を後援する

75　正解 A

What does the speaker ask employees to do?

(A) View some designs
(B) Attend a meeting
(C) Call a client
(D) Make a recommendation

話し手は従業員に何をするよう求めていますか。

(A) デザインを見る
(B) 会議に出席する
(C) 顧客に電話する
(D) 推薦をする

話し手は衣料品工場に作ってもらったスペシャルユニフォームがあることを伝えると、Please take a look at the samples. と聞き手に呼びかけ、I think they look quite nice. と述べている。よって、(A) が正解。

76　正解 D

Why are the listeners directed to a Web site?

(A) To register for an event
(B) To watch a promotional video
(C) To read an article
(D) To order some clothing

聞き手はなぜウェブサイトへ案内されていますか。

(A) イベントに登録するため
(B) プロモーションビデオを見るため
(C) 記事を読むため
(D) 服を注文するため

話し手はスペシャルユニフォームについて話をすると、Right after the meeting, I'd like everyone to visit the manufacturer's Web site and choose their appropriate size. と聞き手に依頼し、その後 Staff members can use this code to place their orders. と説明している。このことから、聞き手はウェブサイト上でユニフォームのサイズを選び注文するようにお願いされていると判断できる。よって、(D) が正解。

語彙チェック □ direct A to B　A を B へ向かわせる

Questions 77 through 79 refer to the following telephone message.

Hello. This is Trevor Mann from Donaldson Building Supplies. I'm calling for Ms. Wilson. You may not have noticed yet, but <u>there was an error in the invoice I sent you this afternoon</u>. <u>You canceled an order of roofing tiles</u>, and I forgot to remove them from the invoice. <u>Please dispose of that invoice or you may end up overpaying. We can't have that</u>. I'll be in Greendale this afternoon, so I plan to drop by the worksite and hand you the new invoice in person. You can call me back on this number if that'll be inconvenient.

問題77-79は次の電話のメッセージに関するものです。

こんにちは。こちらはDonaldson Building Supplies社のTrevor Mannです。Wilsonさんにお電話しております。まだお気付きではないかもしれませんが、今日の午後にお送りした請求書に誤りがございました。お客さまは屋根のタイルの注文をキャンセルされましたが、それを請求書から除くのを失念しておりました。その請求書は処分してください。そうしなければ、必要以上に代金をお支払いいただくことになってしまうかもしれません。当社はそれは受け入れられません。私は今日の午後はGreendaleにおりますので、作業現場に立ち寄って、新しい請求書をお客さまに直接お渡しする予定です。もしご都合が悪ければ、こちらの番号に折り返しお電話していただければと思います。

語彙チェック　□error　誤り、間違い　□invoice　請求書
　　　　　　　　□remove A from B　BからAを取り除く　□dispose of ～　～を処分する
　　　　　　　　□end up doing　ついには～することになる　□overpay　支払い過ぎる
　　　　　　　　□drop by ～　～に立ち寄る　□worksite　仕事場、作業現場
　　　　　　　　□in person　自分で、本人が　□inconvenient　都合の悪い、不便な

77　　　　　　　　　　□□□　正解 D

What is the purpose of the call?　　　　　電話の目的は何ですか。
(A) To explain a shortage of inventory　　　(A) 在庫の不足を説明すること
(B) To request an invoice　　　　　　　　(B) 請求書を依頼すること
(C) To announce a policy change　　　　　(C) 方針変更を知らせること
(D) To report a billing error　　　　　　　(D) 請求書の誤りを報告すること

話し手は自分の名前と所属を述べた後、there was an error in the invoice I sent you this afternoonと説明している。その後、この問題への対処について説明しているので、この問題を伝えることが電話の用件であると判断できる。よって、(D)が正解。

語彙チェック　□shortage　不足　□inventory　在庫　□billing　請求書の作成

78

□□□ 正解 **B**

What did the listener order?

(A) Timber flooring

(B) Roofing tiles

(C) Exterior paint

(D) A shower unit

聞き手は何を注文しましたか。

(A) 木製の床板

(B) 屋根のタイル

(C) 屋外用ペンキ

(D) シャワーユニット

話し手は請求書の誤りについて説明する中で、You canceled an order of roofing tiles と述べている。ここから聞き手が roofing tiles「屋根のタイル」を注文したことが分かるので、正解は (B)。

語彙チェック □timber 材木、木材 □flooring 床板 □exterior 屋外用の

79

□□□ 正解 **D**

What does the speaker mean when he says, "We can't have that"?

(A) Some products are no longer available.

(B) He will avoid a delivery delay.

(C) Some goods will be returned.

(D) A situation would be unacceptable.

話し手は "We can't have that" という発言で、何を意味していますか。

(A) いくつかの商品はもう取り扱っていない。

(B) 彼は配達の遅延を避ける。

(C) いくつかの商品は返品される。

(D) 容認できる状況ではない。

話し手はキャンセルされた注文を請求書から除き忘れたことを伝えると、その後 Please dispose of that invoice or you may end up overpaying. と述べ、「新しい請求書を直接手渡しに行く」と、問題を解決しようとしている様子がうかがえる。これらのことから、お客さんである聞き手が必要以上に料金を払うことに関して「それは受け入れられない」という話し手の意図が読み取れる。よって、正解は (D)。

語彙チェック □no longer 〜 もはや〜ではない
□unacceptable 受け入れられない、容認できない

W 🇬🇧 トーク ▶TRACK_230　問題 ▶TRACK_231

Questions 80 through 82 refer to the following broadcast news.

We have received notification about some roadwork on the northern portion of Lee Road in Scotford. This will be ongoing until June 10. Drivers should avoid the area if possible. There's a detour for people who need to travel in that area. So please follow the signs that have been placed on the road. Try to leave a little earlier than usual if you want to get to work on time. That's it for the traffic update. Now, here's the new single from Linus Webb's latest album.

問題80-82は次のニュース放送に関するものです。

Scotfordの Lee通り北側部分の道路工事についてお知らせが来ています。これは6月10日まで続く予定です。もし可能なら、ドライバーはそのエリアを避けた方がいいでしょう。そのエリアを通る必要がある人のための迂回路があります。ですので、道路に設置された標識に従ってください。時間通りに職場に着きたい場合は、普段より少し早く出発するようにしましょう。最新の交通情報は以上です。それでは、Linus Webbの最新アルバムからニューシングルをお聞きください。

語彙チェック　□notification　通知　□roadwork　道路工事　□portion　部分、一部　□ongoing　進行している　□detour　迂回路　□on time　時間通りに　□update　最新情報

80　□□□　正解 B

What does the speaker say about part of Lee Road?

(A) It has been flooded.
(B) It is being repaired.
(C) It is congested.
(D) It was widened.

話し手は Lee通りの一部について何と言っていますか。

(A) そこは洪水にあった。
(B) そこは補修中である。
(C) そこは渋滞している。
(D) そこは拡張された。

話し手は冒頭で「お知らせが来ている」と述べ、それは some roadwork on the northern portion of Lee Road についてであると説明している。さらに、This will be ongoing until June 10. とも述べていることから、Lee通りでは現在、道路工事が行われている最中であると分かる。よって、(B) が正解。

語彙チェック　□flood　〜を氾濫させる、〜を水浸しにする　□congested　混雑した　□widen　〜を広くする

> 🐾 **ここに注意！**
> (D)は少し紛らわしい選択肢。拡張工事を roadwork と捉えることができたとしても、道路工事は今行われている最中なので、「拡張された」と過去の時制になっているのは不適切。動詞の時制にも注意しよう！

81

□□□ 正解 C

When will road conditions change? 道路の状況はいつ変わりますか。

(A) On June 1 (A) 6月1日

(B) On June 5 (B) 6月5日

(C) On June 10 (C) 6月10日

(D) On June 15 (D) 6月15日

話し手はThis will be ongoing until June 10.と説明しており、このThisはその前の文で説明しているLee通りの道路工事のことを指している。「道路工事は6月10日まで続く」ということは、「6月10日に道路工事が終わる」と考えられる。よって、正解は(C)。

82

□□□ 正解 D

What will the listeners most likely hear next? 聞き手は次に何を聞くと考えられますか。

(A) A weather update (A) 最新の天気情報

(B) An interview (B) インタビュー

(C) Some news (C) ニュース

(D) Some music (D) 音楽

最新の交通情報に関する話題が終わると、話し手は最後にNow, here's the new single from Linus Webb's latest album.と述べている。new single「ニューシングル」やlatest album「最新アルバム」という語句から、これから音楽が流れると判断できる。よって、正解は(D)。

M 🇦🇺

トーク ⏵TRACK_232   問題 ⏵TRACK_233

Questions 83 through 85 refer to the following excerpt from a workshop.

I'm really impressed with the progress you have all made this afternoon. I'm sure the skills you are learning will enhance the shopping experience for our customers. The next activity we're going to do usually takes around one hour to complete. Unfortunately, there isn't enough time for us to do that this afternoon. I have decided that we'll do it tomorrow morning instead. I'd like to give you some time to fill out a questionnaire about today's workshop. It'll be completely anonymous so please evaluate it frankly.

問題83-85は次のワークショップの抜粋に関するものです。

今日の午後の皆さんの進歩には本当に感心しました。皆さんが学んでいるスキルはお客さまのショッピング体験をさらに良いものにするでしょう。私たちが行う予定の次の活動は、完了するのに通常約1時間かかります。あいにく、今日の午後はそれを行う時間が十分にありません。代わりに明日の午前中にやることにしました。今日のワークショップについてのアンケートに記入する時間を取りたいと思います。完全に匿名なので、率直に評価してください。

語彙チェック　□be impressed with 〜　〜に感心する、〜に感動する　□progress　進歩
□enhance　〜を高める　□fill out 〜　〜に記入する
□questionnaire　アンケート用紙　□completely　完全に
□anonymous　匿名の　□evaluate　〜を評価する　□frankly　率直に

83　　□□□　正解 A

What is the topic of the workshop?　ワークショップのトピックは何ですか。

(A) Improving customer satisfaction levels　(A) 顧客満足度を向上させること

(B) Hiring appropriate people for positions　(B) 職種にふさわしい人物を雇用すること

(C) Raising the effectiveness of advertising　(C) 広告の有効性を高めること

(D) Increasing production speed　(D) 生産スピードを上げること

話し手がI'm sure the skills you are learning will enhance the shopping experience for our customers.と述べていることから、顧客の満足度を高めることを目的としたワークショップが行われていると考えられる。よって、(A)が正解。

語彙チェック　□appropriate　ふさわしい、適切な　□effectiveness　有効性

180

84 　□□□　正解 C

What does the speaker say about the next activity?

(A) It is very popular.

(B) It will be performed in teams.

(C) It will take too long.

(D) It has not been tried before.

話し手は次の活動について何と言っていますか。

(A) それはとても人気がある。

(B) それはチームで行われる。

(C) それは時間がかかり過ぎる。

(D) それは今までに試されたことがない。

話し手は次の活動について、「通常約1時間かかる」と説明している。続けて、Unfortunately, there isn't enough time for us to do that this afternoon. とも述べていることから、次の活動は今日行うには長すぎると判断できる。よって、(C)が正解。

85 　□□□　正解 C

What are the listeners asked to do?

(A) Take a break

(B) Talk among each other

(C) Complete a survey

(D) Leave early

聞き手は何をするよう求められていますか。

(A) 休憩をとる

(B) 互いに話をする

(C) アンケートを完成させる

(D) 早く退席する

話し手は次の活動を明日行うことを伝えると、I'd like to give you some time to fill out a questionnaire about today's workshop. と述べている。この fill out a questionnaire を言い換えた (C)が正解。

Questions 86 through 88 refer to the following news.

In business news today, Liontech, an up-and-coming software developer, has announced that its customer support line will be outsourced from June. Company representative Steve Ryan explained that office space in Seattle has become too expensive. He said that the company has grown a lot, and that it didn't make sense to spend money to rent office space when the work could be carried out remotely. According to Ryan, the company they're currently outsourcing to will hire Liontech's help-line staff and allow them to work from home. Other software companies have done the same thing in recent years with different levels of success. The quality of training the staff gets appears to be very important.

問題86-88は次のニュースに関するものです。

今日のビジネスニュースで、将来有望なソフトウェア開発会社であるLiontech社は、6月からカスタマーサポートの電話が外部委託されると発表しました。会社代表のSteve Ryanは、Seattleのオフィススペースは価格が高くなり過ぎてしまったと説明しました。会社が大きく成長しているということと、リモート業務を行えるのに、オフィススペースの賃料を払うのは賢明ではないということを、彼は述べました。Ryanによると、現在の外部委託先の企業がLiontech社の相談窓口のスタッフを雇用し、在宅勤務を許可するとのことです。他のソフトウェア会社も、成功の度合いはさまざまですが、近年同様の取り組みを行っています。スタッフが受ける研修の質が大変重要だと思われます。

語彙チェック	□up-and-coming　有望な　□line　電話回線　□outsource　〜を外部に委託する
	□representative　代表者　□make sense　道理にかなう、賢明である
	□remotely　遠く離れて　□work from home　在宅勤務をする

86　　　　　　　　　　　□□□　正解 C

What is the news mainly about?
(A) The expansion of a local factory
(B) A change in government regulations
(C) A company's cost-cutting measure
(D) The appointment of a new company president

ニュースは主に何についてですか。
(A) 地元工場の拡張
(B) 政府規則の変更
(C) 企業の経費削減策
(D) 企業の新しい社長の発表

まず、冒頭で「Liontech社がカスタマーサポートの電話を外部委託する」ことが述べられている。一方、これに関してLiontech社の代表Steve Ryan氏が述べたoffice space in Seattle has become too expensive や、it didn't make sense to spend money to rent office space when the work could be carried out remotelyといった内容について紹介されている。こうした発言から、Liontech社はオフィスのレンタル費用を削減するために、業務委託を行うと判断できる。よって、正解は(C)。

語彙チェック	□expansion　拡張、拡大　□cost-cutting　経費削減の　□measure　対策、処置

> 🛑 ここに注意！
> 全体で話している内容を問う問題。ここでは特定の単語が選択肢で言い換えられているわけでもないので、文脈の流れをつかんでメインのトピックを読み取る必要がある！

87

□□□ 正解 **B**

What effect will the change have on employees?

(A) They will have a reduced workload.

(B) They will be able to work from home.

(C) They will receive a pay increase.

(D) They will be asked to work in different departments.

変更は従業員にどのような影響を及ぼしますか。

(A) 彼らは仕事量が減る。

(B) 彼らは在宅勤務ができるようになる。

(C) 彼らは賃金が上がる。

(D) 彼らは異なる部署で勤務するよう求められる。

相談窓口のスタッフについて the company they're currently outsourcing to will hire Liontech's help-line staff and allow them to work from home と述べられている。よって、外部委託により従業員は在宅勤務が許されると分かるので、正解は (B)。

語彙チェック □workload **仕事量**

88

□□□ 正解 **D**

What does the speaker say is important?

(A) Planning for changes well in advance

(B) Taking into account the opinions of employees

(C) Ensuring that equipment is properly maintained

(D) Proving adequate training to employees

話し手は何が重要だと言っていますか。

(A) 前もって変更についてよく計画しておくこと

(B) 従業員の意見を考慮に入れること

(C) 機器類が適切に整備されていることを確実にすること

(D) 従業員に十分な研修を提供すること

話し手は「他のソフトウェア会社も、成功の度合いはさまざまだが、近年同様の取り組みをしている」と述べ、その取り組みでの重要な点について The quality of training the staff gets appears to be very important. と説明している。よって、(D) が正解。

語彙チェック □in advance **前もって、事前に** □take into account 〜 **〜を考慮する** □ensure that 〜 **確実に〜するようにする** □maintain **〜を整備する** □adequate **十分な、適切な**

Questions 89 through 91 refer to the following advertisement.

Jack's Grille is Lamington's most popular eatery. We've been in business for many years, and our reputation for delicious food and excellent value has spread around the state. This June, Jack's Grille won Out'n About Magazine's Menu-of-the-Year Award. We're open for business seven days a week. However, Monday through Wednesday are lunch-only days. This month, we're testing some new menu items. It's a great time to come in and try something new and exciting. Reservations are usually necessary for dinner on Friday and Saturday nights. Call us at 246-555-6362 to check availability.

問題89-91は次の広告に関するものです。

Jack's Grille は Lamington で1番人気のレストランです。長年営業しており、おいしい料理と良心的な価格の評判が州中に広がっています。この6月、Jack's Grille は Out'n About Magazine の Menu-of-the-Year 賞を受賞しました。年中無休で営業しております。ただし、月曜日から水曜日はランチのみの営業です。今月は、新メニューの試食を行います。新しくてエキサイティングなことを試しに来るには、とてもいい機会です。通常、金曜日と土曜日の夜のディナーは予約が必要です。246-555-6362に電話して予約状況をご確認ください。

語彙チェック ☐eatery　簡易食堂、レストラン　☐in business　営業中で、事業を行って
☐reputation　評判　☐test　〜を試す
☐availability　利用の可能性、利用できること

89 ☐☐☐ 正解 **A**

What is mentioned about the business?
(A) It has been operating for a long time.
(B) It offers discounts to local residents.
(C) It advertises in a magazine.
(D) It is looking to hire additional staff.

店について何が述べられていますか。
(A) それは長い間営業してきている。
(B) それは地域住民に割引を提供している。
(C) それは雑誌に広告を出している。
(D) それは追加のスタッフを雇おうとしている。

話し手はレストランの名前を述べた後、レストランについて We've been in business for many years と説明している。これを言い換えている (A) が正解。

語彙チェック ☐operate　営業する　☐resident　居住人　☐advertise　広告を出す
☐look to *do*　〜しようとする

90 □□□ 正解 C

What is mentioned about Mondays at the business?

(A) Some entertainment is provided.

(B) It offers discounts.

(C) There is no dinner service.

(D) It requires reservations.

月曜日の営業について何が述べられていますか。

(A) 余興がある。

(B) 割引を提供している。

(C) ディナーサービスがない。

(D) 予約が必要である。

レストランは年中無休としながらも、Monday through Wednesday are lunch-only days と説明されている。ランチのみの営業ということはディナーはやっていないということなので、(C)が正解。

語彙チェック □entertainment 余興、催し物、エンターテイメント □require 〜を必要とする
□reservation 予約

91 □□□ 正解 B

Why does the speaker say, "This month, we're testing some new menu items"?

(A) To explain slower than usual service

(B) To encourage the listeners to come

(C) To celebrate the arrival of a new chef

(D) To inform the listeners of a temporary closure

話し手はなぜ"This month, we're testing some new menu items"と言っていますか。

(A) 通常のサービスより時間がかかると説明するため

(B) 聞き手に来店を促すため

(C) 新しい料理長の到着を祝うため

(D) 聞き手に一時休業を知らせるため

話し手はThis month, we're testing some new menu items.と述べた後、It's a great time to come in and try something new and exciting.と付け加えている。ここから、客の来店を促そうとする話し手の意図がくみ取れる。よって、正解は(B)。

語彙チェック □encourage A to do Aに〜するよう促す □temporary 一時的な
□closure 閉鎖

Questions 92 through 94 refer to the following excerpt from a meeting.

The first thing we have to discuss this afternoon is the Eaton Community Fitness Center. It's one of New South Wales's most popular public fitness centers. To help us keep up with the demand of our patrons, the state government has provided us with a much larger budget this year. We've been instructed to use it to expand the center and update a lot of the exercise equipment. Users have made numerous requests and suggestions over the years, but we lacked the financial resources to carry them out. Now, we're in a position to do something.

問題92-94は次の会議の抜粋に関するものです。

今日の午後に話し合わなくてはいけない最初の事項は、Eaton コミュニティーフィットネスセンターです。それは New South Wales で最も人気のある公営のフィットネスセンターの1つです。私たちが後援者の要望に応えるのを支援するために、州政府は今年かなりの予算をつけてくれました。センターを拡大し、多くの運動器具を最新のものにするためにそれを使うよう指示されています。利用者から長年にわたり多くの要望と提案を頂いてきましたが、それらを実行するには財源が不足していました。今こそ私たちは何かをする局面にあります。

語彙チェック　□keep up with 〜　〜に遅れないで付いていく　□patron　後援者
　　　　　　　□instruct *A* to *do*　Aに〜するよう指示する　□numerous　多数の
　　　　　　　□resources　資源　□carry 〜 out　〜を実行する

92　　　□□□　正解 A

What is mentioned about the organization?

(A) It is publicly owned.
(B) It has multiple locations.
(C) It will hold a publicity event.
(D) It is staffed by volunteers.

組織について何が述べられていますか。

(A) それは公的に所有されている。
(B) それは複数の場所にある。
(C) それは広報イベントを開催する予定である。
(D) ボランティアがスタッフを務めている。

話し手は Eaton コミュニティーフィットネスセンターについて話し合うと述べた後、そのフィットネスセンターについて It's one of New South Wales's most popular public fitness centers. と説明している。よって、(A) が正解。

語彙チェック　□publicly　公的に　□multiple　多数の　□publicity　広報、宣伝
　　　　　　　□staff　〜に職員を配置する

93

□□□　正解 **B**

What will the organization probably do?　組織はおそらく何をする予定ですか。
(A) Hire additional staff　(A) 追加のスタッフを雇用する
(B) Purchase fitness equipment　(B) フィットネス器具を購入する
(C) Offer a new service　(C) 新しいサービスを提供する
(D) Change its operating hours　(D) 営業時間を変更する

州政府の予算について、話し手は We've been instructed to use it to expand the center and update a lot of the exercise equipment. と述べている。よって、この update a lot of the exercise equipment「多くの運動器具を最新のものにする」ことを言い換えた (B) が正解。

語彙チェック　□operating hours　営業時間

94

□□□　正解 **A**

What does the speaker mean when she says, "Now, we're in a position to do something"?　話し手は "Now, we're in a position to do something" という発言で、何を意味していますか。
(A) They have the money to accommodate some requests.　(A) 彼らには要望を受け入れるためのお金がある。
(B) They have moved to a more convenient address.　(B) 彼らはより便利な住所に引っ越した。
(C) They have rearranged the office layout.　(C) 彼らはオフィスのレイアウトを配置し直した。
(D) They have hired experts to improve their services.　(D) 彼らはサービスを向上させるために専門家を雇った。

話し手は「今年は州政府からかなりの予算がついた」と伝え、これまでについては Users have made numerous requests and suggestions over the years, but we lacked the financial resources to carry them out. と述べている。つまり、今年はフィットネスセンターに州政府から予算が下りたことで、財源不足が解消され、利用者の要望や提案を実現できると判断できる。よって、正解は (A)。

語彙チェック　□accommodate　（要求）を受け入れる　□rearrange　～を並べ替える
□layout　配置、レイアウト

M

Questions 95 through 97 refer to the following telephone message and schedule.

Hi Maria. It's Ted. I'm calling about your conference room reservation. A couple of weeks ago, I reserved Room D for a client meeting. Yesterday, I learned that Room D only has seating for six people. In total, we'll have ten people, so I was hoping you could swap with me. I know it's short notice, and your planning meeting is today. If you can't swap, I'll reschedule my meeting, but I need to know as soon as possible. By the way, I heard that David Townsend is transferring here from the Seattle office. We should arrange a welcome party, don't you think?

問題95-97は次の電話のメッセージと予定表に関するものです。

こんにちは Maria。Ted です。あなたの会議室の予約について電話しています。私は2週間前に、顧客との打ち合わせのために Room D を予約しました。昨日、Room D は6人分しか席がないことを知りました。私たちは合計で10人いるので、あなたが私と交換できないかと思いまして。突然のお願いだと承知していますし、あなたの企画会議は今日ですよね。もし交換できないようであれば、私の打ち合わせの予定を変更しますが、それをできるだけ早く知る必要があります。話は変わりますが、David Townsend が Seattle のオフィスからここに転勤してくると聞きました。歓迎会を計画した方がいいですよね？

語彙チェック　□ seating for 〜　〜人分の座席　□ in total　合計で、全部で
□ swap with 〜　〜と交換する　□ short notice　突然のお願い
□ reschedule　〜の予定を変更する　□ as soon as possible　できるだけ早く
□ transfer　転勤する

Conference Room Reservations (TODAY) 11:00 A.M. 〜 12:00 NOON	
Room A	Product Development (Planning)
Room B	Administration (Monthly Meeting)
Room C	Closed for renovations
Room D	Sales (Client Meeting)

会議室の予約(本日) 午前11時〜正午12時	
Room A	製品開発（企画）
Room B	管理（月例会議）
Room C	改装のため閉鎖
Room D	販売（顧客との打ち合わせ）

95

正解 C

When does the speaker say he reserved a conference room?

(A) Yesterday

(B) Two days ago

(C) Two weeks ago

(D) Last month

話し手はいつ会議室を予約したと言っていますか。

(A) 昨日

(B) 2日前

(C) 2週間前

(D) 先月

話し手は冒頭で I'm calling about your conference room reservation. と電話の内容を述べた後、A couple of weeks ago, I reserved Room D for a client meeting. と言っている。よって、(C) が正解。

96

正解 A

Look at the graphic. Which room has the listener reserved?

(A) Room A

(B) Room B

(C) Room C

(D) Room D

図を見てください。聞き手はどの部屋を予約しましたか。

(A) Room A

(B) Room B

(C) Room C

(D) Room D

話し手は当初6人用の Room D を予約したが、実際は10人の参加者がいるため、I was hoping you could swap with me と聞き手の予約している会議室との交換を希望している。your planning meeting is today という発言から、聞き手の会議は企画会議であると分かる。図は今日の会議室の予約状況を示しており、Room A の欄に Planning と記載されていることから、聞き手は Room A を予約したと判断できる。よって、正解は (A)。

97

正解 C

What does the speaker suggest doing?

(A) Hiring an assistant

(B) Requesting some repairs

(C) Organizing a social gathering

(D) Visiting a branch office

話し手は何をすることを提案していますか。

(A) アシスタントを雇うこと

(B) 修理を依頼すること

(C) 懇親会を企画すること

(D) 支社オフィスを訪問すること

話し手は By the way と話題を変え、David Townsend さんが転勤してくることを伝えている。その後、We should arrange a welcome party, don't you think? と発言しているので、「歓迎会を計画する」ことを言い換えている (C) が正解。

語彙チェック □social gathering 懇親会

Questions 98 through 100 refer to the following announcement and notice.

Welcome to Dreamland Park. We hope you're ready for a day of fun, excitement, and adventure. Please note that we need to close certain rides each day to make sure that they're in good running order and that they meet our strict safety guidelines. Today, The Claw will be out of action. If you were looking forward to that one, please come back another day. You can purchase a returner's ticket for just seventeen dollars on your way out. Please make sure to stay hydrated today. The high temperature is going to be thirty four degrees.

問題98-100は次のお知らせと掲示に関するものです。

Dreamland Parkへようこそ。楽しさ、興奮、そして冒険の1日のための準備ができていると思います。乗り物が正常に動くこと、そして私たちの厳格な安全ガイドラインを満たしていることを確実にするために、各日特定の乗り物を休止しなくてはいけないということにご留意ください。今日はThe Clawが動かなくなります。もしその乗り物を楽しみにされていましたら、他の日にまたお越しください。退場する途中でたった17ドルで再来園チケットを購入いただけます。今日は必ず水分補給をするようにしてください。最高気温が34度になる予報です。

語彙チェック □excitement 楽しみ □note 〜に注意する □ride （遊園地の）乗り物
□be in good running order 正常に作動している □strict 厳しい
□safety guideline 安全ガイドライン □out of action 動かなくなって
□look forward to 〜 〜を楽しみにする □returner 戻ってきた人
□on *one's* way 〜 〜の途中で □hydrated 水分を保持して

Dreamland Park
Rides Closed for Inspection This Week

Sunday	Loop-the-Loop
Monday	The Claw
Tuesday	Tri Wing Swing Thing
Wednesday	Wet Wonder
Thursday	Thunder Mountain
Friday	Gravitoni

Dreamland Park
今週点検のため休止となる乗り物

日曜日	Loop-the-Loop
月曜日	The Claw
火曜日	Tri Wing Swing Thing
水曜日	Wet Wonder
木曜日	Thunder Mountain
金曜日	Gravitoni

---

98 □□□ 正解 **B**

Look at the graphic. When is the announcement being made?

(A) On Sunday
(B) On Monday
(C) On Tuesday
(D) On Wednesday

図を見てください。お知らせはいつされていますか。

(A) 日曜日
(B) 月曜日
(C) 火曜日
(D) 水曜日

話し手は「各日特定の乗り物が休止になる」と説明した後、Today, The Claw will be out of action. と述べている。図を見ると、Monday の欄に The Claw と記載があることから、The Claw は月曜日に休止すると分かる。よって、この放送が行われているのは月曜日だと判断できるので、正解は (B)。

> (⚠) ここに注意!
> この問題は1つ目の設問だが、その正答根拠が出てくるのは本文の中盤。1つ目の正答根拠がなかなか出てこないと焦ってしまうことが多いので、次の設問の根拠も同時に待ち構えながら聞くのもポイント!

99　　　　　　　　　□□□　正解 D

What is mentioned about returner's tickets?

再来園チケットについて何が述べられていますか。

(A) They are valid for 12 months.

(A) 12カ月間有効である。

(B) They are only sold to registered members.

(B) 登録済みのメンバーにしか販売されない。

(C) They entitle holders to free refreshments.

(C) 所有者に無料の軽食の特典が与えられる。

(D) They are available at the exit.

(D) 出口で入手できる。

話し手は The Claw の運転休止について、それを楽しみにしていた人は別の機会に来るようにと伝えた後、returner's ticket「再来園チケット」について You can purchase a returner's ticket for just seventeen dollars on your way out. と説明している。「退場する途中で購入できる」ことを「出口で入手できる」と表した (D) が正解。

語彙チェック　□ valid　有効な、期限切れでない　□ entitle *A* to *B*　A に B を得る権利を与える
　　　　　　　□ refreshment　軽食

100　　　　　　　　　□□□　正解 B

What does the speaker remind people to do?

話し手は人々に何をするよう注意していますか。

(A) Hold on to their tickets

(A) チケットを手放さない

(B) Drink enough water

(B) 十分な水を飲む

(C) Enter a contest

(C) コンテストに出場する

(D) Visit the Web site

(D) ウェブサイトにアクセスする

話し手は最後に Please make sure to stay hydrated today. と伝え、その理由を「最高気温が34度になる」と説明している。stay hydrated は「脱水症状にならないように水分補給する」ということなので、水分補給を「十分な水を飲む」と言い換えた (B) が正解。

TEST 4

解答 & 解説

正解一覧

Part 1

問題番号	正解	1	2
1	A	☐	☐
2	A	☐	☐
3	C	☐	☐
4	B	☐	☐
5	C	☐	☐
6	D	☐	☐

Part 2

問題番号	正解	1	2
7	B	☐	☐
8	C	☐	☐
9	C	☐	☐
10	A	☐	☐
11	B	☐	☐
12	B	☐	☐
13	A	☐	☐
14	B	☐	☐
15	C	☐	☐
16	B	☐	☐
17	B	☐	☐
18	A	☐	☐
19	B	☐	☐
20	A	☐	☐
21	C	☐	☐
22	C	☐	☐
23	A	☐	☐
24	A	☐	☐
25	C	☐	☐
26	A	☐	☐
27	B	☐	☐
28	C	☐	☐
29	A	☐	☐
30	B	☐	☐
31	B	☐	☐

Part 3

問題番号	正解	1	2
32	A	☐	☐
33	C	☐	☐
34	C	☐	☐
35	B	☐	☐
36	D	☐	☐
37	D	☐	☐
38	C	☐	☐
39	A	☐	☐
40	D	☐	☐
41	C	☐	☐
42	C	☐	☐
43	B	☐	☐
44	A	☐	☐
45	A	☐	☐
46	D	☐	☐
47	A	☐	☐
48	C	☐	☐
49	B	☐	☐
50	C	☐	☐
51	B	☐	☐
52	A	☐	☐
53	D	☐	☐
54	A	☐	☐
55	D	☐	☐
56	B	☐	☐

Part 4

問題番号	正解	1 2	問題番号	正解	1 2	問題番号	正解	1 2
57	D	☐☐	71	A	☐☐	96	A	☐☐
58	D	☐☐	72	B	☐☐	97	C	☐☐
59	C	☐☐	73	B	☐☐	98	A	☐☐
60	B	☐☐	74	D	☐☐	99	D	☐☐
61	C	☐☐	75	B	☐☐	100	D	☐☐
62	A	☐☐	76	D	☐☐			
63	A	☐☐	77	C	☐☐			
64	D	☐☐	78	A	☐☐			
65	B	☐☐	79	D	☐☐			
66	C	☐☐	80	B	☐☐			
67	B	☐☐	81	C	☐☐			
68	C	☐☐	82	D	☐☐			
69	A	☐☐	83	A	☐☐			
70	B	☐☐	84	C	☐☐			
			85	C	☐☐			
			86	C	☐☐			
			87	B	☐☐			
			88	D	☐☐			
			89	A	☐☐			
			90	B	☐☐			
			91	A	☐☐			
			92	C	☐☐			
			93	A	☐☐			
			94	C	☐☐			
			95	A	☐☐			

Part 1

(A) They're holding a paper down.
(B) They're printing out a copy.
(C) They're paging through a booklet.
(D) They're fixing some equipment.

(A) 彼らは紙を押さえ付けている。
(B) 彼らはコピーをプリントアウトしている。
(C) 彼らはパンフレットのページをめくっている。
(D) 彼らは機器を修理している。

写真に写っている2人の男性は、机の上に広げられた設計図のような紙を手で押さえている。よって、その動作を説明している (A) が正解。

語彙チェック　□print out 〜　〜をプリントアウトする　□page through 〜　〜のページをめくる
　　　　　　　□booklet　小冊子、パンフレット

> 🈲 **ここに注意！**
> 正答の (A) では、hold 〜 down「〜を動かないようにする」という表現が使われている。holdは誰もが知っている基本動詞ではあるが、このように副詞などと一緒に使われると意味を取れなくなる人も多い。基本動詞ほど表現の幅が広いので注意しよう！

(A) Seats are set on either side of the street.
(B) Some dishes are served on a table.
(C) A sign has been placed on the floor.
(D) The road is being paved by a worker.

(A) 座席が道の両側に配置されている。
(B) 料理がテーブルに出されている。
(C) 看板が床に置かれている。
(D) 道路が作業員によって舗装されているところである。

道の両側にはテーブルや椅子があり、座席が配置されていることが分かるので、これを説明している (A) が正解。

語彙チェック　□dish　料理　□pave　〜を舗装する

3 🇺🇸 ☐☐☐ 正解 C ▶TRACK_247

(A) He's pointing at a bottle.

(B) He's pushing a button on the ceiling.

(C) He's wearing safety equipment on his face.

(D) He's opening a drawer in the laboratory.

(A) 彼はボトルを指さしている。

(B) 彼は天井のボタンを押している。

(C) 彼は顔に安全装備を身に着けている。

(D) 彼は実験室にある引き出しを開けている。

保護眼鏡を掛けた男性の状態について説明している (C) が正解。保護眼鏡のことを大きく safety equipment と言い表している。

語彙チェック ☐ point at ～ ～を指さす ☐ laboratory 実験室

4 🇬🇧 ☐☐☐ 正解 B ▶TRACK_248

(A) Signs have been printed on stationery.

(B) Some packages are piled on a cart.

(C) One of the men is emptying a box.

(D) One of the men is opening a door.

(A) 記号が文房具に印刷されている。

(B) 小包がカートの上に積み上げられている。

(C) 男性の1人が箱を空にしている。

(D) 男性の1人がドアを開けている。

写真の中央付近に箱が写っており、この箱がカートの上に積み上げられている状態を説明している (B) が正解。

語彙チェック ☐ stationery 文房具 ☐ package 小包、荷物 ☐ pile ～を積み上げる ☐ empty ～を空にする

⚠ ここに注意！

正答の (B) では段ボールの箱を package「小包」と言い表している一方、誤答の (C) では box「箱」が出てきている。このように、Part 1では同じ物がいろいろな語や語句で言い換えられて出てくるので、言い換えに対応する力も必要になる。1つの物の表し方を複数自分で考えてみるトレーニングで、言い換え力をアップしよう！

(A) One of the women is seated on a sofa.
(B) One of the women is sipping a glass of water.
(C) One of the men is taking an order.
(D) One of the men is tightening his tie.
(A) 女性の1人がソファに座っている。
(B) 女性の1人が1杯の水を少しずつ飲んでいる。
(C) 男性の1人が注文を取っている。
(D) 男性の1人がネクタイを締めている。

レストランでの食事の場面。ウエーターと思われる男性の行動について説明している(C)
が正解。このように、場面から人物の職業を推測できる場合も多い。

語彙チェック　□be seated　座っている　□sip　～を少しずつ飲む　□take an order　注文を取る
　　　　　　　□tighten　～を締める

(A) The door is being held open by a cart.
(B) Cleaning tools have been scattered on the floor.
(C) The woman is sweeping leaves.
(D) The woman is carrying an ID badge.
(A) ドアがカートで開けられている。
(B) 掃除用具が床に散らばっている。
(C) 女性は葉を掃いている。
(D) 女性はIDバッジを持ち歩いている。

女性は首にIDバッジを下げていることが分かるので、これを説明している(D)が正解。
人物の動作とともに、人物が身に着けている物にも注目するようにしよう。

語彙チェック　□scatter　～をまき散らす、～をばらまく　□sweep　～を掃く

Part 2

7 W 🇨🇦 M 🇺🇸 ☐☐☐ 正解 **B** ▶TRACK_252

Why's the north exit of the station crowded?　　なぜ駅の北口が混雑しているのですか。

(A) On the opposite side of the road.　　(A) 道の反対側です。

(B) Some ticket gates are out of order.　　(B) 一部の改札機が故障中です。

(C) The train is bound for London.　　(C) ロンドン行きの電車です。

駅の北口が混雑している理由を尋ねているのに対し、「一部の改札機が故障中だ」と事情を説明している (B) が正解。

語彙チェック　□exit　出口　□crowded　混雑した　□opposite　反対の
□out of order　故障して　□bound for ～　～行きの

> 🐾ここに注意！
>
> 会話では Why's のように、疑問詞と be 動詞が短縮されて発音されることがある。疑問詞の短縮形は聞き取りづらく、聞き間違えも起こりやすいので特に注意しよう！

8 M 🇦🇺 W 🇨🇦 ☐☐☐ 正解 **C** ▶TRACK_253

I wonder if I should buy an annual membership to your theater.　　あなたたちの劇場の年間会員になるべきか悩んでいます。

(A) Some food items are discounted today.　　(A) 今日はいくつかの食品が割引されています。

(B) This movie was released recently.　　(B) この映画は最近公開されました。

(C) How often do you come here?　　(C) どのくらいの頻度でここに来ますか。

問いかけ文では、劇場の年間会員になるべきかどうかを相談している。これに対し、How often ～? と劇場に訪れる頻度を尋ねている (C) が正解。どれくらい劇場に足を運んでいるのかによって、年間会員になるべきかどうかアドバイスしようとしていると考えられる。

語彙チェック　□membership　会員の身分　□release　～を公開する

Who can contact the representative of the construction company?

(A) Mr. James ordered a salad.

(B) It'll be completed by next week.

(C) Is there any problem?

誰が建築会社の代表者と連絡を取ることができますか。

(A) James さんがサラダを注文しました。

(B) 来週までには完了します。

(C) 何か問題がありましたか。

建築会社の代表者と連絡を取ることができる人を尋ねているのに対し、人物の名前を伝えるのではなく、「何か問題があったのか」と聞き返している(C)が正解。

語彙チェック　☐representative　代表者

> 🛑 ここに注意！
> (A)は Mr. James という人名が含まれているが、問いかけに答えている内容ではないので誤り。このように、Who ～?という問いかけに対して、人名を含む選択肢が誤答になるパターンもあるので注意しよう！

Weren't you nervous during the presentation?

(A) I've done it many times.

(B) There're not enough spaces for them.

(C) It took place yesterday.

プレゼンテーションの間、あなたは緊張しなかったのですか。

(A) 何回もやったことがあるのです。

(B) 彼らのための十分な座席がありません。

(C) それは昨日行われました。

「プレゼンテーションの間、緊張しなかったのか」と尋ねる否定疑問文。「何回もやったことがある」と伝えることで、間接的に緊張しなかったということと、その理由を説明している(A)が正解。代名詞の it は the presentation を指している。

語彙チェック　☐nervous　緊張して　☐space　座席、席　☐take place　行われる

Where do you think is the best place for our new branch?

(A) I think it's very easy to use.

(B) Tanya is more familiar with this city.

(C) We usually keep it in the cabinet.

どこが私たちの新しい支店に最適な場所だと思いますか。

(A) 使用するのはとても簡単だと思います。

(B) Tanya の方がこの街をよく知っています。

(C) 通常は戸棚に保管しています。

Where do you think ～?で、新しい支店の場所に関する意見を尋ねているのに対して、「Tanya の方がこの街をよく知っている」と答え、自分以外の人物に聞くよう促している(B)が正解。

語彙チェック　☐branch　支店　☐be familiar with ～　～をよく知っている　☐cabinet　戸棚

12　W 🇬🇧　M 🇦🇺　□□□　正解 B　▶TRACK_257

You could win a gift card by filling out this survey.

(A) These are the gifts from my colleagues.
(B) How long will it take?
(C) The store was filled with customers.

このアンケートに記入していただくとギフトカードを受け取れます。

(A) これらは私の同僚からの贈り物です。
(B) それはどのくらい時間がかかりますか。
(C) 店はお客さまでいっぱいでした。

助動詞の could を使った平叙文で、「アンケートに記入するとギフトカードを受け取れる」ということを提案している。これに対し、アンケートの所要時間を尋ねている (B) が正解。

語彙チェック　□ fill out ～　～に記入する　□ survey　アンケート調査　□ colleague　同僚

13　W 🇬🇧　W 🇨🇦　□□□　正解 A　▶TRACK_258

Haven't the chairs been set up for the training session?

(A) Participants will be standing in this workshop.
(B) I have already registered by e-mail.
(C) Anyone can attend it for free.

研修会用の椅子は準備されていないのですか。

(A) この研修会では、参加者は立っている予定です。
(B) すでに E メールで登録しました。
(C) 誰でも無料で参加できます。

研修会用の椅子が準備されていないことについて否定疑問文で尋ねているのに対し、「参加者は立っている予定だ」と答えることで、間接的に椅子が必要ないことを伝えている (A) が正解。

語彙チェック　□ register　登録する　□ for free　無料で

> 🉐 **ここに注意！**
> (A) の応答は、文の意味を理解するだけでなく、状況や意図を読み取ることができなくては選べない。「この研修会は立って参加する」ということはつまり「椅子が必要ない」ということだ、と瞬時に理解する必要がある！

14　M 🇦🇺　W 🇬🇧　□□□　正解 B　▶TRACK_259

When's the next sale at this store?
(A) This item will be restocked in July.
(B) We haven't announced any yet.
(C) You don't have to pay for shipping.

この店での次のセールはいつですか。
(A) この商品は7月に再入荷されます。
(B) まだ何も発表していません。
(C) 送料をお支払いいただく必要はありません。

問いかけ文では、次のセールの時期を尋ねている。これに対し、次のセールに関しては「まだ何も発表していない」と答えている (B) が正解。

語彙チェック　□ restock　～を再び仕入れる

Should I have this microwave oven
repaired, or purchase a new one?

この電子レンジを修理に出すべきですか、それとも
新しいものを買うべきですか。

(A) Our kitchen is cleaned every day.

(A) 私たちのキッチンは毎日掃除されます。

(B) There's an auto repair shop near here.

(B) この近くに自動車修理店があります。

(C) Let me take a look at it.

(C) それを見せてください。

問いかけ文は、電子レンジを修理に出すのと新しい電子レンジを買うのと、どちらがい
いかを尋ねる選択疑問文。どちらがいいか判断するために、まず電子レンジを見せるよ
うに伝えている(C)が正解。

語彙チェック　□microwave oven　電子レンジ　□auto　自動車

This book signing event doesn't have an
admission fee.

この本のサイン会には入場料はありません。

(A) I have an extra ticket.

(A) 余分なチケットを持っています。

(B) That'll be helpful for young people.

(B) 若者にとっては助かるでしょうね。

(C) There's a road sign over there.

(C) 向こうに道路標識があります。

問いかけ文は平叙文で、サイン会は入場料がかからないということを述べている。その
事実を受けて、入場料がかからないのは「若者にとっては助かるだろう」という自身の
意見を述べている(B)が正解。

語彙チェック　□admission　入場　□fee　料金　□extra　余分の

What brings you to our studio?

どういったご用件で、私たちのスタジオにいらっし
ゃいましたか。

(A) This is a tool box for professionals.

(A) これが専門家の道具箱です。

(B) I'm here to pick up the photos you
took.

(B) あなたたちが撮ってくれた写真を取りに来まし
た。

(C) To all of my clients.

(C) 私のお客さんの全員にです。

問いかけ文を直訳すると、「何があなたを私たちのスタジオに連れて来たのですか」とい
う意味。すなわち、スタジオを訪れた用件を尋ねていることが分かる。これに対し、訪
問の理由を答えている(B)が正解。

語彙チェック　□professional　専門家　□pick up 〜　〜を受け取る

🈲 ここに注意！

この問いかけ文は、What brings you to 〜?で訪問の目的を尋ねている。この表現を知
っていた上で、瞬時に質問の意図を判断しなければならないのが難問ポイント！

18　W 🇨🇦　M 🇺🇸　◻◻◻　正解 A　▶TRACK_263

We can't afford train advertising, can we?

(A) The budget is being reconsidered.

(B) Taking a taxi is the fastest way.

(C) Anyone in the advertising department.

電車広告を出す余裕はないですよね？

(A) 予算が再検討されています。

(B) タクシーに乗ることが最も速い方法です。

(C) 宣伝部の誰でもです。

電車広告を出す余裕があるかどうかを確認している付加疑問文。現在予算が再検討されている最中だと答えることで、電車広告を出す余裕が生まれるかもしれないと示唆している(A)が正解。

語彙チェック　□afford　〜の余裕がある　□reconsider　〜を再び考える

19　M 🇦🇺　M 🇺🇸　◻◻◻　正解 B　▶TRACK_264

Why haven't the instructions for our new game been completed yet?

(A) Because I used to work near here.

(B) Some additional features were added.

(C) It's one of our best sellers.

なぜ私たちの新しいゲームの説明書は、まだ完成していないのですか。

(A) 以前この近くで働いていたからです。

(B) いくつか追加の機能が付け加えられたのです。

(C) 私たちのヒット商品の1つです。

否定疑問文で、新しいゲームの説明書がまだ完成していない理由を尋ねている。これに対し、「追加の機能が付け加えられた」と事情を説明している(B)が正解。

語彙チェック　□instructions　説明書　□additional　追加の　□feature　機能

> 🐾**ここに注意！**
> ①「追加の機能が付け加えられた」→②「追加の機能について、説明書に書き加える必要がある」→③「だから説明書は完成していない」、ということ。②の部分の意図を読み取れるかがポイント！

20　W 🇬🇧　M 🇺🇸　◻◻◻　正解 A　▶TRACK_265

Could you help me find the best accountant?

(A) I'm happy to recommend some.

(B) This is the largest room we have.

(C) My company has a gym for employees.

最も有能な会計士を探すのを手伝っていただけませんか。

(A) 喜んで何人かお薦めいたします。

(B) 私たちが持っている部屋の中でこれが一番大きい部屋です。

(C) 私の会社には従業員のためのジムがあります。

Could you 〜？で会計士を探すのを手伝ってほしいと依頼しているのに対し、会計士を何人かお薦めすることを申し出ている(A)が正解。

語彙チェック　□accountant　会計士

What is your special item this month?

今月の特別メニューは何ですか。

(A) That cooking class was successful.

(A) あの料理教室は成功でした。

(B) You can move to the seats outside.

(B) 外の席に移動することもできますよ。

(C) Oh, there's no menu on your table.

(C) ああ、お客さまのテーブルにはメニューがないですね。

「今月の特別メニューは何か」と尋ねているのに対し、今月の特別メニューが分からないのはテーブルにメニューが置かれていないからだと気付いた発言をしている(C)が正解。

語彙チェック　☐successful　成功した　☐outside　外の

Would it be possible to finish your report ahead of schedule?

予定より早くあなたの報告書を完成させることは可能ですか。

(A) The finish on the desks is great.

(A) 机の仕上がりは素晴らしいです。

(B) That was her first time.

(B) それは彼女にとって初めての経験でした。

(C) I'm almost done.

(C) もう少しで終わります。

予定より早く報告書を完成させることが可能かどうかを尋ねているのに対し、「もう少しで終わる」と作業の進捗を報告している(C)が正解。

語彙チェック　☐ahead of schedule　予定より早く　☐finish　仕上がり

Is there any chance you'll visit your family this year?

今年家族のもとを訪れる可能性はありますか。

(A) I'm not so busy in June.

(A) 6月はそれほど忙しくありません。

(B) You should try it on.

(B) 試着してみるべきです。

(C) We're stuck in traffic.

(C) 渋滞に巻き込まれています。

there is ～構文を使って、今年家族のもとを訪れる可能性について尋ねている。これに対し、「6月はそれほど忙しくない」と答えることで、その時期に訪れる可能性があることを示唆している(A)が正解。

語彙チェック　☐try ～ on　～を試着する

24　W 🇬🇧　M 🇦🇺　□□□　正解 **A**　▶TRACK_269

The applicant sent us her résumé, didn't she?

(A) I'll forward her e-mail to you.
(B) Let's apply for it now.
(C) She will set up the device.

その応募者は自身の履歴書を送ってくれましたよね？

(A) 彼女のEメールをあなたに転送します。
(B) 今応募しましょう。
(C) 彼女が装置を設置してくれます。

問いかけ文は、応募者が履歴書を送ってくれたかどうかを確認する付加疑問文。応募者のEメールを転送すると申し出て、履歴書をすでに受け取ったことを示唆している(A)が正解。

語彙チェック　□applicant　応募者　□forward　～を転送する　□set up～　～を設置する
　　　　　　　□device　装置

25　M 🇺🇸　W 🇨🇦　□□□　正解 **C**　▶TRACK_270

When are you going to finish revising this document?

(A) Actually, I went there yesterday.
(B) Either is fine for me.
(C) Do you have time to review it?

この書類の修正をいつ終わらせる予定ですか。

(A) 実は、そこには昨日行きました。
(B) 私はどちらでも大丈夫です。
(C) それを見直してもらう時間はありますか。

書類の修正について、修正が完了する予定を尋ねているのに対し、「書類を見直してもらう時間はあるか」と質問で返している(C)が正解。itはthis documentを指している。

語彙チェック　□revise　～を修正する　□review　～を見直す

26　M 🇦🇺　W 🇬🇧　□□□　正解 **A**　▶TRACK_271

How different is the new software from the previous one?

(A) It's more cost-effective.
(B) All the participants agreed to that.
(C) By selecting one that you like the most.

新しいソフトウェアは以前のソフトウェアとどう違いますか。

(A) より費用効果が高いです。
(B) 全ての参加者がそれに同意しました。
(C) あなたが一番好きなものを選ぶことによってです。

How different ～?で新しいソフトウェアと以前のソフトウェアの違いを尋ねているのに対し、新しい方は「より費用効果が高い」と異なる点を具体的に述べている(A)が正解。主語のitはthe new softwareを指している。

語彙チェック　□previous　以前の　□cost-effective　費用効果の高い　□participant　参加者

> 🚫 **ここに注意！**
> How different ～?は「どう違うのか」と違いを尋ねる表現。ここでは文頭のHow different
> の部分がかなりさらっと発音されているので、聞き取りにくくなっている！

203

Where's the room you want us to clean? 私たちに掃除してほしい部屋はどこですか。

(A) The room needs booking in advance. (A) その部屋は事前に予約が必要です。

(B) The same one you did last week. (B) 先週掃除したのと同じ部屋です。

(C) You can submit it later. (C) 後で提出できます。

問いかけ文では、掃除してほしい部屋の場所を尋ねている。これに対し、「先週掃除したのと同じ部屋だ」と伝えることで、間接的に部屋の場所を教えている(B)が正解。oneはroomを指し、didはcleanedを意味している。

語彙チェック □in advance 事前に □submit 〜を提出する

⚠ここに注意！
正答の(B)では、roomを指すoneという代名詞や、同じ動詞を繰り返さないためのdidが登場している。置きかえられたり省略されたりしている部分が何を指すのか、整理しながら聞くようにしよう！

How was the trade show last week? 先週の見本市はどうでしたか。

(A) I can't wait for it. (A) 待ちきれないです。

(B) Whichever you can. (B) あなたができる方で構いません。

(C) You should've come. (C) あなたは来るべきでしたよ。

先週行われた見本市の感想を尋ねているのに対し、「あなたは来るべきだった」と自身の意見を伝えている(C)が正解。問いかけをしている人物が見本市に来られなかったことを残念に思うほど、行って良かったと思っていることがうかがえる。

語彙チェック □trade show 見本市

We need someone to analyze our sales data. 売上データを分析する人が必要です。

(A) I used to work as a sales consultant. (A) 以前販売コンサルタントとして働いていました。

(B) Yes, it was already sold out. (B) はい、すでに売り切れました。

(C) Do you want to change the date? (C) 日付を変更したいですか。

問いかけ文は平叙文で、「売上データを分析する人が必要だ」と述べている。これに対し、販売コンサルタントとしての自身の実務経験を伝えることで、自分がデータ分析の業務を引き受けることができることを示唆している(A)が正解。

語彙チェック □analyze 〜を分析する □consultant コンサルタント

30　M🇺🇸　W🇬🇧　□□□　正解 B　▶TRACK_275

Will our new phone model be sold in black only or multiple colors?
(A) Print it in black and white.
(B) Customers can choose from five.
(C) You can make a payment online, too.

私たちの新しい携帯のモデルは黒色のみで売られますか、それとも複数の色で売られますか。
(A) 白黒で印刷してください。
(B) お客さまは5色から選ぶことができます。
(C) オンライン決済もできます。

新しい携帯のモデルのカラーについて、選択疑問文で「黒色のみで売られるか、それとも複数の色で売られるか」と尋ねている。この2択に対し、間接的に複数の色で売られることを伝えている(B)が正解。

語彙チェック　□multiple　複数の　□payment　支払い

31　W🇨🇦　M🇦🇺　□□□　正解 B　▶TRACK_276

Can I take a look at your portfolio?
(A) We met at the airport.
(B) These are my previous works.
(C) It was not very long.

ポートフォリオを見てもよろしいですか。
(A) 私たちは空港で出会いました。
(B) これらが私の以前の作品です。
(C) あまり長くありませんでした。

Can I ～?でポートフォリオを見る許可を求めているのに対し、「これらが私の以前の作品だ」と答えることで、間接的に見ることを承諾している(B)が正解。

語彙チェック　□portfolio　ポートフォリオ　□previous　以前の　□works　作品

M 🇺🇸 **W** 🇬🇧 　　　　　　　　　　　会話 ▶TRACK_278　問題 ▶TRACK_279

Questions 32 through 34 refer to the following conversation.

M: I think it's time we did a cleanup of the storage room. What do you say, Tina?

W: Yes, there's a lot of stuff in there we don't need. The only thing is that garbage collection isn't until Friday. Shouldn't we do it on Thursday afternoon?

M: That's a good point. But, I don't think we can dispose of that much in the regular garbage. We'll have to call someone to come and take it away.

W: In that case, there's no reason why we can't get started today. I'll get a couple of people from my section to come and separate the useful items from things we can throw out.

問題32-34は次の会話に関するものです。

男性：倉庫室の掃除をする時期だと思います。どう思いますか、Tina。

女性：そうですね、そこには必要ない物がたくさんあります。ごみ収集が金曜日までないということだけが問題ですね。木曜日の午後に掃除をするべきではないでしょうか。

男性：それは良いポイントですね。でも、いつものごみに含めてそんなに多くは出せないと思いますよ。回収に来てもらうように電話をしないといけませんね。

女性：その場合は、今日始められない理由はありませんね。私の部署から2、3人来させて、使える物と捨てる物を分別してもらいます。

語彙チェック　　□cleanup　掃除　□What do you say?　あなたはどう思いますか。
　　　　　　　　　　□garbage collection　ごみ収集　□dispose of ~　~を処分する
　　　　　　　　　　□take ~ away　~を運び去る、~を持ち去る
　　　　　　　　　　□separate A from B　AをBから区別する

32　　　　　　　　　　□□□　正解 **A**

What does the man ask the woman about?　　　　男性は女性に何について尋ねていますか。

(A) Her opinion on a suggestion

(B) Her plans for the weekend

(C) The location of a cabinet

(D) The cost of some supplies

(A) 提案についての彼女の意見

(B) 彼女の週末の予定

(C) キャビネットの位置

(D) 備品の値段

男性は冒頭で「倉庫室の掃除をする時期だと思う」と述べ、What do you say, Tina? と女性に意見を求めている。これに対し、女性はYesと男性に同意を示した上で、「必要ない物がたくさんある」と意見を述べている。よって、男性は女性に倉庫室の掃除をすることを提案し、それに対する女性の意見を求めていると分かるので、正解は(A)。

33

□□□　正解 C

When is the next garbage collection?

(A) On Wednesday

(B) On Thursday

(C) On Friday

(D) On Saturday

次のごみ収集はいつですか。

(A) 水曜日

(B) 木曜日

(C) 金曜日

(D) 土曜日

男性の「倉庫室の掃除をする時期だと思う」という提案に同意した女性は、The only thing is that garbage collection isn't until Friday. と懸念点を述べている。金曜日までごみ収集がないということは、すなわち、次のごみ収集は金曜日であるということなので、正解は (C)。

> 🐾 ここに注意！
>
> 女性が Shouldn't we do it on Thursday afternoon? と言っているが、この it は cleanup of the storage room「倉庫室の掃除」のことを指しているので (B) On Thursday は間違い。文脈が取れていないと、選択肢にある単語が登場したときに誘導されてしまうことがあるので要注意！

34

□□□　正解 C

What does the woman say she will do?

(A) Introduce a dependable recycling company

(B) Post a schedule on the company bulletin board

(C) Have some employees sort some items

(D) Ask for an extension on a deadline

女性は何をすると言っていますか。

(A) 信頼できるリサイクル会社を紹介する

(B) 会社の掲示板に予定表を掲示する

(C) 従業員に品物を分類させる

(D) 期限の延長を求める

ごみの回収に来てもらうように電話をする必要があると男性が伝えると、女性は「その場合は、今日始められない理由はない」と述べ、I'll get a couple of people from my section to come and separate the useful items from things we can throw out. と言っている。自分の部署の人に物の分別を頼むということなので、(C) が正解。

> **語彙チェック** □dependable　信頼できる　□post　～を掲示する　□bulletin board　掲示板
> □sort　～を分類する

M 🇦🇺　**W1** 🇨🇦　**W2** 🇬🇧　　　　　　会話 ▶TRACK_280　問題 ▶TRACK_281

Questions 35 through 37 refer to the following conversation with three speakers.

M:　Hi. I'm here about the annual Cross-Town Bicycle Race. Is there still time to sign up?

W1:　Yesterday was the last day, but we might have a cancellation. Cora, could you check if the capacity is full now?

W2:　We just had a cancellation earlier today. As long as you meet the requirements, we can accept your application.

M:　That's great. I've already filled out my application form, and I have the entry fee with me.

W1:　Great. Have you ever taken part in the Cross-Town Bicycle Race before?

M:　No. This will be my first time.

W1:　OK, well there's an orientation session that you'll need to take part in before the race. Make sure you get here by nine A.M. on the day of the race. The race starts at ten thirty.

問題35-37は3人の話し手による次の会話に関するものです。

男性　：こんにちは。毎年開催されるCross-Town自転車レースのことで伺いました。まだ参加登録はできますか。

女性1：昨日が最終日でしたが、キャンセルがあったかもしれません。Cora、定員が現在いっぱいかどうか見てもらえますか。

女性2：今日先ほど、ちょうどキャンセルが出たところです。あなたが条件を満たしてさえいれば、申し込みを受け付けますよ。

男性　：よかったです。もう申込用紙は記入済みで、参加料も持ってきました。

女性1：承知しました。以前にCross-Town自転車レースに参加したことはありますか。

男性　：いいえ。これが初めてになります。

女性1：そうですか、それではレースの前に参加しなければいけない説明会があります。レース当日は必ず午前9時までにここへ着くようにしてください。レースは10時30分スタートです。

語彙チェック　□sign up　参加登録をする　□as long as ～　～さえすれば
　　　　　　　　□meet　（条件）を満たす　□requirement　必要条件　□fill out ～　～を記入する
　　　　　　　　□entry fee　参加料　□orientation session　説明会

35　正解 B

Who most likely are the women?　女性たちは誰だと考えられますか。

(A) City officials　(A) 市の職員

(B) Event organizers　(B) イベントの主催者

(C) Bicycle repairpersons　(C) 自転車修理工

(D) Professional athletes　(D) プロのアスリート

　Cross-Town 自転車レースの参加登録はまだ可能かどうか尋ねている男性に対し、1人目の女性は「昨日が最終日だったが、キャンセルがあったかもしれない」と説明している。また、その後2人目の女性は As long as you meet the requirements, we can accept your application. と男性に伝えている。これらから、女性たちはレースの参加登録受付を行っていると判断でき、イベント主催者であると考えられる。よって、正解は (B)。

36　正解 D

What does the man say he has brought with him?　男性は何を持ってきたと言っていますか。

(A) A bicycle　(A) 自転車

(B) An assistant　(B) アシスタント

(C) Some identification　(C) 身分証明書

(D) Some money　(D) お金

　レースへの参加申し込みを受け付けてもらえることになった男性は、I've already filled out my application form, and I have the entry fee with me. と述べている。the entry fee「参加料」を言い換えている (D) が正解。

37　正解 D

What is the man asked to do?　男性は何をするよう求められていますか。

(A) Give a presentation　(A) プレゼンテーションをする

(B) Write down her address　(B) 彼女の住所を書く

(C) Purchase some equipment　(C) 備品を購入する

(D) Attend a briefing　(D) 説明会に出席する

　レースに出場するのは初めてだと言う男性に、1人目の女性は there's an orientation session that you'll need to take part in before the race と説明している。その後、その説明会に出席するために来るべき時間についても伝えているので、(D) が正解。

語彙チェック　□ briefing　説明会

209

Questions 38 through 40 refer to the following conversation.

W: I think the only way that we can improve our profit is by bringing down the factory's running costs.

M: You're probably right, but perhaps we should hire a consultant to come in and take a look.

W: Well, let's see what we can come up with first. I heard about a new kind of light bulb with motion sensors. They switch off automatically when no one's in the room.

M: Nice idea. I'll put a suggestion box in the break room to see if the staff can come up with any good ways to save money. I'll offer a reward for any ideas we end up using.

問題38-40は次の会話に関するものです。

女性：利益を上げることができる唯一の方法は、工場の維持費を下げることだと思います。

男性：そうかもしれませんが、コンサルタントを雇って見に来てもらった方がいいかもしれません。

女性：それでは、まず何を思い付くか見てみましょう。私は人感センサー付きの新しい種類の電球があると耳にしました。それは部屋に誰もいないときは自動的にスイッチがオフになるのです。

男性：いい考えですね。休憩室に提案箱を置いて、スタッフの皆さんがお金を節約するいい方法を思い付くかどうか見てみますよ。最終的に使用することになったアイデアには褒賞を出しましょう。

語彙チェック　□bring down ～　（費用）を下げる　□running cost　維持費
　　　　　　　　　□consultant　コンサルタント　□come up with ～　～を思い付く
　　　　　　　　　□light bulb　電球　□motion sensor　人感センサー
　　　　　　　　　□switch off　（電灯などが）切れる　□reward　報酬、褒美
　　　　　　　　　□end up *doing*　ついには～することになる

38　　　　　　　　　□□□　正解 **C**

What does the woman want to do?

(A) Provide training

(B) Schedule a vacation

(C) Reduce spending

(D) Hold a banquet

女性は何をしたいと思っていますか。

(A) 研修を提供する

(B) 休暇の予定を組む

(C) 支出を減らす

(D) 宴会を開催する

女性は冒頭でI think the only way that we can improve our profit is by bringing down the factory's running costs.と発言している。「工場の維持費を下げる」ことを「支出を減らす」と言い換えている(C)が正解。その後も、女性は人感センサー付きの電球について述べ、工場の維持費を抑えるために具体的な提案をしている。

語彙チェック　□banquet　宴会

39

What does the man suggest?

(A) Speaking with an expert
(B) Buying some new equipment
(C) Checking a calendar
(D) Calling a venue

正解 A

男性は何を提案していますか。

(A) 専門家と話すこと
(B) 新しい機器を買うこと
(C) 日程表を確認すること
(D) 会場に電話すること

利益を上げることができる唯一の方法は工場の維持費を下げることだという女性の意見に対し、男性は You're probably right と同意を示す一方で、but perhaps we should hire a consultant to come in and take a look と意見を述べている。男性はコンサルタントに見てもらうことを提案しているので、(A) が正解。

語彙チェック □venue　会場

40

What does the man say he will do?

(A) Return from a business trip early
(B) Reserve a conference room
(C) Order some goods from an online store
(D) Encourage employees to share their ideas

正解 D

男性は何をすると言っていますか。

(A) 出張から早く戻る
(B) 会議室を予約する
(C) オンラインストアで商品を注文する
(D) 従業員にアイデアを共有するよう促す

人感センサー付きの電球を導入するという女性の提案を聞くと、男性は I'll put a suggestion box in the break room to see if the staff can come up with any good ways to save money. と言い、また I'll offer a reward for any ideas we end up using. とも述べている。「提案箱を設置すること」と「褒賞を出すこと」は、従業員が節約についてのアイデアを共有するのを促すための方法である。よって、正解は (D)。

語彙チェック □encourage A to do　A に～するよう勧める

M: 🇦🇺 W: 🇬🇧　　　　　　　　　　　　

Questions 41 through 43 refer to the following conversation.

M: Thank you for coming to the radio station to talk about your career in the tech industry. I hope this interview will inspire young people.

W: Thank you for inviting me in. It's interesting that you mentioned young people. I got started in programming when I was in my first year of high school. I created a smartphone app to help students manage their schedules. It was called SSA.

M: I read that you made a lot of money by selling that application. It was how you got funding to start your first company.

W: You've done your homework. Hmm. Impressive... Not many people know that. Yes, the application was quite popular and GeoTech Infoware asked me to sell it to them.

M: It was a good decision for them. They made a lot of money from SSA. It's one of their best-selling products.

問題41-43は次の会話に関するものです。

男性：テクノロジー業界でのあなたの経歴についてお話をするために、ラジオ局へお越しいただきありがとうございます。このインタビューが若者たちに刺激を与えるものになればと思います。

女性：お招きいただきありがとうございます。あなたが若者のことに触れたのは興味深いですね。私は高校1年生の時にプログラミングをやり始めました。学生がスケジュールを管理するのを支援するスマートフォン用アプリを作りました。それはSSAと呼ばれるものでした。

男性：あなたはそのアプリを売ることで大金を稼いだと読みましたよ。そうやって最初の会社を立ち上げるための資金を得たのですね。

女性：あなたは入念な準備をしていますね。うーん。素晴らしい…　そのことを知っている人はあまり多くありませんよ。そうです、アプリはかなり人気があって、GeoTech Infoware 社がそれを売ってほしいと依頼してきました。

男性：彼らは良い決断をしましたね。彼らはSSAから大金を得ました。それは彼らの最も売れている商品のうちの1つですね。

語彙チェック　□tech　テクノロジー、科学技術　□inspire　〜に刺激を与える
□start in 〜　〜を始める　□programming　プログラミング
□funding　財源、資金　□best-selling　最もよく売れている

41　　　□□□　正解 C

What does the woman say she did in high school?

(A) She joined an academic competition.

(B) She became friends with her business partner.

(C) She created a software program.

(D) She founded a club for computer enthusiasts.

女性は高校で何をしたと言っていますか。

(A) 彼女は学問の大会に参加した。

(B) 彼女は彼女のビジネスパートナーと友人になった。

(C) 彼女はソフトウェアプログラムを作った。

(D) 彼女はコンピューター好きの人のためのクラブを設立した。

冒頭の男性の発言から、男性が女性の経歴についてインタビューをする場面だと判断できる。女性は自身の経歴について、I got started in programming when I was in my first year of high school. と述べている。続けて女性は I created a smartphone app と説明を加えているので、この a smartphone app を a software program と言い換えている (C) が正解。

語彙チェック □academic　学問の　□enthusiast　熱中している人、ファン

42　　　　　　　　　　　　正解 C

Why does the woman say, "You've done your homework"?	女性はなぜ "You've done your homework" と言っていますか。
(A) To reassure the man	(A) 男性を安心させるため
(B) To suggest taking a break	(B) 休憩をとることを提案するため
(C) To express admiration	(C) 称賛を言い表すため
(D) To explain an outcome	(D) 結果を説明するため

下線部の発言は、女性が最初の会社を立ち上げる資金を得た方法について、男性が言及した後にされている。その後の Hmm. Impressive... Not many people know that. という発言から、男性が自分のことを調べ上げていることに感心している様子がうかがえる。これらのことから、女性は下線部の発言で、男性がインタビュアーとしての仕事を全うしていることへの称賛の気持ちを表していると考えられる。よって、正解は (C)。

語彙チェック □reassure　〜を安心させる　□admiration　感嘆、称賛
□outcome　結果、成果

43　　　　　　　　　　　　正解 B

What does the man say about SSA?	男性は SSA について何と言っていますか。
(A) It has won awards.	(A) それは賞を受賞した。
(B) It was a good investment.	(B) それは良い投資だった。
(C) It is popular among people of all ages.	(C) それは全ての年代の人々に人気がある。
(D) It has been sold several times.	(D) それは何回か売れたことがある。

GeoTech Infoware 社が女性に SSA というスマートフォン用アプリの売却を依頼してきたことに関して、男性は It was a good decision for them. と発言している。その後の男性の説明から、SSA は GeoTech Infoware 社の人気商品になり、同社が収益を上げたことが分かる。よって、男性は「GeoTech Infoware 社にとって SSA を買ったのは良い投資だった」と考えていると判断できるので、(B) が正解。

語彙チェック □investment　投資

Questions 44 through 46 refer to the following conversation.

W: I heard about you from Margo Day. She's one of the other salespeople here. You helped her sell her house last year. She was really happy with the work you did.

M: I should thank Margo for introducing us, then. Her home sold for much more than she expected; it was a great result. Can I ask why you're selling?

W: I'm moving back to Seattle so I can spend more time with my family.

M: Wow, I'm originally from Seattle, too. What made you leave?

W: At the time, I wanted to live somewhere warmer.

問題44-46は次の会話に関するものです。

女性：御社のことはMargo Dayから伺っています。彼女はここの販売員の1人なのです。御社は、昨年彼女が家を売却するのを手助けしたのですよね。彼女はあなた方の仕事にとても喜んでいましたよ。

男性：それでは、私たちを紹介いただいたことに関して、Margoに感謝しなければいけませんね。彼女の家は彼女が予想していたよりもはるかに高い金額で売れました。素晴らしい結果でしたよ。あなたが売却する理由をお伺いできますか。

女性：家族ともっと時間を過ごせるように、Seattleに戻る予定なのです。

男性：そうですか、私ももともとはSeattle出身です。何がきっかけでそこを出たのですか。

女性：その時は、もっと暖かいところに住みたかったのです。

語彙チェック　□salespeople　販売員　□sell for 〜　〜で売れる　□more than 〜　〜より多い
□originally　もとは、初めは

44　　□□□　正解 A

How did the woman learn about the man's business?

(A) From a colleague

(B) From an advertisement

(C) From a Web site

(D) From a consultant

女性は男性の会社について、どのように知りましたか。

(A) 同僚から

(B) 広告から

(C) ウェブサイトから

(D) コンサルタントから

女性は冒頭でI heard about you from Margo Day.と言い、Margo DayさんについてShe's one of the other salespeople here.と説明している。ここから、女性は同僚であるMargo Dayさんから男性の会社について話を聞いていることが分かるので、正解は(A)。

45

□□□ 正解 **A**

Why does the woman say she will move? 　女性はなぜ引っ越すと言っていますか。

(A) To be closer to her family 　(A) 彼女の家族の近くにいるため
(B) To take a new job 　(B) 新しい仕事に就くため
(C) To save money on rent 　(C) 家賃を節約するため
(D) To have more room 　(D) もっとスペースを手に入れるため

男性がCan I ask why you're selling?と売却理由について尋ねると、女性は「Seattleに戻る予定だ」と明かした後、引っ越しの目的をso I can spend more time with my familyと説明している。よって、正解は(A)。

46

□□□ 正解 **D**

What does the man ask the woman? 　男性は女性に何を尋ねていますか。

(A) How she will pay for a service 　(A) 彼女がどのようにサービス代を支払うのか
(B) How much she made from a sale 　(B) 彼女がどのくらい販売で稼いだのか。
(C) What she will have for lunch 　(C) 彼女が何をランチに食べるのか
(D) Why she left her hometown 　(D) 彼女がなぜ故郷を去ったのか

男性は女性がSeattleに戻る予定だと聞くと、自分もSeattleの出身だと述べた後、女性にWhat made you leave?と尋ねている。「何があなたを（Seattleから）去らせたのですか」とは、すなわち「なぜあなたはSeattleを去ったのですか」ということである。よって、Seattleをhometown「故郷」と表した(D)が正解。

語彙チェック □pay for 〜　〜の代金を支払う

Questions 47 through 49 refer to the following conversation.

W: It's taking me longer than I thought to finish this report. What time will the cruise depart tonight?

M: It leaves at six thirty. We can take a taxi from here to the marina. We should be there in time as long as we leave by six o'clock.

W: OK. Would you mind giving me a hand, then? I need someone to check my calculations before I send the report to the head office.

M: I'm a bit busy, but I think Karen could help you. The client she was supposed to meet canceled at the last moment.

問題47-49は次の会話に関するものです。

女性：この報告書を完成させるのに、思っていたよりも時間がかかっています。今夜クルーズ船が出港するのは何時ですか。

男性：6時30分に出発します。ここからマリーナまでタクシーに乗って行くことができますよ。6時までにここを出さえすれば、間に合うはずです。

女性：分かりました。では、手を貸していただけませんか。本部に報告書を送る前に、誰かに私の計算を確認してもらう必要があるのです。

男性：私はちょっと忙しいのですが、Karen が手伝えると思いますよ。彼女が会うことになっていた顧客が、直前でキャンセルになりましたから。

語彙チェック 　□cruise　クルーズ船　□marina　マリーナ（ヨットやボートなどの停泊所）
　　　　　　　　□in time　間に合って　□as long as 〜　〜さえすれば
　　　　　　　　□give 〜 a hand　〜に手を貸す、〜を手伝う　□calculation　計算
　　　　　　　　□head office　本部　□be supposed to *do*　〜することになっている
　　　　　　　　□at the last moment　直前で、間際で

47　　　　　　　　　　　　　　　　　□□□　正解 **A**

What will the speakers most likely do this evening?

(A) Take part in a dinner cruise

(B) Meet with a client

(C) Attend a theatrical production

(D) Go on a business trip

話し手たちは今晩何をすると考えられますか。

(A) ディナークルーズに参加する

(B) 顧客に会う

(C) 演劇作品を観に行く

(D) 出張に行く

女性は冒頭で、「報告書を完成させるのに、思っていたよりも時間がかかっている」と言うと、What time will the cruise depart tonight? と男性に尋ねている。これに対し、男性は It leaves at six thirty. と答え、We can take a taxi from here to the marina. と付け加えている。これらの発言から、話し手たちは今夜クルーズ船に乗りに行くと考えられる。よって、正解は (A)。

語彙チェック 　□take part in 〜　〜に参加する　□theatrical production　演劇作品

48

□□□ 正解 **C**

By what time does the man say they should leave the office?

(A) 5:00 P.M.

(B) 5:30 P.M.

(C) 6:00 P.M.

(D) 6:30 P.M.

男性は何時までにオフィスを出るべきだと言っていますか。

(A) 午後5時

(B) 午後5時30分

(C) 午後6時

(D) 午後6時30分

男性は「クルーズ船は6時30分に出発する」と述べ、「ここからマリーナまでタクシーに乗って行くことができる」と言った後、We should be there in time as long as we leave by six o'clock. と説明している。よって、正解は(C)。

🐾 **ここに注意！**

男性はIt leaves at six thirty. と発言しているが、これはクルーズ船の出港時間について言っているので(D)は間違い。男性のこの発言には、選択肢にあるキーワード（6:30）に加え、設問文に含まれる動詞（leave）も出てきているため、(D)の選択肢はとても惑わされやすい！

49

□□□ 正解 **B**

What does the woman ask the man to do?

(A) Reserve a vehicle

(B) Review some figures

(C) Order some food

(D) Deliver a document

女性は男性に何をするよう求めていますか。

(A) 乗り物を予約する

(B) 計算を見直す

(C) 食べ物を注文する

(D) 文書を配達する

6時までにここを出発すればクルーズ船に間に合うことを伝えられた女性は、「手を貸していただけませんか」と男性に依頼し、I need someone to check my calculations before I send the report to the head office. と説明している。よって、(B)が正解。

語彙チェック □ figure 数字、計算

Questions 50 through 52 refer to the following conversation.

M: Hi, my name's Kenny Waterhouse. I'd like to talk with someone there about a dishwasher that I bought about a month ago. I've been having a lot of trouble with it.

W: I see. Thank you for calling, Mr. Waterhouse. My name's We Ying. I'm a customer service representative here at Cranston Kitchen Appliances. Depending on the nature of the problem, I might have to ask you to call the manufacturer directly. Naturally, we'll do all we can to fix the situation here, though.

M: I understand. The problem I'm experiencing has been going on since the dishwasher was first installed. Basically, the water pressure doesn't seem to be high enough. The plates are still quite dirty at the end of a cycle.

問題50-52は次の会話に関するものです。

男性：こんにちは、Kenny Waterhouseと申します。1カ月ほど前に購入した食器洗浄機について、そちらにいらっしゃるどなたかとお話ししたいのですが。それに関していろいろと問題がございまして。

女性：承知いたしました。お電話ありがとうございます、Waterhouseさん。私はWe Yingと申します。こちらCranstonキッチン電化製品店のカスタマーサービス担当です。問題の性質によっては、お客さまからメーカーに直接お電話していただくようお願いしなければならないかもしれません。当然、この状況を解決するために当社にできることは全てさせていただきますが。

男性：分かりました。私が今経験している問題は、食器洗浄機が初めて設置されてからずっと起きています。基本的に、水圧が十分高くないようです。運転サイクルが終了しても、お皿がまだかなり汚れています。

語彙チェック　□dishwasher　食器洗浄機　□have trouble with ～　～に問題がある
　□appliance　電化製品　□depending on ～　～によって、～次第で
　□nature　性質　□naturally　当然　□fix　（問題など）を解決する
　□go on　起こる、発生する　□install　～を設置する　□basically　基本的に
　□water pressure　水圧　□cycle　周期、サイクル

50　　　　　　　　□□□　正解 C

When does the man say he purchased the appliance?　　男性はいつ電化製品を購入したと言っていますか。

(A) Yesterday　　　　　　　　　　　(A) 昨日
(B) A week ago　　　　　　　　　　(B) 1週間前
(C) A month ago　　　　　　　　　(C) 1カ月前
(D) A year ago　　　　　　　　　　(D) 1年前

男性は自分の名前を述べた後、I'd like to talk with someone there about a dishwasher that I bought about a month ago.と電話の要件を説明している。この発言から、男性は1カ月前に食器洗浄機を買ったことが分かる。よって、正解は(C)。

51

□□□ 正解 **B**

What does the woman say about her department?

(A) It was founded very recently.

(B) It refers some issues to its suppliers.

(C) It does not provide service to some locations.

(D) It has recently hired some new employees.

女性は彼女の部署について何と言っていますか。

(A) そこはつい最近設立された。

(B) そこは問題を供給元に照会させる。

(C) サービスが提供されていない店舗がある。

(D) そこは最近新しい従業員を雇った。

男性からの問い合わせを受けた女性は、自分の名前と所属を述べた後、Depending on the nature of the problem, I might have to ask you to call the manufacturer directly. と説明している。問題の性質によっては、客自身がメーカーに問い合わなければならない場合があるということなので、(B) が正解。

語彙チェック □refer A to B AをBに照会させる

52

□□□ 正解 **A**

What problem does the man mention?

(A) A device is ineffective.

(B) A delivery is late.

(C) Running costs are too high.

(D) The wrong model was sent.

男性はどのような問題について述べていますか。

(A) 装置は効果がない。

(B) 配達が遅れている。

(C) 維持費が高過ぎる。

(D) 誤ったモデルが送られた。

男性は食器洗浄機の問題について、the water pressure doesn't seem to be high enough と述べ、続いて The plates are still quite dirty at the end of a cycle. と説明している。食器洗浄機を使った後も皿が汚れたままだということは、すなわち食器洗剤機の効果がないと判断できる。よって、(A) が正解。

語彙チェック □ineffective 効果がない、役に立たない □running cost 維持費

Questions 53 through 55 refer to the following conversation.

W: We need to contact the customer about the repair costs before we start ordering parts. The cost is going to be way more than she thought. She might be better off buying a new car.

M: It goes to show. I always tell people that luxury used cars seem cheap to buy, but they cost a lot to maintain.

W: I know. This one's pretty old, so it's going to continue to cost her a lot in the future, too.

M: Can you send her a price list so that she can take her time and make a careful decision? We have all of the customers' e-mail addresses on record. Just ask someone in the office.

問題53-55は次の会話に関するものです。

女性：部品を注文し始める前に、修理費用についてお客さまに連絡を取らなくてはいけません。彼女が思っていたより、はるかに高額な費用がかかることになります。彼女は新しい車を買った方がいいかもしれませんね。

男性：よく分かります。私はいつも、中古高級車は買うのには安いと思われるけれど、維持するのに費用がたくさんかかると、皆さんに伝えています。

女性：そうですね。この車はかなり古いですから、将来的にも費用がたくさんかかり続けますね。

男性：時間をかけて慎重な判断ができるように、彼女に価格表を送ってくれませんか。お客さま全員のEメールアドレスが記録してあります。オフィスにいる人にちょっと聞いてみてください。

語彙チェック　□way　はるかに、ずっと　□be better off *doing*　〜する方がよい
　　　　　　　　□it goes to show 〜　〜だということがよく分かる　□luxury　高級な
　　　　　　　　□pretty　かなり、相当　□take *one's* time　（時間をかけて）ゆっくりやる
　　　　　　　　□make a decision　決定する　□on record　記録して

53　　　　　　　□□□　正解 D

Where do the speakers most likely work?　話し手たちはどこで働いていると考えられますか。

(A) At an online store　　　　　　　(A) オンラインストア

(B) At a hospital　　　　　　　　　(B) 病院

(C) At a utility company　　　　　　(C) 公益事業会社

(D) At a garage　　　　　　　　　　(D) 自動車整備工場

女性は冒頭で We need to contact the customer about the repair costs before we start ordering parts. と述べ、その後 She might be better off buying a new car. と言っている。これらの発言から、話し手たちは自動車の修理に関わる仕事をしていると考えられる。よって、正解は(D)。

54 正解 A

What does the man mean when he says, "It goes to show"?

(A) A situation was just as he expected.

(B) An instruction video was very helpful.

(C) A performance will attract many viewers.

(D) A customer will be surprised.

男性は"It goes to show"という発言で、何を意味していますか。

(A) まさに彼が予想した通りの状況だった。

(B) 説明のビデオはとても役立った。

(C) パフォーマンスは多くの視聴者を引き付けるだろう。

(D) 顧客は驚くだろう。

下線部の発言は「修理費が高額になるから、彼女は新しい車を買った方がいいかもしれない」という女性の意見を受けたものである。男性はその後、I always tell people that luxury used cars seem cheap to buy, but they cost a lot to maintain.と述べていることから、中古高級車を買うことで維持費がたくさんかかってしまうことを男性は見越していたと考えられる。よって、正解は(A)。

語彙チェック □viewer 視聴者

55 正解 D

What does the man suggest?

(A) Requesting a catalog

(B) Providing some contact details

(C) Setting up a meeting

(D) Sending an e-mail

男性は何を提案していますか。

(A) カタログを依頼すること

(B) 連絡先を提供すること

(C) 会議を設定する

(D) Eメールを送ること

男性はCan you send her a price list so that she can take her time and make a careful decision?と女性に依頼した後、We have all of the customers' e-mail addresses on record.と説明している。これらの発言から、男性は価格表をお客さんにEメールで送ることを提案していると判断できる。よって、正解は(D)。

語彙チェック □contact detail 連絡先

Questions 56 through 58 refer to the following conversation with three speakers.

W: We've narrowed the candidates down to three. The next step is to check their references. Which one of you would like to call them and confirm the details?

M1: I don't mind. I know a couple of them, so it'll be nice to catch up.

M2: Thanks, Corey. I'm concerned about Terry White. He just moved back from the UK. All of his references are over there. The time difference might make it difficult.

W: We can't hire him without making sure. You might have to call his references from home.

M1: In that case, would you mind doing it, Jack? I'm going out for dinner tonight with some friends.

M2: I don't mind. I'll let you know what they said tomorrow.

問題56-58は3人の話し手による次の会話に関するものです。

女性　：候補者を3人まで絞り込みました。次の段階は照会先を確認することです。あなた方のどちらかが彼らに電話をして詳細を確認していただけませんか。

男性1：私は構いませんよ。彼らのうちの2、3人を知っているので、久しぶりに連絡を取るにはいい機会です。

男性2：ありがとうございます、Corey。私はTerry Whiteについて心配しています。彼はちょうどイギリスから帰国したところです。彼の照会先は全て向こうです。時差のせいで、連絡を取るのが難しいかもしれません。

女性　：確認せずに彼を雇うことはできません。自宅から彼の照会先に電話をしなくてはいけないかもしれませんね。

男性1：その場合は、それをお願いできませんか、Jack。今夜は友人と夕食に出かける予定なのです。

男性2：構いませんよ。彼らが言っていたことを、明日あなたたちに知らせますね。

語彙チェック　□narrow ～ down　～を狭める、～をしぼる　□catch up　状況を話し合う
　　　　　　　　□be concerned about ～　～について心配している　□time difference　時差

56　　　　□□□　正解 B

What are the speakers discussing?　　話し手たちは何について話し合っていますか。

(A) Foreign branch offices　　(A) 海外支社

(B) Employment references　　(B) 雇用の照会先

(C) Job descriptions　　(C) 職務記述書

(D) Room reservations　　(D) 部屋の予約

冒頭のWe've narrowed the candidates down to three.という女性の発言から、従業員の採用についての会話だと推測できる。また、女性は続けてThe next step is to check their references.と照会先を確認する必要があることについても述べている。これらのことから、正解は(B)。

語彙チェック　□branch office　支店、支社　□description　説明書

57 □□□ 正解 D

What is mentioned about Mr. White?

(A) He was late for an interview.

(B) He has worked with the speakers before.

(C) He will obtain a new qualification.

(D) He has lived abroad.

Whiteさんについて何が述べられていますか。

(A) 彼は面接に遅刻した。

(B) 彼は以前、話し手たちと一緒に仕事をしたことがある。

(C) 彼は新しい資格を取得する予定である。

(D) 彼は海外に住んでいた。

照会先に電話をして詳細を確認してほしいという女性からの依頼に対し、2人目の男性は「Terry Whiteについて心配している」と発言している。その後、WhiteさんについてHe just moved back from the UK.と述べ、All of his references are over there.と説明している。これらから、Whiteさんは今までイギリスで生活しており、最近帰国したことが分かるので、正解は(D)。

語彙チェック □qualification 資格

58 □□□ 正解 D

What does the woman suggest?

(A) Entertaining a client

(B) Promoting an employee

(C) Placing an advertisement

(D) Completing a task at home

女性は何を提案していますか。

(A) 顧客をもてなすこと

(B) 従業員を昇進させること

(C) 広告を掲載すること

(D) 自宅で仕事を終わらせること

「Whiteさんの照会先はイギリスなので、時差のせいで連絡を取るのが難しいかもしれない」という2人目の男性の発言に対し、女性は「確認せずに彼を雇うことはできない」と説明し、You might have to call his references from home.と伝えている。この発言から、女性は照会先と連絡を取るという仕事を、自宅でやるように男性に提案していると分かる。よって、正解は(D)。

語彙チェック □entertain ～をもてなす □promote ～を昇進させる □place ～を掲載する

M 🇦🇺　W 🇬🇧　　　　　　　　　　　　　会話 ▶TRACK_296　問題 ▶TRACK_297

Questions 59 through 61 refer to the following conversation.

M: Hi Mary. <u>I've decided to go to Beaudesert for a few days to look at the new factory's progress.</u> Please show me the plans for the product launch when I get back.

W: I'll make sure everything is ready for you. I was in Beaudesert a few months ago. <u>I don't think you'll be very happy with the accommodations there. The rooms are small and the beds aren't very nice to sleep in.</u>

M: I hadn't thought about that. I've never stayed overnight before. <u>What do you suggest?</u>

W: There are some nice hotels in Dunberg. <u>Why not rent a car and drive to Beaudesert each day?</u> It'll take more than an hour each way, but you'll be glad you did.

問題59-61は次の会話に関するものです。

男性：こんにちは Mary。新しい工場の進捗具合を見に、何日間か Beaudesert に行くことにしました。私が戻ったら、製品発売の計画を見せてください。

女性：全ての準備が整っているようにしておきます。私は数カ月前に Beaudesert にいたのです。あなたはそこの宿泊施設にはあまり満足できないと思いますよ。部屋は小さいし、ベッドは寝るにはあまり良くありません。

男性：それについては考えたことがありませんでした。これまで一度も泊まったことがありませんから。何か提案はありますか。

女性：Dunberg にいいホテルがありますよ。車をレンタルして、毎日 Beaudesert に通ったらどうですか。片道1時間以上かかりますが、やってよかったと思うはずですよ。

語彙チェック　☐progress　進捗、進み具合　☐product launch　製品発売
　　　　　　　　☐accommodations　宿泊施設　☐stay overnight　1泊する

59　　　　　☐☐☐　正解 **C**

Why is the man going to Beaudesert?　　　男性はなぜ Beaudesert に行きますか。

(A) To interview an applicant　　　　　　(A) 応募者の面接をするため

(B) To purchase some land　　　　　　　(B) 土地を買うため

(C) To inspect a facility　　　　　　　　(C) 施設を視察するため

(D) To speak with a client　　　　　　　(D) 顧客と話をするため

男性は冒頭で I've decided to go to Beaudesert for a few days 「何日間か Beaudesert に行くことにした」と述べ、その目的を to look at the new factory's progress 「新しい工場の進捗具合を見るために」と説明している。よって、(C) が正解。

語彙チェック　☐inspect　～を視察する、～を調査する

60 ☐☐☐ 正解 B

What does the woman say about the accommodations in Beaudesert?
(A) They are fully booked.
(B) They are uncomfortable.
(C) They are reasonably priced.
(D) They are convenient.

女性はBeaudesertの宿泊施設について何と言っていますか。
(A) それらは予約でいっぱいである。
(B) それらは快適ではない。
(C) それらは手頃な価格である。
(D) それらは便利である。

Beaudesertに行くと言う男性に対し、女性はI don't think you'll be very happy with the accommodations there. と言い、The rooms are small and the beds aren't very nice to sleep in. と説明している。Beaudesertの宿泊施設は「部屋が小さく、ベッドは寝るにはあまり良くない」ということなので、この状態をuncomfortable「快適ではない」と表した(B)が正解。

語彙チェック ☐fully 完全に ☐book 〜を予約する ☐reasonably 適当に、程よく
☐price 〜に値段を付ける

61 ☐☐☐ 正解 C

What does the woman suggest?
(A) Postponing a visit
(B) Speaking with a colleague
(C) Renting a vehicle
(D) Checking a Web site

女性は何を提案していますか。
(A) 訪問を延期すること
(B) 同僚に話をすること
(C) 乗り物をレンタルすること
(D) ウェブサイトを確認すること

Beaudesertの宿泊施設があまり良くないと聞いた男性は、What do you suggest? と女性に提案を求めている。これに対し、女性は「Dunbergにいいホテルがある」と言うと、Why not rent a car and drive to Beaudesert each day? と提案している。女性は車をレンタルすることを提案しているので、(C)が正解。

M 🇺🇸　**W** 🇨🇦

Questions 62 through 64 refer to the following conversation and table.

M: Hi. I'm in town for a couple of days to catch up with family. Is it possible to get access to the gym on a day-by-day basis?

W: Sure. Here are our short-term fees. Were you hoping to use the sauna?

M: No, that won't be necessary. I just need access to the gym this afternoon.

W: I see. I'll have one of our trainers give you a quick tour of the center so that you know where everything is. The rules are posted on the wall over there. They're very standard gym rules, but please take a look before you begin your workout.

問題62-64は次の会話と表に関するものです。

男性：こんにちは。家族と会うために2、3日この町に滞在します。1日単位でジムを利用することはできますか。

女性：もちろんです。こちらが短期間用の料金です。サウナは利用されるつもりでしたか。

男性：いいえ、それは必要ありません。今日の午後にジムを利用したいだけです。

女性：承知いたしました。全ての物がどこにあるか知っていただくのに、トレーナーの1人にセンターを簡単に案内させますね。ルールは向こうの壁に掲示してあります。とても一般的なジムのルールですが、トレーニングを始める前に確認してください。

語彙チェック　□catch up with 〜　〜と近況を話し合う　□get access to 〜　〜を利用する
□day-by-day　日ごとの　□short-term　短期間　□trainer　トレーナー、指導員
□post　〜を掲示する　□workout　トレーニング、運動

Gainsmax Fitness Center Rates		
One Day Pass	Gym Only	$18
	Gym and Sauna	$24
One Week Pass	Gym Only	$90
	Gym and Sauna	$120
Two Week Pass	Gym Only	$135
	Gym and Sauna	$180

Gainsmax フィットネスセンターの料金		
1 日パス	ジムのみ	18 ドル
	ジムとサウナ	24 ドル
1 週間パス	ジムのみ	90 ドル
	ジムとサウナ	120 ドル
2 週間パス	ジムのみ	135 ドル
	ジムとサウナ	180 ドル

62 □□□ 正解 A

What is the purpose of the man's trip?

(A) To visit relatives

(B) To inspect a venue

(C) To attend a conference

(D) To take part in a contest

男性の旅の目的は何ですか。

(A) 親族を訪ねること

(B) 会場を視察すること

(C) 会議に出席すること

(D) コンテストに参加すること

男性は冒頭で I'm in town for a couple of days to catch up with family. と説明している。よって、男性は家族に会うために町に来たと分かるので、(A) が正解。

語彙チェック □inspect ～を視察する □venue 会場 □take part in ～ ～に参加する

63 □□□ 正解 A

Look at the graphic. How much will the man most likely pay?

(A) $18

(B) $24

(C) $90

(D) $120

図を見てください。男性はいくら支払うと考えられますか。

(A) 18ドル

(B) 24ドル

(C) 90ドル

(D) 120ドル

男性は冒頭で、1日単位でジムを利用することができるかどうかを尋ねている。その後、女性からサウナの利用について質問されると、男性はサウナは必要ないことを伝え、I just need access to the gym this afternoon. と言っている。これらから、男性は今日の午後にサウナは使わずジムだけ利用すると分かる。図を見ると、One Day Pass「1日パス」のうち、Gym Only「ジムのみ」の料金は $18 とある。よって、正解は (A)。

64 □□□ 正解 D

What does the woman say she will do?

(A) Ask the man to sign an agreement

(B) Give the man a discount on some clothing

(C) Watch a televised sporting event

(D) Have a colleague show the man around

女性は何をすると言っていますか。

(A) 男性に同意書に署名をするよう求める

(B) 男性に衣類の割引をする

(C) テレビ中継されているスポーツイベントを見る

(D) 同僚に男性を案内させる

今日の午後ジムを利用したいと言う男性に対し、女性は I'll have one of our trainers give you a quick tour of the center と述べている。one of our trainers「トレーナーの1人」というのは女性の同僚であると言えるので、(D) が正解。

語彙チェック □televised テレビで放送された □sporting スポーツの

Questions 65 through 67 refer to the following conversation and price list.

W: This 900 dollar table won't be large enough for the conference room. We need to buy the next size up.

M: That's fine. We have enough in the budget for that. What shall we do about the chairs?

W: I think we can get by with the current ones. They're in pretty good condition.

M: OK. How about the wall coverings? The current wallpaper is damaged in some areas.

W: Can you get quotes from a couple of companies and choose the one that gives us the best deal?

問題65-67は次の会話と価格表に関するものです。

女性：この900ドルのテーブルは会議室に十分な大きさではありません。1つ上のサイズを買わなくてはいけませんね。

男性：いいですよ。そのための予算は十分あります。椅子はどうしましょうか。

女性：現在のもので何とかできると思いますよ。それらはかなりいい状態ですから。

男性：分かりました。壁紙はどうしましょうか。現在の壁紙は傷んでいる箇所がありますよ。

女性：2、3社から見積もりをもらって、1番お得な取り決めを提示してくれるところを選んでくれませんか。

語彙チェック　□get by with 〜　〜で何とかやっていく　□condition　状態
□wall covering　壁紙　□wallpaper　壁紙　□quote　見積もり
□deal　取り決め、取引

Conference Room Tables	
Ultra-Executive （360cm×120cm)	$1,400
Executive （300cm×120cm)	$1,200
Premium （240cm×120cm)	$900
Standard （200cm×120cm)	$700

会議室テーブル	
Ultra-Executive （360cm×120cm)	1,400ドル
Executive （300cm×120cm)	1,200ドル
Premium （240cm×120cm)	900ドル
Standard （200cm×120cm)	700ドル

65 　　　　　　　正解 B

Look at the graphic. Which table will the speakers most likely buy?
(A) Ultra-Executive
(B) Executive
(C) Premium
(D) Standard

図を見てください。話し手たちはどのテーブルを買うと考えられますか。
(A) Ultra-Executive
(B) Executive
(C) Premium
(D) Standard

女性が冒頭で This 900 dollar table won't be large enough と述べ、We need to buy the next size up. と提案すると、男性はこれに対し That's fine. と了承している。話し手たちは900ドルのテーブルより1つ上のサイズのテーブルを買うと分かるので、図から (B) が正解と判断できる。

> 🐾 ここに注意！
> この問題は、冒頭の900 dollar table というキーワードを逃すと正答を選べない。1問目が図表問題であることも意識した上で、冒頭から集中力を高めて聞くことが大切！

66 　　　　　　　正解 C

What does the woman say about the chairs?
(A) They will arrive within a week.
(B) There are not enough for a meeting.
(C) There is no need to buy new ones.
(D) They cannot be repaired.

女性は椅子について何と言っていますか。
(A) それらは1週間以内に到着する。
(B) それらは会議に使うには数が足りない。
(C) 新しいものを買う必要はない。
(D) それらは修理できない。

テーブルの購入について話した後、男性が What shall we do about the chairs? と椅子について尋ねると、女性は I think we can get by with the current ones. と答え、They're in pretty good condition. と説明している。「現在使っている椅子は状態がいいので、それで何とかできると思う」ということなので、女性は「新しい椅子を買う必要はない」と考えていると判断できる。よって、(C) が正解。

67 　　　　　　　正解 B

What is the man asked to do?
(A) Supply some product samples
(B) Obtain price estimates
(C) Measure a room
(D) Schedule a meeting

男性は何をするよう求められていますか。
(A) 製品見本を供給する
(B) 見積書を手に入れる
(C) 部屋の寸法を測る
(D) 会議の予定を組む

壁紙はどうするかという男性の質問に対し、女性は Can you get quotes from a couple of companies and choose the one that gives us the best deal? と男性に依頼している。女性は複数の会社に見積もりをもらうよう頼んでいるので、(B) が正解。

語彙チェック □price estimate　見積書　□measure　〜の寸法を測る

Questions 68 through 70 refer to the following conversation and seating chart.

W: Hi. My name's Denise Kentucky. I just arrived on Flight 532 from Chicago. It was supposed to be a direct flight to San Francisco, but it was diverted here because of the weather.

M: Good afternoon, Ms. Kentucky. We've arranged another flight to take you to San Francisco. It leaves in an hour. These white ones are the only seats we have available, I'm afraid.

W: I see. Well, I'd prefer not to be on the aisle, and I don't want to be stuck between two other passengers. So, I'll take this one, I suppose.

M: Sure. We'll transfer your luggage onto the new flight. Please listen for updates on the departure time. Oh... and here's a coupon for a free coffee at the Dragon Air Café.

問題68-70は次の会話と座席表に関するものです。

女性：こんにちは。Denise Kentuckyと申します。Chicago発の532便でちょうど到着しました。San Franciscoへの直行便のはずでしたが、天候のせいで、ここに迂回しました。

男性：こんにちは、Kentuckyさん。San Francisco行きの他の便を手配しております。そちらは1時間後に出発いたします。申し訳ございませんが、これらの白い座席のみ、ご利用いただけます。

女性：分かりました。そうですね、通路側でない方がよくて、他の2人の乗客の間に挟まれたくありません。ですから、この席にしようかと思います。

男性：かしこまりました。新しい便にお客さまのお荷物を移動いたします。出発時刻の最新情報を聞くようにお願いします。ああ…それからこちらはDragon Air Caféでのコーヒー無料券でございます。

語彙チェック　□be supposed to *do*　〜することになっている　□direct flight　直行便
　　　　　　　　□divert　〜の進路を変更する、〜を迂回させる　□aisle　通路
　　　　　　　　□be stuck　動きが取れない　□passenger　乗客　□transfer　〜を移動させる
　　　　　　　　□listen for 〜　〜に耳を澄ます　□update　最新情報

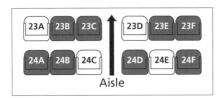

68 　　　　正解 C

What does the woman say happened today?
(A) Her luggage was misplaced.
(B) Her reservation was canceled.
(C) Her flight was redirected.
(D) Her train was delayed.

女性は今日何が起こったと言っていますか。
(A) 彼女の荷物が置き忘れられた。
(B) 彼女の予約がキャンセルになった。
(C) 彼女の便の行き先が変更になった。
(D) 彼女の電車が遅延した。

女性は冒頭で「Chicago発の532便でちょうど到着した」と述べた後、It was supposed to be a direct flight to San Francisco, but it was diverted here と説明している。この発言から、彼女の搭乗便は San Francisco への直行便のはずだったが、迂回したことが分かる。よって、(C) が正解。

語彙チェック □misplace 〜を置き忘れる □redirect 〜の方向を変える

69 　　　　正解 A

Look at the graphic. Where will the woman most likely sit?
(A) In 23A
(B) In 23D
(C) In 24C
(D) In 24E

図を見てください。女性はどこに座ると考えられますか。
(A) 23A
(B) 23D
(C) 24C
(D) 24E

男性が座席について、白い座席のみ空いていることを伝えると、女性は Well, I'd prefer not to be on the aisle, and I don't want to be stuck between two other passengers. と座席の希望を2点伝えている。図を見ると、白色の座席のうち、通路側でなく、かつ他の乗客に挟まれない座席は23Aのみである。よって、正解は (A)。

🐾 **ここに注意！**
この図表問題は、「通路側ではない」→「2人の乗客に挟まれていない」という2段階で絞り込む必要がある。TOEIC本番では問題冊子に書き込むことはできないので、消去法で消える部分を指で隠すなどして、条件を整理できるように工夫しよう！

70 　　　　正解 B

What does the man give to the woman?
(A) Some luggage
(B) A voucher
(C) A schedule
(D) Some labels

男性は女性に何を渡していますか。
(A) 荷物
(B) クーポン券
(C) 予定表
(D) ラベル

座席が確定した後、荷物の移動と出発時刻の最新情報について注意を促した男性は、最後に here's a coupon for a free coffee at the Dragon Air Café と述べている。このことから、男性は女性にコーヒーの無料券を渡していることが分かる。よって、(B) が正解。

Part 4

W 🇬🇧

トーク ▶ TRACK_305   問題 ▶ TRACK_306

Questions 71 through 73 refer to the following telephone message.

Hi James. It's Rosa. I was just looking at the yearly schedule with some of the people in sales and marketing. Umm, we noticed that the family fun day will be at Morison Park. A few complained that it's too far away. And, well... I kind of agree. I'm also worried about the timing. We have an information session for prospective customers on May 4, and everyone's expected to attend. That's the Saturday right before fun day. It's their one day off. The staff probably won't be excited about seeing their workmates. The same thing happened last year, and the turnout wasn't great. How about the following weekend?

問題71-73は次の電話のメッセージに関するものです。

こんにちはJames。Rosaです。営業部の何人かと年間予定表をちょっと見ていました。ええと、ファミリー・ファン・デーがMorison公園で行われると気付いたのですが、そこは遠過ぎではないかと数人から不満が出ました。それで、ええと…私も同感といったところです。私は時期についても心配しています。私たちは5月4日に見込み客向けの説明会があり、全員出席する予定です。それはファン・デーの直前の土曜日です。1日のお休みということになります。おそらく、スタッフは仕事仲間に会いたくないでしょうね。同様のことが昨年も起こって、参加率がよくありませんでした。その次の週末にしてはいかがですか。

語彙チェック　□yearly　1年限りの　□sales and marketing　営業部、販売宣伝部
　　　　　　　　□complain that ～　～であると不満を言う　□far away　遠く離れて
　　　　　　　　□kind of　どちらかというと、ある程度　□timing　タイミング
　　　　　　　　□information session　説明会　□prospective　将来の、見込みのある
　　　　　　　　□expect A to do　Aが～するだろうと思う、Aに～してほしいと思う
　　　　　　　　□workmate　仕事仲間　□turnout　参加者、人出

71
□□□ 正解 **A**

What problem does the speaker mention?　話し手はどんな問題について述べていますか。

(A) A location is inconvenient.　(A) 場所が不便である。

(B) Some products are faulty.　(B) 製品が不良品である。

(C) An employee is late.　(C) 従業員が遅刻している

(D) Sales have been dwindling.　(D) 売り上げが徐々に減少している。

話し手はwe noticed that the family fun day will be at Morison Park**と述べた後、**A few complained that it's too far away.**と言っている。it**はMorison Park**を指していて、ファミリー・ファン・デーの会場である**Morison**公園が遠過ぎることが問題になっていると分かる。よって、(A)**が正解。

語彙チェック　□inconvenient　不便な　□faulty　欠陥のある　□dwindle　次第に減少する

232

72

□□□ 正解 **B**

What does the speaker imply when she says, "<u>It's their one day off</u>"?

(A) Some employees will be grateful.

(B) An event will be unpopular.

(C) Employees should choose what to do.

(D) The schedule has an error.

話し手は "<u>It's their one day off</u>" という発言で、何を示唆していますか。

(A) 一部の従業員は感謝するだろう。

(B) イベントは人気が出ないだろう。

(C) 従業員は何をすべきか選択するべきである。

(D) 予定表に誤りがある。

話し手は、ファン・デーの前日に開催される説明会にスタッフ全員が出席する予定であることを説明した後、It's their one day off. と述べている。続いて、The staff probably won't be excited about seeing their workmates. と言い、昨年もそのせいで参加率がよくなかったと説明している。これらの発言から、ファン・デーの日程がスタッフの貴重な休日と重なっていることにより参加者が集まらないことを話し手は心配していると考えられる。よって、正解は (B)。

語彙チェック □grateful 感謝して □unpopular 人気がない □error 誤り、間違い

73

□□□ 正解 **B**

What does the speaker suggest?

(A) Offering an additional day off

(B) Changing a schedule

(C) Holding a contest

(D) Canceling an information session

話し手は何を提案していますか。

(A) 追加の休日を与えること

(B) 予定を変更すること

(C) コンテストを開催すること

(D) 説明会を中止にすること

話し手は説明会の翌日にファン・デーが開催予定であることから、参加率が良くないことを懸念し、How about the following weekend? と提案している。この発言から、話し手はファン・デーの予定変更を提案していることが分かるので、(B) が正解。

Questions 74 through 76 refer to the following excerpt from a meeting.

Before we end this meeting, I'd like to get everyone's opinion about the five o'clock timeslot. We've been broadcasting *Deal of the Century* in that timeslot for two months, and viewership has been slowly declining. Our advertising revenue has been badly affected. We purchased a hundred episodes of *Deal of the Century*, but I don't think we should bother airing the rest. There's a new cooking show called *Jerry's Bakedown* that we were planning on airing in the mornings. I read about a channel in the United States that's had a lot of success broadcasting it in the afternoons. In short, I'm suggesting replacing *Deal of the Century* with *Jerry's Bakedown*.

問題74-76は次の会議の抜粋に関するものです。

この会議を終える前に、5時の放送枠についての皆さんの意見を伺いたいと思います。2カ月間、その時間枠で Deal of the Century を放送していますが、視聴率が徐々に低下しています。私たちの広告収入にも悪い影響が出ています。Deal of the Century を100話購入しましたが、わざわざ残りを放送するべきではないと私は思います。午前に放送すると予定していた Jerry's Bakedown という新しい料理番組があります。私は、午後にそれを放送してとても成功したというアメリカのチャンネルについて読みました。要するに、Deal of the Century を Jerry's Bakedown に取り替えることを私は提案します。

語彙チェック □timeslot　放送枠　□viewership　視聴率　□decline　低下する
　　　　　　　　□revenue　収益、収入　□bother *doing*　わざわざ～する　□air　～を放送する
　　　　　　　　□rest　残り　□plan on *doing*　～するつもりである　□in short　要するに

74　　　　　　　　☐☐☐　正解 **D**

Where does the speaker most likely work?　話し手はどこで働いていると考えられますか。
(A) At a swimming school　　　　　　　(A) 水泳教室
(B) At a real estate agency　　　　　　(B) 不動産会社
(C) At an auction house　　　　　　　(C) オークション会社
(D) At a television station　　　　　　(D) テレビ局

話し手は冒頭で I'd like to get everyone's opinion about the five o'clock timeslot と述べた後、Deal of the Century という番組の視聴率が下がっていると伝えている。その後も、新番組について提案を行っていることから、話し手はテレビ放送に関連した仕事をしていると考えられる。よって、正解は (D)。

75

正解 **B**

What problem does the speaker mention?

(A) The business is short-staffed.

(B) The business has lost some income.

(C) Advertising costs have been increasing.

(D) Some equipment needs to be replaced.

話し手はどんな問題について述べていますか。

(A) 会社は人員不足である。

(B) 会社は収入が減っている。

(C) 宣伝費が増加している。

(D) 機材の取り換えが必要である。

話し手はDeal of the Centuryの放送について「視聴率が徐々に低下している」と述べ、Our advertising revenue has been badly affected. と説明している。広告収入が悪影響を受けているということは会社の収入が減っているということなので、(B)が正解。

語彙チェック □short-staffed　人手不足の

76

正解 **D**

What does the speaker suggest?

(A) Requesting assistance from an expert

(B) Testing some product samples

(C) Relocating to a more suitable address

(D) Adopting the strategy of another business

話し手は何を提案していますか。

(A) 専門家に援助を要求すること

(B) 製品サンプルを試験すること

(C) もっと適切な住所に移転すること

(D) 他の会社の戦略を導入すること

話し手は、5時の放送枠で放送しているDeal of the Centuryの視聴率が下がっていることを説明すると、新しく午前に放送する予定の料理番組Jerry's Bakedownについて「午後にそれを放送してとても成功したというアメリカのチャンネルについて読んだ」と言い、I'm suggesting replacing *Deal of the Century* with *Jerry's Bakedown*と述べている。つまり話し手は、成功を収めたアメリカのチャンネルに倣って、午後の時間にJerry's Bakedownを放送することを提案している。よって、正解は(D)。

語彙チェック □request *A* from *B*　BにAを要求する　□test　～を試験する、～を試す
　　　　　　□relocate　移転する　□adopt　～を導入する

Questions 77 through 79 refer to the following announcement.

Good evening patrons. We will be closing in just under fifteen minutes. If you would like to borrow a book, please make your way to the check-out desk as soon as possible. You are welcome to continue reading up until nine P.M., but we do ask that you leave as soon as you hear the nine o'clock chime. Please be sure to take any personal belongings with you when you leave. If you do leave anything behind, you will be unable to retrieve it until ten A.M. tomorrow. Please note that lost items are not stored here. We deliver them to the council office at 34 Collins Street every evening. Please contact the staff there if you are searching for lost property.

問題77-79は次のお知らせに関するものです。

こんばんは、ご利用の皆さま。当館はあと15分足らずで閉館いたします。本を借りたい場合は、できるだけ早く貸出し部へお進みください。午後9時までは読書を続けていただけますが、9時のチャイムが聞こえましたら、速やかにお帰りいただきますよう、お願いいたします。お帰りの際は、必ず全てのお荷物をお持ちください。もし忘れ物をされますと、明日午前10時まで、取りに戻ることはできなくなります。紛失物はこちらには保管しておりませんので、ご注意ください。私たちは毎晩、Collins通り34番地の市議会のオフィスにそれらを届けております。遺失物をお探しの場合は、そちらのスタッフにご連絡ください。

語彙チェック　□patron　（施設の）利用者　□make *one's* way to ～　～に向かって進む
□check-out desk　（図書館の）貸出し部　□welcome to *do*　自由に～してよい
□up until　～まで　□chime　チャイム　□belongings　所有物
□leave ～ behind　～を置き忘れる　□retrieve　～を取り戻す、～を回収する
□store　～を保管する　□lost property　遺失物

77　　　　　　□□□　正解 C

Where is the announcement being made?　お知らせはどこでされていますか。
(A) At an Internet café　(A) インターネットカフェ
(B) At a fitness club　(B) フィットネスクラブ
(C) At a library　(C) 図書館
(D) At a restaurant　(D) レストラン

話し手はGood evening patrons. と呼びかけ、「あと15分足らずで閉まる」と伝えた後、If you would like to borrow a book, please make your way to the check-out deskと発言している。本を借りたい場合は貸出し部へ行くよう伝えていることから、このお知らせは図書館で流れていると判断できる。よって、正解は(C)。

78　　　　□□□　正解 A

What is one purpose of the announcement?

(A) To inform people about a closing time

(B) To thank guests for attending an event

(C) To announce a change in policy

(D) To request assistance with a task

お知らせの1つの目的は何ですか。

(A) 閉館時間について人々に知らせること

(B) イベントへの参加についてお客さんに感謝すること

(C) 方針の変更について知らせること

(D) 仕事の支援を要請すること

話し手は冒頭でGood evening patrons. と呼びかけると、We will be closing in just under fifteen minutes. と述べている。また、we do ask that you leave as soon as you hear the nine o'clock chime とも述べている。これらのことから、このお知らせは閉館時間について知らせることを1つの目的としていると判断できる。よって、正解は (A)。

79　　　　□□□　正解 D

What does the speaker say about lost property?

(A) It should be handed to a manager.

(B) It will be disposed of after a week.

(C) It has been reported more often recently.

(D) It is kept at a different location.

話し手は遺失物について何と言っていますか。

(A) それは管理者に手渡されるべきである。

(B) それは1週間後に処分される。

(C) それの報告が最近増えている。

(D) それは別の場所に保管されている。

話し手は「お帰りの際は、必ず全てのお荷物をお持ちください」と述べた後、Please note that lost items are not stored here. と言い、We deliver them to the council office at 34 Collins Street every evening. と説明している。遺失物は図書館で保管されるのではなく、市議会のオフィスに届けられるということなので、正解は (D)。

語彙チェック　□hand *A* to *B*　AをBに手渡す　□dispose of〜　〜を処分する

Questions 80 through 82 refer to the following broadcast announcement.

I'm sad to say, that was the last news update we'll hear from Ralph Wilson. He's been a popular member of the staff here at Radio 7TR for almost 15 years and we're all really sorry to see him go. We wish him all the best in his retirement, though, and hope that he stays in touch. Moving on to brighter topics — in a few minutes, I'll be talking with Judy Chow. She's been in California all week interviewing celebrities. She's there for the annual Hollywood Filmmakers' Awards. Today is the big day, and she's going to tell us about which films are tipped to win.

問題80-82は次の放送のお知らせに関するものです。

残念ですが、私たちがRalph Wilsonから聞く最新のニュース情報はそれで最後となりました。彼はここRadio 7TRでほぼ15年間、人気のあるスタッフメンバーでしたので、彼を見送るのを私たち全員が本当に残念に思っています。しかし、退職後の彼の幸運をお祈りするとともに、これからも連絡を取り合えればうれしく思います。明るい話に移りまして―数分後、私はJudy Chowとお話しする予定です。彼女はこの1週間ずっとCaliforniaにいて、有名人にインタビューしています。彼女は毎年行われるHollywood Filmmakers' Awardsのためにそこにいます。今日は重要な日で、彼女はどの映画が受賞すると予想されているかということについて、私たちに教えてくれます。

語彙チェック   □wish 〜 all the best 〜の幸運を祈る   □stay in touch 連絡を取り合う
           □all week 1週間ずっと   □big day 重要な日
           □tip 〜を予想する、〜を有力候補として挙げる

80   □□□   正解 **B**

Who is Ralph Wilson?

(A) A musician
(B) A news reporter
(C) A filmmaker
(D) A sports person

Ralph Wilsonとは誰ですか。

(A) 音楽家
(B) ニュースリポーター
(C) 映画製作者
(D) スポーツ選手

話し手は冒頭でthat was the last news update we'll hear from Ralph Wilsonと述べているので、Ralph Wilsonさんは最新ニュースを伝えていた人物だと分かる。このことから、Ralph Wilsonさんの職業はニュースリポーターだと判断できるので、正解は(B)。

81

□□□ 正解 C

What does the speaker mention about Ms. Chow?

話し手はChowさんについて何と述べていますか。

(A) She took part in a contest.

(B) She will replace a retiring employee.

(C) She is on a business trip.

(D) She has a lot of experience.

(A) 彼女はコンテストに参加した。

(B) 彼女は退職する従業員の後任となる。

(C) 彼女は出張中である。

(D) 彼女は経験が豊富である。

話し手は Moving on to brighter topics と話題を変え、in a few minutes, I'll be talking with Judy Chow と言った後、その Chow さんについて She's been in California all week interviewing celebrities. と説明している。これを「彼女は出張中である」と言い換えている (C) が正解。

語彙チェック □take part in 〜 〜に参加する □replace 〜の後任となる

82

□□□ 正解 D

What will probably take place today?

おそらく今日何が行われますか。

(A) A fashion show

(B) A retirement party

(C) A sporting event

(D) An award ceremony

(A) ファッションショー

(B) 退職記念パーティー

(C) スポーツイベント

(D) 授賞式

話し手は、Chow さんが California にいる理由を for the annual Hollywood Filmmakers' Awards と説明している。また、その後の Today is the big day, and she's going to tell us about which films are tipped to win. という発言から、今日は Hollywood Filmmakers' Awards の受賞作品が決定する日であると考えられる。よって、(D) が正解。

Questions 83 through 85 refer to the following talk.

This just about concludes our historical tour of Boston. I hope you've all had a wonderful time and learned a lot about this fascinating city. <u>I'll come by in a few minutes with a satisfaction survey.</u> Of course, you don't have to fill it out if you don't want to. However, <u>those who do will be automatically entered into a competition to win a trip for two to New York. It includes all transportation, accommodations, and meals.</u> Oh, I almost forgot to mention — You have a choice of two places to get off the bus. First, we'll be making a brief stop on Leichardt Street. <u>People who are interested in browsing the stores should get off there.</u> After that, we'll head to Rigley Station. That's where you all got on the bus this morning.

問題83-85は次の話に関するものです。

これでBoston歴史ツアーは終了です。皆さまに楽しい時間をお過ごしいただき、この魅力的な街について多くのことを知っていただけたのならばうれしく思います。数分後に満足度調査をお持ちいたします。もちろん、もし記入したくないということでしたら、記入していただかなくても結構です。しかし、ご記入いただいた方は、New Yorkへのペア旅行が当たる抽選に自動的にエントリーされます。こちらには、交通手段、宿泊、食事全てが含まれています。ああ、お話しし忘れるところでした―バスの降車地は2か所からお選びいただけます。まず、Leichardt通りに一時停車いたします。お店を見て回ることに興味がある方はそこでお降りください。その後、Rigley駅へ向かいます。こちらは、皆さまが今朝バスに乗車したところです。

語彙チェック　□fascinating　魅力的な　□come by　ちょっと来る、立ち寄る
　　　　　　　　□fill 〜 out　〜を記入する　□enter　〜をエントリーさせる
　　　　　　　　□accommodations　宿泊　□brief stop　一時停車
　　　　　　　　□browse　（店や品物）を見て回る　□head to 〜　〜へ向かう

83　☐☐☐　正解 **A**

What does the speaker want the listeners to do?

(A) Complete a questionnaire
(B) Attend an information session
(C) Put away personal items
(D) Take note of some contact details

話し手は聞き手に何をしてほしいと思っていますか。

(A) アンケート用紙に記入する
(B) 説明会に出席する
(C) 自分の荷物を片付ける
(D) 連絡先をメモに取る

話し手はツアーの終了を告げ、I'll come by in a few minutes with a satisfaction survey. と伝えている。この調査については、記入した人は旅行が当たる抽選に自動的にエントリーされると説明している。これらの発言から、話し手は聞き手に対して、満足度調査の用紙に記入することに協力してもらいたいと思っていると考えられるので、正解は(A)。

語彙チェック　□questionnaire　アンケート用紙　□information session　説明会
　　　　　　　　□put away 〜　〜を片付ける

84

□□□ 正解 **C**

What can the listeners win?

(A) Concert tickets

(B) A meal with a celebrity

(C) A travel package

(D) Clothing items

聞き手は何を獲得することができますか。

(A) コンサートのチケット

(B) 有名人との食事

(C) パッケージツアー

(D) 衣料品

話し手は満足度調査について、「記入した人は、New Yorkへのペア旅行が当たる抽選に自動的にエントリーされる」と述べている。この旅行については、その後It includes all transportation, accommodations, and meals. と説明している。これらから、満足度調査の用紙に記入した人の中から、交通手段、宿泊、食事が付いたパッケージツアーが当たると分かる。よって、正解は(C)。

85

□□□ 正解 **C**

What is implied about Leichardt Street?

(A) It has a major train station.

(B) It has some important historical landmarks.

(C) It is in a shopping district.

(D) It is known for its unique architecture.

Leichardt通りについて何が示唆されていますか。

(A) そこには主要な電車の駅がある。

(B) そこには重要な歴史的名所がある。

(C) そこはショッピング街にある。

(D) そこはユニークな建築様式で有名である。

話し手は降車地について「2か所から選べる」と言い、「まずLeichardt 通りに一時停車する」と伝えている。そして、Leichardt通りについてPeople who are interested in browsing the stores should get off there. と説明している。この発言から、Leichardt通りは繁華街で店が並んでいると考えられる。よって、正解は(C)。

語彙チェック □major　主要な　□landmark　名所　□district　地域、街

Questions 86 through 88 refer to the following telephone message.

Hi. This is Rod McKenzie from Freemantle Green Pros. I'm returning a call from Helen Thornton regarding an estimate for some work at Thornton Clinic. I was there earlier this morning before the clinic opened. I measured the size of the lawn and assessed the amount of care required. I have a fair idea of the amount of work now, and I feel confident that I can give an accurate estimate. Unfortunately, I'll be away from work for the rest of the week. I've left the details with my assistant. I'll ask her to get in touch with you and set up an appointment to discuss scheduling. I recommend that you have your property taken care of at least every two weeks.

問題86-88は次の電話のメッセージに関するものです。

こんにちは。Freemantle Green Pros 社の Rod McKenzie と申します。Helen Thornton からの Thornton クリニックでの作業の見積もりのお問い合わせについて、折り返しお電話しております。今朝、クリニックが開く前にそこを伺ってきました。芝生のサイズを測って、必要な手入れの量を査定しました。現在、作業量の見当が付きましたので、正確な見積もりがお出しできると思います。あいにく、私は今週の残りは仕事から離れております。私の助手に詳細を残してあります。彼女に、あなたと連絡を取って、スケジュールを話し合うために面会の約束を取るよう、頼んでおきます。少なくとも2週間ごとにお客さまの所有地を見てもらうことをお勧めいたします。

語彙チェック　□measure　～を測る　□lawn　芝生　□assess　～を査定する　□fair　適正な
□rest　残り　□get in touch with ～　～と連絡を取る
□set up ～　～の日時を決める　□property　所有物、地所

86　□□□　正解 C

What does the speaker say he has done?

(A) Delivered some materials

(B) Evaluated a care facility

(C) Visited Ms. Thornton's place of work

(D) Rescheduled an appointment

話し手は何をしたと言っていますか。

(A) 資材を配達した

(B) 介護施設を評価した

(C) Thornton さんの仕事場を訪れた

(D) 予約の予定を変更した

冒頭の発言から、聞き手は Thornton クリニックでの作業の見積もりを問い合わせていたことが分かる。その問い合わせを受け、話し手は I was there earlier this morning before the clinic opened. と述べている。この発言から、話し手は今朝聞き手の仕事場であるクリニックを訪ねたと分かる。よって、正解は (C)。

語彙チェック　□evaluate　～を評価する　□care facility　介護施設
□reschedule　～の予定を変更する

87

□□□ 正解 **B**

What kind of work does the speaker most likely do?

(A) Painting
(B) Gardening
(C) Construction
(D) Medicine

話し手はどんな仕事をしていると考えられますか。

(A) 塗装
(B) 造園
(C) 建設
(D) 医療

見積もりの問い合わせに対し、話し手は現場であるクリニックを訪ね、I measured the size of the lawn and assessed the amount of care required. と芝生のサイズを測って手入れの量を査定したことを説明している。続いて「作業量の見当がついて、正確な見積もりが出せる」とも言っている。これらから、男性は庭の管理をする仕事をしていると考えられる。よって、正解は (B)。

88

□□□ 正解 **D**

What will the speaker's assistant do?

(A) Provide some computer graphics
(B) Order some pharmaceuticals
(C) Install a device
(D) Arrange a meeting

話し手の助手は何をしますか。

(A) コンピューターグラフィックを提供する
(B) 薬を注文する
(C) 機器を取り付ける
(D) 打ち合わせを手配する

話し手は、今週の残りは仕事から離れるために助手に詳細を残してあると説明すると、I'll ask her to get in touch with you and set up an appointment to discuss scheduling. と伝えている。この発言から、助手はこの後聞き手に連絡をし、スケジュールについて打ち合わせするために面会の約束を取ると考えられる。よって、(D) が正解。

語彙チェック □pharmaceuticals 薬、調合薬 □install ～を設置する、～を取り付ける

Questions 89 through 91 refer to the following advertisement.

If you're looking for something fun to do this weekend, why not come to the first Annual Fitness and Fun Day at Southbank Parklands? To encourage residents to engage in more physical activity and eat more nutritious food, the city council is providing free workshops and demonstrations of a wide variety of fitness activities. All will be led by top professionals from respected institutions. This is part of the City Council's Fitness First campaign, which was launched last year by Mayor Goldy Garland. You can't afford to miss out. The information will change your life and help you live longer and better.

問題89-91は次の広告に関するものです。

今週末何か楽しいことをお探しなら、Southbank Parklandsで初めて開催されるAnnual Fitness and Fun Dayに来てはいかがですか。より身体的な活動に参加し、より栄養価が高い食べ物を食べることを地域の人々に促すため、市議会が無料のワークショップや種々さまざまなフィットネス活動のデモンストレーションを提供いたします。これらは全て、評判の高い施設の一流プロによって指導されます。これはGoldy Garland市長によって昨年始められた、市議会のFitness Firstキャンペーンの一部です。この機会を逃すわけにはいきません。この情報はあなたの生活を変え、より長く、より良く生きるために役立つでしょう。

語彙チェック　□encourage *A* to *do*　Aに〜するよう促す　□engage in 〜　〜に携わる
□physical　身体の　□nutritious　栄養のある　□city council　市議会
□a wide variety of〜　種々さまざまな〜　□professional　プロ
□respected　評判の高い　□afford to *do*　〜する余裕がある、〜しても困らない
□miss out　（良いチャンスなどを）見送る

89　　□□□　正解 A

What is the purpose of the event?
(A) To promote healthy lifestyles
(B) To raise some money
(C) To attract more tourists
(D) To celebrate an anniversary

イベントの目的は何ですか。
(A) 健康的な生活スタイルを促進すること
(B) お金を集めること
(C) より多くの観光客を引き付けること
(D) 記念日を祝うこと

話し手は、今週末Annual Fitness and Fun Dayに来てはどうかと勧めた後、そのイベントの目的をTo encourage residents to engage in more physical activity and eat more nutritious foodと述べ、内容について「市議会が無料のワークショップや種々さまざまなフィットネス活動のデモンストレーションを提供する」と説明している。よって、これは地域住民の健康促進のためのイベントだと判断できるので、(A)が正解。

90 　　　　　正解 B

Who is Goldy Garland?

(A) An educator

(B) A politician

(C) An event organizer

(D) A workshop facilitator

Goldy Garland とは誰ですか。

(A) 教育者

(B) 政治家

(C) イベント企画者

(D) ワークショップの進行役

話し手はイベントについて、「市議会の Fitness First キャンペーンの一部だ」と述べた後、さらにこのキャンペーンについて which was launched last year by Mayor Goldy Garland と説明している。この発言から、Goldy Garland さんは Mayor「市長」だと分かるので、(B) が正解。

語彙チェック　□ facilitator　進行役

91 　　　　　正解 A

Why does the speaker say, "You can't afford to miss out"?

(A) To stress the benefits of an event

(B) To explain the cost of admission

(C) To encourage people to lead workshops

(D) To offer people an affordable alternative

話し手はなぜ "You can't afford to miss out" と言っていますか。

(A) イベントのメリットを強調するため

(B) 入場料について説明するため

(C) 人々にワークショップを指導するよう促すため

(D) 人々に手頃な料金の他の選択肢を提供するため

話し手は下線部の発言の後、The information will change your life and help you live longer and better. と述べている。このことから、イベントで得られる情報は生活や今後の人生にとても役立つと強調するために、下線部の発言をしていると考えられる。よって、正解は (A)。

語彙チェック　□ affordable　手頃な

> (注) ここに注意！
> 1つ前の設問90.のキーワードは Goldy Garland という人物となるが、この91.で問われているのはその人物名が出てきた直後の発言なので聞き逃しやすい。先読みの際に、設問で引用されているセリフを頭の片隅に入れて構えておくようにしよう！

M 🇺🇸

トーク ▶TRACK_319　問題 ▶TRACK_320

Questions 92 through 94 refer to the following talk.

In the next exercise, I would like you to practice taking calls from customers who are having trouble with their orders. You will be speaking with experienced customer support officers who will ask you for help with typical issues. As is the case with real calls, your conversation will be saved in an audio file. I know it can make people anxious to go before everyone else, but would anyone like to volunteer? This is just for practice; you're not being evaluated.

問題92-94は次の話に関するものです。

次の練習では、注文に問題を抱えているお客さまからの電話を受ける練習をしていただきます。あなた方には経験豊富なカスタマーサポートの職員と話してもらいますが、彼らは典型的な問題について助けを求めてきます。実際の電話の場合と同様に、あなた方の会話は音声ファイルに保存されます。他の皆さんよりも先にやることは心配になってしまうと思いますが、誰かやってくれる人はいますか。これはただの練習で、評価はされません。

語彙チェック　□take a call　電話を受ける　□ask *A* for *B*　AにBを求める　□typical　典型的な
□as is the case with 〜　〜と同様に　□audio　音声の
□anxious　心配な、不安な　□volunteer　進んで引き受ける、進んで申し出る
□evaluate　〜を評価する

92　□□□　正解 **C**

Where does the talk most likely take place?

(A) At a client meeting
(B) At a press conference
(C) At a training workshop
(D) At a company banquet

話はどこで行われていると考えられますか。

(A) 顧客との会議
(B) 記者会見
(C) 研修会
(D) 会社の祝宴

話し手は、冒頭で In the next exercise, I would like you to practice taking calls from customers who are having trouble with their orders. と述べているので、聞き手はこれから顧客の電話対応の練習をすると分かる。また、その練習は経験のあるカスタマーサポートの職員とロールプレイ形式で行うことを続けて説明している。これらから、研修で顧客からの電話対応の練習をしている場面だと判断できる。よって、正解は(C)。

93

正解 **A**

What does the speaker say about telephone calls?

(A) They are recorded.

(B) They must be answered quickly.

(C) They are not cost-effective.

(D) They take less time than e-mail.

話し手は電話について何と言っていますか。

(A) それらは録音される。

(B) それらに素早く出なければならない。

(C) それらは費用効果がよくない。

(D) それらはEメールよりも時間がかからない。

話し手は電話対応の練習について、As is the case with real calls, your conversation will be saved in an audio file. と説明している。この発言から、電話での会話は録音されることが分かる。よって、(A)が正解。

語彙チェック □cost-effective 費用効果の高い、経済的な

94

正解 **C**

What does the speaker mean when he says, "would anyone like to volunteer"?

(A) He needs some people to represent the company.

(B) He would like some assistance with an environmental project.

(C) He hopes someone will choose to go first.

(D) He wonders when to schedule a vacation.

話し手は"would anyone like to volunteer"という発言で、何を意味していますか。

(A) 彼は会社を代表する人を必要としている。

(B) 彼は環境保護プロジェクトにおける支援が欲しい。

(C) 彼は誰かが最初に行うと選択してくれることを望んでいる。

(D) 彼は休暇をいつ予定に入れるか考えている。

話し手は、これから行う電話対応の練習についてI know it can make people anxious to go before everyone else「誰よりも先にやることは心配になると思う」と言いながらも、下線部の発言を聞き手に投げかけている。この流れから「1番初めにやることに躊躇する気持ちは分かるが、誰かに進んで練習をやってほしい」という話し手の意図がくみ取れる。よって、正解は(C)。

語彙チェック □go first 最初にやる

Questions 95 through 97 refer to the following advertisement and Web page.

Today is the first day of Sampson Electrical's four-day clearance sale, and we have some amazing bargains. We need to sell all our current stock to make room for next year's models. So, there's up to forty percent off on major items in a different department each day of the sale. We have unbelievable deals on kitchen appliances, game devices, computers, televisions, and much more. We're open until seven P.M. daily until the sale ends on December 16. Visit the Sampson Electrical Web site for details on our inventory. You can find us by searching for Sampson Electrical in your favorite search engine.

問題95-97は次の広告とウェブページに関するものです。

今日はSampson Electricalの4日間にわたる在庫一掃セールの初日で、驚くようなお買い得品をご用意しております。来年のモデルのためのスペースを作るため、現在の在庫を全て売らなくてはなりません。ですから、セール期間中は毎日異なる売り場で主要な商品が最大40パーセント引きになります。キッチン用品、ゲーム機器、コンピューター、テレビ、さらにたくさんの商品が信じられないくらいお得です。12月16日のセール終了まで、毎日午後7時まで営業しております。在庫の詳細につきましては、Sampson Electricalのウェブサイトにアクセスしてください。お気に入りの検索エンジンでSampson Electricalを検索すると、ご覧いただけます。

語彙チェック　□clearance sale　在庫一掃セール　□bargain　お買い得品、特価品
　　　　　　　□up to 〜　〜まで、最大〜　□unbelievable　信じられない
　　　　　　　□appliance　電気器具　□daily　毎日　□inventory　在庫

www.sampsonelectrical.com/ycs	
Televisions Thursday, December 13	Computers and Phones Friday, December 14
Kitchen Appliances Saturday, December 15	Gaming Devices Sunday, December 16

www.sampsonelectrical.com/ycs	
テレビ 12月13日、木曜日	コンピューターと電話 12月14日、金曜日
キッチン家電 12月15日、土曜日	ゲーム機器 12月16日、日曜日

95

□□□ 正解 A

Look at the graphic. What is on sale today?

(A) Televisions
(B) Computers and Phones
(C) Kitchen Appliances
(D) Gaming Devices

図を見てください。今日は何がセール中ですか。

(A) テレビ
(B) コンピューターと電話
(C) キッチン家電
(D) ゲーム機器

話し手は冒頭で Today is the first day of Sampson Electrical's four-day clearance sale と述べているので、今日が4日間のセールの初日だと判断できる。その後、「セール期間中は毎日異なる売り場で主要な商品が最大40パーセント引きになる」と説明しているので、このセールでは日によって安くなる商品が変わることが分かる。図を見ると、セール初日の12月13日には Televisions「テレビ」と書かれているので、正解は(A)。

96

□□□ 正解 A

What is the maximum discount the listeners can expect?

(A) 40 percent
(B) 30 percent
(C) 20 percent
(D) 10 percent

聞き手が期待できる最大の割引率はどれですか。

(A) 40パーセント
(B) 30パーセント
(C) 20パーセント
(D) 10パーセント

話し手は、在庫一掃セールについて there's up to forty percent off on major items in a different department each day of the sale と説明している。最大40パーセント引きと言っているので、正解は(A)。

97

□□□ 正解 C

What can the listeners do by visiting the Web site?

(A) Reserve items for later purchase
(B) Register as a customer
(C) Learn more about items for sale
(D) Check the nearest store location

聞き手はウェブサイトにアクセスすることで何ができますか。

(A) 後日購入のために商品を予約する
(B) お客さま登録をする
(C) 売られている商品についてもっと詳しく知る
(D) 最寄りの店舗を確認する

話し手は在庫一掃セールの内容やその間の営業時間などについて説明した後、Visit the Sampson Electrical Web site for details on our inventory. と述べている。この発言から、ウェブサイト上で在庫の詳細を確認できることが分かる。よって、(C)が正解。

トーク ▶TRACK_323   問題 ▶TRACK_324

Questions 98 through 100 refer to the following talk and sign.

Welcome to Shandling Circus. With over seventy years in the industry, we're Australia's oldest and most exciting circus. Today's final performance will commence at one P.M. You have about twenty minutes to buy refreshments at our food stand or browse the gift shop. If you don't have a ticket yet, you can get one at the ticket booth at the main entrance. If you'd like to use the free shuttle bus to get back into town after the performance, please make a reservation by visiting the administration booth on the southern side of the main tent.

問題98-100は次の話と看板に関するものです。

Shandlingサーカスにようこそ。この業界で70年以上の歴史を持つ私たちは、オーストラリアで最も古く、最も刺激的なサーカスです。本日の最終公演は午後1時に始まります。あと20分ほどは、食べ物の屋台で軽食を買ったり、ギフトショップを見て回ったりしていただけます。もしまだチケットをお持ちでない場合は、正面玄関のチケット売り場でご購入いただけます。公演後、町へ戻るのに無料シャトルバスをご利用になりたい場合は、メインテントの南側にある管理ブースへ行って予約してください。

語彙チェック　□commence　始まる　□refreshment　軽食　□stand　屋台、売店
　　　　　　　　□browse　（店など）を見て歩く　□make a reservation　予約する
　　　　　　　　□administration　管理、運営　□southern　南の

Shandling Circus	**Shandlingサーカス**
performing at	Johanna通り 787番地
787 Johanna Road	にて上演
From June 6 **to** June 10	6月6日から6月10日まで
Show times	**ショーの時間**
6:00 P.M. (Tuesday to Friday)	午後6時（火曜日から金曜日）
10:00 A.M. 1:00 P.M., and 8:00 P.M. (Saturday)	午前10時、午後1時、午後8時（土曜日）
10:30 A.M. and 1:00 P.M. (Sunday)	午前10時30分、午後1時（日曜日）

🔶**ここに注意！**

本問の図表は情報量が多く見えるので、混乱してしまう可能性が高い。先読みをする際に書かれている要素を確認しておき、その要素に触れた内容が出てきたら図表を確認するのがポイント！この図表の場合、「開催場所」「開催期間」「曜日ごとのショーの時間」という要素に分けて整理できる。

98

□□□ 正解 A

What does the speaker mention about the circus?

(A) It has a long history.

(B) It is a family business.

(C) It advertises on the radio.

(D) It travels internationally.

話し手はサーカスについて何と述べていますか。

(A) それは長い歴史がある。

(B) それは家族経営である。

(C) それはラジオで宣伝をしている。

(D) それは国際的に巡演している。

話し手はWelcome to Shandling Circus.と言って話し始め、With over seventy years in the industry, we're Australia's oldest and most exciting circus.と説明している。70年以上続いているオーストラリアで最も古いサーカスということは、長い歴史があると言えるので、(A)が正解。

99

□□□ 正解 D

Look at the graphic. When does the talk most likely take place?

(A) On Tuesday

(B) On Friday

(C) On Saturday

(D) On Sunday

図を見てください。話はいつ行われていると考えられますか。

(A) 火曜日

(B) 金曜日

(C) 土曜日

(D) 日曜日

話し手はToday's final performance will commence at one P.M.と述べている。図のShow times「ショーの時間」を見ると、午後1時の公演が1日の最後の公演になるのは、日曜日だと分かる。よって、正解は(D)。

100

□□□ 正解 D

Why are some people advised to visit an administration booth?

(A) To apply for a position

(B) To retrieve lost property

(C) To have their parking validated

(D) To reserve some transportation

何人かの人々はなぜ管理ブースに行くよう勧められていますか。

(A) 職務に応募するため

(B) 遺失物を回収するため

(C) 駐車を認証してもらうため

(D) 交通手段を予約するため

話し手は最後にIf you'd like to use the free shuttle bus 〜 please make a reservation by visiting the administration boothと説明している。この発言から、管理ブースへ行くと無料のシャトルバスの予約ができると分かる。よって、正解は(D)。

語彙チェック □retrieve 〜を回収する □lost property 遺失物
□validate 〜を有効にする、〜を認証する

TEST 5

解答＆解説

正解一覧

Part 1

問題番号	正解	1	2
1	A	☐	☐
2	C	☐	☐
3	B	☐	☐
4	C	☐	☐
5	D	☐	☐
6	A	☐	☐

Part 2

問題番号	正解	1	2
7	C	☐	☐
8	B	☐	☐
9	B	☐	☐
10	A	☐	☐
11	B	☐	☐
12	A	☐	☐
13	C	☐	☐
14	C	☐	☐
15	B	☐	☐
16	B	☐	☐
17	A	☐	☐
18	C	☐	☐
19	A	☐	☐
20	C	☐	☐
21	B	☐	☐
22	C	☐	☐
23	A	☐	☐
24	B	☐	☐
25	C	☐	☐
26	C	☐	☐
27	B	☐	☐
28	A	☐	☐
29	A	☐	☐
30	C	☐	☐
31	B	☐	☐

Part 3

問題番号	正解	1	2
32	A	☐	☐
33	B	☐	☐
34	C	☐	☐
35	C	☐	☐
36	A	☐	☐
37	D	☐	☐
38	B	☐	☐
39	D	☐	☐
40	D	☐	☐
41	A	☐	☐
42	B	☐	☐
43	C	☐	☐
44	A	☐	☐
45	D	☐	☐
46	A	☐	☐
47	D	☐	☐
48	C	☐	☐
49	A	☐	☐
50	C	☐	☐
51	B	☐	☐
52	C	☐	☐
53	D	☐	☐
54	A	☐	☐
55	D	☐	☐
56	B	☐	☐

Part 4

問題番号	正解	1	2
57	D	☐	☐
58	D	☐	☐
59	C	☐	☐
60	B	☐	☐
61	C	☐	☐
62	A	☐	☐
63	B	☐	☐
64	B	☐	☐
65	A	☐	☐
66	A	☐	☐
67	D	☐	☐
68	C	☐	☐
69	C	☐	☐
70	B	☐	☐

問題番号	正解	1	2
71	B	☐	☐
72	D	☐	☐
73	D	☐	☐
74	C	☐	☐
75	A	☐	☐
76	D	☐	☐
77	B	☐	☐
78	C	☐	☐
79	D	☐	☐
80	A	☐	☐
81	C	☐	☐
82	C	☐	☐
83	C	☐	☐
84	B	☐	☐
85	D	☐	☐
86	A	☐	☐
87	B	☐	☐
88	A	☐	☐
89	A	☐	☐
90	C	☐	☐
91	B	☐	☐
92	D	☐	☐
93	B	☐	☐
94	D	☐	☐
95	C	☐	☐

問題番号	正解	1	2
96	A	☐	☐
97	B	☐	☐
98	A	☐	☐
99	D	☐	☐
100	B	☐	☐

Part 1

1 □□□ 正解 A ▶TRACK_326

(A) Some workers are facing the same direction.
(B) Some ingredients are arranged in a refrigerator.
(C) A kitchen worker is opening an oven.
(D) A tray of food is being carried in the kitchen.

(A) 作業員が同じ方向を向いている。
(B) 材料が冷蔵庫の中に並べられている。
(C) キッチン作業員がオーブンを開けているところである。
(D) 食べ物のトレーがキッチンで運ばれているところである。

厨房で、作業員が同じ方向に体を向けて作業をしている。よって、彼らが向いている方向が同じであることを説明している (A) が正解。

語彙チェック □face 〜に向き合う □ingredient 材料 □arrange 〜を並べる

> 🐾 ここに注意！
>
> be facing each other「お互いに向き合っている」という表現も Part 1によく登場するが、ここでは the same direction とあるので「同じ方向を向いている」という意味になる！ちなみに、be facing the other way だと「別の方を向いている」となる。

---

2 □□□ 正解 C ▶TRACK_327

(A) Building materials are loaded on a car.
(B) A lamp is being installed to light the walkway.
(C) A path of bricks has been laid down.
(D) Some trees are being trimmed.

(A) 建築資材が車に詰め込まれている。
(B) 散歩道を照らすために照明装置が設置されているところである。
(C) れんがの道が敷かれている。
(D) 木が手入れされているところである。

写真の手前から奥に向かってれんがの道が続いているので、(C) が正解。lay down 〜は「〜を横たえる」という意味の他、このように「〜を敷く」という意味で使われることもあるので覚えておこう。

語彙チェック □walkway 散歩道 □path 小道、通り道 □brick れんが
□lay down〜 〜を横たえる、〜を敷く □trim 〜の手入れをする

3 🍁 　　　　　　　☐☐☐　正解 B　　▶TRACK_328

(A) Some shopping carts are being pushed.
(B) Some merchandise is displayed in barrels.
(C) A customer is crouching on the ground.
(D) A canopy is being folded outside of the store.

(A) ショッピングカートが押されている。
(B) 商品がたるの中に陳列されている。
(C) お客さんが地面にしゃがんでいる。
(D) 天蓋が店の外で折り畳まれているところである。

屋外の写真。たるが並べられており、その中に商品が陳列されているので、(B)が正解。merchandiseは集合的に「商品」を指す単語であり、今回のように青果物のようなものも指すことができる。

語彙チェック ☐barrel　たる　☐crouch　しゃがむ　☐canopy　天蓋　☐fold　〜を折り畳む

4 🇦🇺 　　　　　　　☐☐☐　正解 C　　▶TRACK_329

(A) The woman is pouring water into a bottle.
(B) The woman is leaning against a wall.
(C) Containers are kept in a cupboard.
(D) Some appliance is being plugged in.

(A) 女性は水をボトルに注いでいる。
(B) 女性は壁に寄りかかっている。
(C) 容器が戸棚にしまわれている。
(D) 電化製品がコンセントにつながれているところである。

写真の上部に注目すると、戸棚の中にいくつか容器が収納されている。よって、これを説明している(C)が正解。

語彙チェック ☐pour　〜を注ぐ　☐lean against 〜　〜に寄りかかる　☐appliance　電化製品
☐plug in 〜　〜をコンセントにつなぐ

> 🚧ここに注意！
> 女性は水を注いでいるが、ボトルに注いではいないので(A)は誤り。飲み物を注いでいる女性の動作が一番目に入りやすいが、写真の中で目立っているものほど、選択肢での引っ掛けに気を付けよう！

5   正解 D ⏵TRACK_330

(A) He is stacking some boxes.
(B) He is filling a container with beans.
(C) He is watering plants.
(D) He is harvesting outside.
(A) 彼は箱を積み重ねている。
(B) 彼は容器に豆を詰めている。
(C) 彼は植物に水をあげている。
(D) 彼は屋外で作物を収穫している。

男性は屋外で、果物のようなものをかごの中に集めている。よって、これを「屋外で作物を収穫している」と説明している (D) が正解。harvestには、「〜を収穫する」という他動詞の用法と「作物を収穫する」という自動詞の用法がある。

語彙チェック　□stack　〜を積み重ねる　□water　〜に水をやる　□harvest　作物を収穫する

> 🐾 ここに注意！
> この問題は、男性の動作を部分的に見るだけでは正解を導くことができない。周りの植物に果物のようなものが実っていることなどから、「男性が作物を収穫している」という状況を判断する必要がある！

6  正解 A ⏵TRACK_331

(A) The women are descending a staircase.
(B) The women are talking on the phone.
(C) One of the women is holding a door knob.
(D) One of the women is using medical equipment.
(A) 女性たちは階段を降りている。
(B) 女性たちは電話で話をしている。
(C) 女性の1人はドアノブをつかんでいる。
(D) 女性の1人は医療機器を使っている。

女性たちは階段を降りているところなので、これを説明している (A) が正解。descendは難易度の高い語彙だが、接頭辞のde-が「下へ」という意味を表すことを押さえておくと覚えやすい。

語彙チェック　□descend　〜を降りる　□staircase　階段　□medical　医療の

Part 2

7 M 🇺🇸 W 🇬🇧 　　　 正解 **C** ▶TRACK_333

When's the due date for submission of these application documents?

(A) In the main building.

(B) Mr. Rogers will arrange our accommodations.

(C) Let me check the schedule.

これらの申込書類の提出期限はいつですか。

(A) 本館です。

(B) Rogers さんが私たちの宿泊の手配をしてくれる予定です。

(C) 予定を確認させてください。

　問いかけ文では、申込書類の提出期限を尋ねている。これに対し、その期限を調べるためにスケジュールを確認させてほしいと伝えている (C) が正解。

語彙チェック　□due　締め切りの　□submission　提出　□arrange　〜を手配する
□accommodations　宿泊施設

> 🈳 ここに注意！
> 問いかけ文の文頭の When's は、Where's と似た音で発音されるので注意。Where's と聞き取ってしまった場合、場所を答えている (A) のような選択肢を選んでしまう！

8 M 🇦🇺 W 🇬🇧 　　　 正解 **B** ▶TRACK_334

I should register to attend this writing workshop.

(A) Something to write with.

(B) Registration begins next week.

(C) They've already arrived.

私はこのライティング講習会に参加するための登録をしなければなりません。

(A) 何か書くための物です。

(B) 登録は来週から始まります。

(C) 彼らはもうすでに到着しました。

　問いかけ文は平叙文で、「ライティング講習会に参加するための登録をしなければならない」と述べている。これに対し、登録が開始するのは来週からだと登録のスケジュールについて伝えている (B) が正解。

語彙チェック　□register to do　〜するための登録をする　□registration　登録

9 W 🇨🇦 M 🇺🇸 　　　 正解 **B** ▶TRACK_335

Haven't you created the final draft of the design yet?

(A) Yes, they were.

(B) We still have a lot of time.

(C) I've never been there.

デザインの最終案はまだ作っていないのですか。

(A) はい、そうでした。

(B) まだ時間はたくさんあります。

(C) 私は一度もそこに行ったことがありません。

　「デザインの最終案はまだ作っていないのか」と尋ねているのに対し、「まだ時間はたくさんある」と述べることで、最終案はまだ作成していないが時間的には問題ないことを示唆している (B) が正解。

語彙チェック　□draft　草案、下書き

10

M 🇺🇸 W 🇬🇧 　□□□ 正解 A 　▶TRACK_336

What's the theme of your presentation? あなたのプレゼンテーションのテーマは何ですか。
(A) I was asked to change the original one. (A) 元のテーマを変えるよう頼まれたのです。
(B) It was presented here in New York. (B) それはここニューヨークで贈呈されました。
(C) On the third shelf from the top. (C) 上から3番目の棚です。

プレゼンテーションのテーマを尋ねているのに対し、具体的なテーマについて答えるのではなく、テーマ変更の依頼があったことを伝えている(A)が正解。代名詞のone は問いかけ文のtheme を指している。

語彙チェック □theme　テーマ　□original　元の　□present　〜を贈呈する　□shelf　棚

11

W 🇬🇧 M 🇦🇺 　□□□ 正解 B 　▶TRACK_337

Do you think we should change the font of the title? タイトルのフォントを変えるべきだと思いますか。
(A) I couldn't change the date. (A) 日付を変更できませんでした。
(B) Just enlarge it, please. (B) ただ大きくしてください。
(C) Mr. Ryan's first book. (C) Ryan さんの初めての著書です。

タイトルのフォントを変えるべきかどうかについて意見を求めているのに対し、フォントはそのままで、フォントのサイズのみ変更を依頼していることが分かる(B)が正解。代名詞のit はthe font of the title を指している。

語彙チェック □font　フォント　□enlarge　〜を大きくする

12

W 🇨🇦 M 🇦🇺 　□□□ 正解 A 　▶TRACK_338

Should we arrange the chairs in a circle or in a line? 椅子を円にして並べるべきですか、それとも列にして並べるべきですか。
(A) It will be a group discussion. (A) グループディスカッションをする予定です。
(B) This table needs to be repaired. (B) このテーブルは修理する必要があります。
(C) At the entrance, please. (C) エントランスでお願いします。

椅子の並べ方に関して、円にして並べるのと列にして並べるのとどちらがいいかを選択疑問文で尋ねている。「グループディスカッションをする予定である」と伝えることで、間接的に、円にして並べたいという要望を伝えている(A)が正解。

語彙チェック □arrange　〜を並べる　□entrance　入り口、エントランス

> ⚠️ **ここに注意！**
> 「グループディスカッションをする」ということを受けて、複数人がグループになって話し合うなら机は円にして並べた方がいい、という相手の意図をくみ取る。ある程度、想像力が必要になる難問！

13 M 🇺🇸 W 🏴󠁧󠁢󠁥󠁮󠁧󠁿

Why don't we use more illustrations?　　イラストをもっと使いませんか。

(A) I don't live in the financial district.　　(A) 私は金融街には住んでいません。

(B) Because of the weather.　　(B) 天候が原因です。

(C) We have a limited budget.　　(C) 予算に限りがあります。

Why don't we ～? で、「イラストをもっと使わないか」と提案している。それに対し、「予算に限りがある」と答えることで、予算の制約上イラストを増やすことは難しいということを示唆している(C)が正解。

語彙チェック □district　地域、街　□limited　限られた

---

14 M 🇦🇺　M 🇺🇸　　　　　| | | | 正解 B → C | ⊙ TRACK_340

The event information on the Web site is not clear.　　ウェブサイトにあるイベント情報が不明瞭です。

(A) At the information counter.　　(A) 問い合わせ窓口です。

(B) It comes in eight colors.　　(B) 8色あります。

(C) What did you want to know?　　(C) 何を知りたかったのですか。

問いかけ文は平叙文で、「ウェブサイトにあるイベント情報が不明瞭だ」と報告している。これに対し、ウェブサイトを通じて何を知りたかったのかを聞き返している(C)が正解。

語彙チェック □clear　明瞭な

---

15 W 🏴󠁧󠁢󠁥󠁮󠁧󠁿　M 🇦🇺　　　　| | | | 正解 B | ⊙ TRACK_341

Weren't there enough copies of the agenda?　　アジェンダのコピーの数が十分ではなかったのですか。

(A) It was far from here.　　(A) ここからは遠かったです。

(B) I needed a few extra.　　(B) もう少し必要でした。

(C) About the cost reduction.　　(C) 費用削減についてです。

アジェンダのコピーの数が十分ではなかったのかと尋ねているのに対し、「もう少し必要だった」とコピーが少し足りなかったことを伝えている(B)が正解。

語彙チェック □reduction　削減

Is Lucia out of the office this week?
(A) No, I'll do that next week.
(B) She'll be back on Friday.
(C) Yes, you can use mine.

Luciaは今週オフィスにいませんか。
(A) いいえ、来週それをする予定です。
(B) 彼女は金曜日に戻ってくる予定です。
(C) はい、私のを使っていいですよ。

Luciaさんが今週オフィスを不在にしているかどうかを尋ねている。これに対し、「彼女は金曜日に戻ってくる予定だ」とLuciaさんの戻りの予定を伝えている (B) が正解。

How can I access the internet in my room?
(A) I'm afraid it's not free.
(B) Here's your room key.
(C) Please check out by eleven.

どうしたら私の部屋でインターネットにアクセスできますか。
(A) 申し訳ないのですが、無料ではありません。
(B) こちらがあなたの部屋の鍵です。
(C) 11時までにチェックアウトをお願いします。

自分の部屋でインターネットにアクセスする方法を尋ねているのに対し、I'm afraid「申し訳ないのですが」と前置きした後、it's not free「それは無料ではない」と事情を説明している (A) が正解。

語彙チェック □access 〜にアクセスする □check out チェックアウトする

Who is supposed to make the presentation slides?
(A) Isabelle gets to work by train.
(B) It's easy enough to access.
(C) They've already been completed.

誰がプレゼンテーションのスライドを作成することになっていますか。
(A) Isabelleは電車通勤です。
(B) アクセスするのは十分簡単です。
(C) すでに完成しています。

プレゼンテーションのスライドを作成することになっている人物について尋ねている。これに対し、「スライドはすでに完成している」と答えている (C) が正解。主語である代名詞のtheyは、問いかけ文のthe presentation slidesを指している。

語彙チェック □be supposed to do 〜することになっている

> ⚒ここに注意！
> 問いかけをしている人物はこれからスライドの作成をすると思っていることがうかがえるが、実際はその作業はすでに終わっているという状況。この問題のように、相手の認識や情報を訂正するような応答もよく出るので押さえておこう！

19　W 🇨🇦　M 🇺🇸　□□□　正解 A　▶TRACK_345

Has today's shipment already arrived?

(A) I saw the lorry coming in.

(B) No, that is our policy.

(C) They work at the warehouse.

今日の発送品はもう届きましたか。

(A) トラックが入ってくるのを見ました。

(B) いいえ、それは私たちの方針です。

(C) 彼らは倉庫で働いています。

今日の発送品がもう届いたかどうかを尋ねているのに対し、「トラックが入ってくるのを見た」と答えることで、発送品がすでに到着したことを示唆している(A)が正解。

語彙チェック □shipment　発送品　□lorry　トラック　□policy　方針　□warehouse　倉庫

🐾 **ここに注意！**

(A)のlorryはイギリス英語で使われる単語。「トラック」という意味で、アメリカ英語ではtruckとなる！

20　M 🇦🇺　W 🇨🇦　□□□　正解 C　▶TRACK_346

Where's the dentist you usually go to?

(A) I've already made an appointment.

(B) Monday through Friday.

(C) It's a twenty-minute drive from here.

あなたがいつも行く歯医者はどこにありますか。

(A) すでに予約しました。

(B) 月曜日から金曜日までです。

(C) ここから車で20分のところです。

かかりつけの歯医者がどこにあるのか、その場所を尋ねている。それに対し、その歯医者までのここからの距離を伝えている(C)が正解。

語彙チェック □dentist　歯医者　□make an appointment　予約する

21　W 🇬🇧　M 🇺🇸　□□□　正解 B　▶TRACK_347

Isn't your department holding a welcome party for new employees?

(A) She specializes in marketing.

(B) We did it on their first day.

(C) You have to fold it up.

あなたの部署は、新入社員の歓迎会を開かないのですか。

(A) 彼女はマーケティングを専攻しています。

(B) 彼らの出勤初日に開催しました。

(C) 折り畳む必要があります。

否定疑問文で、新入社員歓迎会の開催予定について尋ねている。相手の部署は歓迎会を開かないのかと確認しているのに対し、実は初日にすでに開催したことを伝えている(B)が正解。didはheldを意味しており、itはa welcome party for new employeesを指している。

語彙チェック □specialize in 〜　〜を専攻する　□fold 〜 up　〜を折り畳む

🐾 **ここに注意！**

(C)は問いかけ文のholdと音が似ている単語foldを含む誤答。fとhの発音は区別しづらく、聞き間違えやすいので注意しよう！

What made you visit our store?	なぜ当店に来店してくれたのですか。
(A) Thank you for your input.	(A) ご意見ありがとうございます。
(B) In the center of the city.	(B) 街の中心でです。
(C) My company is near here.	(C) 私の会社がこの近くにあるのです。

問いかけ文は、直訳すると「何があなたを私たちの店に来店させたのですか」という意味で、すなわち来店の理由を尋ねている。これに対し、「会社がここの近くにある」と理由を説明している(C)が正解。

語彙チェック ☐input 意見

🚨**ここに注意！**
この問いかけ文では、What made you *do* ～?で「理由」を尋ねている。文頭の疑問詞はWhyではなくWhatなので、それに惑わされずに定型表現として聞き取る必要がある！

Would you prefer meeting us in person or joining online?	私たちと直接お会いする方がいいですか、それともオンラインで参加する方がいいですか。
(A) I'm worried about the internet connection.	(A) インターネット接続が心配です。
(B) Yes, I was looking forward to it.	(B) はい、それを楽しみにしていました。
(C) It's about digital marketing strategies.	(C) デジタルマーケティング戦略についてです。

Would you prefer *doing* ～?で、相手の意向を伺っている選択疑問文。「直接会うのとオンラインで参加するのとどちらがいいか」という質問に対し、インターネット接続に不安があると伝えることで、直接会う方がいいことを示唆している(A)が正解。

語彙チェック ☐in person 自分で、本人が ☐connection 接続 ☐strategy 戦略

Why's Billy concerned about leading the event for the local community?	なぜBillyは地域社会のイベントを仕切ることについて心配しているのですか。
(A) At Beacon Park, I think.	(A) Beacon公園でだと思います。
(B) He has just moved to this area.	(B) 彼はこの地域に引っ越してきたばかりなのです。
(C) I can show you around.	(C) 私が案内できますよ。

Billyさんが地域社会のイベントを仕切ることについて心配している理由を尋ねている。これに対し、「彼はこの地域に引っ越してきたばかりである」という事情を説明することで、その理由を伝えている(B)が正解。

語彙チェック ☐move to ～ ～に引っ越す ☐show ～ around ～を案内する

25　M🇺🇸　W🇬🇧　☐☐☐　正解 C　▶TRACK_351

We need feedback on our transportation service from residents.

(A) It's easy to maintain.

(B) We can use a bus to get there.

(C) Let's conduct an online survey.

私たちの交通サービスについての住民からの意見が必要です。

(A) 維持するのは簡単です。

(B) そこに着くにはバスが利用できます。

(C) オンライン調査を行いましょう。

交通サービスに関して住民からの意見が必要だと述べている平叙文。これに対し、意見をもらう方法としてオンライン調査を行うことを提案している(C)が正解。

語彙チェック　☐feedback　意見　☐transportation　輸送機関　☐resident　住民
☐maintain　〜を維持する

26　M🇦🇺　M🇺🇸　☐☐☐　正解 C　▶TRACK_352

When will this ceiling light be automatically turned off?

(A) They'll visit us at noon.

(B) This model is the latest one.

(C) In about thirty minutes.

このシーリングライトはいつ自動的に消えるのですか。

(A) 彼らは正午に私たちのところに訪ねてくる予定です。

(B) このモデルは最新のものです。

(C) 約30分後です。

シーリングライトが自動的に消えるのはいつなのか尋ねている。これに対し、「約30分後だ」と具体的な時間を答えている(C)が正解。前置詞inには「〜の後に、〜経って」という意味を表す用法もある。

語彙チェック　☐automatically　自動的に　☐turn off 〜　〜を消す　☐latest　最新の

27　W🇬🇧　W🇨🇦　☐☐☐　正解 B　▶TRACK_353

The accounting seminar tomorrow is filled up, isn't it?

(A) Participants are required to show it.

(B) You can attend online.

(C) It's twenty dollars.

明日の会計セミナーは満員ですよね？

(A) 参加者はそれを見せる必要があります。

(B) オンラインで参加できますよ。

(C) 20ドルです。

付加疑問文で明日の会計セミナーが満員かどうかを確認しているのに対し、「オンラインで参加できる」と答えている(B)が正解。満員かどうかははっきりと答えていないが、セミナーに参加する方法はあるということを伝えている。

語彙チェック　☐accounting　会計　☐fill up 〜　〜を満員にする　☐participant　参加者
☐attend　出席する

Where did you get your bookmark?　どこでそのしおりを手に入れたのですか。

(A) It was a present.　(A) これは贈り物でした。

(B) I bought a bookshelf.　(B) 本棚を買いました。

(C) Just a week ago.　(C) ちょうど1週間前です。

しおりを手に入れた場所を尋ねているのに対し、実は自身で購入したものではなく、しおりは贈り物であったことを説明している(A)が正解。主語となっている代名詞のitは、問いかけ文のbookmarkを指している。

語彙チェック ☐bookmark　しおり　☐bookshelf　本棚

The guest speaker is arriving in about ten minutes.　ゲストスピーカーは約10分後に到着します。

(A) He's known to be so punctual.　(A) 彼は時間厳守な人で知られています。

(B) It was very informative.　(B) それはとても有益でした。

(C) I've worked as an engineer.　(C) エンジニアとして働いたことがあります。

問いかけ文は平叙文で、ゲストスピーカーの到着時刻を伝えている。これに対し、そのゲストスピーカーがとても時間厳守な人として知られていることを説明している(A)が正解。

語彙チェック ☐punctual　時間を守る　☐informative　有益な

How long is my loyalty card valid?　私のポイントカードはどのくらいの間有効ですか。

(A) About twenty kilometers.　(A) 約20キロメートルです。

(B) Since I graduated from college.　(B) 大学を卒業して以来です。

(C) Do you have it with you now?　(C) 今そちらをお持ちですか。

How long ～?でポイントカードの有効期間を尋ねているのに対し、期間を教えるのではなく今ポイントカードを持っているかを聞き返している(C)が正解。

語彙チェック ☐loyalty card　ポイントカード　☐valid　有効な

🐾 **ここに注意！**

誤答の(A)と(B)はどちらも、How long ～?という問いかけに対する応答としてよくある形になっているので注意！　何かの距離を尋ねていれば(A)が、現時点までに何かが継続している期間を尋ねていれば(B)が正解になりうる。

31　M 🇦🇺　W 🇨🇦　　　　□□□　正解 **B**　　▶TRACK_357

You're assigned to the section manager, right?	あなたは部長に任命されていますよね？
(A) No, Ms. Long will leave us.	(A) いいえ、Longさんは辞職する予定です。
(B) I have to prepare a lot for that.	(B) そのために準備しなければならないことがたくさんあります。
(C) Here's the ID card reader.	(C) これがIDカード読み取り機です。

　話しかけている相手が部長に任命されていることを確認している。これに対し、「そのために準備しなければならないことがたくさんある」と答え、部長の役割を担う上で準備するべきことが多いことを示唆している(B)が正解。

語彙チェック　□assign *A* to *B*　AをBに任命する　□reader　読み取り機

Part 3

M ▆ W ▆ 　　　　　　　　　 会話 ▶TRACK_359 　問題 ▶TRACK_360
Questions 32 through 34 refer to the following conversation.

M: Jenny, I need to talk to you about <u>this new adhesive we're using for the soles</u>. The people in quality control say that the rubber is coming off much earlier than it should.

W: I see. <u>We're using the same glue on the upper parts of the boots</u>, too. Did they mention any problems there?

M: No. Perhaps it sticks to some materials better than others. I know <u>we still have some of the old glue</u> in the warehouse. <u>Let's switch back to that until we sort out the problem.</u>

W: Sure. I think there's only enough for one week of production, though. <u>We can't order more because IGK Chemicals has closed down.</u>

問題32-34は次の会話に関するものです。

男性：Jenny、私たちが靴底に使っている、この新しい接着剤について話があります。品質管理の人たちによると、本来よりもはるかに早くゴムが剥がれてしまうそうです。

女性：そうですか。ブーツの上部にも同じ接着剤を使っています。そこについては何か問題があると言っていましたか。

男性：いいえ。たぶん他の素材よりもよくくっつく素材があるのかもしれません。まだ倉庫に古い接着剤がありますよね。問題を解決するまでそれに戻しましょう。

女性：いいですよ。でも1週間の製造分だけしかないと思います。IGK化学会社が廃業してしまったので、これ以上は注文できません。

語彙チェック　□adhesive　接着剤　□sole　靴底　□quality control　品質管理　□rubber　ゴム　□come off　剥がれる　□glue　接着剤　□upper　上部の　□stick to 〜　〜にくっつく　□material　素材　□switch to 〜　〜に切り替える　□sort out 〜　〜を解決する　□close down　廃業する

32 　　　　　　　□□□　正解 A

Where do the speakers most likely work?	話し手たちはどこで働いていると考えられますか。
(A) At a shoe factory	(A) 靴工場
(B) At a shipping company	(B) 配送会社
(C) At a hardware store	(C) ホームセンター
(D) At an equipment rental firm	(D) 機器レンタル会社

男性のthis new adhesive we're using for the soles「私たちが靴底に使っている、この新しい接着剤」という発言や、女性のWe're using the same glue on the upper parts of the boots「ブーツの上部にも同じ接着剤を使っている」という発言から、2人は靴類を作る仕事をしていると考えられる。よって、正解は(A)。

> ⚠ ここに注意！
> このような話し手の職業を問う問題は、会話の中ではっきりと述べられるわけではないので、全体で話されている情報をもとに予測する必要がある。1問目に気をとられて、次の問題の根拠を聞き逃してしまわないように注意しよう！

33 □□□ 正解 B

What does the man suggest?

(A) Spending more on advertising
(B) Reverting to a previously used product
(C) Conducting a satisfaction survey
(D) Redesigning a product

男性は何を提案していますか。

(A) 広告にもっとお金をかけること
(B) 以前に使用されていた製品に戻ること
(C) 満足度調査を行うこと
(D) 製品を設計し直すこと

靴底に使用している接着剤が剥がれやすいという問題を受けて、男性はwe still have some of the old glueと言い、Let's switch back to that until we sort out the problem.と提案している。男性は、問題を解決するまで古い接着剤を使うことを提案しているので、正解は(B)。

語彙チェック □ revert to 〜 〜に戻る □ satisfaction survey 満足度調査
□ redesign 〜を再設計する

34 □□□ 正解 C

Why are the speakers unable to order an item?

(A) The Web site is temporarily unavailable.
(B) A product was discontinued.
(C) A supplier has gone out of business.
(D) There was a supply chain issue.

話し手たちはなぜ商品を注文できませんか。

(A) ウェブサイトが一時的に利用できない。
(B) 商品が製造中止になった。
(C) 供給業者が廃業した。
(D) サプライチェーンに問題があった。

古い接着剤を使うという男性の提案に対し、女性は「1週間の製造分だけしかないと思う」と述べ、理由をWe can't order more because IGK Chemicals has closed down.と説明している。IGK化学会社は話し手たちが接着剤を注文していた会社なので、これをsupplier「供給業者」と言い換えている (C) が正解。

語彙チェック □ temporarily 一時的に □ unavailable 利用できない
□ discontinue 〜をやめる、〜を中止する
□ go out of business 廃業する、倒産する

W [🇨🇦]　M [🇦🇺]　　　　　　　　　　会話 ▶TRACK_361　問題 ▶TRACK_362

Questions 35 through 37 refer to the following conversation.

W: Hi. I've just purchased a new car, and I'd like to find out how much it will cost to insure it. Can I do that over the phone?

M: You sure can. Can you give me the make and model of the vehicle please?

W: Um... It's a Venturi STR. It's uh... this year, no... last year's model.

M: What is the purpose of the vehicle? I mean, will you be using it for commuting or just on the weekends and holidays?

W: I'll be using it to get to work every day.

問題35-37は次の会話に関するものです。

女性：こんにちは。ちょうど新しい車を買ったところで、それに保険をかけるのにいくらかかるのか知りたいと思っています。電話で伺うことはできますか。

男性：もちろんできますよ。自動車のメーカーとモデルを教えていただけますか。

女性：ええと… Venturi STR です。それは、ええと…今年、いえ…去年のモデルです。

男性：自動車の使用目的は何ですか。つまり、通勤にお使いになりますか、それとも週末と休日だけお使いになりますか。

女性：毎日仕事に行くのに使う予定です。

語彙チェック　□find out 〜　〜について知る　□insure　〜に保険をかける
　　　　　　　　□over the phone　電話で　□make　メーカー、製造会社
　　　　　　　　□commute　通勤する、通学する　□get to 〜　〜に到着する

35　　　　　　　　□□□　正解 C

What is the purpose of the call?　　　電話の目的は何ですか。

(A) To request permission for a purchase　(A) 購入許可を頼むこと

(B) To recommend a model　　　　　　(B) モデルを勧めること

(C) To check on a price　　　　　　　(C) 値段を調べること

(D) To make a reservation　　　　　　(D) 予約を取ること

女性は冒頭で「新しい車を買ったところだ」と伝えた後、I'd like to find out how much it will cost to insure it と述べ、Can I do that over the phone? と尋ねている。ここから、女性は自動車保険の値段を調べるために電話をかけてきていると判断できる。よって、(C) が正解。

語彙チェック　□permission　許可　□check on 〜　〜を調べる

36 □□□ 正解 A

What does the man request?

(A) A brand name

(B) The proof of purchase

(C) The number of passengers

(D) Contact details

男性は何を求めていますか。

(A) ブランド名

(B) 購入の証明

(C) 乗客の人数

(D) 連絡先

女性からの自動車保険料に関する問い合わせに対し、男性は Can you give me the make and model of the vehicle please? と尋ねている。男性は、the make and model of the vehicle「自動車のメーカーとモデル」を知りたがっていると分かるので、(A) が正解。

37 □□□ 正解 D

What does the woman say about the vehicle?

(A) It is in need of some repairs.

(B) It was purchased from a dealer.

(C) It will be kept in a company garage.

(D) It will be used for commuting.

女性は自動車について何と言っていますか。

(A) それは修理が必要である。

(B) それは販売業者から購入した。

(C) それは会社の車庫に保管される。

(D) それは通勤に使用される。

男性が What is the purpose of the vehicle? と自動車の使用目的を尋ねると、女性は I'll be using it to get to work every day. と答えている。この発言から、車は仕事に行くために使われるということが分かる。よって、(D) が正解。

語彙チェック □be in need of 〜　〜を必要とする　□dealer　ディーラー、販売業者
□garage　車庫

269

Questions 38 through 40 refer to the following conversation.

W: Walter, I think we need to source our timber somewhere new. The company we're relying on now has been sending us low quality wood.

M: Well, let's not be too hasty. I mean, we've been using Solomon's for years, and they give us a pretty good rate. Let them know in writing that we'll look elsewhere if the quality doesn't improve.

W: That sounds reasonable. I've mentioned it to the drivers a few times, but you're right. The message may not have gotten back to their management.

M: Right. By the way, I'm going to meet some of the board members at Memorial Hospital this afternoon. We'll be discussing their expansion plans. Would you like to come along? You could help me put together our bid.

問題38-40は次の会話に関するものです。

女性：Walter、私たちの木材をどこか新しいところから調達しなければいけないと思います。現在私たちが頼っている会社は、品質の低い木材を送ってきています。

男性：まあ、そんなに急ぎすぎないようにしましょう。というのも、私たちはSolomon社のものを何年も使っていて、彼らはかなり良い価格を提供してくれているのです。品質が改善されなければどこか他を探すと彼らに文書で知らせましょう。

女性：それは妥当ですね。このことについて数回運転手に話したのですが、あなたの言う通りですね。向こうの経営陣にメッセージが伝わっていなかったのかもしれません。

男性：そうですね。ところで、今日の午後に記念病院の役員に会う予定があります。私たちは彼らの拡張計画について話し合います。あなたも一緒に来ませんか。入札をまとめるのを手伝ってください。

語彙チェック   □source 〜を調達する   □timber 木材、材木   □rely on 〜 〜に頼る
       □hasty 軽率な、早まった   □rate 料金、値段   □in writing 文書で
       □board member 重役、役員   □come along 一緒に行く、同行する
       □put together 〜 〜をまとめる   □bid 入札

38   □□□   正解 **B**

What are the speakers mainly discussing?   話し手たちは主に何について話し合っていますか。

(A) Testing some products   (A) 製品の検査をすること

(B) Changing a supplier   (B) 供給業者を変更すること

(C) Choosing a restaurant   (C) レストランを選ぶこと

(D) Reading some reviews   (D) レビューを読むこと

女性は冒頭でI think we need to source our timber somewhere newと発言し、理由をThe company we're relying on now has been sending us low quality wood.と説明している。それに対して男性は「急ぎすぎないようにしましょう」と声をかけた後、Let them know in writing that we'll look elsewhere if the quality doesn't improve.と言っている。これらの発言から、2人は木材を仕入れる会社を変更するかどうかについて話し合っていると判断できる。よって、(B)が正解。

39 □□□ 正解 D

What does the man suggest?

(A) Raising production capacity

(B) Updating a manual

(C) Requesting a meeting

(D) Giving a warning

男性は何を提案していますか。

(A) 生産能力を上げること

(B) マニュアルを更新すること

(C) 打ち合わせを要請すること

(D) 警告をすること

「現在私たちが頼っている会社は、品質の低い木材を送ってきている」という女性の発言に対し、男性は「Solomon 社のものを何年も使っていて、彼らはかなり良い価格を提供してくれている」と説明した後、Let them know in writing that we'll look elsewhere if the quality doesn't improve. と提案している。この「品質が改善されなければどこか他を探すと文書で知らせる」ことを「警告をする」と表している (D) が正解。

語彙チェック □capacity　能力

40 □□□ 正解 D

What will the man do this afternoon?

(A) Attend an industry conference

(B) Assemble some office furniture

(C) Get a medical checkup

(D) Speak with a prospective customer

男性は今日の午後に何をしますか。

(A) 産業会議に出席する

(B) オフィス家具を組み立てる

(C) 健康診断を受ける

(D) 見込み客と話す

男性は By the way と話題を変え、今日の午後に記念病院の役員に会う予定があり、病院の拡張計画について話し合うと伝えている。その後の You could help me put together our bid. という発言から、これから入札が行われると判断でき、この病院の拡張計画は将来的な事業であると考えられる。よって、(D) が正解。

語彙チェック □assemble　〜を組み立てる　□prospective　将来の、見込みのある

Questions 41 through 43 refer to the following conversation.

W: Look at this traffic. I don't think we're going to get to the airport on time. Perhaps we should take the train from here.

M: That might be a good call. Can you find out how long it will take by train from here? I would but the battery is running out on my phone.

W: I already did. We could be there in about 30 minutes. That gives us plenty of time to check in and get to the boarding gate.

M: OK. Driver, could you let us out at Gleeson Station? Glenda, I'll get the bags from the trunk. Would you mind paying?

問題41-43は次の会話に関するものです。

女性：この交通量を見てください。空港に予定通りに到着しそうもないですよ。たぶんここから電車に乗った方がいいと思います。

男性：それは良い考えかもしれません。ここから電車でどのくらいかかるか調べてもらえませんか。調べようと思ったのですが、私の携帯電話は充電が切れそうで。

女性：すでに調べましたよ。約30分で空港に到着できそうです。それだと、チェックインして搭乗口へ行くのにたっぷり時間があります。

男性：分かりました。運転手さん、Gleeson駅で降ろしていただけますか。Glenda、私はトランクからバッグを取ってきます。あなたは支払いをしてもらえませんか。

語彙チェック　□traffic　交通量　□on time　時間通りに、予定通りに
□good call　正しい判断、良い考え　□run out　尽きる、終わる
□plenty of 〜　たくさんの〜、十分な〜　□boarding　搭乗
□let 〜 out　〜を外に出す　□trunk　(車の) トランク

41　□□□　正解 A

Where does the conversation most likely take place?

(A) In a taxi

(B) At an airport

(C) In an office

(D) On a train

会話はどこで行われていると考えられますか。

(A) タクシー

(B) 空港

(C) オフィス

(D) 電車

冒頭の Look at this traffic. I don't think we're going to get to the airport on time. Perhaps we should take the train from here. という女性の発言から、話し手たちは道路を走る乗り物に乗車していて、交通渋滞にはまっていると考えられる。また、空港に電車で行くことについて話し合った後、Driver, could you let us out at Gleeson Station? と男性は運転手に声をかけ、支払いをするように女性にお願いしている。これらのことから、話し手たちはタクシーに乗っていると判断できるので、正解は (A)。

🐾 **ここに注意！**
会話が行われている場所を答える問題。ここでは、タクシーの中にいることははっきりと述べられていないので、話し手の発言から状況を予測する必要がある。会話を聞きながら状況をイメージする癖を付けよう！

42 □□□ 正解 B

What does the man ask the woman to do?	男性は女性に何をするよう求めていますか。
(A) Call a colleague	(A) 同僚に電話する
(B) Check a schedule	(B) 時刻表を確認する
(C) Install an application	(C) アプリケーションをインストールする
(D) Charge his phone	(D) 彼の携帯電話を充電する

「ここから電車に乗った方がいい」という女性の提案に、男性は That might be a good call. と同意を示し、Can you find out how long it will take by train from here? と女性に依頼している。「ここから電車でどのくらいかかるか調べる」ことを「時刻表を確認する」と言い換えている (B) が正解。

語彙チェック □install ～をインストールする □charge ～を充電する

43 □□□ 正解 C

What does the man say he will do?	男性は何をすると言っていますか。
(A) Purchase some tickets	(A) チケットを購入する
(B) Check in at a hotel	(B) ホテルにチェックインする
(C) Retrieve some luggage	(C) 手荷物を回収する
(D) Reserve a vehicle	(D) 乗り物を予約する

男性は運転手にタクシーから降ろしてもらうよう頼むと、女性に Glenda, I'll get the bags from the trunk. と伝えている。この発言から、この後に男性はトランクから荷物を取ってくると判断できる。よって、(C) が正解。

語彙チェック □retrieve ～を取り戻す、～を回収する

Questions 44 through 46 refer to the following conversation.

M: Hi Chloe. You haven't seen my 3D scanner, have you? I need it for a job in Wilcox this afternoon.

W: Sorry, Fred. I'd lend you mine, but I'm using it all day. If the job in Wilcox isn't too big, I could take care of it for you.

M: Thanks, Chloe. I might take you up on that. I have a feeling I left the scanner in Havertown when I was there yesterday. Do you have time, though?

W: No problem at all. I pass through Wilcox every evening when I go home.

問題44-46は次の会話に関するものです。

男性：こんにちはChloe。私の3Dスキャナーを見ていませんよね？　今日の午後Wilcoxでの仕事にそれが必要なのです。

女性：ごめんなさい、Fred。私のものを貸してあげたいのですが、私も1日中それを使う予定なのです。Wilcoxでの仕事がそれほど大きくなければ、私が代わりに引き受けることもできますよ。

男性：ありがとうございます、Chloe。それをお願いするかもしれません。昨日Havertownに行ったときにスキャナーを忘れてきた気がします。でもあなたは時間がありますか。

女性：全く問題ありませんよ。毎晩家に帰るときに、Wilcoxを通りますから。

語彙チェック　□ all day　1日中　□ take care of ～　～を引き受ける
□ take *A* up on *B*　*A*の*B*（申し出など）を受け入れる
□ pass through ～　～を通る

44　　　　　　　　□□□　正解 A

Why is the man concerned?　　　男性はなぜ心配していますか。

(A) He has misplaced some equipment.　(A) 彼は機器を置き忘れてきた。

(B) He does not have time to finish a project.　(B) 彼はプロジェクトを終える時間がない。

(C) His department needs a bigger budget.　(C) 彼の部署はもっと予算が必要である。

(D) His computer has been malfunctioning.　(D) 彼のコンピューターは調子が悪い。

男性は冒頭でHi Chloe. と女性に声をかけると、You haven't seen my 3D scanner, have you? と尋ねている。その後、「今日の午後Wilcoxでの仕事にそれが必要だ」と言っているので、男性は今日の午後に使う予定の3Dスキャナーをどこかに置き忘れてきたことを心配していると考えられる。よって、正解は(A)。

語彙チェック　□ misplace　～を置き忘れる　□ malfunction　うまく機能しない

45 　　　□□□　正解 D

What does the man mean when he says, "I might take you up on that"?

(A) He may ask the woman to accompany him.

(B) He hopes to give the woman a promotion.

(C) He would like to show the woman his new car.

(D) He may accept the woman's offer.

男性は "I might take you up on that" という発言で、何を意味していますか。

(A) 彼は女性に同行してもらうよう求めるかもしれない。

(B) 彼は女性を昇進させたいと思っている。

(C) 彼は女性に彼の新しい車を見せたいと思っている。

(D) 彼は女性の申し出を受け入れるかもしれない。

女性の If the job in Wilcox isn't too big, I could take care of it for you. という申し出に対し、男性は下線部の発言をしている。その後、男性は I have a feeling I left the scanner in Havertown when I was there yesterday. と言っていることから、男性は仕事ができないかもしれないことが示唆される。これらのことから、下線部の発言は、女性の申し出を受け入れる可能性があるという男性の意図を表していると考えられる。よって、正解は (D)。

語彙チェック　□give 〜 a promotion　〜を昇進させる

46 　　　□□□　正解 A

What does the woman say about Wilcox?

(A) It is on her way home.

(B) It is the location of a supplier.

(C) It will host an important event.

(D) It has cheap rent.

女性は Wilcox について何と言っていますか。

(A) そこは帰宅する途中にある。

(B) そこは供給業者の所在地である。

(C) そこは重要なイベントを主催する。

(D) そこは賃料が安い。

男性の仕事を引き受けるという女性に、「時間がありますか」と男性が尋ねると、女性は No problem at all. と答え、理由を I pass through Wilcox every evening when I go home. と説明している。この発言から Wilcox は女性の帰り道の途中にあると判断できる。よって、正解は (A)。

語彙チェック　□on one's way　途中で、途中にある

Questions 47 through 49 refer to the following conversation.

W: I met one of your old workmates from Vandelay Technology yesterday. She was one of the applicants for the chief programmer position. Do you remember Ingrid Thompson?

M: Yes. She was one of the programmers there — Really talented and very easy to get along with.

W: I'm glad to hear that. I've decided to offer her the position. Could you give her a call and let her know the good news?

問題47-49は次の会話に関するものです。

女性：昨日、Vandelayテクノロジー社のあなたの昔の同僚の1人に会いましたよ。彼女は主任プログラマーの職の応募者の1人でした。Ingrid Thompsonを覚えていますか。

男性：はい。彼女はそこのプログラマーの1人でしたよ―かなり有能で、とても付き合いやすい人でした。

女性：それを聞けて良かったです。彼女にその職をお願いすることに決めました。彼女に電話をして、この良い知らせを伝えてあげてもらえませんか。

語彙チェック　□workmate　同僚、仕事仲間　□chief　（組織の）長
　　　　　　　　□talented　有能な、才能のある　□get along with 〜　〜と仲良くやっていく
　　　　　　　　□give 〜 a call　〜に電話する

47　　　　　　　□□□　正解 D

What did the woman do yesterday?

(A) She visited a competitor.

(B) She installed some software.

(C) She had a client meeting.

(D) She interviewed a candidate.

女性は昨日何をしましたか。

(A) 彼女は競合会社を訪ねた。

(B) 彼女はソフトウェアをインストールした。

(C) 彼女は顧客との打ち合わせがあった。

(D) 彼女は志願者を面接した。

女性は冒頭でI met one of your old workmates from Vandelay Technology yesterday. と述べた後、会った相手について She was one of the applicants for the chief programmer position. と説明している。この発言から、女性は昨日仕事の応募者と会って話をしたと判断できる。よって、正解は (D)。

語彙チェック　□install　〜をインストールする

48

□□□ 正解 C

What does the man say about Ms. Thompson?

(A) She is a company founder.
(B) She introduced him to the company.
(C) She is good at her job.
(D) She likes to travel.

男性はThompsonさんについて何と言っていますか。

(A) 彼女は会社の創業者である。
(B) 彼女は彼を会社に紹介した。
(C) 彼女は自分の仕事が得意である。
(D) 彼女は旅行が好きだ。

女性が Do you remember Ingrid Thompson? と尋ねると、男性は Yes. She was one of the programmers there と答え、続けて Really talented と説明している。Really talented「かなり有能な」と言っているので、これを言い換えている (C) が正解。

語彙チェック □ be good at ～　～が得意である

49

□□□ 正解 A

What does the woman ask the man to do?

(A) Announce a decision
(B) Advertise a position
(C) Write a news article
(D) Send an e-mail

女性は男性に何をするよう求めていますか。

(A) 決定事項を知らせる
(B) 求人広告を出す
(C) 新聞記事を書く
(D) Eメールを送る

男性から Ingrid Thompson さんについて聞いた女性は「それを聞けて良かった」と言い、「彼女にその職をお願いすることに決めた」と述べている。続けて Could you give her a call and let her know the good news? と男性に頼んでいる。この発言から、女性は男性に、Thompson さんに電話をして採用決定を伝えるよう依頼していることが分かる。よって、正解は (A)。

Questions 50 through 52 refer to the following conversation.

M: Hi. I bought a used vehicle a couple of days ago, and I'd like to have the mechanics take a look at it. Just to check the safety features and make sure the fluids are OK.

W: That's always a good idea with a used vehicle. I'm afraid we can't take a look at it today. You need to make a reservation. We're quite busy these days.

M: Oh... I didn't expect that. I was hoping to leave it with you and pick it up in a few days.

W: Well, in that case, we could check it tomorrow. I can't offer you a replacement vehicle, though.

M: That's fine. I'll take the bus. My office is only a couple of stops from here.

問題50-52は次の会話に関するものです。

男性：こんにちは。2、3日前に中古車を買ったので、整備士の方に見ていただきたいと思っています。ちょっと安全機能を点検して、液体類が大丈夫か確認していただきたくて。

女性：中古車に関して言えば、それがいつだって正しい考えですね。申し訳ございませんが、今日は点検ができません。予約が必要になります。最近かなり混んでいるのです。

男性：ああ…それは予想外でした。こちらに車を預けて、数日後に受け取れたらいいなと思っていたのですが。

女性：そうですか、その場合は、明日点検できると思います。代車をお貸しすることはできませんが。

男性：それは大丈夫です。バスを使いますから。私のオフィスはここからたった2、3個行ったバス停のところなのです。

語彙チェック　□mechanic　機械工　□safety feature　安全機能　□fluid　液体
　　　　　　　　□quite　かなり　□pick 〜 up　〜を受け取る　□in that case　その場合には

50　　　　　　　□□□ 正解 **C**

What is the purpose of the man's visit?　　男性の訪問の目的は何ですか。

(A) To pick up his car　　　　　　　(A) 彼の車を受け取ること

(B) To apply for a position　　　　　(B) 仕事に応募すること

(C) To have a vehicle inspected　　　(C) 車を点検してもらうこと

(D) To sell a used item　　　　　　　(D) 中古品を売ること

男性は冒頭で「2、3日前に中古車を買った」と述べ、I'd like to have the mechanics take a look at it と伝えている。続けて、Just to check the safety features and make sure the fluids are OK. と説明している。これらの発言から、男性は購入した中古車を点検してもらうために訪れたと判断できる。よって、正解は (C)。

語彙チェック　□inspect　〜を点検する、〜を検査する

51

□□□ 正解 **B**

Why is the woman unable to accept the man's request?

(A) Some work has not been completed.

(B) An appointment is necessary.

(C) A meeting has been rescheduled.

(D) There is a shortage of some supplies.

なぜ女性は男性の依頼を受けることができませんか。

(A) 完了していない仕事がある。

(B) 予約が必要である。

(C) 会議の予定が変更された。

(D) 不足している供給品がある。

車の点検に訪れた男性に対し、女性は I'm afraid we can't take a look at it today. と伝えると、理由を You need to make a reservation. と説明している。よって、これを言い換えている (B) が正解。

語彙チェック □be unable to *do* 〜することができない □shortage 不足

52

□□□ 正解 **C**

What does the man say he will do?

(A) Check his schedule

(B) Wait in reception

(C) Use public transportation

(D) Try another dealership

男性は何をすると言っていますか。

(A) 彼の予定を確認する

(B) 受付で待つ

(C) 公共交通機関を使う

(D) 他の販売代理店を試してみる

女性が、明日点検できると思うが代車を貸すことはできないことを伝えると、男性は That's fine. と答え、続けて I'll take the bus. と言っている。よって、男性はバスを使うことが分かるので、(C) が正解。

語彙チェック □reception 受付 □dealership 販売代理店

Questions 53 through 55 refer to the following conversation.

W: Hi, Harley. <u>I was checking the employee handbook last night, and I found a few errors.</u> There were some spelling mistakes and a couple of extension numbers that have been changed.

M: Good work. You know, it's time we reprinted them and handed them out to all of the employees. <u>When you've finished, call Red Simms at Colorworld.</u> He always gives us a good deal on this kind of printing work.

W: I will. Um, perhaps we should wait a couple of weeks, though. The marketing section is moving to the ground floor, and I'm sure that'll lead to a few more changes.

M: Good point. Well, <u>I'll leave the rest to you.</u> <u>It looks like you've thought of everything.</u>

問題53-55は次の会話に関するものです。

女性：こんにちは、Harley。昨夜、従業員ハンドブックを確認していて、いくつか間違いを見つけました。いくつかスペルの間違いがあったのと、変更になった内線番号が2、3個ありました。

男性：よく見つけましたね。そろそろそれを印刷し直して、全従業員に配布する頃ですからね。終わったら、Colorworld社のRed Simmsに電話してください。この種類の印刷の仕事に、彼はいつも良い価格を提示してくれます。

女性：そうします。ええと、でもたぶん、2、3週間待った方がいいかもしれません。マーケティング部が1階に移動するので、絶対にもう少し変更が出ると思います。

男性：良いポイントですね。では、残りはあなたにお任せします。あなたは全部考えてあるようですから。

語彙チェック □error　間違い　□spelling　つづり、スペル　□extension number　内線番号　□reprint　〜を再び印刷する　□hand *A* out to *B*　AをBに配る　□deal　取引　□lead to 〜　〜を引き起こす、〜の原因となる　□leave *A* to *B*　AをBに任せる　□rest　残り

---

53   □□□ 正解 D

What did the woman do yesterday?   女性は昨日何をしましたか。

(A) She looked at some applications.   (A) 彼女は申込書を見た。

(B) She submitted a report.   (B) 彼女は報告書を提出した。

(C) She updated employee files.   (C) 彼女は従業員ファイルを更新した。

(D) She proofread a manual.   (D) 彼女はマニュアルを校正した。

女性はI was checking the employee handbook last nightと発言するとI found a few errorsと伝え、続けてその詳細を報告している。これらの発言から、女性は昨日、従業員ハンドブックの校正作業をしていたと判断できる。よって、**(D)** が正解。

語彙チェック □proofread　〜を校正する　□manual　マニュアル、手引書

54 ☐☐☐ 正解 A

What does the man ask the woman to do?

(A) Call a printing company
(B) Resubmit a report
(C) Meet with a client
(D) Schedule some interviews

男性は女性に何をするよう求めていますか。

(A) 印刷会社に電話する
(B) 報告書を再提出する
(C) 顧客に会う
(D) 面接の予定を組む

男性は従業員ハンドブックについて「そろそろ印刷し直して、全従業員に配布する頃だ」と言うと、女性にWhen you've finished, call Red Simms at Colorworld.と指示している。また、Red Simmsさんについて He always gives us a good deal on this kind of printing work.と述べていることから、Simmsさんは印刷業者だと考えられる。これらから、男性は印刷会社に電話するよう女性に指示していると判断できる。よって、正解は(A)。

語彙チェック ☐ resubmit 〜を再提出する

55 ☐☐☐ 正解 D

Why does the man say, "I'll leave the rest to you"?

(A) To suggest that the woman take a break
(B) To offer the woman some food
(C) To allow the woman to use some space
(D) To put the woman in charge of a task

男性はなぜ "I'll leave the rest to you" と言っていますか。

(A) 女性が休憩をとることを提案するため
(B) 女性に食べ物を提供するため
(C) 女性が場所を使うことを許可するため
(D) 女性に仕事を任せるため

印刷会社に電話するよう指示された女性は「たぶん、2、3週間待った方がいいかもしれない」と述べ、理由を「マーケティング部が1階に移動するため、絶対にもう少し変更が出ると思う」と説明している。これに対し、男性は下線部の発言をした後、最後に It looks like you've thought of everything.と述べている。これらの流れから、男性は女性が仕事の詳細について理解しているのを見て、女性にこの仕事を任せようとしていると考えられる。よって、正解は(D)。

語彙チェック ☐ allow A to do Aが〜することを許可する

W 🇬🇧　**M1** 🇦🇺　**M2** 🇺🇸　　　　　　　　　 会話 ▶TRACK_375　　問題 ▶TRACK_376

Questions 56 through 58 refer to the following conversation with three speakers.

W: Ken, I need you to translate these apartment profiles into Japanese. Bill Yapp at Kruger Real Estate wants to show them to a Japanese investor tomorrow afternoon.

M1: I'm busy with this financial report. Can you see if Yutaka is available?

W: Sure. Oh, there he is.

M2: I heard you. I'm a bit pressed for time at the moment myself. It looks like there's two profiles. How about doing one each?

W: I don't mind. How does that sound Ken?

M1: Sure. I'll have it ready by about noon tomorrow.

M2: That goes for me, too.

W: OK, I'll give Mr. Yapp a call now to make sure that's ok.

問題56-58は3人の話し手による次の会話に関するものです。

女性　：Ken、あなたにこれらのアパート情報を日本語に翻訳してもらいたいのですが。Kruger不動産のBill Yappが明日の午後、日本人の投資家にそれらを見せたいそうです。

男性1：私はこの会計報告書で忙しくて。Yutakaが手が空いているかどうか、確認してくれませんか。

女性　：もちろんです。あら、彼ですよ。

男性2：聞こえましたよ。今はちょっと時間がなくて困っています。アパート情報は2つあるようですね。1つずつやるのはどうですか。

女性　：私は構いませんよ。Kenはどうですか。

男性1：いいですよ。明日の正午ごろまでに準備しておきます。

男性2：私もそれで大丈夫です。

女性　：分かりました。それで問題ないか確認するためにYappさんに今電話をしますね。

語彙チェック　　□translate *A* into *B*　AをBに翻訳する　□investor　投資家
　　　　　　　　　□financial report　会計報告書　□be pressed for ～　～がなくて困っている
　　　　　　　　　□go for ～　～に当てはまる

⚠️ ここに注意！

2人目の男性の最初の発言に、I'm a bit pressed for time at the moment myself. とある。be pressed for ～「～がなくて困っている」はあまりなじみがない表現なので、この文の意味をつかめなかった人もいるかもしれない。難しい表現があったときはそこに固執し過ぎず、文脈の流れからなんとなくで意味を予測することも大切！

56　正解 B

Who most likely are the men?

(A) Real estate agents

(B) Translators

(C) Investors

(D) Financial experts

男性たちは誰だと考えられますか。

(A) 不動産業者

(B) 翻訳家

(C) 投資家

(D) 財務の専門家

女性は冒頭でI need you to translate these apartment profiles into Japaneseと男性に伝えている。この発言から、1人目の男性は日本語に翻訳する仕事をしていると考えられる。その後、男性2人がこの翻訳業務を分担するという流れになることから、2人目の男性も同じ仕事をしていると判断できる。よって、正解は(B)。

57　正解 D

What does Yutaka suggest?

(A) Outsourcing some help

(B) Asking for an extension

(C) Offering a discount

(D) Dividing some work

Yutakaは何を提案していますか。

(A) 支援を外部委託すること

(B) 延長を求めること

(C) 値引きすること

(D) 仕事を分担すること

女性から翻訳作業を頼まれた1人目の男性は、会計報告書で忙しいことを伝えると、Can you see if Yutaka is available?と尋ねている。その後、Yutakaと呼ばれるもう1人の男性が登場する。この男性は「今はちょっと時間がなくて困っている」と伝えた後、It looks like there's two profiles.と言い、How about doing one each?と提案している。この発言から、Yutakaさんは2つあるアパート情報を、もう1人の男性とそれぞれ1つずつ分担して翻訳することを提案していることが分かる。よって、正解は(D)。

語彙チェック □outsource　〜を外部に委託する　□ask for 〜　〜を求める

58　正解 D

What will the woman do next?

(A) Register for a workshop

(B) Confirm a price

(C) Send an invitation

(D) Speak with a client

女性は次に何をしますか。

(A) ワークショップに登録する

(B) 価格を確認する

(C) 招待状を送る

(D) 顧客と話す

男性たちがそれぞれ翻訳作業を分担して行い、明日の正午ごろまでに完了させると言うと、最後に女性はI'll give Mr. Yapp a call now to make sure that's okと述べている。Yappさんについては冒頭の発言で言及されており、アパート情報の翻訳を依頼してきたと考えられる人物である。よって、正解は(D)。

語彙チェック □register for 〜　〜に登録する

Questions 59 through 61 refer to the following conversation with three speakers.

M: I was recently in South Hamilton to visit some family. The area is really starting to grow. <u>I think we should consider it for our new location. There aren't many places to eat there yet.</u>

W1: Good to know. Why don't we take a trip there this week?

W2: Good idea. <u>We should go to city hall and see if they have any future development plans.</u> If the population is set to grow, we should get in fast.

M: We're closed on Thursday, so how about then?

W1: Great. It's a bit too far to drive, though. <u>Let's take the train. Get us a private cabin so we can discuss ideas on the way up.</u>

問題59-61は3人の話し手による次の会話に関するものです。

男性　：家族に会いに、最近South Hamiltonに行ってきました。その地域はとても成長し始めていますよ。私たちの新店舗を出すのに、そこを考慮に入れるべきだと思います。そこにはまだ食事をするところはあまりありませんし。

女性1：知れてよかったです。今週そこへ行ってみませんか。

女性2：いい考えですね。市役所へ行って、将来的な開発計画があるかどうか確認した方がいいです。もし人口が増える予定なら、急がないといけません。

男性　：木曜日は休業ですから、そのときはどうですか。

女性1：いいですね。でも車で行くには少し遠過ぎますね。電車に乗りましょう。向かう途中でアイデアを話し合えるように、個室のキャビンを取ってください。

語彙チェック　□be set to *do*　〜する予定である　□get in　先手を取る　□private　個人の
　　　　　　　□cabin　キャビン、客室　□on the way　途中で、その間に

59　　　　　　　　□□□　正解 C

What is the conversation mainly about?　会話は主に何についてですか。

(A) Hiring a gardener　　　　　　　　(A) 庭師を雇うこと

(B) Entertaining a visitor　　　　　　(B) 訪問客をもてなすこと

(C) Opening a restaurant　　　　　　(C) レストランを開店すること

(D) Conducting a survey　　　　　　　(D) 調査を実施すること

男性は冒頭でSouth Hamiltonについて「その地域はとても成長し始めている」と言うと、I think we should consider it for our new location. There aren't many places to eat there yet.と述べている。これらから、話し手たちは飲食関係の仕事をしていると考えられ、新店舗の出店について話をしていることが分かる。よって、正解は(C)。

語彙チェック　□entertain　〜をもてなす、〜を楽しませる

60　正解 B

What will the speakers most likely do this week?

話し手たちは今週何をすると考えられますか。

(A) Advertise a new service
(B) Go to a government office
(C) Reward some employees
(D) Try a new menu item

(A) 新サービスを宣伝する
(B) 行政のオフィスへ行く
(C) 従業員に報酬を与える
(D) 新メニューを試す

男性から South Hamilton への出店計画について聞いて、1人目の女性は「今週そこへ行ってみないか」と提案している。それに対し、2人目の女性は賛成して We should go to city hall and see if they have any future development plans. と付け加えている。その後も日程や交通手段について話しているので、話し手たちは今週市役所に行くと考えられる。よって、(B) が正解。

語彙チェック □ reward ～に報酬を与える

61　正解 C

Where will the speakers discuss ideas?

話し手たちはどこでアイデアを話し合いますか。

(A) In a plane
(B) In a car
(C) In a train
(D) In a bus

(A) 飛行機
(B) 車
(C) 電車
(D) バス

South Hamilton へ行く日程決めに続いて、1人目の女性はその場所について「車で行くには少し遠過ぎる」と述べ、Let's take the train. と電車で行くことを提案している。その後、Get us a private cabin so we can discuss ideas on the way up. と言っているので、(C) が正解。

W 🇬🇧　M 🇦🇺　　　　　　　　　　　

Questions 62 through 64 refer to the following conversation and graph.

W: We've put together all of the data from the regional offices and made a graph showing the growth. This is only in terms of sales. Naturally, <u>farm machinery sales are affected by many factors</u>. So, it's not necessarily the fault of sales people in these offices.

M: Sure. We couldn't measure growth in this one because it's the first year in business. But, <u>I'm interested to know why there's been negative growth here.</u>

W: According to their head of sales, <u>they stopped advertising in print media and tried other forms such as social media and search engine marketing.</u>

M: I see. Well, we can learn from what happened there. <u>I'm in favor of trying new things, but we should exercise caution.</u>

問題62-64は次の会話とグラフに関するものです。

女性：地方オフィスからのデータを全てまとめて、成長率を表すグラフを作成しました。これは売り上げに関してのみですが。当然、農業機械の売り上げは、多くの要因によって影響を受けます。ですから、これは必ずしもこれらのオフィスの販売員の責任とは限りません。

男性：分かりました。事業を始めて最初の年ですから、これだけで成長率を測ることはできないでしょう。しかし、ここでなぜマイナス成長があるのか知るのは興味深いですね。

女性：そこの販売部長によると、印刷媒体で広告を出すのをやめ、ソーシャルメディアやサーチエンジンンマーケティングといった他の形を試したそうです。

男性：そうですか。では、そこで起きたことから学ぶことができますね。新しいことを試すには賛成ですが、私たちは用心すべきです。

語彙チェック　□put together ～　～をまとめる　□growth　成長（率）
□in terms of ～　～に関して、～の点から　□naturally　もちろん、当然
□machinery　機械、機器　□not necessarily　必ずしも～とは限らない
□fault　責任　□measure　～を測る　□negative growth　マイナス成長
□print media　印刷媒体　□form　形、形態　□in favor of ～　～に賛成の
□exercise caution　用心する

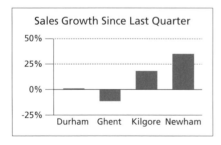

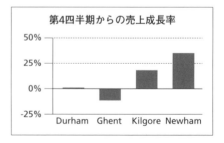

62 | 正解 A

What kind of products does the company sell?	会社はどのような製品を売っていますか。
(A) Agricultural equipment	(A) 農業機器
(B) Recreational vehicles	(B) RV車
(C) Farm produce	(C) 農作物
(D) Factory machinery	(D) 工場用機械

女性は冒頭で「地方オフィスからのデータを全てまとめて、成長率を表すグラフを作成した」と述べ、farm machinery sales are affected by many factors と説明している。この発言から、この会社は農業機械を販売していると判断できる。よって、(A) が正解。

63 | 正解 B

Look at the graphic. Which office switched to online advertising?	図を見てください。どのオフィスがオンライン広告に切り替えましたか。
(A) Durham	(A) Durham
(B) Ghent	(B) Ghent
(C) Kilgore	(C) Kilgore
(D) Newham	(D) Newham

売り上げの成長率を表すグラフを見て、男性は「ここでなぜマイナス成長があるのか知るのは興味深い」と発言している。これに対し、女性は「そこの販売部長によると、印刷媒体で広告を出すのをやめ、ソーシャルメディアやサーチエンジンマーケティングといった他の形を試した」と説明している。つまり、売り上げがマイナス成長になったオフィスがオンライン広告を試したということなので、図から Ghent のオフィスだと分かる。よって、正解は(B)。

語彙チェック □ switch to 〜 〜に切り替える

64 | 正解 B

What does the man say the company should do?	男性は会社は何をすべきだと言っていますか。
(A) Encourage employees to exercise more	(A) 従業員にもっと運動するよう促す
(B) Be careful when adopting new strategies	(B) 新しい戦略を採用するときは気を付ける
(C) Ask for advice from a consultant	(C) コンサルタントの助言を求める
(D) Share ideas with staff at other offices	(D) 他のオフィスのスタッフとアイデアを共有する

従来の印刷媒体での広告からオンライン広告に切り替えたオフィスの売り上げが減少したことについて女性が共有した後、男性は I'm in favor of trying new things, but we should exercise caution. と述べている。よって、(B) が正解。

Questions 65 through 67 refer to the following conversation and illustration.

M: Hi. I'm here for a company banquet, but I'm not sure which restaurant they're in. I left my invitation at home. Perhaps you could check for me.

W: Sure. What name would the reservation be under, sir?

M: Um... Probably the company name. Try Arch Engineering.

W: Found it. They're in Schooners. Take the stairs over there.

M: Thanks.

W: Not at all. The reservation is for six thirty, though. The rest of your party might not be here yet. You're welcome to wait in the lobby if you like.

問題65-67は次の会話と説明図に関するものです。

男性：こんにちは。会社の宴会に来たのですが、どのレストランが会場か分からなくて。招待状を家に置いてきてしまいましたし。たぶんこちらで確認していただけるかと思いまして。

女性：かしこまりました。お客さま、どちらのお名前で予約されているかお分かりですか。

男性：うーん…　たぶん会社の名前です。Arch Engineeringを試してみてください。

女性：見つかりました。Schoonersが会場です。向こうの階段をお上がりください。

男性：ありがとうございます。

女性：どういたしまして。しかし予約は6時30分です。お客さまのグループの残りの方はまだいらっしゃっていないかもしれません。もしよろしければ、ロビーでお待ちいただけます。

語彙チェック　□banquet　宴会　□under *one's* name　〜の名義で、〜の名前で
□take the stairs　階段で行く　□rest　残り　□party　グループ、一団
□be welcome to *do*　自由に〜してよい

Premiere Inn Restaurant Locations			
	8	Cloud 9	Pierre's
	7		
	6		
	5		Sea Captain
	4		
	3		
Schooners	2		
	1	Reception	Entry

Premiere Innレストランの場所			
	8	Cloud 9	Pierre's
	7		
	6		
	5		Sea Captain
	4		
	3		
Schooners	2		
	1	受付	入り口

65 正解 A

What is the purpose of the man's visit?

(A) To attend an event

(B) To repair some equipment

(C) To meet with a client

(D) To have a job interview

男性の訪問の目的は何ですか。

(A) イベントに出席すること

(B) 機器を修理すること

(C) 顧客に会うこと

(D) 仕事の面接を受けること

男性は冒頭で、I'm here for a company banquetと述べ、その後I left my invitation at home.と発言している。これらから、男性は会社の宴会に招待されており、それに出席するために来たと判断できる。よって、正解は(A)。

66 正解 A

Look at the graphic. Which floor will the man go to next?

(A) The 2nd Floor

(B) The 4th Floor

(C) The 5th Floor

(D) The 8th Floor

図を見てください。男性は次にどの階に行きますか。

(A) 2階

(B) 4階

(C) 5階

(D) 8階

女性は男性の会社名から予約を調べると、They're in Schooners.と宴会会場を特定し、男性にTake the stairs over there.と伝えている。図を見るとSchoonersは2階にあることが分かる。よって、正解は(A)。

67 正解 D

What does the woman say?

(A) The hotel has a vacancy.

(B) A reservation has been changed.

(C) A manager is in a meeting.

(D) The man has arrived early.

女性は何と言っていますか。

(A) ホテルには空室がある。

(B) 予約が変更されている。

(C) 支配人は会議中である。

(D) 男性は早く到着した。

女性は男性に宴会会場の場所を案内した一方で、「予約は6時30分だ」と言い、The rest of your party might not be here yet.と他の参加者がまだ来ていないことを伝えている。これらの発言から、男性は予約時間よりも早く会場に到着したと分かる。よって、正解は(D)。

語彙チェック □vacancy　空室

Questions 68 through 70 refer to the following conversation and list.

W: I've decided that we should take six people to the top of Mt. Montego to assess the area and calculate the cost of constructing a lookout there.

M: OK. I'll rent a minivan. A six-seater should be large enough, shouldn't it?

W: Don't forget that the engineers will want to take a bunch of gear. I'd get one with a couple of extra seats.

M: Fair enough. I suppose we'll have to stay overnight. I'll look for some accommodations somewhere near the base of the mountain.

W: Good idea. Find somewhere with a good restaurant. I'd like to have a meeting over dinner to discuss the project, and I imagine that everyone will be pretty tired.

問題68-70は次の会話とリストに関するものです。

女性：その地域を査定し、そこに展望台を建設する費用を算出するために、Montego山の頂上に6人を連れていくことにしました。

男性：分かりました。私がミニバンをレンタルしますよ。大きさは6人乗りで十分ですよね？

女性：エンジニアがたくさんの道具を持っていきたがることを忘れてはいけませんよ。私が余分に2席ある車を用意します。

男性：そうですね。私たちはそこで一泊しなければいけないと思います。私はどこか山の麓の近くで宿泊施設を探しますよ。

女性：良い考えですね。いいレストランがあるところを見つけてください。プロジェクトを話し合うために夕食のときに打ち合わせをしたいのと、全員かなり疲れていると思います。

語彙チェック　□assess　〜を査定する　□calculate　〜を計算する、〜を算出する
□lookout　展望台　□minivan　ミニバン　□a bunch of 〜　たくさんの〜
□gear　道具、用具　□fair enough　賛成だ、あなたの言う通りだ
□stay overnight　一泊する　□accommodations　宿泊施設
□base　（山の）麓

Bolian	5 Seater	$50 per day
Portlander	6 Seater	$63 per day
Tavarish	8 Seater	$72 per day
Hoovie	10 Seater	$80 per day

Bolian	5人乗り	1日あたり50ドル
Portlander	6人乗り	1日あたり63ドル
Tavarish	8人乗り	1日あたり72ドル
Hoovie	10人乗り	1日あたり80ドル

68

□□□ 正解 **C**

Where do the speakers most likely work?

(A) At a production company
(B) At a software developer
(C) At a construction company
(D) At a real estate agency

話し手たちはどこで働いていると考えられますか。

(A) プロダクション会社
(B) ソフトウェア開発会社
(C) 建設会社
(D) 不動産業社

女性は冒頭で we should take six people to the top of Mt. Montego と発言すると、その目的を to assess the area and calculate the cost of constructing a lookout there と述べている。「その地域を査定し、そこに展望台を建設する費用を算出する」という内容から、話し手たちは建設関係の仕事をしていると考えられる。よって、正解は (C)。

69

□□□ 正解 **C**

Look at the graphic. Which car will the speakers most likely choose?

(A) Bolian
(B) Portlander
(C) Tavarish
(D) Hoovie

図を見てください。話し手たちはどの車を選ぶと考えられますか。

(A) Bolian
(B) Portlander
(C) Tavarish
(D) Hoovie

男性は I'll rent a minivan. と言った後、A six-seater should be large enough, shouldn't it? と尋ねているが、これに対し女性は「エンジニアがたくさんの道具を持っていきたがることを忘れてはいけない」と忠告し、I'd get one with a couple of extra seats. と申し出ている。これらの発言から、話し手たちは、6人乗りからさらに余分な座席が2席ある車を選ぶと判断できる。図を見ると Tavarish の欄に 8 Seater「8人乗り」とあるので、正解は (C)。

70

□□□ 正解 **B**

What does the woman want at the accommodation?

(A) A meeting space
(B) Pleasant dining facilities
(C) High-speed Internet access
(D) Scenic views

女性は宿泊施設に何が欲しいと思っていますか。

(A) 会議の場所
(B) 快適な食事施設
(C) 高速インターネット回線
(D) 眺めの良い景色

男性が I'll look for some accommodations と申し出ると、女性は Find somewhere with a good restaurant. と依頼している。よって、この a good restaurant を言い換えている (B) が正解。

語彙チェック □ dining　食事　□ scenic　眺めの良い

Part 4

M 🇺🇸 トーク ▶TRACK_386　問題 ▶TRACK_387

Questions 71 through 73 refer to the following talk.

Good morning and <u>welcome to the first day of our investment workshop</u>. Our first instructor is Glenda Day. <u>She used to work as a financial advisor at Conway Associates.</u> <u>She was there for 18 years</u>, so she has a lot of experience. She's retired now, and she enjoys sharing her knowledge with people like us. I know you're all looking forward to hearing her speak, <u>but first, I'd like to show you a short animation</u>. It will help you understand some of the topics she will be talking about.

問題71-73は次の話に関するものです。

おはようございます、そして当社の投資ワークショップの1日目へようこそ。最初のインストラクターは Glenda Day です。彼女は以前 Conway Associates 社で財務顧問として勤務していました。彼女は18年間 そこにいましたので、経験が大変豊富です。彼女は現在は退職し、私たちのような人々と自身の知識を 共有することを楽しんでいます。彼女の話を聞くのを皆さま楽しみにしているとは思いますが、まず短 いアニメーションをご覧いただきたいと思います。こちらは彼女が話す予定であるトピックのいくつか を理解するのに役立つでしょう。

語彙チェック □investment　投資　□financial advisor　財務顧問
　　　　　　　　□share *A* with *B*　AをBと共有する
　　　　　　　　□look forward to *doing*　～することを楽しみにする

71　□□□ 正解 B

Where does the talk most likely take place?

(A) At a press conference
(B) At a finance seminar
(C) At a retirement party
(D) At an employee orientation

話はどこで行われていると考えられますか。

(A) 記者会見
(B) 財務セミナー
(C) 退職パーティー
(D) 従業員説明会

話し手は冒頭で welcome to the first day of our investment workshop と発言している。 また、インストラクターである Glenda Day さんについて、She used to work as a financial advisor at Conway Associates. と説明している。よって、(B) が正解。

語彙チェック □orientation　オリエンテーション、説明会

72　正解 D

Why does the speaker say, "<u>She was there for 18 years</u>"?

(A) To express gratitude to Ms. Day

(B) To explain Ms. Day's decision to retire

(C) To suggest hiring Ms. Day for a position

(D) To stress Ms. Day's qualifications

話し手はなぜ"<u>She was there for 18 years</u>"と言っていますか。

(A) Dayさんに感謝を表すため

(B) Dayさんの退職の決定を説明するため

(C) Dayさんをある職務に雇用することを提案するため

(D) Dayさんの資質を強調するため

話し手はGlenda Dayさんをインストラクターとして紹介し、彼女について She used to work as a financial advisor at Conway Associates. と説明している。その後、下線部の発言に続いて so she has a lot of experience と述べている。これらから、下線部の発言は直後の「彼女は経験が豊富だ」ということを裏付けるものだと判断でき、Dayさんにインストラクターの資質があることを強調していると言える。よって、正解は (D)。

語彙チェック　□gratitude　感謝　□qualification　資格、資質

73　正解 D

What will the listeners do next?

(A) Complete a survey

(B) Greet a visitor

(C) Read some documents

(D) Watch a video

聞き手は次に何をしますか。

(A) アンケートに記入する

(B) 訪問客にあいさつする

(C) 文書を読む

(D) ビデオを見る

話し手は I know you're all looking forward to hearing her speak と述べた後、but first, I'd like to show you a short animation と伝えている。この発言から、聞き手はこの後、Dayさんの話を聞く前にアニメーションを見ると判断できる。よって、(D) が正解。

語彙チェック　□greet　～にあいさつする

M 🏴

トーク ⏵TRACK_388　問題 ⏵TRACK_389

Questions 74 through 76 refer to the following advertisement.

The Kingsmill electric screwdriver is all you need for most small repairs around the home and office. It comes with sixteen adapters, which means it can be used on a wide variety of screws, nuts, and bolts. The powerful 16-volt battery can be charged in under twenty minutes. We're so sure of the quality that it comes with a five-year warranty. Learn more about the features of this amazingly popular new product at the Dex 10 Web site.

問題74-76は次の広告に関するものです。

ご自宅やオフィス周りの小さな修繕のほとんどには、Kingsmill 電動ドライバーさえあれば十分です。16個のアダプター付きで、多種多様なねじ、ナット、そしてボルトに使うことができます。パワフルな16ボルトのバッテリーは20分未満で充電できます。品質には大変自信があり、5年保証が付いています。この驚くほど人気な新商品の特徴については、Dex 10のウェブサイトで詳細をご確認ください。

語彙チェック　□electric　電動の　□screwdriver　ドライバー、ねじ回し
□come with 〜　〜を伴う　□adapter　アダプター
□a wide variety of 〜　多種多様な〜　□screw　ねじ　□nut　ナット
□bolt　ボルト　□volt　ボルト（電圧の単位）　□charge　〜を充電する
□be sure of 〜　〜に自信がある　□feature　特徴

74　　　　　□□□□　正解 C

What is being advertised?　　　　何が宣伝されていますか。
(A) A kitchen utensil　　　　(A) キッチン用品
(B) Some fishing equipment　　　　(B) 釣り道具
(C) A power tool　　　　(C) 電動工具
(D) Some clothing　　　　(D) 衣類

冒頭のThe Kingsmill electric screwdriver is all you need for most small repairs around the home and office.という発言から、これは電動ドライバーの広告だと判断できる。その後も「16個のアダプター付きで、多種多様なねじ、ナット、そしてボルトに使うことができる」と説明されており、この商品は工具であると分かるので、(C)が正解。

語彙チェック　□utensil　用具、器具

75

☐☐☐　正解 **A**

What does the speaker say about the product?

(A) It is guaranteed to work for a long time.

(B) It has sold out in many stores.

(C) It was advertised on television.

(D) It has won some design awards.

話し手は製品について何と言っていますか。

(A) それは長期間動くことが保証されている。

(B) それは多くの店で売り切れている。

(C) それはテレビで宣伝された。

(D) それはデザイン賞を受賞した。

話し手は電動ドライバーについて We're so sure of the quality that it comes with a five-year warranty. と説明している。「5年保証が付いている」ということから、この製品は5年間は壊れずに動くはずだと考えられる。よって、正解は (A)。

語彙チェック　☐guarantee *A* to *do*　Aが〜することを保証する　☐sell out　売り切れる

76

☐☐☐　正解 **D**

Why does the speaker mention the Web site?

(A) An operation manual can be downloaded there.

(B) Customer reviews are posted there.

(C) The product can be purchased there.

(D) A product description is available there.

話し手はなぜウェブサイトについて述べていますか。

(A) そこで取扱説明書をダウンロードできる。

(B) そこでお客さまレビューを投稿できる。

(C) そこで製品を買うことができる。

(D) そこで製品の説明を入手できる。

話し手は最後に Learn more about the features of this amazingly popular new product at the Dex 10 Web site. と述べている。この発言から、ウェブサイト上で製品の特徴についてさらに見ることができると分かる。よって、**(D)** が正解。

語彙チェック　☐operation manual　取扱説明書　☐post　〜を投稿する

⚠ **ここに注意！**

76. の正答根拠は75. の正答根拠のすぐ後に登場しているので、聞き逃してしまった人もいるかもしれない。さらに、75. も76. も選択肢が長いので、解答に時間がかかってしまう可能性が高い。先読みの際に長い選択肢が続いていたら、設問の内容をより頭に刻み込むようにしっかり読んでおこう！

Questions 77 through 79 refer to the following excerpt from a meeting.

I was contacted this week by Professor Winter at Horizons University. She's asked us to take interns from their course on natural history. I'm confident in the quality of their students. Indeed, our head curator and a few of the other employees graduated from Horizons. What I need to know from each of you is how many interns you can use in your departments. I hope that you'll agree to take at least one or two. Please don't worry about the cost. We will get a subsidy from the government for every intern we take.

問題77-79は次の会議の抜粋に関するものです。

今週、Horizons大学のWinter教授から連絡がありました。大学の博物学のコースから実習生を受け入れてほしいとお願いされました。学生の質は大丈夫だと思います。実際に、私たちの主任学芸員と他の従業員の数名がHorizons大学を卒業しています。皆さんそれぞれから伺う必要があるのは、あなたの部署で何人の実習生を使えるかということです。少なくとも1人か2人は受け入れていただくことに同意してもらいたいと思います。費用については心配いりません。受け入れるどの実習生に対しても、政府から助成金をもらえます。

語彙チェック □professor　教授　□intern　インターン、実習生　□natural history　博物学　□indeed　実際に　□curator　学芸員　□subsidy　助成金、補助金

77

□□□　正解 B

Where does the speaker most likely work?　話し手はどこで働いていると考えられますか。

(A) At a college　(A) 大学
(B) At a museum　(B) 博物館
(C) At an art gallery　(C) 美術館
(D) At a financial institution　(D) 金融機関

話し手は冒頭で、Horizons大学のWinter教授から博物学コースの実習生を受け入れてほしいと依頼があったことを説明し、また「私たちの主任学芸員と他の従業員の数名がHorizons大学を卒業している」と述べている。natural history「博物学」の実習生を受け入れることや、our head curator「私たちの主任学芸員」という言葉から、話し手は博物館で働いていると考えられる。よって、正解は(B)。

> 🐾 **ここに注意！**
> 4文目に出てきているcuratorは、「（博物館・美術館の）学芸員、館長」や「（動物園の）園長」を意味する語。こういった語は、話し手の働く場所や会話の状況を絞ることができる要素になるので、関連する情報とともに覚えておこう！

78

☐☐☐ 正解 C

Who most likely are the listeners?

(A) Financial contributors

(B) Art students

(C) Department managers

(D) University lecturers

聞き手は誰だと考えられますか。

(A) 資金提供者

(B) 画学生

(C) 部長

(D) 大学講師

実習生を受け入れることについて、話し手は What I need to know from each of you is how many interns you can use in your departments. と聞き手に伝えている。聞き手は「自分の部署で何人の実習生を使えるか」について聞かれていることから、それぞれの部署の責任者だと考えられる。よって、正解は (C)。

語彙チェック ☐contributor 寄付者、貢献者 ☐lecturer 講師

79

☐☐☐ 正解 D

What does the speaker say about the organization?

(A) It was forced to raise its prices.

(B) It employed additional staff recently.

(C) It will close temporarily.

(D) It will receive financial assistance.

話し手は組織について何と言っていますか。

(A) それは価格を上げさせられた。

(B) それは最近追加のスタッフを雇った。

(C) それは一時的に休業する。

(D) それは資金援助を受ける。

実習生の受け入れに関して、話し手は「費用については心配ない」と言い、We will get a subsidy from the government for every intern we take. と説明している。この subsidy「助成金」を financial assistance と言い換えている (D) が正解。

語彙チェック ☐force A to do Aに〜することを強いる

Questions 80 through 82 refer to the following talk.

We've had complaints from some of our clients that the candidates we have been sending them lack certain qualifications. We need to be doubly sure that they meet all of the criteria outlined in the requirements. To that end, I will be assigning each of you a buddy. When you have a list of candidates that you are ready to send to a client, you must first submit it to your buddy for review. Any unsatisfactory applications should be removed. I will e-mail a letter I received from a client to each of you. Please read it so that you better understand the problems sending unqualified people causes.

問題80-82は次の話に関するものです。

私たちが派遣している候補者たちに特定の必要条件が足りていないと、一部の顧客から苦情がありました。彼らが必要条件に概説されている全ての基準を満たすよう、二重に確認しなければいけません。そのために、あなた方それぞれにバディを割り振ります。顧客に送る準備ができている候補者のリストがあるときは、見直しのためにまずバディにそれを提出しなければいけません。不十分な申し込みは取り除いてください。顧客から受け取った手紙をあなた方それぞれにEメールで送ります。不適任な人々を送ることが引き起こす問題についてより良く理解するよう、それを読んでください。

語彙チェック　□lack　〜が不足している　□certain　特定の　□qualification　資格、必要条件
　　　　　　　□doubly　二重に　□criteria　基準　□outline　〜を概説する
　　　　　　　□to that end　その目的のために　□assign A B　AにBを割り当てる
　　　　　　　□buddy　相棒、バディ　□be ready to do　〜する準備ができている
　　　　　　　□submit A to B　AをBに提出する　□unsatisfactory　不十分な
　　　　　　　□unqualified　不適任な、資格のない

80　　　　　　□□□　正解 A

Where does the speaker most likely work?　話し手はどこで働いていると考えられますか。

(A) At a recruiting agency　　　　　(A) 人材派遣会社
(B) At a vocational college　　　　 (B) 専門学校
(C) At a training center　　　　　　(C) 研修センター
(D) At a newspaper company　　　 (D) 新聞社

冒頭の We've had complaints from some of our clients that the candidates we have been sending them lack certain qualifications. という発言から、話し手の会社は顧客に対して、必要条件を満たす人を派遣していると考えられる。このことから、話し手は人材派遣会社で働いていると判断できる。よって、正解は(A)。

81 　　　　正解 C

What is the purpose of the talk?　話の目的は何ですか。
(A) To thank employees for hard work　(A) 従業員の懸命な働きに感謝すること
(B) To introduce a new employee　(B) 新しい従業員を紹介すること
(C) To announce a new procedure　(C) 新しい手順を知らせること
(D) To invite employees to an event　(D) 従業員をイベントに招待すること

話し手は顧客から苦情が来ていることを伝えると、「彼らが必要条件に概説されている全ての基準を満たすよう、二重に確認しなければいけない」と述べている。その後、To that end「そのために」に続けて、「それぞれにバディを割り振る」ことや、「候補者のリストを作ったら、見直しのためにまずバディにそれを提出する」ことなど、より詳しい手順について説明している。よって、(C)が正解。

82 　　　　正解 C

What will the speaker attach to an e-mail?　話し手は何をEメールに添付しますか。
(A) A copy of the new employee handbook　(A) 新しい従業員ハンドブックのコピー
(B) A list of contest winners　(B) コンテストの入賞者のリスト
(C) Some communication from a client　(C) 顧客からの手紙
(D) Updates to a yearly schedule　(D) 年間スケジュールの最新版

話し手は候補者の必要条件を確認する手順について説明した後、I will e-mail a letter I received from a client to each of you. と伝えているので、(C)が正解。communicationには「手紙」という意味もある。

語彙チェック □attach A to B　AをBに添付する　□communication　手紙

Questions 83 through 85 refer to the following telephone message.

Hi. Umm. It's Rosa Popov at Lamington Sports Center. <u>Earlier today, you came out to look at one of the photocopiers here. I just found a piece of equipment you must have left behind. It's a meter of some kind.</u> We have it in the administration office, which is open between ten A.M. and seven P.M. <u>Unfortunately, we'll be closed tomorrow and Friday, so I recommend that you come and get it today. Please just call our main number and ask to speak with my assistant if you need to. I'll be in a meeting for the rest of the afternoon.</u>

問題83-85は次の電話のメッセージに関するものです。

こんにちは。えっと、LamingtonスポーツセンターのRosa Popovです。先ほど、こちらにコピー機を見に来ていただきましたよね。あなたが置き忘れていってしまったに違いない機器をちょうど見つけました。何らかの計量器です。管理事務所でそれをお預かりしていますが、空いている時間は午前10時から午後7時です。あいにく、明日と金曜日は休業ですので、今日取りに来られることをお勧めします。もし必要であれば、代表番号に電話して、私の助手と話すようお願いしてください。私は午後の残りの時間は会議に入っています。

語彙チェック　□photocopier　コピー機　□leave 〜 behind　〜を置き忘れる　□meter　計量器　□administration　管理　□main number　代表電話番号　□rest　残り

83 □□□ 正解 C

Who is the message most likely intended for?

(A) An editor
(B) A fitness trainer
(C) A technician
(D) A delivery driver

メッセージは誰に向けられていると考えられますか。

(A) 編集者
(B) スポーツトレーナー
(C) 技術者
(D) 配達員

話し手の Earlier today, you came out to look at one of the photocopiers here. という発言から、聞き手はコピー機の確認をしに話し手のところに行ったと判断できる。また、I just found a piece of equipment you must have left behind. It's a meter of some kind. から、聞き手は計量器を使う仕事をしていると分かる。これらから、聞き手は機器類を取り扱う仕事をしていると考えられる。よって、正解は(C)。

語彙チェック　□be intended for 〜　〜に向けられている

84

□□□ 正解 **B**

Why does the speaker suggest that the listener come today?

(A) A product is likely to sell out.

(B) The business will not be open tomorrow.

(C) A discount offer will end.

(D) Her belongings will be transferred to another location.

話し手はなぜ聞き手に今日来ることを勧めていますか。

(A) 製品が売り切れそうである。

(B) 会社が明日は開いていない。

(C) 割引の提供が終了する。

(D) 彼女の持ち物が別の場所に移される。

話し手は聞き手の忘れ物を管理事務所で預かっていると伝えた後、Unfortunately, we'll be closed tomorrow and Friday と述べ、それを理由に so I recommend that you come and get it today と提案している。よって、明日が休業日のため今日来るように勧めていると分かるので、**(B)** が正解。

語彙チェック □ be likely to *do* ～しそうである □ sell out 売り切れる
□ belongings 所有物

85

□□□ 正解 **D**

What does the speaker mean when she says, "I'll be in a meeting for the rest of the afternoon"?

(A) The listener should wait for her.

(B) She asks the listener for help.

(C) She has to reschedule an appointment.

(D) The listener won't be able to call her back.

話し手は "I'll be in a meeting for the rest of the afternoon" という発言で、何を意味していますか。

(A) 聞き手は彼女を待つべきである。

(B) 彼女は聞き手に支援を求めている。

(C) 彼女は予約を変更しなければいけない。

(D) 聞き手は彼女に折り返し電話ができない。

話し手は Please just call our main number and ask to speak with my assistant if you need to. と伝えた後に下線部の発言をしている。すなわち、話し手はこの後は会議に入り、電話に応対できないため、必要があれば助手と話してほしいと言っていると判断できる。このことから、聞き手は話し手と電話で話すことができなくなると考えられるので、**(D)** が正解。

語彙チェック □ ask *A* for *B* A に B を求める □ reschedule ～の予定を変更する

W 🇬🇧

トーク ▶TRACK_396　問題 ▶TRACK_397

Questions 86 through 88 refer to the following radio broadcast.

Today is the first day that the new dedicated bus lanes have been in use on the South East Freeway. There are heavy fines for drivers who use the lanes without authorization. The lanes have been created to speed up travel times for bus users. The council expects that bus services into the city will be up to thirty minutes faster. I recommend that you all try it out. You might find that you save both time and money. The Gladstone Bus Service Web site has detailed information on travel times and scheduling. There's even a handy calculator. It'll help you work out how much money you'll save.

問題86-88は次のラジオ放送に関するものです。

今日は South East 高速道路の新しいバス専用レーンが使用される初日です。無許可でそのレーンを使った運転手には重い罰金が科されます。レーンはバス利用者の移動時間を短縮するために作られました。議会は街へのバスサービスが最大30分速くなると予想しています。あなたもそれを試してみることをお勧めします。時間とお金の両方を節約できると分かるかもしれません。Gladstone バスサービスのウェブサイトでは、移動時間と時刻表の詳しい情報をご覧いただけます。便利な計算機もございます。こちらはいくら節約できるか算出するのにお役立ていただけます。

語彙チェック　□dedicated　専用の　□lane　レーン、車線　□be in use　使用されている
　　　　　　　□freeway　高速道路　□fine　罰金　□authorization　許可
　　　　　　　□speed up ～　～の速度を上げる　□up to ～　最大～、～まで
　　　　　　　□try ～ out　～を試験的に使ってみる　□handy　便利な
　　　　　　　□work out ～　～を計算する

86　□□□　正解 A

What is the broadcast mainly about?　放送は主に何についてですか。

(A) New road rules　(A) 新しい交通規則

(B) A construction plan　(B) 建設計画

(C) Environmental issues　(C) 環境問題

(D) Some road repairs　(D) 道路工事

冒頭の Today is the first day that the new dedicated bus lanes have been in use という発言から、新しいバス専用レーンが開通したことが分かる。続けて、There are heavy fines for drivers who use the lanes without authorization. と、無許可でのレーンの使用には罰金が科されることが説明されている。これらから、新しいバス専用レーンに関する規則について述べられていると判断できる。よって、正解は (A)。

302

87 ☐☐☐ 正解 B

What are the listeners advised to do?

(A) Take an online course
(B) Use bus services
(C) Leave home early
(D) Check the weather forecast

聞き手は何をするよう勧められていますか。

(A) オンラインコースを受講する
(B) バスサービスを利用する
(C) 家を早く出る
(D) 天気予報を確認する

話し手は新しいバス専用レーンについて The council expects that bus services into the city will be up to thirty minutes faster. と述べた後、I recommend that you all try it out. と街へのバスサービスを試すことを勧めている。よって、正解は (B)。

語彙チェック ☐weather forecast　天気予報

88 ☐☐☐ 正解 A

What can the listeners do on a Web site?

(A) View a time table
(B) Schedule a meeting
(C) Read reviews
(D) Watch some videos

聞き手はウェブサイト上で、何をすることができますか。

(A) 時刻表を見る
(B) 会議の予定を組む
(C) 評価を読む
(D) 動画を見る

話し手はウェブサイトについて、The Gladstone Bus Service Web site has detailed information on travel times and scheduling. と説明している。この発言から、ウェブサイトでは移動時間と時刻表の詳しい情報が見られると分かる。よって、正解は (A)。

Questions 89 through 91 refer to the following radio advertisement.

It seems like the cost of living is going up every day, but there's one place you can count on to keep prices low. McGillicutty's Diner has been feeding hungry families all over California for almost 50 years. Our amazing menu and reasonable prices keep people coming back again and again. To celebrate our fiftieth year, we're offering an exciting new service. Now, you can order your meal from a convenient smartphone app and have it brought to your door in under 30 minutes. And this month, delivery's free! McGillicutty's is always the right decision, but don't trust me. Ask your family! See what they say.

問題89-91は次のラジオ広告に関するものです。

毎日生活費が上がっているように思われますが、価格を抑えるために頼れる場所が1か所あります。McGillicutty's Dinerは50年近くの間、California中のお腹を空かせた家族に食事を提供してきました。私たちの驚きのメニューと手頃な価格に人々は何度も何度も戻ってきます。私たちの50周年を祝うために、わくわくする新しいサービスを提供いたします。今では便利なスマートフォン用アプリから食事を注文でき、30分足らずで自宅にお届けすることができます。そして今月はお届けが無料です！ McGillicutty'sはいつだって正しい判断ですが、私を信用しないでください。家族に聞いてください！ 彼らが何と言うか確認してください。

語彙チェック □cost of living 生活費 □count on 〜 〜を頼る □diner レストラン、食堂 □feed 〜に食べ物を与える □convenient 便利な □trust 〜を信用する

89   □□□ 正解 A

What kind of business is being advertised?

(A) A restaurant
(B) A fashion store
(C) A fitness club
(D) A hardware store

どのような店が宣伝されていますか。

(A) レストラン
(B) ファッション店
(C) フィットネスクラブ
(D) ホームセンター

McGillicutty's Diner has been feeding hungry families all over California 「McGillicutty's DinerはCalifornia中のお腹を空かせた家族に食事を提供してきた」や、Our amazing menu and reasonable prices 「私たちの驚きのメニューと手頃な価格」といった発言から、McGillicutty's DinerはCalifornia中で展開しているレストランだと考えられる。よって、正解は(A)。

90 □□□ 正解 C

What can customers receive this month?

(A) A product sample
(B) A discount coupon
(C) Free home delivery
(D) Training advice

お客さんは今月何を受け取ることができますか。

(A) 製品見本
(B) 割引券
(C) 無料宅配
(D) トレーニングのアドバイス

50周年を祝うための新しいサービスとして、話し手は you can order your meal from a convenient smartphone app and have it brought to your door と述べ、そのサービスについて And this month, delivery's free! と説明している。よって、正解は(C)。

91 □□□ 正解 B

What does the speaker imply when he says, "See what they say"?

(A) He wants to hear the listeners' opinions.
(B) He believes the business is popular.
(C) He hopes people will write down their comments.
(D) He recommends the listeners take some time.

話し手は "See what they say" という発言で、何を示唆していますか。

(A) 彼は聞き手の意見を聞きたいと思っている。
(B) 彼は店が人気だと思っている。
(C) 彼は人々にコメントを書いてもらいたいと思っている。
(D) 彼は聞き手に少し時間をかけてみるよう勧めている。

話し手は McGillicutty's is always the right decision と述べた後、but don't trust me. Ask your family! と伝えている。この発言から、信用できる家族に店について聞けば、「McGillicutty's はいつだって正しい判断だ」ということが本当であると分かるはずだという、話し手の自信が感じ取れる。よって、正解は(B)。

語彙チェック　□write down 〜　〜を書く

W 🇨🇦

Questions 92 through 94 refer to the following announcement.

Good morning, everyone. To make it easier for the accounting department to calculate everyone's hours and make sure you're being paid correctly, we've decided to adopt a new system. These new identification cards have a chip that'll record your arrival when you get here in the morning and your departure the last time you leave the building in the afternoon. Today, I'll give one to each of you, and I'll collect your old ones for disposal. The scanners will be operational from tomorrow morning. If you're going to be away from your desk, please come and see me in the administration office by ten A.M. I'm going to be in a meeting after that.

問題92-94は次のお知らせに関するものです。

おはようございます、皆さん。会計部が皆さんの勤務時間を計算するのを簡単にし、正確に給与の支払いがされるために、新システムを導入することにしました。これらの新しいIDカードにはチップが付いていて、午前に出勤したときの到着と、午後に最後に建物を出たときの退出を記録します。今日は、皆さん1人ずつにカードをお渡して、古いものは処分するために回収します。スキャナーは明日の朝から使用できます。もしデスクから離れる予定がある場合は、午前10時までに管理事務所の私のところへ来てください。私はその後に会議に入る予定です。

語彙チェック　□accounting　会計　□calculate　～を計算する　□adopt　～を採用する
　　　　　　　　□identification card　身分証明書、IDカード　□chip　チップ
　　　　　　　　□record　～を記録する　□collect　～を集める、～を回収する　□disposal　処分
　　　　　　　　□scanner　スキャナー　□operational　操作可能な、運転中の
　　　　　　　　□administration　管理、運営

92　□□□　正解 **D**

According to the speaker, what is being changed?

(A) How security is ensured
(B) Where employees can take breaks
(C) What time employees can leave
(D) How wages are calculated

話し手によると、何が変更されますか。

(A) どのように安全が保障されるか
(B) どこで従業員が休憩を取れるか
(C) 何時に従業員が退勤できるか
(D) どのように賃金が計算されるか

話し手は we've decided to adopt a new system と伝えているが、その目的を冒頭部分で To make it easier for the accounting department to calculate everyone's hours and make sure you're being paid correctly と説明している。「勤務時間の計算を簡単にし、正確に給与が支払われるよう新システムを導入する」ということから、これを言い換えている (D) が正解。

語彙チェック　□security　安全　□ensure　～を保証する　□wage　賃金

93

□□□ 正解 **B**

What are the listeners instructed to do today?

(A) Leave the office early

(B) Exchange identification cards

(C) Update their software

(D) Dispose of confidential documents

聞き手は今日何をするよう指示されていますか。

(A) 早くオフィスを出る

(B) IDカードを交換する

(C) ソフトウェアを更新する

(D) 機密文書を処分する

話し手は新システムを導入すると述べ、チップ付きのIDカードについて説明した後、Today, I'll give one to each of you, and I'll collect your old ones for disposal. と伝えている。この発言から、聞き手は今日新しいIDカードを受け取り、古いカードは回収されることが分かる。よって、これを「IDカードを交換する」と表した(B)が正解。

語彙チェック □instruct *A* to *do* Aに～するよう指示する □dispose of ～ ～を処分する
□confidential 機密の

94

□□□ 正解 **D**

What will happen at 10:00 A.M.?

(A) The speaker will leave on a business trip.

(B) Some equipment will be replaced.

(C) A new procedure will be implemented.

(D) The speaker will become unavailable.

午前10時に何が起こりますか。

(A) 話し手が出張に出る。

(B) 機器が交換される。

(C) 新しい手順が実施される。

(D) 話し手は応対できなくなる。

話し手は If you're going to be away from your desk, please come and see me in the administration office by ten A.M. と伝えた後、I'm going to be in a meeting after that. と述べている。このことから、午前10時を過ぎると、話し手は会議が始まり応対ができなくなると判断できる。よって、正解は(D)。

語彙チェック □implement ～を実施する

Questions 95 through 97 refer to the following talk and map.

Tomorrow is the first day of the annual Software Conference at the Dougal Conference Center. We've made a special deal with the organizers whereby conference attendees get large discounts on their accommodation. Nearly forty percent of tonight's guests will be here for the conference. You're sure to be asked about getting to the conference center in Peters. In that case, please advise against using the Pink Line. The subway is generally crowded and the station is hard for first-timers to navigate. So, it is the best for them to use the Silver and Green Lines.

問題95-97は次の話と地図に関するものです。

明日はDougal Conference Centerで毎年開催されるSoftware Conferenceの初日です。私たちは会議の主催者と、会議の出席者が宿泊施設の大幅な割引を受けられる特別な取引をしました。今夜の宿泊者の40パーセント近くがその会議のために当ホテルへいらっしゃいます。皆さんはPetersにある会議場へ行くことについて必ず聞かれると思います。その場合は、Pink線は使わないようにアドバイスしてください。その地下鉄はたいてい混雑していて、駅は初めての人にとっては通り抜けるのが大変です。ですから、Silver線とGreen線を使うのが彼らにとって1番良い方法です。

語彙チェック □make a deal with 〜　〜と取引する　□whereby　それによって（〜する）
□accommodation　宿泊施設　□be sure to *do*　きっと〜する
□advise against *doing*　〜しないよう忠告する　□first-timer　初めての人
□navigate　〜を通り抜ける

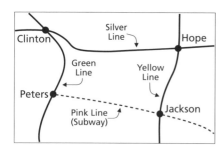

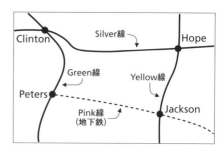

95 　　　　　正解 C

Who most likely is the speaker?

(A) An event organizer

(B) A tour guide

(C) A hotel manager

(D) A business traveler

話し手は誰だと考えられますか。

(A) イベント主催者

(B) ツアーガイド

(C) ホテル支配人

(D) 出張者

話し手は「明日はSoftware Conferenceの初日だ」と述べると、We've made a special deal with the organizers whereby conference attendees get large discounts on their accommodation.と伝えている。「会議の主催者と取引をして、会議の参加者が宿泊施設の割引を受けられるようにした」という内容から、話し手は宿泊施設の関係者だと考えられる。よって、正解は (C)。

96

□□□ 正解 **A**

What does the speaker say about conference attendees?

(A) They will make up a large portion of the hotel's guests.

(B) They have weeklong reservations.

(C) They will arrive on a tour bus.

(D) They have had their luggage delivered separately.

話し手は会議の出席者について、何と言っていますか。

(A) 彼らはホテルの宿泊客の大部分を構成する。

(B) 彼らは1週間にわたる予約をしている。

(C) 彼らは観光バスで到着する。

(D) 彼らは荷物を別で送ってもらった。

話し手は、会議の出席者は宿泊割引が受けられると説明した後、Nearly forty percent of tonight's guests will be here for the conference. と述べている。よって、これを言い換えている (A) が正解。

語彙チェック □make up 〜 〜を構成する □portion 部分 □weeklong 1週間にわたる

97

□□□ 正解 **B**

Look at the graphic. Where is the hotel?

(A) In Clinton

(B) In Hope

(C) In Peters

(D) In Jackson

図を見てください。ホテルはどこですか。

(A) Clinton

(B) Hope

(C) Peters

(D) Jackson

まず、You're sure to be asked about getting to the conference center in Peters. という発言から、会議場は Peters にあると分かる。話し手は please advise against using the Pink Line と忠告した後、最後に it is the best for them to use the Silver and Green Lines と発言していることから、ホテルから会議場へは Silver 線と Green 線を乗り継いで行くことが分かる。地図によると、Peters まで Silver 線と Green 線を乗り継いで行く場合の出発地は Hope である。よって、正解は (B)。

⚠ ここに注意！

中盤から後半にかけて会議場への行き方の説明をしているが、4文目の the conference center in Peters から、会議場が Peters にあることを把握していないと正解を絞りだすのは難しくなる。この問題は、図表の中のキーワードを聞き取るだけでなく、全体の内容や会話の流れを理解していないと解けない難問！

Questions 98 through 100 refer to the following announcement and schedule.

OK, everyone. Welcome aboard the Scarborough Tour Bus. Today you're coming with us on an exciting tour of Landsborough's biggest attractions. I should apologize in advance because there's been a small change to our schedule. We were going to get to the art gallery at ten, but it won't open until ten thirty today. So, we've decided to switch it with Tully Castle. The other times will remain the same; only the order will change. It'll take us about forty five minutes to get to our first stop. Some inclement weather has been forecast, so it might take a little longer than usual. One of the passengers has asked me to talk a little about the town's foundation, and its growth over the years. We can discuss these before we arrive at the first stop.

問題98-100は次のお知らせと予定表に関するものです。

では、皆さん。Scarboroughツアーバスにようこそ。本日はLandsboroughの最大の観光名所を巡るわくわくするツアーに皆さまをお連れいたします。私たちの予定に小さな変更点があることをあらかじめお詫び申し上げます。10時に美術館に到着する予定でしたが、そちらは本日は10時30分まで開館しません。ですから、それとTully城を入れ替えることにいたしました。その他の時間は同じままです。順番のみ変更いたします。最初の見学地に到着するのに約45分かかります。荒れた天気が予想されていますので、通常より少し長くかかるかもしれません。乗客の1人から、町の創設と長年にわたる成長について少し話してほしいとお願いがありました。最初の見学地に到着する前に、それらについてお話ししましょう。

語彙チェック　□aboard　〜に乗って　□attraction　観光名所、人々を引き付けるもの
　　　□in advance　前もって、あらかじめ　□switch *A* with *B*　A を B と交換する
　　　□inclement　荒れ模様の　□forecast　〜を予想する、〜を予報する
　　　□passenger　乗客

Tour Schedule	
Friedrich Art Gallery	10:00 A.M.
Harington's (Lunch)	12:10 P.M.
River Cruise	1:30 P.M.
Tully Castle	3:30 P.M.

ツアースケジュール	
Friedrich 美術館	午前10:00
Harington's（昼食）	午後12:10
リバークルーズ	午後1:30
Tully 城	午後3:30

98

□□□　正解 **A**

Look at the graphic. What is the final stop on the tour today?

(A) Friedrich Art Gallery
(B) Harington's
(C) River Cruise
(D) Tully Castle

図を見てください。今日のツアーの最後の見学地は何ですか。

(A) Friedrich 美術館
(B) Harington's
(C) リバークルーズ
(D) Tully 城

話し手は変更点があると伝えると、We were going to get to the art gallery at ten, but it won't open until ten thirty today. と言い、So, we've decided to switch it with Tully Castle. と説明している。また、「その他の時間は同じままで、順番のみ変更する」とも述べている。これらの発言から、美術館とTully城の順番が入れ替わることが分かる。図によると、Tully Castle が最後の見学地になっているが、これが美術館と入れ替わるので、Friedrich 美術館が最後の見学地となる。よって、正解は(A)。

ここに注意！
この本文では、予定表に書かれている内容に変更があったことが説明されている。このように、図表に書かれていることが実際のものではないパターンもあるので、注意してよく聞こう！

99　　　　　正解 D

What does the speaker say may happen?

(A) One of the destinations may be crowded.
(B) A passenger may arrive late.
(C) The lunch menu may change.
(D) The weather may be unfavorable.

話し手は何が起こるかもしれないと言っていますか。

(A) 目的地の1つが混んでいるかもしれない。
(B) 乗客が遅れて到着するかもしれない。
(C) 昼食のメニューが変更されるかもしれない。
(D) 天気が良くないかもしれない。

話し手は「最初の見学地に到着するまで約45分かかる」と述べると、Some inclement weather has been forecast, so it might take a little longer than usual. と伝えている。「荒れた天気が予想されている」と言っているので、(D)が正解。

語彙チェック □unfavorable　不都合な、好ましくない

100　　　　　正解 B

What has the speaker been asked to talk about?

(A) A famous person
(B) Some local history
(C) A popular food item
(D) Some interesting geography

話し手は何について話すよう求められましたか。

(A) 有名人
(B) 地域の歴史
(C) 人気の食べ物
(D) 興味深い地形

話し手は終盤でOne of the passengers has asked me to talk a little about the town's foundation, and its growth over the years. と述べている。このthe town's foundation, and its growth over the years「町の創設と長年にわたる成長」を「地域の歴史」と言い換えている(B)が正解。

語彙チェック □geography　地形、地理

990点獲得
Part 1~4専用マークシート
（コピーしてお使いください）

TEST 1からTEST 5までのマークシートと、フリーで使える2回分のマークシートを用意しました。本番さながらにマークシートを使って問題を解くようにしましょう。

TEST 1

Part 1

No.	A	B	C	D
1	Ⓐ	Ⓑ	Ⓒ	Ⓓ
2	Ⓐ	Ⓑ	Ⓒ	Ⓓ
3	Ⓐ	Ⓑ	Ⓒ	Ⓓ
4	Ⓐ	Ⓑ	Ⓒ	Ⓓ
5	Ⓐ	Ⓑ	Ⓒ	Ⓓ
6	Ⓐ	Ⓑ	Ⓒ	Ⓓ
7	Ⓐ	Ⓑ	Ⓒ	Ⓓ
8	Ⓐ	Ⓑ	Ⓒ	Ⓓ
9	Ⓐ	Ⓑ	Ⓒ	Ⓓ
10	Ⓐ	Ⓑ	Ⓒ	Ⓓ

Part 2

No.	A	B	C		No.	A	B	C
11	Ⓐ	Ⓑ	Ⓒ		21	Ⓐ	Ⓑ	Ⓒ
12	Ⓐ	Ⓑ	Ⓒ		22	Ⓐ	Ⓑ	Ⓒ
13	Ⓐ	Ⓑ	Ⓒ		23	Ⓐ	Ⓑ	Ⓒ
14	Ⓐ	Ⓑ	Ⓒ		24	Ⓐ	Ⓑ	Ⓒ
15	Ⓐ	Ⓑ	Ⓒ		25	Ⓐ	Ⓑ	Ⓒ
16	Ⓐ	Ⓑ	Ⓒ		26	Ⓐ	Ⓑ	Ⓒ
17	Ⓐ	Ⓑ	Ⓒ		27	Ⓐ	Ⓑ	Ⓒ
18	Ⓐ	Ⓑ	Ⓒ		28	Ⓐ	Ⓑ	Ⓒ
19	Ⓐ	Ⓑ	Ⓒ		29	Ⓐ	Ⓑ	Ⓒ
20	Ⓐ	Ⓑ	Ⓒ		30	Ⓐ	Ⓑ	Ⓒ

Part 3

No.	A	B	C		No.	A	B	C	D
31	Ⓐ	Ⓑ	Ⓒ		41	Ⓐ	Ⓑ	Ⓒ	Ⓓ
32	Ⓐ	Ⓑ	Ⓒ		42	Ⓐ	Ⓑ	Ⓒ	Ⓓ
33	Ⓐ	Ⓑ	Ⓒ		43	Ⓐ	Ⓑ	Ⓒ	Ⓓ
34	Ⓐ	Ⓑ	Ⓒ		44	Ⓐ	Ⓑ	Ⓒ	Ⓓ
35	Ⓐ	Ⓑ	Ⓒ		45	Ⓐ	Ⓑ	Ⓒ	Ⓓ
36	Ⓐ	Ⓑ	Ⓒ		46	Ⓐ	Ⓑ	Ⓒ	Ⓓ
37	Ⓐ	Ⓑ	Ⓒ		47	Ⓐ	Ⓑ	Ⓒ	Ⓓ
38	Ⓐ	Ⓑ	Ⓒ		48	Ⓐ	Ⓑ	Ⓒ	Ⓓ
39	Ⓐ	Ⓑ	Ⓒ		49	Ⓐ	Ⓑ	Ⓒ	Ⓓ
40	Ⓐ	Ⓑ	Ⓒ		50	Ⓐ	Ⓑ	Ⓒ	Ⓓ

Part 4

No.	A B C D	No.	A B C D	No.	A B C D	No.	A B C D	No.	A B C D
51	Ⓐ Ⓑ Ⓒ Ⓓ	61	Ⓐ Ⓑ Ⓒ Ⓓ	71	Ⓐ Ⓑ Ⓒ Ⓓ	81	Ⓐ Ⓑ Ⓒ Ⓓ	91	Ⓐ Ⓑ Ⓒ Ⓓ
52	Ⓐ Ⓑ Ⓒ Ⓓ	62	Ⓐ Ⓑ Ⓒ Ⓓ	72	Ⓐ Ⓑ Ⓒ Ⓓ	82	Ⓐ Ⓑ Ⓒ Ⓓ	92	Ⓐ Ⓑ Ⓒ Ⓓ
53	Ⓐ Ⓑ Ⓒ Ⓓ	63	Ⓐ Ⓑ Ⓒ Ⓓ	73	Ⓐ Ⓑ Ⓒ Ⓓ	83	Ⓐ Ⓑ Ⓒ Ⓓ	93	Ⓐ Ⓑ Ⓒ Ⓓ
54	Ⓐ Ⓑ Ⓒ Ⓓ	64	Ⓐ Ⓑ Ⓒ Ⓓ	74	Ⓐ Ⓑ Ⓒ Ⓓ	84	Ⓐ Ⓑ Ⓒ Ⓓ	94	Ⓐ Ⓑ Ⓒ Ⓓ
55	Ⓐ Ⓑ Ⓒ Ⓓ	65	Ⓐ Ⓑ Ⓒ Ⓓ	75	Ⓐ Ⓑ Ⓒ Ⓓ	85	Ⓐ Ⓑ Ⓒ Ⓓ	95	Ⓐ Ⓑ Ⓒ Ⓓ
56	Ⓐ Ⓑ Ⓒ Ⓓ	66	Ⓐ Ⓑ Ⓒ Ⓓ	76	Ⓐ Ⓑ Ⓒ Ⓓ	86	Ⓐ Ⓑ Ⓒ Ⓓ	96	Ⓐ Ⓑ Ⓒ Ⓓ
57	Ⓐ Ⓑ Ⓒ Ⓓ	67	Ⓐ Ⓑ Ⓒ Ⓓ	77	Ⓐ Ⓑ Ⓒ Ⓓ	87	Ⓐ Ⓑ Ⓒ Ⓓ	97	Ⓐ Ⓑ Ⓒ Ⓓ
58	Ⓐ Ⓑ Ⓒ Ⓓ	68	Ⓐ Ⓑ Ⓒ Ⓓ	78	Ⓐ Ⓑ Ⓒ Ⓓ	88	Ⓐ Ⓑ Ⓒ Ⓓ	98	Ⓐ Ⓑ Ⓒ Ⓓ
59	Ⓐ Ⓑ Ⓒ Ⓓ	69	Ⓐ Ⓑ Ⓒ Ⓓ	79	Ⓐ Ⓑ Ⓒ Ⓓ	89	Ⓐ Ⓑ Ⓒ Ⓓ	99	Ⓐ Ⓑ Ⓒ Ⓓ
60	Ⓐ Ⓑ Ⓒ Ⓓ	70	Ⓐ Ⓑ Ⓒ Ⓓ	80	Ⓐ Ⓑ Ⓒ Ⓓ	90	Ⓐ Ⓑ Ⓒ Ⓓ	100	Ⓐ Ⓑ Ⓒ Ⓓ

TEST 2

Part 1

No.	ANSWER			
	A	B	C	D
1	Ⓐ	Ⓑ	Ⓒ	Ⓓ
2	Ⓐ	Ⓑ	Ⓒ	Ⓓ
3	Ⓐ	Ⓑ	Ⓒ	Ⓓ
4	Ⓐ	Ⓑ	Ⓒ	Ⓓ
5	Ⓐ	Ⓑ	Ⓒ	Ⓓ
6	Ⓐ	Ⓑ	Ⓒ	Ⓓ
7	Ⓐ	Ⓑ	Ⓒ	
8	Ⓐ	Ⓑ	Ⓒ	
9	Ⓐ	Ⓑ	Ⓒ	
10	Ⓐ	Ⓑ	Ⓒ	

Part 2

No.	ANSWER			No.	ANSWER			No.	ANSWER			No.	ANSWER		
	A	B	C		A	B	C		A	B	C		A	B	C
11	Ⓐ	Ⓑ	Ⓒ	21	Ⓐ	Ⓑ	Ⓒ	31	Ⓐ	Ⓑ	Ⓒ				
12	Ⓐ	Ⓑ	Ⓒ	22	Ⓐ	Ⓑ	Ⓒ	32	Ⓐ	Ⓑ	Ⓒ				
13	Ⓐ	Ⓑ	Ⓒ	23	Ⓐ	Ⓑ	Ⓒ	33	Ⓐ	Ⓑ	Ⓒ				
14	Ⓐ	Ⓑ	Ⓒ	24	Ⓐ	Ⓑ	Ⓒ	34	Ⓐ	Ⓑ	Ⓒ				
15	Ⓐ	Ⓑ	Ⓒ	25	Ⓐ	Ⓑ	Ⓒ	35	Ⓐ	Ⓑ	Ⓒ				
16	Ⓐ	Ⓑ	Ⓒ	26	Ⓐ	Ⓑ	Ⓒ	36	Ⓐ	Ⓑ	Ⓒ				
17	Ⓐ	Ⓑ	Ⓒ	27	Ⓐ	Ⓑ	Ⓒ	37	Ⓐ	Ⓑ	Ⓒ				
18	Ⓐ	Ⓑ	Ⓒ	28	Ⓐ	Ⓑ	Ⓒ	38	Ⓐ	Ⓑ	Ⓒ				
19	Ⓐ	Ⓑ	Ⓒ	29	Ⓐ	Ⓑ	Ⓒ	39	Ⓐ	Ⓑ	Ⓒ				
20	Ⓐ	Ⓑ	Ⓒ	30	Ⓐ	Ⓑ	Ⓒ	40	Ⓐ	Ⓑ	Ⓒ				

Part 3

No.	ANSWER				No.	ANSWER				No.	ANSWER			
	A	B	C	D		A	B	C	D		A	B	C	D
41	Ⓐ	Ⓑ	Ⓒ	Ⓓ	51	Ⓐ	Ⓑ	Ⓒ	Ⓓ	61	Ⓐ	Ⓑ	Ⓒ	Ⓓ
42	Ⓐ	Ⓑ	Ⓒ	Ⓓ	52	Ⓐ	Ⓑ	Ⓒ	Ⓓ	62	Ⓐ	Ⓑ	Ⓒ	Ⓓ
43	Ⓐ	Ⓑ	Ⓒ	Ⓓ	53	Ⓐ	Ⓑ	Ⓒ	Ⓓ	63	Ⓐ	Ⓑ	Ⓒ	Ⓓ
44	Ⓐ	Ⓑ	Ⓒ	Ⓓ	54	Ⓐ	Ⓑ	Ⓒ	Ⓓ	64	Ⓐ	Ⓑ	Ⓒ	Ⓓ
45	Ⓐ	Ⓑ	Ⓒ	Ⓓ	55	Ⓐ	Ⓑ	Ⓒ	Ⓓ	65	Ⓐ	Ⓑ	Ⓒ	Ⓓ
46	Ⓐ	Ⓑ	Ⓒ	Ⓓ	56	Ⓐ	Ⓑ	Ⓒ	Ⓓ	66	Ⓐ	Ⓑ	Ⓒ	Ⓓ
47	Ⓐ	Ⓑ	Ⓒ	Ⓓ	57	Ⓐ	Ⓑ	Ⓒ	Ⓓ	67	Ⓐ	Ⓑ	Ⓒ	Ⓓ
48	Ⓐ	Ⓑ	Ⓒ	Ⓓ	58	Ⓐ	Ⓑ	Ⓒ	Ⓓ	68	Ⓐ	Ⓑ	Ⓒ	Ⓓ
49	Ⓐ	Ⓑ	Ⓒ	Ⓓ	59	Ⓐ	Ⓑ	Ⓒ	Ⓓ	69	Ⓐ	Ⓑ	Ⓒ	Ⓓ
50	Ⓐ	Ⓑ	Ⓒ	Ⓓ	60	Ⓐ	Ⓑ	Ⓒ	Ⓓ	70	Ⓐ	Ⓑ	Ⓒ	Ⓓ

Part 4

No.	ANSWER				No.	ANSWER				No.	ANSWER			
	A	B	C	D		A	B	C	D		A	B	C	D
71	Ⓐ	Ⓑ	Ⓒ	Ⓓ	81	Ⓐ	Ⓑ	Ⓒ	Ⓓ	91	Ⓐ	Ⓑ	Ⓒ	Ⓓ
72	Ⓐ	Ⓑ	Ⓒ	Ⓓ	82	Ⓐ	Ⓑ	Ⓒ	Ⓓ	92	Ⓐ	Ⓑ	Ⓒ	Ⓓ
73	Ⓐ	Ⓑ	Ⓒ	Ⓓ	83	Ⓐ	Ⓑ	Ⓒ	Ⓓ	93	Ⓐ	Ⓑ	Ⓒ	Ⓓ
74	Ⓐ	Ⓑ	Ⓒ	Ⓓ	84	Ⓐ	Ⓑ	Ⓒ	Ⓓ	94	Ⓐ	Ⓑ	Ⓒ	Ⓓ
75	Ⓐ	Ⓑ	Ⓒ	Ⓓ	85	Ⓐ	Ⓑ	Ⓒ	Ⓓ	95	Ⓐ	Ⓑ	Ⓒ	Ⓓ
76	Ⓐ	Ⓑ	Ⓒ	Ⓓ	86	Ⓐ	Ⓑ	Ⓒ	Ⓓ	96	Ⓐ	Ⓑ	Ⓒ	Ⓓ
77	Ⓐ	Ⓑ	Ⓒ	Ⓓ	87	Ⓐ	Ⓑ	Ⓒ	Ⓓ	97	Ⓐ	Ⓑ	Ⓒ	Ⓓ
78	Ⓐ	Ⓑ	Ⓒ	Ⓓ	88	Ⓐ	Ⓑ	Ⓒ	Ⓓ	98	Ⓐ	Ⓑ	Ⓒ	Ⓓ
79	Ⓐ	Ⓑ	Ⓒ	Ⓓ	89	Ⓐ	Ⓑ	Ⓒ	Ⓓ	99	Ⓐ	Ⓑ	Ⓒ	Ⓓ
80	Ⓐ	Ⓑ	Ⓒ	Ⓓ	90	Ⓐ	Ⓑ	Ⓒ	Ⓓ	100	Ⓐ	Ⓑ	Ⓒ	Ⓓ

TEST 3

Part 1

No.	ANSWER
	A B C D
1	Ⓐ Ⓑ Ⓒ Ⓓ
2	Ⓐ Ⓑ Ⓒ Ⓓ
3	Ⓐ Ⓑ Ⓒ Ⓓ
4	Ⓐ Ⓑ Ⓒ Ⓓ
5	Ⓐ Ⓑ Ⓒ Ⓓ
6	Ⓐ Ⓑ Ⓒ Ⓓ
7	Ⓐ Ⓑ Ⓒ
8	Ⓐ Ⓑ Ⓒ
9	Ⓐ Ⓑ Ⓒ
10	Ⓐ Ⓑ Ⓒ

Part 2

No.	ANSWER
	A B C
11	Ⓐ Ⓑ Ⓒ
12	Ⓐ Ⓑ Ⓒ
13	Ⓐ Ⓑ Ⓒ
14	Ⓐ Ⓑ Ⓒ
15	Ⓐ Ⓑ Ⓒ
16	Ⓐ Ⓑ Ⓒ
17	Ⓐ Ⓑ Ⓒ
18	Ⓐ Ⓑ Ⓒ
19	Ⓐ Ⓑ Ⓒ
20	Ⓐ Ⓑ Ⓒ

No.	ANSWER
	A B C
21	Ⓐ Ⓑ Ⓒ
22	Ⓐ Ⓑ Ⓒ
23	Ⓐ Ⓑ Ⓒ
24	Ⓐ Ⓑ Ⓒ
25	Ⓐ Ⓑ Ⓒ
26	Ⓐ Ⓑ Ⓒ
27	Ⓐ Ⓑ Ⓒ
28	Ⓐ Ⓑ Ⓒ
29	Ⓐ Ⓑ Ⓒ
30	Ⓐ Ⓑ Ⓒ

No.	ANSWER
	A B C D
31	Ⓐ Ⓑ Ⓒ
32	Ⓐ Ⓑ Ⓒ Ⓓ
33	Ⓐ Ⓑ Ⓒ Ⓓ
34	Ⓐ Ⓑ Ⓒ Ⓓ
35	Ⓐ Ⓑ Ⓒ Ⓓ
36	Ⓐ Ⓑ Ⓒ Ⓓ
37	Ⓐ Ⓑ Ⓒ Ⓓ
38	Ⓐ Ⓑ Ⓒ Ⓓ
39	Ⓐ Ⓑ Ⓒ Ⓓ
40	Ⓐ Ⓑ Ⓒ Ⓓ

Part 3

No.	ANSWER
	A B C D
41	Ⓐ Ⓑ Ⓒ Ⓓ
42	Ⓐ Ⓑ Ⓒ Ⓓ
43	Ⓐ Ⓑ Ⓒ Ⓓ
44	Ⓐ Ⓑ Ⓒ Ⓓ
45	Ⓐ Ⓑ Ⓒ Ⓓ
46	Ⓐ Ⓑ Ⓒ Ⓓ
47	Ⓐ Ⓑ Ⓒ Ⓓ
48	Ⓐ Ⓑ Ⓒ Ⓓ
49	Ⓐ Ⓑ Ⓒ Ⓓ
50	Ⓐ Ⓑ Ⓒ Ⓓ

No.	ANSWER
	A B C D
51	Ⓐ Ⓑ Ⓒ Ⓓ
52	Ⓐ Ⓑ Ⓒ Ⓓ
53	Ⓐ Ⓑ Ⓒ Ⓓ
54	Ⓐ Ⓑ Ⓒ Ⓓ
55	Ⓐ Ⓑ Ⓒ Ⓓ
56	Ⓐ Ⓑ Ⓒ Ⓓ
57	Ⓐ Ⓑ Ⓒ Ⓓ
58	Ⓐ Ⓑ Ⓒ Ⓓ
59	Ⓐ Ⓑ Ⓒ Ⓓ
60	Ⓐ Ⓑ Ⓒ Ⓓ

No.	ANSWER
	A B C D
61	Ⓐ Ⓑ Ⓒ Ⓓ
62	Ⓐ Ⓑ Ⓒ Ⓓ
63	Ⓐ Ⓑ Ⓒ Ⓓ
64	Ⓐ Ⓑ Ⓒ Ⓓ
65	Ⓐ Ⓑ Ⓒ Ⓓ
66	Ⓐ Ⓑ Ⓒ Ⓓ
67	Ⓐ Ⓑ Ⓒ Ⓓ
68	Ⓐ Ⓑ Ⓒ Ⓓ
69	Ⓐ Ⓑ Ⓒ Ⓓ
70	Ⓐ Ⓑ Ⓒ Ⓓ

Part 4

No.	ANSWER
	A B C D
71	Ⓐ Ⓑ Ⓒ Ⓓ
72	Ⓐ Ⓑ Ⓒ Ⓓ
73	Ⓐ Ⓑ Ⓒ Ⓓ
74	Ⓐ Ⓑ Ⓒ Ⓓ
75	Ⓐ Ⓑ Ⓒ Ⓓ
76	Ⓐ Ⓑ Ⓒ Ⓓ
77	Ⓐ Ⓑ Ⓒ Ⓓ
78	Ⓐ Ⓑ Ⓒ Ⓓ
79	Ⓐ Ⓑ Ⓒ Ⓓ
80	Ⓐ Ⓑ Ⓒ Ⓓ

No.	ANSWER
	A B C D
81	Ⓐ Ⓑ Ⓒ Ⓓ
82	Ⓐ Ⓑ Ⓒ Ⓓ
83	Ⓐ Ⓑ Ⓒ Ⓓ
84	Ⓐ Ⓑ Ⓒ Ⓓ
85	Ⓐ Ⓑ Ⓒ Ⓓ
86	Ⓐ Ⓑ Ⓒ Ⓓ
87	Ⓐ Ⓑ Ⓒ Ⓓ
88	Ⓐ Ⓑ Ⓒ Ⓓ
89	Ⓐ Ⓑ Ⓒ Ⓓ
90	Ⓐ Ⓑ Ⓒ Ⓓ

No.	ANSWER
	A B C D
91	Ⓐ Ⓑ Ⓒ Ⓓ
92	Ⓐ Ⓑ Ⓒ Ⓓ
93	Ⓐ Ⓑ Ⓒ Ⓓ
94	Ⓐ Ⓑ Ⓒ Ⓓ
95	Ⓐ Ⓑ Ⓒ Ⓓ
96	Ⓐ Ⓑ Ⓒ Ⓓ
97	Ⓐ Ⓑ Ⓒ Ⓓ
98	Ⓐ Ⓑ Ⓒ Ⓓ
99	Ⓐ Ⓑ Ⓒ Ⓓ
100	Ⓐ Ⓑ Ⓒ Ⓓ

TEST 4

Part 1

No.	ANSWER
	A B C D
1	Ⓐ Ⓑ Ⓒ Ⓓ
2	Ⓐ Ⓑ Ⓒ Ⓓ
3	Ⓐ Ⓑ Ⓒ Ⓓ
4	Ⓐ Ⓑ Ⓒ Ⓓ
5	Ⓐ Ⓑ Ⓒ Ⓓ
6	Ⓐ Ⓑ Ⓒ Ⓓ
7	Ⓐ Ⓑ Ⓒ
8	Ⓐ Ⓑ Ⓒ
9	Ⓐ Ⓑ Ⓒ
10	Ⓐ Ⓑ Ⓒ

Part 2

No.	ANSWER	No.	ANSWER
	A B C		A B C
11	Ⓐ Ⓑ Ⓒ	21	Ⓐ Ⓑ Ⓒ
12	Ⓐ Ⓑ Ⓒ	22	Ⓐ Ⓑ Ⓒ
13	Ⓐ Ⓑ Ⓒ	23	Ⓐ Ⓑ Ⓒ
14	Ⓐ Ⓑ Ⓒ	24	Ⓐ Ⓑ Ⓒ
15	Ⓐ Ⓑ Ⓒ	25	Ⓐ Ⓑ Ⓒ
16	Ⓐ Ⓑ Ⓒ	26	Ⓐ Ⓑ Ⓒ
17	Ⓐ Ⓑ Ⓒ	27	Ⓐ Ⓑ Ⓒ
18	Ⓐ Ⓑ Ⓒ	28	Ⓐ Ⓑ Ⓒ
19	Ⓐ Ⓑ Ⓒ	29	Ⓐ Ⓑ Ⓒ
20	Ⓐ Ⓑ Ⓒ	30	Ⓐ Ⓑ Ⓒ

Part 3

No.	ANSWER	No.	ANSWER
	A B C D		A B C D
31	Ⓐ Ⓑ Ⓒ Ⓓ	41	Ⓐ Ⓑ Ⓒ Ⓓ
32	Ⓐ Ⓑ Ⓒ Ⓓ	42	Ⓐ Ⓑ Ⓒ Ⓓ
33	Ⓐ Ⓑ Ⓒ Ⓓ	43	Ⓐ Ⓑ Ⓒ Ⓓ
34	Ⓐ Ⓑ Ⓒ Ⓓ	44	Ⓐ Ⓑ Ⓒ Ⓓ
35	Ⓐ Ⓑ Ⓒ Ⓓ	45	Ⓐ Ⓑ Ⓒ Ⓓ
36	Ⓐ Ⓑ Ⓒ Ⓓ	46	Ⓐ Ⓑ Ⓒ Ⓓ
37	Ⓐ Ⓑ Ⓒ Ⓓ	47	Ⓐ Ⓑ Ⓒ Ⓓ
38	Ⓐ Ⓑ Ⓒ Ⓓ	48	Ⓐ Ⓑ Ⓒ Ⓓ
39	Ⓐ Ⓑ Ⓒ Ⓓ	49	Ⓐ Ⓑ Ⓒ Ⓓ
40	Ⓐ Ⓑ Ⓒ Ⓓ	50	Ⓐ Ⓑ Ⓒ Ⓓ

No.	ANSWER	No.	ANSWER
	A B C D		A B C D
51	Ⓐ Ⓑ Ⓒ Ⓓ	61	Ⓐ Ⓑ Ⓒ Ⓓ
52	Ⓐ Ⓑ Ⓒ Ⓓ	62	Ⓐ Ⓑ Ⓒ Ⓓ
53	Ⓐ Ⓑ Ⓒ Ⓓ	63	Ⓐ Ⓑ Ⓒ Ⓓ
54	Ⓐ Ⓑ Ⓒ Ⓓ	64	Ⓐ Ⓑ Ⓒ Ⓓ
55	Ⓐ Ⓑ Ⓒ Ⓓ	65	Ⓐ Ⓑ Ⓒ Ⓓ
56	Ⓐ Ⓑ Ⓒ Ⓓ	66	Ⓐ Ⓑ Ⓒ Ⓓ
57	Ⓐ Ⓑ Ⓒ Ⓓ	67	Ⓐ Ⓑ Ⓒ Ⓓ
58	Ⓐ Ⓑ Ⓒ Ⓓ	68	Ⓐ Ⓑ Ⓒ Ⓓ
59	Ⓐ Ⓑ Ⓒ Ⓓ	69	Ⓐ Ⓑ Ⓒ Ⓓ
60	Ⓐ Ⓑ Ⓒ Ⓓ	70	Ⓐ Ⓑ Ⓒ Ⓓ

Part 4

No.	ANSWER	No.	ANSWER	No.	ANSWER
	A B C D		A B C D		A B C D
71	Ⓐ Ⓑ Ⓒ Ⓓ	81	Ⓐ Ⓑ Ⓒ Ⓓ	91	Ⓐ Ⓑ Ⓒ Ⓓ
72	Ⓐ Ⓑ Ⓒ Ⓓ	82	Ⓐ Ⓑ Ⓒ Ⓓ	92	Ⓐ Ⓑ Ⓒ Ⓓ
73	Ⓐ Ⓑ Ⓒ Ⓓ	83	Ⓐ Ⓑ Ⓒ Ⓓ	93	Ⓐ Ⓑ Ⓒ Ⓓ
74	Ⓐ Ⓑ Ⓒ Ⓓ	84	Ⓐ Ⓑ Ⓒ Ⓓ	94	Ⓐ Ⓑ Ⓒ Ⓓ
75	Ⓐ Ⓑ Ⓒ Ⓓ	85	Ⓐ Ⓑ Ⓒ Ⓓ	95	Ⓐ Ⓑ Ⓒ Ⓓ
76	Ⓐ Ⓑ Ⓒ Ⓓ	86	Ⓐ Ⓑ Ⓒ Ⓓ	96	Ⓐ Ⓑ Ⓒ Ⓓ
77	Ⓐ Ⓑ Ⓒ Ⓓ	87	Ⓐ Ⓑ Ⓒ Ⓓ	97	Ⓐ Ⓑ Ⓒ Ⓓ
78	Ⓐ Ⓑ Ⓒ Ⓓ	88	Ⓐ Ⓑ Ⓒ Ⓓ	98	Ⓐ Ⓑ Ⓒ Ⓓ
79	Ⓐ Ⓑ Ⓒ Ⓓ	89	Ⓐ Ⓑ Ⓒ Ⓓ	99	Ⓐ Ⓑ Ⓒ Ⓓ
80	Ⓐ Ⓑ Ⓒ Ⓓ	90	Ⓐ Ⓑ Ⓒ Ⓓ	100	Ⓐ Ⓑ Ⓒ Ⓓ

TEST 5

Part 1

No.	ANSWER
	A B C D
1	Ⓐ Ⓑ Ⓒ Ⓓ
2	Ⓐ Ⓑ Ⓒ Ⓓ
3	Ⓐ Ⓑ Ⓒ Ⓓ
4	Ⓐ Ⓑ Ⓒ Ⓓ
5	Ⓐ Ⓑ Ⓒ Ⓓ
6	Ⓐ Ⓑ Ⓒ Ⓓ
7	Ⓐ Ⓑ Ⓒ
8	Ⓐ Ⓑ Ⓒ
9	Ⓐ Ⓑ Ⓒ
10	Ⓐ Ⓑ Ⓒ

Part 2

No.	ANSWER
	A B C
11	Ⓐ Ⓑ Ⓒ
12	Ⓐ Ⓑ Ⓒ
13	Ⓐ Ⓑ Ⓒ
14	Ⓐ Ⓑ Ⓒ
15	Ⓐ Ⓑ Ⓒ
16	Ⓐ Ⓑ Ⓒ
17	Ⓐ Ⓑ Ⓒ
18	Ⓐ Ⓑ Ⓒ
19	Ⓐ Ⓑ Ⓒ
20	Ⓐ Ⓑ Ⓒ

No.	ANSWER
	A B C
21	Ⓐ Ⓑ Ⓒ
22	Ⓐ Ⓑ Ⓒ
23	Ⓐ Ⓑ Ⓒ
24	Ⓐ Ⓑ Ⓒ
25	Ⓐ Ⓑ Ⓒ
26	Ⓐ Ⓑ Ⓒ
27	Ⓐ Ⓑ Ⓒ
28	Ⓐ Ⓑ Ⓒ
29	Ⓐ Ⓑ Ⓒ
30	Ⓐ Ⓑ Ⓒ

No.	ANSWER
	A B C D
31	Ⓐ Ⓑ Ⓒ
32	Ⓐ Ⓑ Ⓒ Ⓓ
33	Ⓐ Ⓑ Ⓒ Ⓓ
34	Ⓐ Ⓑ Ⓒ Ⓓ
35	Ⓐ Ⓑ Ⓒ Ⓓ
36	Ⓐ Ⓑ Ⓒ Ⓓ
37	Ⓐ Ⓑ Ⓒ Ⓓ
38	Ⓐ Ⓑ Ⓒ Ⓓ
39	Ⓐ Ⓑ Ⓒ Ⓓ
40	Ⓐ Ⓑ Ⓒ Ⓓ

Part 3

No.	ANSWER
	A B C D
41	Ⓐ Ⓑ Ⓒ Ⓓ
42	Ⓐ Ⓑ Ⓒ Ⓓ
43	Ⓐ Ⓑ Ⓒ Ⓓ
44	Ⓐ Ⓑ Ⓒ Ⓓ
45	Ⓐ Ⓑ Ⓒ Ⓓ
46	Ⓐ Ⓑ Ⓒ Ⓓ
47	Ⓐ Ⓑ Ⓒ Ⓓ
48	Ⓐ Ⓑ Ⓒ Ⓓ
49	Ⓐ Ⓑ Ⓒ Ⓓ
50	Ⓐ Ⓑ Ⓒ Ⓓ

No.	ANSWER
	A B C D
51	Ⓐ Ⓑ Ⓒ Ⓓ
52	Ⓐ Ⓑ Ⓒ Ⓓ
53	Ⓐ Ⓑ Ⓒ Ⓓ
54	Ⓐ Ⓑ Ⓒ Ⓓ
55	Ⓐ Ⓑ Ⓒ Ⓓ
56	Ⓐ Ⓑ Ⓒ Ⓓ
57	Ⓐ Ⓑ Ⓒ Ⓓ
58	Ⓐ Ⓑ Ⓒ Ⓓ
59	Ⓐ Ⓑ Ⓒ Ⓓ
60	Ⓐ Ⓑ Ⓒ Ⓓ

No.	ANSWER
	A B C D
61	Ⓐ Ⓑ Ⓒ Ⓓ
62	Ⓐ Ⓑ Ⓒ Ⓓ
63	Ⓐ Ⓑ Ⓒ Ⓓ
64	Ⓐ Ⓑ Ⓒ Ⓓ
65	Ⓐ Ⓑ Ⓒ Ⓓ
66	Ⓐ Ⓑ Ⓒ Ⓓ
67	Ⓐ Ⓑ Ⓒ Ⓓ
68	Ⓐ Ⓑ Ⓒ Ⓓ
69	Ⓐ Ⓑ Ⓒ Ⓓ
70	Ⓐ Ⓑ Ⓒ Ⓓ

Part 4

No.	ANSWER
	A B C D
71	Ⓐ Ⓑ Ⓒ Ⓓ
72	Ⓐ Ⓑ Ⓒ Ⓓ
73	Ⓐ Ⓑ Ⓒ Ⓓ
74	Ⓐ Ⓑ Ⓒ Ⓓ
75	Ⓐ Ⓑ Ⓒ Ⓓ
76	Ⓐ Ⓑ Ⓒ Ⓓ
77	Ⓐ Ⓑ Ⓒ Ⓓ
78	Ⓐ Ⓑ Ⓒ Ⓓ
79	Ⓐ Ⓑ Ⓒ Ⓓ
80	Ⓐ Ⓑ Ⓒ Ⓓ

No.	ANSWER
	A B C D
81	Ⓐ Ⓑ Ⓒ Ⓓ
82	Ⓐ Ⓑ Ⓒ Ⓓ
83	Ⓐ Ⓑ Ⓒ Ⓓ
84	Ⓐ Ⓑ Ⓒ Ⓓ
85	Ⓐ Ⓑ Ⓒ Ⓓ
86	Ⓐ Ⓑ Ⓒ Ⓓ
87	Ⓐ Ⓑ Ⓒ Ⓓ
88	Ⓐ Ⓑ Ⓒ Ⓓ
89	Ⓐ Ⓑ Ⓒ Ⓓ
90	Ⓐ Ⓑ Ⓒ Ⓓ

No.	ANSWER
	A B C D
91	Ⓐ Ⓑ Ⓒ Ⓓ
92	Ⓐ Ⓑ Ⓒ Ⓓ
93	Ⓐ Ⓑ Ⓒ Ⓓ
94	Ⓐ Ⓑ Ⓒ Ⓓ
95	Ⓐ Ⓑ Ⓒ Ⓓ
96	Ⓐ Ⓑ Ⓒ Ⓓ
97	Ⓐ Ⓑ Ⓒ Ⓓ
98	Ⓐ Ⓑ Ⓒ Ⓓ
99	Ⓐ Ⓑ Ⓒ Ⓓ
100	Ⓐ Ⓑ Ⓒ Ⓓ

TEST

Part 1	ANSWER				Part 2	ANSWER					ANSWER				Part 3	ANSWER					ANSWER				Part 4	ANSWER					ANSWER					ANSWER			
No.	A	B	C	D	No.	A	B	C		No.	A	B	C	D	No.	A	B	C	D	No.	A	B	C	D	No.	A	B	C	D	No.	A	B	C	D	No.	A	B	C	D
1	Ⓐ	Ⓑ	Ⓒ	Ⓓ	11	Ⓐ	Ⓑ	Ⓒ		21	Ⓐ	Ⓑ	Ⓒ		31	Ⓐ	Ⓑ	Ⓒ	Ⓓ	41	Ⓐ	Ⓑ	Ⓒ	Ⓓ	51	Ⓐ	Ⓑ	Ⓒ	Ⓓ	61	Ⓐ	Ⓑ	Ⓒ	Ⓓ	71	Ⓐ	Ⓑ	Ⓒ	Ⓓ	81	Ⓐ	Ⓑ	Ⓒ	Ⓓ	91	Ⓐ	Ⓑ	Ⓒ	Ⓓ
2	Ⓐ	Ⓑ	Ⓒ	Ⓓ	12	Ⓐ	Ⓑ	Ⓒ		22	Ⓐ	Ⓑ	Ⓒ		32	Ⓐ	Ⓑ	Ⓒ	Ⓓ	42	Ⓐ	Ⓑ	Ⓒ	Ⓓ	52	Ⓐ	Ⓑ	Ⓒ	Ⓓ	62	Ⓐ	Ⓑ	Ⓒ	Ⓓ	72	Ⓐ	Ⓑ	Ⓒ	Ⓓ	82	Ⓐ	Ⓑ	Ⓒ	Ⓓ	92	Ⓐ	Ⓑ	Ⓒ	Ⓓ
3	Ⓐ	Ⓑ	Ⓒ	Ⓓ	13	Ⓐ	Ⓑ	Ⓒ		23	Ⓐ	Ⓑ	Ⓒ		33	Ⓐ	Ⓑ	Ⓒ	Ⓓ	43	Ⓐ	Ⓑ	Ⓒ	Ⓓ	53	Ⓐ	Ⓑ	Ⓒ	Ⓓ	63	Ⓐ	Ⓑ	Ⓒ	Ⓓ	73	Ⓐ	Ⓑ	Ⓒ	Ⓓ	83	Ⓐ	Ⓑ	Ⓒ	Ⓓ	93	Ⓐ	Ⓑ	Ⓒ	Ⓓ
4	Ⓐ	Ⓑ	Ⓒ	Ⓓ	14	Ⓐ	Ⓑ	Ⓒ		24	Ⓐ	Ⓑ	Ⓒ		34	Ⓐ	Ⓑ	Ⓒ	Ⓓ	44	Ⓐ	Ⓑ	Ⓒ	Ⓓ	54	Ⓐ	Ⓑ	Ⓒ	Ⓓ	64	Ⓐ	Ⓑ	Ⓒ	Ⓓ	74	Ⓐ	Ⓑ	Ⓒ	Ⓓ	84	Ⓐ	Ⓑ	Ⓒ	Ⓓ	94	Ⓐ	Ⓑ	Ⓒ	Ⓓ
5	Ⓐ	Ⓑ	Ⓒ	Ⓓ	15	Ⓐ	Ⓑ	Ⓒ		25	Ⓐ	Ⓑ	Ⓒ		35	Ⓐ	Ⓑ	Ⓒ	Ⓓ	45	Ⓐ	Ⓑ	Ⓒ	Ⓓ	55	Ⓐ	Ⓑ	Ⓒ	Ⓓ	65	Ⓐ	Ⓑ	Ⓒ	Ⓓ	75	Ⓐ	Ⓑ	Ⓒ	Ⓓ	85	Ⓐ	Ⓑ	Ⓒ	Ⓓ	95	Ⓐ	Ⓑ	Ⓒ	Ⓓ
6	Ⓐ	Ⓑ	Ⓒ	Ⓓ	16	Ⓐ	Ⓑ	Ⓒ		26	Ⓐ	Ⓑ	Ⓒ		36	Ⓐ	Ⓑ	Ⓒ	Ⓓ	46	Ⓐ	Ⓑ	Ⓒ	Ⓓ	56	Ⓐ	Ⓑ	Ⓒ	Ⓓ	66	Ⓐ	Ⓑ	Ⓒ	Ⓓ	76	Ⓐ	Ⓑ	Ⓒ	Ⓓ	86	Ⓐ	Ⓑ	Ⓒ	Ⓓ	96	Ⓐ	Ⓑ	Ⓒ	Ⓓ
7	Ⓐ	Ⓑ	Ⓒ	Ⓓ	17	Ⓐ	Ⓑ	Ⓒ		27	Ⓐ	Ⓑ	Ⓒ		37	Ⓐ	Ⓑ	Ⓒ	Ⓓ	47	Ⓐ	Ⓑ	Ⓒ	Ⓓ	57	Ⓐ	Ⓑ	Ⓒ	Ⓓ	67	Ⓐ	Ⓑ	Ⓒ	Ⓓ	77	Ⓐ	Ⓑ	Ⓒ	Ⓓ	87	Ⓐ	Ⓑ	Ⓒ	Ⓓ	97	Ⓐ	Ⓑ	Ⓒ	Ⓓ
8	Ⓐ	Ⓑ	Ⓒ	Ⓓ	18	Ⓐ	Ⓑ	Ⓒ		28	Ⓐ	Ⓑ	Ⓒ		38	Ⓐ	Ⓑ	Ⓒ	Ⓓ	48	Ⓐ	Ⓑ	Ⓒ	Ⓓ	58	Ⓐ	Ⓑ	Ⓒ	Ⓓ	68	Ⓐ	Ⓑ	Ⓒ	Ⓓ	78	Ⓐ	Ⓑ	Ⓒ	Ⓓ	88	Ⓐ	Ⓑ	Ⓒ	Ⓓ	98	Ⓐ	Ⓑ	Ⓒ	Ⓓ
9	Ⓐ	Ⓑ	Ⓒ	Ⓓ	19	Ⓐ	Ⓑ	Ⓒ		29	Ⓐ	Ⓑ	Ⓒ		39	Ⓐ	Ⓑ	Ⓒ	Ⓓ	49	Ⓐ	Ⓑ	Ⓒ	Ⓓ	59	Ⓐ	Ⓑ	Ⓒ	Ⓓ	69	Ⓐ	Ⓑ	Ⓒ	Ⓓ	79	Ⓐ	Ⓑ	Ⓒ	Ⓓ	89	Ⓐ	Ⓑ	Ⓒ	Ⓓ	99	Ⓐ	Ⓑ	Ⓒ	Ⓓ
10	Ⓐ	Ⓑ	Ⓒ	Ⓓ	20	Ⓐ	Ⓑ	Ⓒ		30	Ⓐ	Ⓑ	Ⓒ		40	Ⓐ	Ⓑ	Ⓒ	Ⓓ	50	Ⓐ	Ⓑ	Ⓒ	Ⓓ	60	Ⓐ	Ⓑ	Ⓒ	Ⓓ	70	Ⓐ	Ⓑ	Ⓒ	Ⓓ	80	Ⓐ	Ⓑ	Ⓒ	Ⓓ	90	Ⓐ	Ⓑ	Ⓒ	Ⓓ	100	Ⓐ	Ⓑ	Ⓒ	Ⓓ

TEST

Part 1

No.	ANSWER
1	A B C D
2	A B C D
3	A B C D
4	A B C D
5	A B C D
6	A B C D
7	A B C D
8	A B C D
9	A B C D
10	A B C D

Part 2

No.	ANSWER	No.	ANSWER
11	A B C	21	A B C
12	A B C	22	A B C
13	A B C	23	A B C
14	A B C	24	A B C
15	A B C	25	A B C
16	A B C	26	A B C
17	A B C	27	A B C
18	A B C	28	A B C
19	A B C	29	A B C
20	A B C	30	A B C

No.	ANSWER
31	A B C D
32	A B C D
33	A B C D
34	A B C D
35	A B C D
36	A B C D
37	A B C D
38	A B C D
39	A B C D
40	A B C D

Part 3

No.	ANSWER	No.	ANSWER
41	A B C D	51	A B C D
42	A B C D	52	A B C D
43	A B C D	53	A B C D
44	A B C D	54	A B C D
45	A B C D	55	A B C D
46	A B C D	56	A B C D
47	A B C D	57	A B C D
48	A B C D	58	A B C D
49	A B C D	59	A B C D
50	A B C D	60	A B C D

No.	ANSWER
61	A B C D
62	A B C D
63	A B C D
64	A B C D
65	A B C D
66	A B C D
67	A B C D
68	A B C D
69	A B C D
70	A B C D

Part 4

No.	ANSWER	No.	ANSWER
71	A B C D	81	A B C D
72	A B C D	82	A B C D
73	A B C D	83	A B C D
74	A B C D	84	A B C D
75	A B C D	85	A B C D
76	A B C D	86	A B C D
77	A B C D	87	A B C D
78	A B C D	88	A B C D
79	A B C D	89	A B C D
80	A B C D	90	A B C D

No.	ANSWER
91	A B C D
92	A B C D
93	A B C D
94	A B C D
95	A B C D
96	A B C D
97	A B C D
98	A B C D
99	A B C D
100	A B C D

著者紹介

株式会社メディアビーコン（Media Beacon）

1999 年創業。語学教材に特化した教材制作会社。TOEIC、英検、TOEFL をはじめとする英語の資格試験から、子供英語、中学英語、高校英語、英会話、ビジネス英語まで、英語教材全般の制作を幅広く行う。特に TOEIC の教材制作には定評があり、『TOEIC® テスト新公式問題集 Vol. 5』の編集制作ほか、TOEIC 関連企画を多数担当している。出版物以外にも英語学習アプリ、英会話学校のコース設計から指導マニュアルの開発、大手進学塾の教材開発まで、多角的な教材制作が可能な数少ない制作会社。「語学の力で世界中の人々の幸せに貢献する」をモットーに、社員一同、学習者の笑顔を想いながら教材の研究開発を行っている。また、同時に TOEIC® L&R テストのスコアアップを目指す方のための指導も行っている。

著書に『TOEIC® L&R TEST 990 点獲得　Part 5&6 難問模試』、『TOEIC® L&R TEST 990 点獲得最強 Part 7 模試』（以上、ベレ出版）、『寝る前 5 分暗記ブック TOEIC テスト単語＆フレーズ』、『寝る前 5 分暗記ブック TOEIC テスト英文法』、『寝る前 5 分暗記ブック 英会話フレーズ集〈基礎編〉』、『寝る前 5 分暗記ブック 英会話フレーズ集〈海外旅行編〉』、『寝る前 5 分暗記ブック 英会話フレーズ集〈接客編〉』、『寝る前 5 分暗記ブック 英会話フレーズ集〈おもてなし編〉』（以上、学研プラス）がある。

YouTube「ビーコン イングリッシュ チャンネル」にて英語学習者のために役立つ情報を配信中。
メディアビーコンの公式 LINE にて、TOEIC テストのスコアアップに役立つ情報を発信中。

◉ ── カバーデザイン	竹内 雄二
◉ ── 編集	株式会社メディアビーコン（山田優月）
◉ ── DTP	株式会社秀文社
◉ ── 校正、ネイティブチェック	渡邉真理子、Jonathan Nacht
◉ ── 音声・ナレーション	Howard Colefield、Nadia McKechnie、Carolyn Miller、Stuart O ／ 時間・約225分

［音声DL付］TOEIC® L&R TEST 990点獲得 Part 1 – 4 難問模試

| 2022 年 6 月 25 日 | 初版発行 |
| 2023 年 3 月 25 日 | 第 3 刷発行 |

著者	メディアビーコン
発行者	内田 真介
発行・発売	ベレ出版
	〒162-0832　東京都新宿区岩戸町12 レベッカビル TEL.03-5225-4790 FAX.03-5225-4795 ホームページ　https://www.beret.co.jp/
印刷	モリモト印刷株式会社
製本	根本製本株式会社

落丁本・乱丁本は小社編集部あてにお送りください。送料小社負担にてお取り替えします。
本書の無断複写は著作権法上での例外を除き禁じられています。購入者以外の第三者による本書のいかなる電子複製も一切認められておりません。

ISBN 978-4-86064-693-6 C2082　　　　　　　　　　　　　担当　綿引ゆか

[音声 DL 付] TOEIC L&R TEST
990点獲得 最強 Part 7模試

メディアビーコン 著

B5 変形／定価 2420 円（税込）■ 208 頁＋ 96 頁
ISBN978-4-86064-596-0 C2082

英文の意味はとれていながら正解の根拠を探すのに時間がかかってしまい、結果的に間違える、最後まで終わらないという悩みを解決。新テストでは拾い読みやテクニックだけで全問正解をするのが困難なため、精読が必須。その対策として本書では、長文を正確に素早く読むことができる実力をつけるために、2 か月間計画的にトレーニングを行います。本番に近いクオリティの問題と、徹底した精読と速読の実力をつけるための解説と特訓で、Part7 全問正解を確実にします。速読トレーニング用音声付き。

[音声 DL 付] TOEIC L&R TEST
990 点獲得 Part 5&6 難問模試

メディアビーコン 著

A5 並製／定価 2200 円（税込）■ 280 頁＋ 100 頁
ISBN978-4-86064-668-4 C2082

Part 5&6 の難問ばかりを集めた一冊。今回も狙うは満点獲得です。Part 7 に時間をかけるために正確に素早く解きたい Part 5&6 ですが、実際の問題には難問と言われる問題が必ず数問含まれています。それらに時間をかけてしまうと Part 7 を解く時間に余裕がなくなり、満点から遠のいてしまいます。本書は、そんな難問のパターンを研究し、全ての問題を難問にして高所トレーニングのように最大の負荷をかけた練習をすることで、1 問もとりこぼすことなく、全問正解を狙える実力をつけていきます。

Part 1-4 模試

ベレ出版

TEST 1

LISTENING TEST

In the Listening test, your ability to understand spoken English will be tested. The Listening test has four parts and will take approximately 45 minutes. Directions are given for each part. You need to mark your answers on the answer sheet. Nothing must be written in your test book.

PART 1

Directions: In this part, you will hear four statements about a picture in your test book. After hearing the statements, you must select the one statement that best describes what can be seen in the picture. Then mark your answer on your answer sheet. The statements will be spoken only one time and will not be written in your test book.

Answer (C), "They're wearing suits," best describes the picture. You should mark answer (C) on your answer sheet.

1.

2.

GO ON TO THE NEXT PAGE

3.

4.

5.

6.

GO ON TO THE NEXT PAGE

Directions: In this part, you will hear a question or statement followed by three responses. All of them will be spoken in English. They will be spoken only one time and will not be written in your test book. Select the best response to each question or statement and mark answer (A), (B), or (C) on your answer sheet.

7. Mark your answer.	**20.** Mark your answer.
8. Mark your answer.	**21.** Mark your answer.
9. Mark your answer.	**22.** Mark your answer.
10. Mark your answer.	**23.** Mark your answer.
11. Mark your answer.	**24.** Mark your answer.
12. Mark your answer.	**25.** Mark your answer.
13. Mark your answer.	**26.** Mark your answer.
14. Mark your answer.	**27.** Mark your answer.
15. Mark your answer.	**28.** Mark your answer.
16. Mark your answer.	**29.** Mark your answer.
17. Mark your answer.	**30.** Mark your answer.
18. Mark your answer.	**31.** Mark your answer.
19. Mark your answer.	

Directions: In this part, you will hear conversations between two or more people. You must answer three questions about what is said in each conversation. Select the best response to each question and mark answer (A), (B), (C), or (D) on your answer sheet. The conversations will be spoken only one time and will not be written in your test book.

32. Where does the conversation most likely take place?
(A) At a reception desk
(B) At a bus stop
(C) At a movie theater
(D) At a parking garage

33. What does the woman say about Ms. Harper?
(A) She will be late.
(B) She is meeting one of her clients.
(C) She has changed the meeting location.
(D) She is on a business trip.

34. What does the woman offer the man?
(A) A brochure
(B) A pen
(C) A beverage
(D) An invitation

GO ON TO THE NEXT PAGE

35. Who most likely is the woman?
(A) An engineer
(B) A politician
(C) A tour guide
(D) A park ranger

36. What does the man ask about?
(A) Throwing out some garbage
(B) Inviting some colleagues
(C) Changing a schedule
(D) Planning an event

37. What does the man say he would like to do?
(A) Eat a meal
(B) Take a break
(C) Take some photographs
(D) Do some shopping

38. Who most likely is the woman?
(A) A mechanic
(B) A doctor
(C) A construction worker
(D) A film producer

39. What does the man ask about?
(A) When some work will be completed
(B) Who will be invited to an event
(C) What will be served at a dinner
(D) Where some guests will be seated

40. What does the man mean when he says, "It might be beyond me"?
(A) He may not be able to attend a meeting.
(B) He is not qualified to carry out a task.
(C) He does not have enough time.
(D) He may not understand the woman's explanation.

41. What does the woman ask the man about?
(A) The duration of an event
(B) The purpose of his visit
(C) The opening hours of a business
(D) The deadline of an assignment

42. What is the woman invited to do?
(A) Become a club member
(B) Sample a product
(C) Attend a conference
(D) Have something to eat

43. What does the woman say she will do today?
(A) Review a product
(B) Meet a client
(C) Leave work early
(D) Complete a report

44. What does the woman offer to do?
    (A) Introduce a client
    (B) Teach a course
    (C) Arrange a function
    (D) Check some reviews

45. Why is the woman asked to meet Mr. Rose?
    (A) To express gratitude
    (B) To get some documents
    (C) To return some equipment
    (D) To provide some feedback

46. What will the woman most likely do?
    (A) Send an e-mail
    (B) Place an advertisement
    (C) Make a phone call
    (D) Complete a report

47. Why does the man say, "There's a lot to it"?
    (A) They should distribute an instruction manual.
    (B) A shipment will be very heavy.
    (C) There are several routes to choose from.
    (D) Some preparations will be complicated.

48. What does the man say he has done?
    (A) Written a manual
    (B) Interviewed a candidate
    (C) Sent an e-mail
    (D) Read a book

49. What does the woman say she would like to do?
    (A) Ask some questions
    (B) Order some food
    (C) Look at a menu
    (D) Speak with an expert

50. What does the man say is inconvenient?
    (A) The bathrooms
    (B) The dining room
    (C) The entryway
    (D) The parking lot

51. When does the woman say they will submit the plans?
    (A) On Tuesday
    (B) On Wednesday
    (C) On Thursday
    (D) On Friday

52. What does the man say he will do?
    (A) Call an architect
    (B) Visit the council building
    (C) Speak with employees
    (D) Sit by the window

GO ON TO THE NEXT PAGE

53. What does the man say will happen tomorrow?
    (A) A conference room will be used.
    (B) Invitations will be sent out.
    (C) Some products will be delivered.
    (D) The staff will have a day off.

54. What does the woman say she has to do?
    (A) Obtain some product samples
    (B) Prepare a presentation
    (C) Review a production schedule
    (D) Do some vehicle maintenance

55. What does the woman say she has prepared?
    (A) A meeting schedule
    (B) A shipping label
    (C) A product catalog
    (D) A room layout

56. Where does the man work?
    (A) At a catering company
    (B) At a golf course
    (C) At a travel agency
    (D) At a sports store

57. How many people will participate in the event?
    (A) 10
    (B) 20
    (C) 30
    (D) 40

58. What does the man ask about?
    (A) The woman's contact details
    (B) An event location
    (C) The size of a budget
    (D) Dining requirements

59. Why does the man speak to Helen?
- (A) He wants to see a guest list.
- (B) He needs a client's contact details.
- (C) He is looking for a mobile phone.
- (D) He would like her to work additional hours.

60. What does Helen say about the projector?
- (A) It was recently installed.
- (B) It was malfunctioning.
- (C) It is a well-known brand.
- (D) It has been removed.

61. What do the women agree about?
- (A) Hiring temporary staff members
- (B) Refurbishing a building
- (C) Using a wireless connection
- (D) Rescheduling a meeting

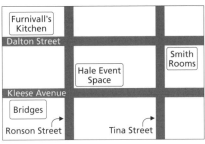

62. What are the speakers planning?
- (A) A dinner
- (B) A clearance sale
- (C) An information session
- (D) A reunion

63. Look at the graphic. Which venue will the speakers most likely choose?
- (A) Furnivall's Kitchen
- (B) Bridges
- (C) Hale Event Space
- (D) Smith Rooms

64. What is the woman instructed to do?
- (A) Check their product inventory
- (B) Get a price estimate
- (C) Update a Web site
- (D) Schedule a holiday

GO ON TO THE NEXT PAGE

Program	Average Viewer Age
Brighton Bake Off	68
Home Reno Challenge	45
This Week Today	30
Fun and Games Show	22

65. What is mentioned about two of the branches?
(A) They are using a new marketing strategy.
(B) They will hire new staff members this month.
(C) They will have their offices renovated.
(D) They have hired an analyst.

66. Look at the graphic. Which sales team will be invited to the head office?
(A) Portland
(B) Seattle
(C) Hartford
(D) Durant

67. Who most likely is Mr. Hargraves?
(A) A sales representative
(B) An accountant
(C) A new recruit
(D) A company president

68. What product do the speakers want to sell?
(A) Mobile phones
(B) Desserts
(C) Motorcycles
(D) Fashion items

69. Look at the graphic. Which program are the speakers most likely to choose?
(A) Brighton Bake Off
(B) Home Reno Challenge
(C) This Week Today
(D) Fun and Games Show

70. What does the woman suggest?
(A) Asking for a discount
(B) Viewing an advertisement
(C) Conducting a survey
(D) Visiting a broadcaster

PART 4

▶TRACK_061～▶TRACK_081

Directions: In this part, you will hear talks given by one speaker. You must answer three questions about what is said in each talk. Select the best response to each question and mark answer (A), (B), (C), or (D) on your answer sheet. The talks will be spoken only one time and will not be written in your test book.

71. Who is the speaker?
    (A) A real estate agent
    (B) A security guard
    (C) A taxi driver
    (D) A plumber

72. What does the speaker say about the property at 45 Wilcox Street?
    (A) The gate is hard to find.
    (B) He cannot gain access.
    (C) The power is disconnected.
    (D) Some guests have arrived.

73. Why does the speaker mention Carrara?
    (A) His company is based there.
    (B) It is outside his territory.
    (C) There is a traffic jam in the area.
    (D) He has to go there for his next job.

74. What is the purpose of the talk?
    (A) To promote a product
    (B) To explain an installation procedure
    (C) To attract new investors
    (D) To thank an employee

75. Why are the solar panels perfect for residential use?
    (A) They are lightweight.
    (B) They are highly customizable.
    (C) They can be purchased in small lots.
    (D) They are easy to install.

76. What does the speaker mean when she says, "You can't go wrong"?
    (A) The product is a safe investment.
    (B) The instructions are easy to follow.
    (C) The store is conveniently located.
    (D) The company provides free shipping.

GO ON TO THE NEXT PAGE

77. Who most likely is the listener?
(A) An actor
(B) A scientist
(C) An author
(D) A musician

78. What is the purpose of the call?
(A) To announce a decision
(B) To describe an offer
(C) To explain a condition
(D) To congratulate a colleague

79. When is the listener invited to the speaker's office?
(A) Today
(B) Tomorrow
(C) Next week
(D) Next month

80. Where does the speaker most likely work?
(A) At an educational institution
(B) At a printing firm
(C) At a construction company
(D) At a cruise provider

81. What will happen at the end of this month?
(A) A deadline will pass.
(B) A payment will be made.
(C) A new rule will be created.
(D) An employee will retire.

82. What does the speaker say listeners should do?
(A) Spend money on upgrading a bridge
(B) Send a document to the speaker
(C) Reduce spending on a project
(D) Dispatch workers to a certain project

83. What does the speaker say about the event?
(A) He helped organize it.
(B) He did not expect to be invited.
(C) He likes the new venue.
(D) He will leave before the end.

84. When did the speaker first attend the event?
(A) One year ago
(B) Two years ago
(C) Three years ago
(D) Four years ago

85. What will the listeners most likely do next?
(A) Open an envelope
(B) Take a seat
(C) Ask questions
(D) Watch a video

86. What does the speaker mean when she says, "you should visit it first"?
    (A) She needs the listener to confirm the location's suitability.
    (B) There is no time to consider other choices.
    (C) The listener must lead a group in the future.
    (D) There is a discount for first-time visitors.

87. What benefit does the speaker mention?
    (A) Modern design
    (B) High visibility
    (C) Low cost
    (D) Popular area

88. What is the listener asked to do?
    (A) Stock a product
    (B) Return a call
    (C) Get a qualification
    (D) Provide a reference

89. What does the speaker mention about White Car Wash locations?
    (A) They are easy to get to.
    (B) They all have the same equipment.
    (C) They are looking for new staff members.
    (D) They have luxurious waiting rooms.

90. What is the company celebrating this week?
    (A) An anniversary
    (B) The completion of a merger
    (C) A grand opening
    (D) The launch of a new service

91. How can listeners get a members card?
    (A) By filling out an online application form
    (B) By purchasing one from a vending machine
    (C) By telling staff that they heard the commercial
    (D) By introducing a customer to the business

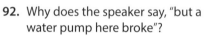

92. Why does the speaker say, "but a water pump here broke"?
    (A) To suggest a change of location
    (B) To ask the listener for some assistance
    (C) To encourage a quick response
    (D) To explain why he can't make an appointment

93. What does the speaker say he will do tomorrow morning?
    (A) Meet with Kate
    (B) Visit the bank
    (C) Work on the farm
    (D) Complete some paperwork

94. Who does the speaker say he will bring to the meeting?
    (A) A colleague
    (B) An accountant
    (C) A relative
    (D) A neighbor

GO ON TO THE NEXT PAGE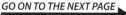

Annual County Fair Schedule			
Friday	Saturday	Sunday	Monday
Set up	Day One	Day Two	Cleanup

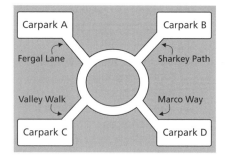

95. Look at the graphic. When does the announcement take place?
(A) On Friday
(B) On Saturday
(C) On Sunday
(D) On Monday

96. Why does the speaker mention 2:00 P.M.?
(A) The parking lot may be full.
(B) The main event will take place.
(C) An announcement will be made.
(D) Ticket booths should be fully staffed.

97. What will the speaker most likely do next?
(A) Inspect some venues
(B) Hold a meeting
(C) Explain a procedure
(D) Introduce a guest

98. What is mentioned about Hampton Gardens?
(A) It has won an award.
(B) It charges an admission fee.
(C) It has historical significance.
(D) It is publicly owned.

99. Look at the graphic. Where will the listeners get on the bus?
(A) At Carpark A
(B) At Carpark B
(C) At Carpark C
(D) At Carpark D

100. What time will the bus depart?
(A) At 2:20 P.M.
(B) At 3:00 P.M.
(C) At 3:20 P.M.
(D) At 4:00 P.M.

This is the end of the Listening test.

TEST 2

LISTENING TEST

In the Listening test, your ability to understand spoken English will be tested. The Listening test has four parts and will take approximately 45 minutes. Directions are given for each part. You need to mark your answers on the answer sheet. Nothing must be written in your test book.

PART 1

Directions: In this part, you will hear four statements about a picture in your test book. After hearing the statements, you must select the one statement that best describes what can be seen in the picture. Then mark your answer on your answer sheet. The statements will be spoken only one time and will not be written in your test book.

Answer (C), "They're wearing suits," best describes the picture. You should mark answer (C) on your answer sheet.

1.

2.

GO ON TO THE NEXT PAGE ▶

3.

4.

5.

6.

GO ON TO THE NEXT PAGE

Directions: In this part, you will hear a question or statement followed by three responses. All of them will be spoken in English. They will be spoken only one time and will not be written in your test book. Select the best response to each question or statement and mark answer (A), (B), or (C) on your answer sheet.

7. Mark your answer.	**20.** Mark your answer.
8. Mark your answer.	**21.** Mark your answer.
9. Mark your answer.	**22.** Mark your answer.
10. Mark your answer.	**23.** Mark your answer.
11. Mark your answer.	**24.** Mark your answer.
12. Mark your answer.	**25.** Mark your answer.
13. Mark your answer.	**26.** Mark your answer.
14. Mark your answer.	**27.** Mark your answer.
15. Mark your answer.	**28.** Mark your answer.
16. Mark your answer.	**29.** Mark your answer.
17. Mark your answer.	**30.** Mark your answer.
18. Mark your answer.	**31.** Mark your answer.
19. Mark your answer.	

PART 3

▶TRACK_115～▶TRACK_141

Directions: In this part, you will hear conversations between two or more people. You must answer three questions about what is said in each conversation. Select the best response to each question and mark answer (A), (B), (C), or (D) on your answer sheet. The conversations will be spoken only one time and will not be written in your test book.

32. What does the man say he is waiting for?
    (A) A visitor
    (B) A delivery
    (C) A taxi
    (D) A broadcast

33. What does the woman say about the clock?
    (A) It was recently installed.
    (B) It may be showing the wrong time.
    (C) It is the same model as hers.
    (D) It needs new batteries.

34. What does the woman offer to do?
    (A) Call a client
    (B) Purchase an item
    (C) Supply some beverages
    (D) Schedule a meeting

GO ON TO THE NEXT PAGE

35. Where does the man most likely work?
(A) At a construction company
(B) At the city council
(C) At a second-hand store
(D) At a fitness center

36. What does the man say about Ms. Cranston?
(A) He has worked with her before.
(B) He spoke with her today.
(C) She was nominated for an award.
(D) She is taking a day off from work.

37. What does the woman say she will do?
(A) Rent a vehicle
(B) Provide a map
(C) Call a colleague
(D) Confirm a schedule

38. What does the woman say about the advertisement?
(A) It will appear tomorrow.
(B) It was published accidentally.
(C) It was larger than expected.
(D) It has been very successful.

39. What is the man concerned about?
(A) The expense
(B) The timing
(C) An error
(D) A delay

40. What is the woman instructed to do?
(A) Purchase a newspaper
(B) Cancel an advertisement
(C) Conduct a customer survey
(D) Allocate some work

41. Where does the man most likely work?
(A) At an equipment rental company
(B) At a carpet cleaning business
(C) At a clothing manufacturer
(D) At a furniture store

42. What does the man say he forgot to do?
(A) Provide some directions
(B) Take a reservation
(C) Return some goods
(D) Charge the woman

43. Why does the woman say, "That's a new one"?
(A) To introduce a colleague
(B) To assign some work
(C) To recommend an item
(D) To express surprise

44. What does the man ask about?
(A) The length of a presentation
(B) A meeting location
(C) A presentation topic
(D) An accounting seminar

45. When will the man be available?
(A) In 5 minutes
(B) In 10 minutes
(C) In 20 minutes
(D) In 30 minutes

46. Where will the woman most likely go next?
(A) To a bathroom
(B) To a restaurant
(C) To a garage
(D) To a kitchen

47. What does the man ask about?
(A) Vehicle parking
(B) Luggage storage
(C) A key return system
(D) A payment method

48. Why did the man ask for a change of room?
(A) His room was too noisy.
(B) He wanted to stay near a colleague.
(C) He was unsatisfied with the scenery.
(D) His room was smaller than he expected.

49. What does the woman say about the hotel?
(A) It is unusual to have a vacancy.
(B) It only accepts online bookings.
(C) It has locations in most cities.
(D) It is popular among vacationers.

50. Where does the conversation most likely take place?
(A) At a hardware store
(B) At an educational institution
(C) At a radio station
(D) At a supermarket

51. What does Jane ask about?
(A) A rental service
(B) A discount coupon
(C) Advertising rates
(D) Home delivery

52. When did Jane last come to the business?
(A) 1 month ago
(B) 2 months ago
(C) 3 months ago
(D) 4 months ago

GO ON TO THE NEXT PAGE

53. What does the woman mean when she says, "It wasn't the best"?
(A) She preferred another movie.
(B) She wanted to go to another cinema.
(C) She disagreed with a review.
(D) She disliked the movie.

54. What does the man say about Jennifer?
(A) She is in charge of a team.
(B) She has already gone home.
(C) She has a new qualification.
(D) She regularly goes to the movies.

55. What does the man say he has been doing?
(A) Watching a movie
(B) Speaking with a client
(C) Fixing some machinery
(D) Preparing for a sporting event

56. What are the speakers discussing?
(A) A photography exhibition
(B) A charity event
(C) A musical performance
(D) An award ceremony

57. What do the men say about the plans?
(A) They will be expensive.
(B) They have been distributed.
(C) They include entertainment.
(D) They have been finalized.

58. What does the woman say she has done?
(A) Approved a purchase
(B) Reserved some equipment
(C) Met with a guest
(D) Provided some information

59. Why did the man call the woman?
    (A) He would like her to take over a project.
    (B) He will arrive at work late today.
    (C) He needs someone with a certain skill.
    (D) He forgot to take a map of the area.

60. What does the woman mention about Mr. Tanaka?
    (A) He is on a business trip this afternoon.
    (B) He is no longer employed at the company.
    (C) He has experience in hospitality.
    (D) He is a factory employee.

61. What will the woman most likely do next?
    (A) Pick up a colleague
    (B) Search for a bus service
    (C) Call Mr. Tanaka
    (D) Cancel a visit

Truman
Three-draw
Filing Cabinet

Height: 110cm
Depth: 42cm

Four width options
Slim: 35cm
Regular: 45cm
Wide: 55cm
Ultra-Wide: 65cm

62. Where do the speakers most likely work?
    (A) At a clinic
    (B) At an appliance store
    (C) At an office supply store
    (D) At a publishing house

63. Look at the graphic. Which filing cabinet will the woman probably order?
    (A) Slim
    (B) Regular
    (C) Wide
    (D) Ultra-Wide

64. What does the woman suggest?
    (A) Scanning some documents
    (B) Ending some subscriptions
    (C) Purchasing some magazines
    (D) Refurbishing an office

GO ON TO THE NEXT PAGE

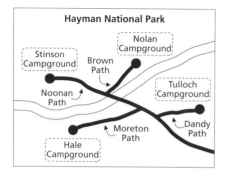

Hayman National Park

Nolan Campground
Stinson Campground
Brown Path
Noonan Path
Tulloch Campground
Moreton Path
Dandy Path
Hale Campground

Morning Tour Options		
8:00	Breakfast Tour	$155.00 per person
9:30	Historical Tour	$145.00 per person
10:00	Pop Culture Tour	$133.00 per person
10:00	Landmark Tour	$130.00 per person

65. Look at the graphic. Which path are the speakers discussing?
(A) Noonan Path
(B) Brown Path
(C) Moreton Path
(D) Dandy Path

66. What does the man say about Truck 4?
(A) It is in the main garage.
(B) It needs some repairs.
(C) It is out of fuel.
(D) It has been taken by a colleague.

67. What does the man say he will do this morning?
(A) Check a fence
(B) Guide some visitors
(C) Purchase some tires
(D) Plant some trees

68. What does the woman ask about?
(A) A menu option
(B) A pickup location
(C) A tour duration
(D) A departure time

69. Look at the graphic. Which tour will the woman take?
(A) Breakfast Tour
(B) Historical Tour
(C) Pop Culture Tour
(D) Landmark Tour

70. What does the woman mention about her accommodations?
(A) It provides a shuttle service.
(B) She is staying nearby.
(C) She will change hotels.
(D) It will not store her luggage.

PART 4   ▶TRACK_142～▶TRACK_162

Directions: In this part, you will hear talks given by one speaker. You must answer three questions about what is said in each talk. Select the best response to each question and mark answer (A), (B), (C), or (D) on your answer sheet. The talks will be spoken only one time and will not be written in your test book.

71. What does the speaker mean when she says, "We have a big day planned"?
(A) A lot of changes will be made.
(B) Employees will be very busy.
(C) A popular event will be held.
(D) A product will be launched.

72. What are employees asked to do?
(A) Package some items
(B) Call a moving company
(C) Fill out a form
(D) Purchase some furniture

73. What does the speaker say about lunch?
(A) It will be provided by the company.
(B) Employees can take extra time.
(C) Food and beverages will be sold at booths.
(D) A receipt is needed for reimbursements.

74. Who is the speaker?
(A) A training officer
(B) A waiter
(C) A bus driver
(D) A tour guide

75. What will happen on May 17?
(A) The listeners will attend a performance.
(B) The listeners will check out of a hotel.
(C) The listeners will be assigned positions.
(D) The listeners will receive a discount.

76. What does the speaker say he will do next?
(A) Deliver some drinks
(B) Explain a procedure
(C) Hand out a guidebook
(D) Take a meal order

GO ON TO THE NEXT PAGE ▶

77. Where does the speaker most likely work?
(A) At a concert venue
(B) At a garage
(C) At a music store
(D) At a construction firm

78. Why did the work take longer than expected?
(A) Some parts were shipped internationally.
(B) Some employees were on holiday.
(C) There was some inclement weather.
(D) The work was complicated.

79. What can the speaker provide for an additional fee?
(A) An accessory
(B) Some clothing
(C) After-hours service
(D) Home delivery

80. What does the speaker say about the meeting?
(A) It will end soon.
(B) It was called suddenly.
(C) Some people did not attend.
(D) The location was changed.

81. What does the speaker say about a product launch?
(A) It will be handled by a new employee.
(B) It has had a budget cut.
(C) It has been rescheduled.
(D) It will be attended by a journalist.

82. What kind of products does the company produce?
(A) Motor vehicles
(B) Sporting goods
(C) Software titles
(D) Office equipment

83. Who is the listener?
(A) A dental patient
(B) A cleaner
(C) A salesperson
(D) A business consultant

84. Why does the speaker mention Toronto?
(A) He will open a new branch there.
(B) He will meet the listener there.
(C) His employer is currently there.
(D) His flight will stop there.

85. What does the speaker suggest?
(A) Meeting at the airport
(B) Registering for a conference
(C) Providing some contact details
(D) Obtaining a qualification

86. Why does the speaker say, "They're not the kind of thing you wear to a fancy dinner"?
(A) To avoid a misunderstanding
(B) To explain a dress requirement
(C) To recommend a different option
(D) To stress the reasonable price

87. How long is the product warranty?
(A) One month
(B) Six months
(C) One year
(D) Two years

88. How can people buy the product?
(A) By ordering from a catalog
(B) By going to a specialty store
(C) By attending a special event
(D) By visiting an online store

89. Who is the speaker?
(A) A musician
(B) A scientist
(C) A radio personality
(D) A talent agent

90. What is the purpose of Mr. Porteous' trip?
(A) To help develop new chemicals
(B) To promote a fiction publication
(C) To speak at a conference
(D) To attend a ceremony

91. What does the speaker ask Mr. Porteous about?
(A) An employment contract
(B) A work schedule
(C) A film adaptation
(D) A career change

92. What is the purpose of the gathering?
(A) To praise an employee
(B) To celebrate a retirement
(C) To show appreciation to a client
(D) To launch a new service

93. What does the speaker imply when he says, "We've been receiving inquiries from all around the state"?
(A) Ms. Forbes has been asked to speak at other firms.
(B) The firm had been put up for sale by its owners.
(C) Ms. Forbes has made the firm more attractive to clients.
(D) The new products have been getting positive reviews.

94. What will the speaker most likely do next?
(A) Distribute a document
(B) Convey a message
(C) Introduce a guest
(D) Explain a schedule

GO ON TO THE NEXT PAGE

Small	1m x 1m	$2,000
Standard	1m x 2m	$2,500
Roomy	2m x 2m	$3,500
Extra Roomy	2m x 3m	$4,000

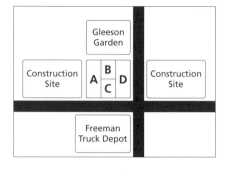

95. Where does the listener most likely work?
(A) At an appliance store
(B) At a supermarket
(C) At a construction firm
(D) At a restaurant

96. What does the speaker ask the listener to do?
(A) Call a supplier
(B) Sign a form
(C) Read a contract
(D) Write a review

97. Look at the graphic. Which model does the speaker recommend?
(A) Small
(B) Standard
(C) Roomy
(D) Extra Roomy

98. When did the construction work probably start?
(A) On Tuesday
(B) On Wednesday
(C) On Thursday
(D) On Friday

99. Look at the graphic. In which office is the accounting department?
(A) In Office A
(B) In Office B
(C) In Office C
(D) In Office D

100. What suggestion does the speaker mention?
(A) Allowing flexible work hours
(B) Having some employees work remotely
(C) Moving some employees to a different office
(D) Postponing the construction work

This is the end of the Listening test.

TEST 3

In the Listening test, your ability to understand spoken English will be tested. The Listening test has four parts and will take approximately 45 minutes. Directions are given for each part. You need to mark your answers on the answer sheet. Nothing must be written in your test book.

PART 1

Directions: In this part, you will hear four statements about a picture in your test book. After hearing the statements, you must select the one statement that best describes what can be seen in the picture. Then mark your answer on your answer sheet. The statements will be spoken only one time and will not be written in your test book.

Answer (C), "They're wearing suits," best describes the picture. You should mark answer (C) on your answer sheet.

1.

2.

GO ON TO THE NEXT PAGE

3.

4.

5.

6.

GO ON TO THE NEXT PAGE ▶

Directions: In this part, you will hear a question or statement followed by three responses. All of them will be spoken in English. They will be spoken only one time and will not be written in your test book. Select the best response to each question or statement and mark answer (A), (B), or (C) on your answer sheet.

7. Mark your answer.	**20.** Mark your answer.
8. Mark your answer.	**21.** Mark your answer.
9. Mark your answer.	**22.** Mark your answer.
10. Mark your answer.	**23.** Mark your answer.
11. Mark your answer.	**24.** Mark your answer.
12. Mark your answer.	**25.** Mark your answer.
13. Mark your answer.	**26.** Mark your answer.
14. Mark your answer.	**27.** Mark your answer.
15. Mark your answer.	**28.** Mark your answer.
16. Mark your answer.	**29.** Mark your answer.
17. Mark your answer.	**30.** Mark your answer.
18. Mark your answer.	**31.** Mark your answer.
19. Mark your answer.	

Directions: In this part, you will hear conversations between two or more people. You must answer three questions about what is said in each conversation. Select the best response to each question and mark answer (A), (B), (C), or (D) on your answer sheet. The conversations will be spoken only one time and will not be written in your test book.

32. What does the woman say about Ms. Carter?
    (A) She will leave the company.
    (B) She has broken a sales record.
    (C) She did some volunteer work.
    (D) She has been promoted.

33. What does the man agree to do?
    (A) Change a date
    (B) Contribute some money
    (C) Order some flowers
    (D) Make a speech

34. What does the woman say about the party?
    (A) It has been postponed.
    (B) An employee will perform a song.
    (C) The company will pay the bill.
    (D) It will be held at a hotel.

GO ON TO THE NEXT PAGE

35. What is the purpose of the phone call?
(A) To inquire about some furnishings
(B) To suggest a venue
(C) To schedule an interview
(D) To introduce an artist

36. How long is the exhibition?
(A) Two weeks
(B) One week
(C) Three days
(D) One day

37. What does the woman offer to do?
(A) Send some free tickets
(B) Sell some artwork
(C) Take a photograph
(D) Provide contact details

38. Who most likely is the woman?
(A) An event planner
(B) A florist
(C) A mechanic
(D) A hotel manager

39. What does the man say has happened?
(A) Some parcels were mislabeled.
(B) A delivery arrived late.
(C) A meeting has been rescheduled.
(D) Some goods have been damaged.

40. What does the woman say she will do?
(A) Offer a discount
(B) Load a vehicle
(C) Speak with a colleague
(D) Call a customer

41. What does the man say they should do?
(A) Provide feedback on a presentation
(B) Discuss a sales report
(C) Choose a candidate
(D) Revise a travel schedule

42. Why are the women concerned?
(A) There are too few candidates.
(B) They do not have enough time.
(C) There are not any rooms available.
(D) They have already spent their budget.

43. What does the man mean when he says, "I'm sure we can manage"?
(A) He thinks they can find a solution.
(B) He does not want to hire a new manager.
(C) He will start a new business.
(D) He does not need assistance.

44. What type of business does the man work for?
(A) An architecture firm
(B) A financial institution
(C) A clothing manufacturer
(D) A travel agency

45. What does the man say about Ms. Crenshaw?
(A) She is unavailable.
(B) She has a new phone number.
(C) She will give a speech.
(D) She is dependable.

46. What does the woman want to discuss?
(A) The design of an award
(B) A magazine subscription
(C) The cost of a construction project
(D) An invitation to an event

47. What does the man say will happen today?
(A) Some food will be delivered.
(B) An athletic event will be held.
(C) He will make a presentation.
(D) An inspection will take place.

48. What problem does the woman mention?
(A) There is a shortage of ingredients.
(B) Some reservations were canceled.
(C) An employee is absent.
(D) Some equipment is malfunctioning.

49. What does the man say he will do?
(A) Call a town office
(B) Attend a banquet
(C) Speak with an athlete
(D) Take part in a tour

50. What kind of event are the speakers attending?
(A) An employee orientation
(B) A shareholders' meeting
(C) A product launch
(D) A business conference

51. Why does the man address the woman?
(A) He plans to leave early.
(B) He has not been given a document.
(C) He does not have anywhere to sit.
(D) He would like to ask a question.

52. What will the woman talk about this afternoon?
(A) Timeline of an event
(B) New features of an item
(C) Some company policies
(D) Some membership benefits

GO ON TO THE NEXT PAGE

53. Why does the woman speak to the man?
    (A) She wants to see a catalog.
    (B) She would like to exchange an item.
    (C) She needs an instruction manual.
    (D) She cannot find a product.

54. Why does the woman say, "I only have a small van"?
    (A) To request an alternative
    (B) To make a suggestion
    (C) To explain an expense
    (D) To turn down an offer

55. Who will the man ask for assistance?
    (A) A warehouse worker
    (B) A sales assistant
    (C) A mechanic
    (D) A store manager

56. Where do the men most likely work?
    (A) At a catering company
    (B) At a moving company
    (C) At a construction firm
    (D) At an accounting firm

57. What does the woman offer the men?
    (A) An invitation
    (B) A contract
    (C) A ride
    (D) A beverage

58. Where does the woman direct the men?
    (A) To a loading bay
    (B) To a dining room
    (C) To a waiting room
    (D) To a meeting room

59. What does the man ask about?
   (A) Admission fees
   (B) Dress recommendations
   (C) Guided tours
   (D) Accommodation availability

60. What does the woman offer to do?
   (A) Reserve a room
   (B) Provide an introduction
   (C) Check a timetable
   (D) Recommend a restaurant

61. What does the woman say she is unsure of?
   (A) Operating hours
   (B) A maintenance schedule
   (C) Language skills
   (D) Weather conditions

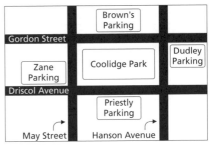

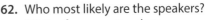

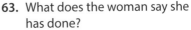

62. Who most likely are the speakers?
   (A) Conference attendees
   (B) Restaurant patrons
   (C) Film critics
   (D) Financial experts

63. What does the woman say she has done?
   (A) Purchased some tickets
   (B) Invited a colleague to an event
   (C) Left one of her belongings behind
   (D) Sent some product samples

64. Look at the graphic. Where will the speakers probably go next?
   (A) To Zane Parking
   (B) To Brown's Parking
   (C) To Priestly Parking
   (D) To Dudley Parking

GO ON TO THE NEXT PAGE

Room / Incident	
Hoover (457)	Noise
Bobson (1041)	Broken air conditioner
Kelly (987)	Luggage sent to the wrong room
Oda (546)	Room too small

Meeting Room A	Meeting Room B	●▭● Lounge
Meeting Room C	Meeting Room D	●▭●
Restaurant	Reception	
▭ ▭ ✕ ✕ ✕		Gift Shop

65. What does the woman say about the man?
(A) He has been hired to repair a device.
(B) He works in the evenings.
(C) He is at the beginning of his shift.
(D) He reported a problem to reception.

66. Look at the graphic. Which guest was moved to another room?
(A) Hoover
(B) Bobson
(C) Kelly
(D) Oda

67. What does the man say he will do?
(A) Order a device
(B) Cancel a reservation
(C) Request some repairs
(D) Apologize to a guest

68. What does the woman say she will do?
(A) Interview some candidates
(B) Have confidential meetings
(C) Make a presentation
(D) Arrange an event

69. Look at the graphic. Which room will the woman probably rent?
(A) Meeting Room A
(B) Meeting Room B
(C) Meeting Room C
(D) Meeting Room D

70. What is mentioned about the meeting rooms?
(A) They have projectors installed in them.
(B) Hotel guests can get a discount.
(C) They are available 24-hours a day.
(D) Furniture must be rented separately.

PART 4

▶TRACK_223～▶TRACK_243

Directions: In this part, you will hear talks given by one speaker. You must answer three questions about what is said in each talk. Select the best response to each question and mark answer (A), (B), (C), or (D) on your answer sheet. The talks will be spoken only one time and will not be written in your test book.

71. What is mentioned about AM Drive?
(A) It has multiple presenters.
(B) It does not have any advertisements.
(C) It features a competition.
(D) It lasts three hours.

72. Who is Ms. Singh?
(A) An entertainer
(B) An athlete
(C) A politician
(D) A scientist

73. What will Ms. Singh most likely speak about?
(A) Her recent discovery
(B) Her upcoming holiday
(C) Her retirement plans
(D) Her volunteer activity

74. What is the company going to do soon?
(A) Open a new store
(B) Relocate to another city
(C) Sponsor an event
(D) Release a product

75. What does the speaker ask employees to do?
(A) View some designs
(B) Attend a meeting
(C) Call a client
(D) Make a recommendation

76. Why are the listeners directed to a Web site?
(A) To register for an event
(B) To watch a promotional video
(C) To read an article
(D) To order some clothing

GO ON TO THE NEXT PAGE

77. What is the purpose of the call?
    (A) To explain a shortage of
        inventory
    (B) To request an invoice
    (C) To announce a policy change
    (D) To report a billing error

78. What did the listener order?
    (A) Timber flooring
    (B) Roofing tiles
    (C) Exterior paint
    (D) A shower unit

79. What does the speaker mean
    when he says, "We can't have
    that"?
    (A) Some products are no longer
        available.
    (B) He will avoid a delivery delay.
    (C) Some goods will be returned.
    (D) A situation would be
        unacceptable.

80. What does the speaker say about
    part of Lee Road?
    (A) It has been flooded.
    (B) It is being repaired.
    (C) It is congested.
    (D) It was widened.

81. When will road conditions
    change?
    (A) On June 1
    (B) On June 5
    (C) On June 10
    (D) On June 15

82. What will the listeners most likely
    hear next?
    (A) A weather update
    (B) An interview
    (C) Some news
    (D) Some music

83. What is the topic of the
    workshop?
    (A) Improving customer
        satisfaction levels
    (B) Hiring appropriate people for
        positions
    (C) Raising the effectiveness of
        advertising
    (D) Increasing production speed

84. What does the speaker say about
    the next activity?
    (A) It is very popular.
    (B) It will be performed in teams.
    (C) It will take too long.
    (D) It has not been tried before.

85. What are the listeners asked to
    do?
    (A) Take a break
    (B) Talk among each other
    (C) Complete a survey
    (D) Leave early

86. What is the news mainly about?
(A) The expansion of a local factory
(B) A change in government regulations
(C) A company's cost-cutting measure
(D) The appointment of a new company president

87. What effect will the change have on employees?
(A) They will have a reduced workload.
(B) They will be able to work from home.
(C) They will receive a pay increase.
(D) They will be asked to work in different departments.

88. What does the speaker say is important?
(A) Planning for changes well in advance
(B) Taking into account the opinions of employees
(C) Ensuring that equipment is properly maintained
(D) Proving adequate training to employees

89. What is mentioned about the business?
(A) It has been operating for a long time.
(B) It offers discounts to local residents.
(C) It advertises in a magazine.
(D) It is looking to hire additional staff.

90. What is mentioned about Mondays at the business?
(A) Some entertainment is provided.
(B) It offers discounts.
(C) There is no dinner service.
(D) It requires reservations.

91. Why does the speaker say, "This month, we're testing some new menu items"?
(A) To explain slower than usual service
(B) To encourage the listeners to come
(C) To celebrate the arrival of a new chef
(D) To inform the listeners of a temporary closure

92. What is mentioned about the organization?
(A) It is publicly owned.
(B) It has multiple locations.
(C) It will hold a publicity event.
(D) It is staffed by volunteers.

93. What will the organization probably do?
(A) Hire additional staff
(B) Purchase fitness equipment
(C) Offer a new service
(D) Change its operating hours

94. What does the speaker mean when she says, "Now, we're in a position to do something"?
(A) They have the money to accommodate some requests.
(B) They have moved to a more convenient address.
(C) They have rearranged the office layout.
(D) They have hired experts to improve their services.

GO ON TO THE NEXT PAGE

Conference Room Reservations (TODAY)	
11:00 A.M. ~ 12:00 NOON	
Room A	Product Development (Planning)
Room B	Administration (Monthly Meeting)
Room C	Closed for renovations
Room D	Sales (Client Meeting)

Dreamland Park

Rides Closed for Inspection This Week

Sunday	Loop-the-Loop
Monday	The Claw
Tuesday	Tri Wing Swing Thing
Wednesday	Wet Wonder
Thursday	Thunder Mountain
Friday	Gravitoni

95. When does the speaker say he reserved a conference room?
(A) Yesterday
(B) Two days ago
(C) Two weeks ago
(D) Last month

96. Look at the graphic. Which room has the listener reserved?
(A) Room A
(B) Room B
(C) Room C
(D) Room D

97. What does the speaker suggest doing?
(A) Hiring an assistant
(B) Requesting some repairs
(C) Organizing a social gathering
(D) Visiting a branch office

98. Look at the graphic. When is the announcement being made?
(A) On Sunday
(B) On Monday
(C) On Tuesday
(D) On Wednesday

99. What is mentioned about returner's tickets?
(A) They are valid for 12 months.
(B) They are only sold to registered members.
(C) They entitle holders to free refreshments.
(D) They are available at the exit.

100. What does the speaker remind people to do?
(A) Hold on to their tickets
(B) Drink enough water
(C) Enter a contest
(D) Visit the Web site

This is the end of the Listening test.

TEST 4

In the Listening test, your ability to understand spoken English will be tested. The Listening test has four parts and will take approximately 45 minutes. Directions are given for each part. You need to mark your answers on the answer sheet. Nothing must be written in your test book.

PART 1

Directions: In this part, you will hear four statements about a picture in your test book. After hearing the statements, you must select the one statement that best describes what can be seen in the picture. Then mark your answer on your answer sheet. The statements will be spoken only one time and will not be written in your test book.

Answer (C), "They're wearing suits," best describes the picture. You should mark answer (C) on your answer sheet.

1.

2.

GO ON TO THE NEXT PAGE

3.

4.

5.

6.

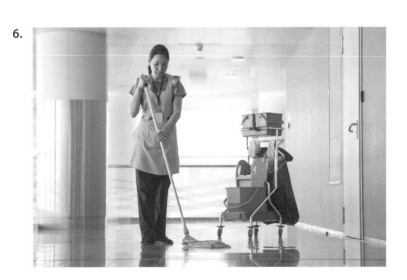

GO ON TO THE NEXT PAGE

Directions: In this part, you will hear a question or statement followed by three responses. All of them will be spoken in English. They will be spoken only one time and will not be written in your test book. Select the best response to each question or statement and mark answer (A), (B), or (C) on your answer sheet.

7. Mark your answer.

8. Mark your answer.

9. Mark your answer.

10. Mark your answer.

11. Mark your answer.

12. Mark your answer.

13. Mark your answer.

14. Mark your answer.

15. Mark your answer.

16. Mark your answer.

17. Mark your answer.

18. Mark your answer.

19. Mark your answer.

20. Mark your answer.

21. Mark your answer.

22. Mark your answer.

23. Mark your answer.

24. Mark your answer.

25. Mark your answer.

26. Mark your answer.

27. Mark your answer.

28. Mark your answer.

29. Mark your answer.

30. Mark your answer.

31. Mark your answer.

Directions: In this part, you will hear conversations between two or more people. You must answer three questions about what is said in each conversation. Select the best response to each question and mark answer (A), (B), (C), or (D) on your answer sheet. The conversations will be spoken only one time and will not be written in your test book.

32. What does the man ask the woman about?
    (A) Her opinion on a suggestion
    (B) Her plans for the weekend
    (C) The location of a cabinet
    (D) The cost of some supplies

33. When is the next garbage collection?
    (A) On Wednesday
    (B) On Thursday
    (C) On Friday
    (D) On Saturday

34. What does the woman say she will do?
    (A) Introduce a dependable recycling company
    (B) Post a schedule on the company bulletin board
    (C) Have some employees sort some items
    (D) Ask for an extension on a deadline

GO ON TO THE NEXT PAGE

35. Who most likely are the women?
(A) City officials
(B) Event organizers
(C) Bicycle repairpersons
(D) Professional athletes

36. What does the man say he has brought with him?
(A) A bicycle
(B) An assistant
(C) Some identification
(D) Some money

37. What is the man asked to do?
(A) Give a presentation
(B) Write down her address
(C) Purchase some equipment
(D) Attend a briefing

38. What does the woman want to do?
(A) Provide training
(B) Schedule a vacation
(C) Reduce spending
(D) Hold a banquet

39. What does the man suggest?
(A) Speaking with an expert
(B) Buying some new equipment
(C) Checking a calendar
(D) Calling a venue

40. What does the man say he will do?
(A) Return from a business trip early
(B) Reserve a conference room
(C) Order some goods from an online store
(D) Encourage employees to share their ideas

41. What does the woman say she did in high school?
(A) She joined an academic competition.
(B) She became friends with her business partner.
(C) She created a software program.
(D) She founded a club for computer enthusiasts.

42. Why does the woman say, "You've done your homework"?
(A) To reassure the man
(B) To suggest taking a break
(C) To express admiration
(D) To explain an outcome

43. What does the man say about SSA?
(A) It has won awards.
(B) It was a good investment.
(C) It is popular among people of all ages.
(D) It has been sold several times.

44. How did the woman learn about the man's business?
(A) From a colleague
(B) From an advertisement
(C) From a Web site
(D) From a consultant

45. Why does the woman say she will move?
(A) To be closer to her family
(B) To take a new job
(C) To save money on rent
(D) To have more room

46. What does the man ask the woman?
(A) How she will pay for a service
(B) How much she made from a sale
(C) What she will have for lunch
(D) Why she left her hometown

---

47. What will the speakers most likely do this evening?
(A) Take part in a dinner cruise
(B) Meet with a client
(C) Attend a theatrical production
(D) Go on a business trip

48. By what time does the man say they should leave the office?
(A) 5:00 P.M.
(B) 5:30 P.M.
(C) 6:00 P.M.
(D) 6:30 P.M.

49. What does the woman ask the man to do?
(A) Reserve a vehicle
(B) Review some figures
(C) Order some food
(D) Deliver a document

---

50. When does the man say he purchased the appliance?
(A) Yesterday
(B) A week ago
(C) A month ago
(D) A year ago

51. What does the woman say about her department?
(A) It was founded very recently.
(B) It refers some issues to its suppliers.
(C) It does not provide service to some locations.
(D) It has recently hired some new employees.

52. What problem does the man mention?
(A) A device is ineffective.
(B) A delivery is late.
(C) Running costs are too high.
(D) The wrong model was sent.

GO ON TO THE NEXT PAGE

53. Where do the speakers most likely work?
(A) At an online store
(B) At a hospital
(C) At a utility company
(D) At a garage

54. What does the man mean when he says, "It goes to show"?
(A) A situation was just as he expected.
(B) An instruction video was very helpful.
(C) A performance will attract many viewers.
(D) A customer will be surprised.

55. What does the man suggest?
(A) Requesting a catalog
(B) Providing some contact details
(C) Setting up a meeting
(D) Sending an e-mail

56. What are the speakers discussing?
(A) Foreign branch offices
(B) Employment references
(C) Job descriptions
(D) Room reservations

57. What is mentioned about Mr. White?
(A) He was late for an interview.
(B) He has worked with the speakers before.
(C) He will obtain a new qualification.
(D) He has lived abroad.

58. What does the woman suggest?
(A) Entertaining a client
(B) Promoting an employee
(C) Placing an advertisement
(D) Completing a task at home

59. Why is the man going to Beaudesert?
   (A) To interview an applicant
   (B) To purchase some land
   (C) To inspect a facility
   (D) To speak with a client

60. What does the woman say about the accommodations in Beaudesert?
   (A) They are fully booked.
   (B) They are uncomfortable.
   (C) They are reasonably priced.
   (D) They are convenient.

61. What does the woman suggest?
   (A) Postponing a visit
   (B) Speaking with a colleague
   (C) Renting a vehicle
   (D) Checking a Web site

Gainsmax Fitness Center Rates		
One Day Pass	Gym Only	$18
	Gym and Sauna	$24
One Week Pass	Gym Only	$90
	Gym and Sauna	$120
Two Week Pass	Gym Only	$135
	Gym and Sauna	$180

62. What is the purpose of the man's trip?
   (A) To visit relatives
   (B) To inspect a venue
   (C) To attend a conference
   (D) To take part in a contest

63. Look at the graphic. How much will the man most likely pay?
   (A) $18
   (B) $24
   (C) $90
   (D) $120

64. What does the woman say she will do?
   (A) Ask the man to sign an agreement
   (B) Give the man a discount on some clothing
   (C) Watch a televised sporting event
   (D) Have a colleague show the man around

GO ON TO THE NEXT PAGE ▶

Conference Room Tables	
Ultra-Executive (360cm × 120cm)	$1,400
Executive (300cm × 120cm)	$1,200
Premium (240cm × 120cm)	$900
Standard (200cm × 120cm)	$700

23A	23B	23C	23D	23E	23F
24A	24B	24C	24D	24E	24F

Aisle

65. Look at the graphic. Which table will the speakers most likely buy?
(A) Ultra-Executive
(B) Executive
(C) Premium
(D) Standard

66. What does the woman say about the chairs?
(A) They will arrive within a week.
(B) There are not enough for a meeting.
(C) There is no need to buy new ones.
(D) They cannot be repaired.

67. What is the man asked to do?
(A) Supply some product samples
(B) Obtain price estimates
(C) Measure a room
(D) Schedule a meeting

68. What does the woman say happened today?
(A) Her luggage was misplaced.
(B) Her reservation was canceled.
(C) Her flight was redirected.
(D) Her train was delayed.

69. Look at the graphic. Where will the woman most likely sit?
(A) In 23A
(B) In 23D
(C) In 24C
(D) In 24E

70. What does the man give to the woman?
(A) Some luggage
(B) A voucher
(C) A schedule
(D) Some labels

PART 4

⊙TRACK_304~⊙TRACK_324

TEST 1
TEST 2
TEST 3
TEST 4
TEST 5

Directions: In this part, you will hear talks given by one speaker. You must answer three questions about what is said in each talk. Select the best response to each question and mark answer (A), (B), (C), or (D) on your answer sheet. The talks will be spoken only one time and will not be written in your test book.

71. What problem does the speaker mention?
(A) A location is inconvenient.
(B) Some products are faulty.
(C) An employee is late.
(D) Sales have been dwindling.

72. What does the speaker imply when she says, "It's their one day off"?
(A) Some employees will be grateful.
(B) An event will be unpopular.
(C) Employees should choose what to do.
(D) The schedule has an error.

73. What does the speaker suggest?
(A) Offering an additional day off
(B) Changing a schedule
(C) Holding a contest
(D) Canceling an information session

74. Where does the speaker most likely work?
(A) At a swimming school
(B) At a real estate agency
(C) At an auction house
(D) At a television station

75. What problem does the speaker mention?
(A) The business is short-staffed.
(B) The business has lost some income.
(C) Advertising costs have been increasing.
(D) Some equipment needs to be replaced.

76. What does the speaker suggest?
(A) Requesting assistance from an expert
(B) Testing some product samples
(C) Relocating to a more suitable address
(D) Adopting the strategy of another business

GO ON TO THE NEXT PAGE

77. Where is the announcement being made?
(A) At an Internet café
(B) At a fitness club
(C) At a library
(D) At a restaurant

78. What is one purpose of the announcement?
(A) To inform people about a closing time
(B) To thank guests for attending an event
(C) To announce a change in policy
(D) To request assistance with a task

79. What does the speaker say about lost property?
(A) It should be handed to a manager.
(B) It will be disposed of after a week.
(C) It has been reported more often recently.
(D) It is kept at a different location.

80. Who is Ralph Wilson?
(A) A musician
(B) A news reporter
(C) A filmmaker
(D) A sports person

81. What does the speaker mention about Ms. Chow?
(A) She took part in a contest.
(B) She will replace a retiring employee.
(C) She is on a business trip.
(D) She has a lot of experience.

82. What will probably take place today?
(A) A fashion show
(B) A retirement party
(C) A sporting event
(D) An award ceremony

83. What does the speaker want the listeners to do?
(A) Complete a questionnaire
(B) Attend an information session
(C) Put away personal items
(D) Take note of some contact details

84. What can the listeners win?
(A) Concert tickets
(B) A meal with a celebrity
(C) A travel package
(D) Clothing items

85. What is implied about Leichardt Street?
(A) It has a major train station.
(B) It has some important historical landmarks.
(C) It is in a shopping district.
(D) It is known for its unique architecture.

86. What does the speaker say he has done?
(A) Delivered some materials
(B) Evaluated a care facility
(C) Visited Ms. Thornton's place of work
(D) Rescheduled an appointment

87. What kind of work does the speaker most likely do?
(A) Painting
(B) Gardening
(C) Construction
(D) Medicine

88. What will the speaker's assistant do?
(A) Provide some computer graphics
(B) Order some pharmaceuticals
(C) Install a device
(D) Arrange a meeting

89. What is the purpose of the event?
(A) To promote healthy lifestyles
(B) To raise some money
(C) To attract more tourists
(D) To celebrate an anniversary

90. Who is Goldy Garland?
(A) An educator
(B) A politician
(C) An event organizer
(D) A workshop facilitator

91. Why does the speaker say, "You can't afford to miss out"?
(A) To stress the benefits of an event
(B) To explain the cost of admission
(C) To encourage people to lead workshops
(D) To offer people an affordable alternative

92. Where does the talk most likely take place?
(A) At a client meeting
(B) At a press conference
(C) At a training workshop
(D) At a company banquet

93. What does the speaker say about telephone calls?
(A) They are recorded.
(B) They must be answered quickly.
(C) They are not cost-effective.
(D) They take less time than e-mail.

94. What does the speaker mean when he says, "would anyone like to volunteer"?
(A) He needs some people to represent the company.
(B) He would like some assistance with an environmental project.
(C) He hopes someone will choose to go first.
(D) He wonders when to schedule a vacation.

GO ON TO THE NEXT PAGE

www.sampsonelectrical.com/ycs	
Televisions	Computers and Phones
Thursday, December 13	Friday, December 14
Kitchen Appliances	Gaming Devices
Saturday, December 15	Sunday, December 16

Shandling Circus

performing at
787 Johanna Road
From June 6 to June 10

Show times

6:00 P.M. (Tuesday to Friday)
10:00 A.M. 1:00 P.M., and 8:00 P.M. (Saturday)
10:30 A.M. and 1:00 P.M. (Sunday)

95. Look at the graphic. What is on sale today?
(A) Televisions
(B) Computers and Phones
(C) Kitchen Appliances
(D) Gaming Devices

96. What is the maximum discount the listeners can expect?
(A) 40 percent
(B) 30 percent
(C) 20 percent
(D) 10 percent

97. What can the listeners do by visiting the Web site?
(A) Reserve items for later purchase
(B) Register as a customer
(C) Learn more about items for sale
(D) Check the nearest store location

98. What does the speaker mention about the circus?
(A) It has a long history.
(B) It is a family business.
(C) It advertises on the radio.
(D) It travels internationally.

99. Look at the graphic. When does the talk most likely take place?
(A) On Tuesday
(B) On Friday
(C) On Saturday
(D) On Sunday

100. Why are some people advised to visit an administration booth?
(A) To apply for a position
(B) To retrieve lost property
(C) To have their parking validated
(D) To reserve some transportation

This is the end of the Listening test.

TEST 5

In the Listening test, your ability to understand spoken English will be tested. The Listening test has four parts and will take approximately 45 minutes. Directions are given for each part. You need to mark your answers on the answer sheet. Nothing must be written in your test book.

PART 1

Directions: In this part, you will hear four statements about a picture in your test book. After hearing the statements, you must select the one statement that best describes what can be seen in the picture. Then mark your answer on your answer sheet. The statements will be spoken only one time and will not be written in your test book.

Answer (C), "They're wearing suits," best describes the picture. You should mark answer (C) on your answer sheet.

1.

2.

GO ON TO THE NEXT PAGE

3.

4.

5.

6.

GO ON TO THE NEXT PAGE ▸

Directions: In this part, you will hear a question or statement followed by three responses. All of them will be spoken in English. They will be spoken only one time and will not be written in your test book. Select the best response to each question or statement and mark answer (A), (B), or (C) on your answer sheet.

7. Mark your answer.	**20.** Mark your answer.
8. Mark your answer.	**21.** Mark your answer.
9. Mark your answer.	**22.** Mark your answer.
10. Mark your answer.	**23.** Mark your answer.
11. Mark your answer.	**24.** Mark your answer.
12. Mark your answer.	**25.** Mark your answer.
13. Mark your answer.	**26.** Mark your answer.
14. Mark your answer.	**27.** Mark your answer.
15. Mark your answer.	**28.** Mark your answer.
16. Mark your answer.	**29.** Mark your answer.
17. Mark your answer.	**30.** Mark your answer.
18. Mark your answer.	**31.** Mark your answer.
19. Mark your answer.	

PART 3 ⏵TRACK_358~⏵TRACK_384

Directions: In this part, you will hear conversations between two or more people. You must answer three questions about what is said in each conversation. Select the best response to each question and mark answer (A), (B), (C), or (D) on your answer sheet. The conversations will be spoken only one time and will not be written in your test book.

32. Where do the speakers most likely work?
(A) At a shoe factory
(B) At a shipping company
(C) At a hardware store
(D) At an equipment rental firm

33. What does the man suggest?
(A) Spending more on advertising
(B) Reverting to a previously used product
(C) Conducting a satisfaction survey
(D) Redesigning a product

34. Why are the speakers unable to order an item?
(A) The Web site is temporarily unavailable.
(B) A product was discontinued.
(C) A supplier has gone out of business.
(D) There was a supply chain issue.

GO ON TO THE NEXT PAGE

35. What is the purpose of the call?
  (A) To request permission for a purchase
  (B) To recommend a model
  (C) To check on a price
  (D) To make a reservation

36. What does the man request?
  (A) A brand name
  (B) The proof of purchase
  (C) The number of passengers
  (D) Contact details

37. What does the woman say about the vehicle?
  (A) It is in need of some repairs.
  (B) It was purchased from a dealer.
  (C) It will be kept in a company garage.
  (D) It will be used for commuting.

38. What are the speakers mainly discussing?
  (A) Testing some products
  (B) Changing a supplier
  (C) Choosing a restaurant
  (D) Reading some reviews

39. What does the man suggest?
  (A) Raising production capacity
  (B) Updating a manual
  (C) Requesting a meeting
  (D) Giving a warning

40. What will the man do this afternoon?
  (A) Attend an industry conference
  (B) Assemble some office furniture
  (C) Get a medical checkup
  (D) Speak with a prospective customer

41. Where does the conversation most likely take place?
  (A) In a taxi
  (B) At an airport
  (C) In an office
  (D) On a train

42. What does the man ask the woman to do?
  (A) Call a colleague
  (B) Check a schedule
  (C) Install an application
  (D) Charge his phone

43. What does the man say he will do?
  (A) Purchase some tickets
  (B) Check in at a hotel
  (C) Retrieve some luggage
  (D) Reserve a vehicle

44. Why is the man concerned?
    (A) He has misplaced some equipment.
    (B) He does not have time to finish a project.
    (C) His department needs a bigger budget.
    (D) His computer has been malfunctioning.

45. What does the man mean when he says, "I might take you up on that"?
    (A) He may ask the woman to accompany him.
    (B) He hopes to give the woman a promotion.
    (C) He would like to show the woman his new car.
    (D) He may accept the woman's offer.

46. What does the woman say about Wilcox?
    (A) It is on her way home.
    (B) It is the location of a supplier.
    (C) It will host an important event.
    (D) It has cheap rent.

47. What did the woman do yesterday?
    (A) She visited a competitor.
    (B) She installed some software.
    (C) She had a client meeting.
    (D) She interviewed a candidate.

48. What does the man say about Ms. Thompson?
    (A) She is a company founder.
    (B) She introduced him to the company.
    (C) She is good at her job.
    (D) She likes to travel.

49. What does the woman ask the man to do?
    (A) Announce a decision
    (B) Advertise a position
    (C) Write a news article
    (D) Send an e-mail

50. What is the purpose of the man's visit?
    (A) To pick up his car
    (B) To apply for a position
    (C) To have a vehicle inspected
    (D) To sell a used item

51. Why is the woman unable to accept the man's request?
    (A) Some work has not been completed.
    (B) An appointment is necessary.
    (C) A meeting has been rescheduled.
    (D) There is a shortage of some supplies.

52. What does the man say he will do?
    (A) Check his schedule
    (B) Wait in reception
    (C) Use public transportation
    (D) Try another dealership

GO ON TO THE NEXT PAGE

53. What did the woman do yesterday?
    (A) She looked at some applications.
    (B) She submitted a report.
    (C) She updated employee files.
    (D) She proofread a manual.

54. What does the man ask the woman to do?
    (A) Call a printing company
    (B) Resubmit a report
    (C) Meet with a client
    (D) Schedule some interviews

55. Why does the man say, "I'll leave the rest to you"?
    (A) To suggest that the woman take a break
    (B) To offer the woman some food
    (C) To allow the woman to use some space
    (D) To put the woman in charge of a task

56. Who most likely are the men?
    (A) Real estate agents
    (B) Translators
    (C) Investors
    (D) Financial experts

57. What does Yutaka suggest?
    (A) Outsourcing some help
    (B) Asking for an extension
    (C) Offering a discount
    (D) Dividing some work

58. What will the woman do next?
    (A) Register for a workshop
    (B) Confirm a price
    (C) Send an invitation
    (D) Speak with a client

59. What is the conversation mainly about?
    (A) Hiring a gardener
    (B) Entertaining a visitor
    (C) Opening a restaurant
    (D) Conducting a survey

60. What will the speakers most likely do this week?
    (A) Advertise a new service
    (B) Go to a government office
    (C) Reward some employees
    (D) Try a new menu item

61. Where will the speakers discuss ideas?
    (A) In a plane
    (B) In a car
    (C) In a train
    (D) In a bus

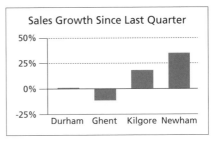

Sales Growth Since Last Quarter

62. What kind of products does the company sell?
    (A) Agricultural equipment
    (B) Recreational vehicles
    (C) Farm produce
    (D) Factory machinery

63. Look at the graphic. Which office switched to online advertising?
    (A) Durham
    (B) Ghent
    (C) Kilgore
    (D) Newham

64. What does the man say the company should do?
    (A) Encourage employees to exercise more
    (B) Be careful when adopting new strategies
    (C) Ask for advice from a consultant
    (D) Share ideas with staff at other offices

GO ON TO THE NEXT PAGE

Premiere Inn Restaurant Locations

8	Cloud 9	Pierre's
7		
6		
5		Sea
4		Captain
3		
Schooners 2		
1	Reception	Entry

Bolian	5 Seater	$50 per day
Portlander	6 Seater	$63 per day
Tavarish	8 Seater	$72 per day
Hoovie	10 Seater	$80 per day

65. What is the purpose of the man's visit?
(A) To attend an event
(B) To repair some equipment
(C) To meet with a client
(D) To have a job interview

66. Look at the graphic. Which floor will the man go to next?
(A) The 2nd Floor
(B) The 4th Floor
(C) The 5th Floor
(D) The 8th Floor

67. What does the woman say?
(A) The hotel has a vacancy.
(B) A reservation has been changed.
(C) A manager is in a meeting.
(D) The man has arrived early.

68. Where do the speakers most likely work?
(A) At a production company
(B) At a software developer
(C) At a construction company
(D) At a real estate agency

69. Look at the graphic. Which car will the speakers most likely choose?
(A) Bolian
(B) Portlander
(C) Tavarish
(D) Hoovie

70. What does the woman want at the accommodation?
(A) A meeting space
(B) Pleasant dining facilities
(C) High-speed Internet access
(D) Scenic views

Directions: In this part, you will hear talks given by one speaker. You must answer three questions about what is said in each talk. Select the best response to each question and mark answer (A), (B), (C), or (D) on your answer sheet. The talks will be spoken only one time and will not be written in your test book.

71. Where does the talk most likely take place?
(A) At a press conference
(B) At a finance seminar
(C) At a retirement party
(D) At an employee orientation

72. Why does the speaker say, "She was there for 18 years"?
(A) To express gratitude to Ms. Day
(B) To explain Ms. Day's decision to retire
(C) To suggest hiring Ms. Day for a position
(D) To stress Ms. Day's qualifications

73. What will the listeners do next?
(A) Complete a survey
(B) Greet a visitor
(C) Read some documents
(D) Watch a video

74. What is being advertised?
(A) A kitchen utensil
(B) Some fishing equipment
(C) A power tool
(D) Some clothing

75. What does the speaker say about the product?
(A) It is guaranteed to work for a long time.
(B) It has sold out in many stores.
(C) It was advertised on television.
(D) It has won some design awards.

76. Why does the speaker mention the Web site?
(A) An operation manual can be downloaded there.
(B) Customer reviews are posted there.
(C) The product can be purchased there.
(D) A product description is available there.

GO ON TO THE NEXT PAGE

77. Where does the speaker most likely work?
(A) At a college
(B) At a museum
(C) At an art gallery
(D) At a financial institution

78. Who most likely are the listeners?
(A) Financial contributors
(B) Art students
(C) Department managers
(D) University lecturers

79. What does the speaker say about the organization?
(A) It was forced to raise its prices.
(B) It employed additional staff recently.
(C) It will close temporarily.
(D) It will receive financial assistance.

80. Where does the speaker most likely work?
(A) At a recruiting agency
(B) At a vocational college
(C) At a training center
(D) At a newspaper company

81. What is the purpose of the talk?
(A) To thank employees for hard work
(B) To introduce a new employee
(C) To announce a new procedure
(D) To invite employees to an event

82. What will the speaker attach to an e-mail?
(A) A copy of the new employee handbook
(B) A list of contest winners
(C) Some communication from a client
(D) Updates to a yearly schedule

83. Who is the message most likely intended for?
(A) An editor
(B) A fitness trainer
(C) A technician
(D) A delivery driver

84. Why does the speaker suggest that the listener come today?
(A) A product is likely to sell out.
(B) The business will not be open tomorrow.
(C) A discount offer will end.
(D) Her belongings will be transferred to another location.

85. What does the speaker mean when she says, "I'll be in a meeting for the rest of the afternoon"?
(A) The listener should wait for her.
(B) She asks the listener for help.
(C) She has to reschedule an appointment.
(D) The listener won't be able to call her back.

86. What is the broadcast mainly about?
(A) New road rules
(B) A construction plan
(C) Environmental issues
(D) Some road repairs

87. What are the listeners advised to do?
(A) Take an online course
(B) Use bus services
(C) Leave home early
(D) Check the weather forecast

88. What can the listeners do on a Web site?
(A) View a time table
(B) Schedule a meeting
(C) Read reviews
(D) Watch some videos

89. What kind of business is being advertised?
(A) A restaurant
(B) A fashion store
(C) A fitness club
(D) A hardware store

90. What can customers receive this month?
(A) A product sample
(B) A discount coupon
(C) Free home delivery
(D) Training advice

91. What does the speaker imply when he says, "See what they say"?
(A) He wants to hear the listeners' opinions.
(B) He believes the business is popular.
(C) He hopes people will write down their comments.
(D) He recommends the listeners take some time.

92. According to the speaker, what is being changed?
(A) How security is ensured
(B) Where employees can take breaks
(C) What time employees can leave
(D) How wages are calculated

93. What are the listeners instructed to do today?
(A) Leave the office early
(B) Exchange identification cards
(C) Update their software
(D) Dispose of confidential documents

94. What will happen at 10:00 A.M.?
(A) The speaker will leave on a business trip.
(B) Some equipment will be replaced.
(C) A new procedure will be implemented.
(D) The speaker will become unavailable.

GO ON TO THE NEXT PAGE

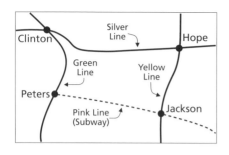

Tour Schedule	
Friedrich Art Gallery	10:00 A.M.
Harington's (Lunch)	12:10 P.M.
River Cruise	1:30 P.M.
Tully Castle	3:30 P.M.

95. Who most likely is the speaker?
(A) An event organizer
(B) A tour guide
(C) A hotel manager
(D) A business traveler

96. What does the speaker say about conference attendees?
(A) They will make up a large portion of the hotel's guests.
(B) They have weeklong reservations.
(C) They will arrive on a tour bus.
(D) They have had their luggage delivered separately.

97. Look at the graphic. Where is the hotel?
(A) In Clinton
(B) In Hope
(C) In Peters
(D) In Jackson

98. Look at the graphic. What is the final stop on the tour today?
(A) Friedrich Art Gallery
(B) Harington's
(C) River Cruise
(D) Tully Castle

99. What does the speaker say may happen?
(A) One of the destinations may be crowded.
(B) A passenger may arrive late.
(C) The lunch menu may change.
(D) The weather may be unfavorable.

100. What has the speaker been asked to talk about?
(A) A famous person
(B) Some local history
(C) A popular food item
(D) Some interesting geography

This is the end of the Listening test.